Shame

Shame

Jasvinder Sanghera

W F HOWES LTD

This large print edition published in 2007 by
W F Howes Ltd
Unit 4, Rearsby Business Park, Gaddesby Lane,
Rearsby, Leicester LE7 4YH

1 3 5 7 9 10 8 6 4 2

First published in the United Kingdom in 2007
by Hodder & Stoughton

A CIP catalogue record for this book is available
from the British Library

ISBN 978 1 40740 540 7

Typeset by Palimpsest Book Production Limited,
Grangemouth, Stirlingshire
Printed and bound in Great Britain
by Antony Rowe Ltd, Chippenham, Wilts.

To Robina, whose life was sadly taken away, and to Mum and Dad, who I now know wanted what they thought to be best for me.

This is my story. However, some of the names and personal information about other people in the book have been changed to protect their identities.

PROLOGUE

It wasn't too bad in the phone box. It wasn't like the city phone boxes I was used to where you had to hold your breath against the stench of wee and fags. I was glad to be inside it because I'd felt quite conspicuous walking through the village. There were other people wandering about, going up to the pub or buying their tea in the little corner shop, there were kids skidding around on bikes, but there were no other Asian people. Jassey noticed that too, he mentioned it to me. He was leaning up against the wall outside now and I could feel him watching me through the glass. I looked up and smiled at him, pretending I was still fumbling for ten-pence coins in my purse.

I took a deep breath to steady myself. I'd been wanting to make this call for so many weeks now; I'd ached for the sound of familiar voices, for news, for reassurance that all was well. That morning I'd woken up and found the longing was so great I couldn't stand it any longer, I couldn't go another day without speaking to someone from my family. I wanted to talk to my mum, to hear her voice ring with pleasure and relief as she said my name, to know that she and Dad were missing me.

I couldn't admit this to Jassey, but I wanted Mum to tell me to come home. On the drive out from Newcastle I'd had this fantasy that she would say, 'Stay right where you are, *putt*, we're coming to get you.' *Putt* means darling. My dad used to say it to me sometimes. I wished I could hear him say it now. In my imagination I was sitting on the back seat of Dad's old Cortina, Mum looking round to check on me, Dad with his eyes on the road as he drove me safely back to Derby.

I looked at my watch. It was just after seven p.m. I knew Mum would be standing in the kitchen, stirring something on the cooker. I could almost feel the heat and smell the turmeric. Lucy would be in the living-room watching telly. I wondered if the teachers at school had asked her where I was. And Dad would have gone to the foundry. Had he told his friends about me running away? They'd know anyway, of course; in the two months since I'd left home the gossip would have filtered through from our Sikh temple, the *gurdwara*. I hoped I hadn't hurt him too badly. I hoped he missed me as much as I missed him.

Jassey tapped softly on the glass and mouthed 'go on'. I shivered; the evenings were getting cooler and I'd forgotten to bring a jacket. There were goose bumps on my arms and a trickle of cold sweat running down the middle of my back. My heart was beating double time and I could feel the courage draining out of me as I lifted the receiver and fed in the first of my coins.

Mum answered almost immediately. I said, 'Mum, it's me . . .'

She was off straight away, screaming and crying down the phone, and the voice I'd yearned to hear was harsh and shrill. 'What have you done to us? How could you do this? You've shamed us. Why should we suffer this disgrace?'

My dreams of a happy family reunion were instantly shattered. I'd been so stupid. Shame and dishonour were what Mum dreaded more than anything. I should have known she wouldn't forgive me that. But some stubborn part of me was still determined to defend myself. I was crying too by then, but I managed to say, 'Mum, you know why I left.'

But she wouldn't have any of that. The way she saw it I'd defiled the family name by running off with a *chamar*. My mum always told me that *chamars* are the lowest caste, they are the people who pick up dung in the fields; some people call them untouchables. My family are *jats*; back in India *jats* are landowners and no matter that the only land my dad owns in Derby is the patch of grass behind our terraced house, being high caste was a very big thing for us. Through all the shouting and hysterics I couldn't make out if Mum was most cross about my associating with someone of such low birth or the fact that I'd left my intended husband – 'a good match, a *jat*, like us' – in the lurch.

'Thanks to you I can't walk the streets of Derby any more; I can't go to the *gurdwara* because people are talking. People spit at me.' There was a pause; I thought she'd finished but she was just catching her breath. 'You'll get what you deserve for ruining your family. You'll see. In a few months' time you and your *chamar* boyfriend will be rolling round in the gutter which is no more than you deserve. You will amount to nothing, *nothing*, do you hear me? I hope you give birth to a daughter who does to you what you have done to me, then you'll know what it feels like to raise a prostitute.'

I was so shocked by the viciousness of her attack that I was shaking. I couldn't believe it was turning out like this. I wanted her to stop. I wanted more than anything for the conversation to take a better turn, for her to say something – anything – that showed she loved me or even that she cared a little. I wanted her to know that I loved her. My voice was thick with tears.

'I'll come back, Mum. I want to come back. But I won't marry that man. I'm only just sixteen. I want to live my own life. I want to go to college.' I was talking as quickly as I could, trying to get my explanation out, but she started shouting over me and her voice was full of scorn.

'Live your own life then, and good luck to you. In our eyes you're dead!' And with that she slammed the phone down.

4

My legs seemed to give way beneath me. I was still holding the receiver, staring into it as if I needed visual proof that Mum had cut me off. I slid down the wall and crouched on the floor of the phone box. My chest felt so tight it was as if someone was crushing me. I was literally choking on my sobs. Jassey came in and put his arms around me and tried to comfort me, but for all his kind words and kisses, I had never felt so alone. It was as if someone had taken all my childhood memories and ripped them apart. In the next few days the conversation played over and over in my mind until I thought I would go mad.

'You've shamed us . . .'

'You are dead in our eyes . . .'

'You've shamed us . . .'

'You are dead in our eyes . . .'

Had I really done something so terrible that my parents could disown me? Had they really stopped loving me? Was it such a crime to want my own life?

CHAPTER 1

At five-thirty every morning my mum would put her prayers on, full-blast. '*Ik-cum-kar, ik-cum-kar* . . .' The noise went wailing round the house and you couldn't get away from it. You'd put a pillow over your head and think, *stop, p-l-e-a-s-e stop*, but you never blocked it out.

There were four of us in our bed: me, Lucy, Robina and Yasmin, sleeping two at the top and two at the bottom. At bedtime we wriggled and giggled and it was 'you kicked me' and 'move over' and 'that's my space' until we settled down.

There were three other girls in our family. Bachanu, my half-sister, who stayed in India, when Mum came over, Prakash who lived in London, and Ginda, who was about ten years older than me. She slept in the other bed in our room. Ginda was a huge influence in our lives; you could almost say she brought us up. She used to look after us while Mum was at work, and on bath nights she would put us all in the tub together and wash our hair. We all had very long hair, and afterwards she would cover it with jasmine and almond oil which made it greasy and horrible. Your hair would be plastered flat on your head and I hated the feel of that, and the smell. Sometimes, as we got bigger, there wasn't room for all of us in the bath and one person would have to take a bowl of warm water and wash down in the toilet outside. We all dreaded doing that in winter.

Our first house had two bedrooms in it and my brother Balbir slept in the other one. Mum sometimes slept in there too, sometimes downstairs on the sofa. I'd left home before I wondered why there wasn't a bed where she slept with Dad. They must have had a physical relationship: they had seven children together. But there wasn't any sign of it by the time I was old enough to notice; I never saw them kiss one another, not even a peck on the cheek. They didn't seem close; it was just like a practical arrangement. I don't even remember them talking much beyond the questions and answers it takes to get through everyday life.

Balbir was the one who had my mum's attention. He was treated completely differently from us girls. Mum would prepare his food and encourage him to eat it, and she'd wash his clothes, whereas we were expected to wash our own clothes and get our uniforms ready and get our food when we felt like it.

We never all sat down to share a meal. Mum would leave a big pan of curry on the cooker and it was help yourself and take it in front of the TV. We'd sit there cross-legged, balancing our plates on our laps. We had a black and white TV but when we were little we used to spread those transparent Lucozade wrappers across the screen to make it feel like colour.

I was about seven when I started asking why everything was different for Balbir. Why is he allowed out on his own and we're not? Why do I have to learn to cook when he doesn't? Then I started questioning other aspects of our life. If Sikhs think everyone is equal, why do we look down on people of a lower caste?

Just near our house was a *gurdwara*, which was important to my mum because her faith was very strong. Our old house has been knocked down now, but the *gurdwara* is still there, a big red-brick building with silvery domes and tinsel decorations on the front.

Mum left the house at six-thirty every morning and she'd feed the birds on the stretch of grass next to the *gurdwara* and then go in and say her prayers before she went to work. In the evenings she'd go again and she'd bring back holy water and sprinkle it around the house. My sisters and I would be watching *Charlie's Angels* and she'd be sprinkling water all over us and lighting joss sticks and chanting.

The *gurdwara* was – to me still is – the local gossip shop. You see the women standing in huddles with their scarves round their heads.

'Did you know that Zeeta's oldest son has got a wife coming over from the Punjab?'

'Have you heard Hasina's daughter-in-law has had *another* girl? I think Hasina is really regretting that match.'

'What about Zainab Singh? Her mother caught her at the bus stop, talking to a boy. That was three weeks ago and Mira hasn't let her out of the house since. I said to her, "Mira, you have only yourself to blame. Let her mix with white girls and she will pick up white girl ways."'

The worst thing you can say to an Asian girl is that she is behaving like a white person. We weren't allowed to mix with white people because Mum said they didn't have any morals or self-respect. She said whites were dirty people with dirty ways. That's what all the women I called Aunty thought too, and everyone else in our community. An Asian boy might have a bit of fun with white girls – 'white meat', that's what they'd say – while he was growing up, but when it came to settling down, his family would find him a good Asian bride. If an Asian girl went out with a white boy that was different, that was bad. Her brothers or her uncles would find him and beat him up and then they would beat her too, for bringing shame on the family. Then she would be ruined; no decent Asian man would ever want her. Everyone in the community knew that. I knew it by the time I was eight. No one handed me a book of rules but I knew the particular way in which I was supposed to act, walk, talk, even breathe. I knew that with every bad word said a reputation could die.

* * *

We lived in Northumberland Street in Derby. When I was small I used to stand at the top of the street and look down and it seemed so long. All the doors would be open and it was really busy and bustling; people would be wandering from house to house. Now the whole area is Asian, but then it was a very mixed community; there were Asians, Irish and Italian – Pakis, Paddies and Eyeties – all the people that nobody else wanted.

There was a Polish woman we called Mrs Funny and another neighbour we called Mrs Nosey Parker because she was a real curtain-twitcher. We used to play 'Knock out Ginger' on her door. There was an empty house at the top of the street which we told ourselves was haunted; we used to run round it to scare ourselves silly. There were hardly any cars and we played hopscotch and skip-ping on the pavements and we used to run away from a bad-tempered dog that always seemed to be sitting in the middle of the road. At one o'clock we'd hear the siren from the foundry telling the day shift it was time for their dinner.

My dad worked nights in that foundry. He got his job there on the day I was born, and stayed until he retired. On weekdays I used to make his tea in the morning when he came home; from the age of eight or nine that was my job, and so was sweeping the stairs. We all had jobs, except Balbir of course. In the afternoons when I came home from school I would wake Dad up and pack up his lunch in a steel container like a tower. It had three layers; you'd put different food in each – curry in one, salad in another and chapattis in the third. Mum would make the curries, but I had to do the chapattis.

It used to take me about an hour to make Dad's lunch and his flask of tea. I did it because I loved my dad dearly and doing that for him was a very small thing. I liked sitting with him while he had his tea; sometimes I'd tell him things about my day, but often we just sat, keeping each other company. When it was finished he'd go off to work and I'd stand at the door waiting for him to turn back and wave to me. He always did.

Mum would come in a bit later. She did what work she could get, mostly in textile factories. She always carried a big bag of woven plastic, covered with flowers, and when she came home me and my sisters used to dive for that bag because there was always something nice in it like a sweet or a chocolate. She'd be laughing and saying, 'Let me get in first, let me get my coat off . . .' and we'd all be giggling and grabbing. If I ever got that bag to myself I'd explore it really thoroughly. I didn't want to think I was missing a chocolate. Once I found a tiny little bottle buried right at the bottom and when I took the lid off and smelt it I fell backwards. They were smelling salts and the smell was terrible, it hit the back of your throat and made your eyes water. Mum and my sisters thought that was hilarious.

That bag is the happiest memory I have of childhood with Mum. I don't really remember being close to her. Not in the way my brother was. To me, she was the one that put you in your place and reprimanded you. She didn't like us mucking about or making too much noise and laughing upset her. 'You shouldn't laugh so much, stop that. If you laugh so much you are going to cry.' That's what she used to say.

Of all of us girls I was the tomboy; I loved running in the street and climbing on walls, but if Mum ever saw me she would call me in immediately and I never dared ignore her, I always came straight away. 'Don't you care what people think of you? Are you trying to shame us?' she'd say, holding my shoulders too tightly and peering into my face. 'Seven daughters to bring up . . . that has been my fate. Are you trying to make it harder still? Must you always be different?'

Because I was a breech birth, I was the only one of all Mum's children born in hospital. She spent six days there and she hated it. 'Born with your feet first, pah!' she used to say when she was angry with me. 'You were difficult from the start.'

Her main concern was always that we maintain the family's good name and grow up to be good daughters-in-law who were respectful, subservient and knew how to cook. 'Come here to the stove, stand by me and learn,' she'd say as she got out her cooking pots, and my heart would sink. I remember her recipes now, but those lessons left other, equally vivid memories: my legs aching as I stood beside her, my face hot and flushed by steam, my arm stinging where she slapped me when I let my eyes wander. 'No daughter of mine will go ignorant to her mother-in-law's house.'

Mum was the dominant one in our house. Dad was very quiet and followed what she said. He spent all week working to provide for his family, and then at the weekends he would go to our local pub, the Byron, and get drunk. Sometimes he'd come home happy and sit down in the living-room and ask us to search his hair for nits. We'd all cluster round his chair and he'd sit there telling us jokes and stories as we raked our fingers through his oily black hair, squealing when we caught one and crushed it between our nails. When we were done he'd give us all ten pence pocket money, which doesn't sound like much, but it was a lot for us. Despite the nits, I loved those times because we were all together and even Mum seemed to soften up. She didn't join in but she'd be sat there, watching us all with Dad. It was like our family was the only thing that mattered then, whereas most of the time there would be other people around, aunties and uncles, and Mum would be worrying that we behaved properly in front of them.

Keeping a good face in the community was a very big thing for her. From when we were little she taught us that no matter what was going on in your life you kept your head held high and presented a perfect front. A trouble shared is a trouble talked about by each and every gossip in the *gurdwara*, that's what my mum thought. Better to keep things private and then you can't be judged or shamed.

Sometimes on Saturdays I went with my dad to his allotment. We went up there just the two of us because the others weren't interested. It had huge, rusty iron gates and I would hop out of the car and heave them open so Dad could drive through. He grew potatoes, onions, garlic, marrows, and he showed me how to water them and stake them up. I watched him loosening the soil between his fingers with a faraway look in his eyes and sometimes he started singing softly to himself.

When he was done he sat in his deckchair, smoking a cigarette. Usually he had a can of Tennents lager in the pocket of his coat. That's what made him chatty. I sat beside him on the grass and he told me about his farm in the Punjab and this big shady tree in the middle of his village, Kang Sabhu, where at the end of the day he and the other men used to sit.

'Would I have sat there with you, like I do here?' I said. I knew the answer, we'd had the conversation many times before, but I was relishing the moment, having Dad all to myself. I leant my head against his knees and let his soft, low voice wash over me, filling my mind with exotic images of the life I might have led.

'Goodness me, no. In the daytime, when your chores were done, you might have played under the tree. In fact I remember a rope swing dangling down from one of the branches; as I recall it was Dalbir's son Govind who climbed up to put it there, climbed like a monkey that boy did. You little ones might play there in the day, but in the evening the shade it provided was for the men, it was where we relaxed or, if needs be, discussed the affairs of the village. Your place then was with the women. You would have been minding Lucy, or helping your mother grind the grain. I remember Bachanu when she was only five or six, pulling a wooden stool up to the grain bin which was twice her size and trying to reach down into it with the scoop. She wanted to be like the bigger girls, a helper to her mum.'

'But she couldn't help with the water, could she, Dad.'

'No, *putt*. The pot that your mum took to the well was much too heavy for little girls, it was bronze, you see. If we'd stayed Ginda and Yasmin could do it now, possibly Robina, but you had to be big enough to carry it properly, to lift it up onto your head without spilling any drop.

'Water was precious there. Not like here where you turn on the tap and nobody minds if it runs away useless. Back home we had to carry every drop of water that we used, even the crops weren't irrigated like your uncles' are now. They brought in those irrigation systems two years after I left and I'm telling you it made a difference. I read that productivity has gone sky-high with all that watering.'

15

His voice was dreamy now and although I could still feel his hand on the back of my head I could tell that in his mind he'd travelled miles away from me. He was back under the big shady tree with his mates.

'You know, I believe that one of your uncles has a tractor now. A mechanical tractor, can you believe that? For us it was ploughs pulled by bullocks. I had some excellent bullocks in my time, but one of them – oh my – that was the most stubborn, obstinate creature ever born and driving him on nearly broke my back.'

'You liked it there, Dad, didn't you. Why didn't you stay?'

This part of the story always made me feel a bit sad. I could picture the great big ship that brought Dad from the Punjab to Liverpool. He and men from other villages round about set off in their crisp cotton shirts and pyjamas, squinting in the bright sunshine as they waved goodbye to their families on the dock. The boat steamed out to sea and by the time India was just a memory lost on the horizon Dad was waking up cold and finding each day was darker than the one before.

He never said this, but I think he found it hard to hold onto his hope as he stood shivering on the deck in the middle of the ocean. He'd told me before that, to cheer themselves up, he and the other men did *bangrha*, a wild traditional dance that was supposed to celebrate the harvest. I couldn't imagine him doing that. In his drab brown clothes he seemed too quiet and serious. I couldn't imagine him wearing earrings either, but he had the holes in his ears.

'Why did you come here, Dad?' I banged the toe of his shoe with the heel of my hand, prompting him to tell the next part of the story.

'It was the 1950s, things were changing, it's always important to keep up to date. I didn't want any son of mine driving a bullock-drawn plough all his life; I dreamt of more for my daughters than the drudgery of carrying water on their heads. Besides the British government was asking us to come, they needed workers, they offered favourable conditions. We were told we would have a wonderful life.'

But what my dad found when he got here wasn't all that wonderful. When he first arrived he shared a house with other Asian men, sometimes as many as twelve crammed into one room. They found it difficult to find places to stay because landlords didn't want to rent to them; there were signs saying NO IRISH, NO BLACKS. They'd come expecting to be welcomed and instead they found hostility. People stopped talking and stared when they went into pubs or shops. Once, my dad was told to get off a bus because he was a Paki. It's not surprising that they stuck together.

Lots of them lived near us in Derby. That's where my mum came to, almost seven years after Dad. She'd married him when she was fifteen; she was told she had to when his first wife, her older sister, died from a snake bite. That was the tradition where they lived. She married her sister's husband and took on Bachanu, her sister's child.

Bachanu was already married by the time Mum came to England, so she stayed behind. What must it have been like for Mum coming all the way to Derby? She never talked about it the way Dad did, but I knew from what he said that before she came to England she'd lived in the same tiny village all her life. She'd never been further than she could walk from that village; she'd never been to town. Before she left the farm my mum had never seen a proper toilet; the only kitchen she had known was in the open air. She never really got the hang of English furniture; when I think of Mum now I think of her sitting cross-legged on the floor, peeling onions.

She must have been lonely when she came here. On the farm she'd have had her in-laws, other women in the house, everybody's kids. When Dad described this household full of people it sounded jolly but I realize now that, more than that, it must have felt safe. Mum would have known her place and her responsibilities; she'd have known where she sat.

I expect she missed that. She didn't know anyone in England. She didn't speak English. She never learnt English, right up until the day she died. Dad learnt enough to get by outside but at home we always spoke Punjabi. We ate Punjabi food, we had Punjabi friends and, although we wore our uniforms to school, we were expected to put on our Indian suits as soon as we came home. It was like you came home and shut the door on Derby and all the white people with their dirty white ways.

Often Dad and I would sit up at the allotment until it was dusk, and as we drove home under the yellow city sky he'd tell me how dark the sky is at night in India and how bright the stars.

Weekends for us were mostly about people coming to our house, or us visiting them. When we went visiting, Ginda used to plait our hair and put ribbons in it and dress us up in really frilly, girly western dresses, like we'd seen the posh kids wear in Asian films. We were so proud of those dresses; mine was green. Once we'd got them on we weren't allowed to go outside or play or do anything except sit still and keep them clean and uncreased so everyone could see how smart we were. The visits were always very formal. The men would be in one room, drinking whisky and smoking, and the women would be in another having the same old conversations.

'Did you see the sari Suki's new daughter-in-law was wearing at the *gurdwara*? So much gold; I hear she is from a rich family. And there she was washing the pots, so she is dutiful too. Suki is very pleased with her.'

'But what of her daughter? Nineteen now and still not married. Why has there been no match?'

'Did you not hear? A match was made, but before the marriage had taken place the groom pulled out because his mother heard that Suki's daughter was dancing with another man at a wedding. Showing herself off. The groom's family wanted nothing more to do with her . . .'

After a while the women would move to the kitchen and continue their gossip while they chopped onions and chillis, ground spices and washed rice. We children were expected to sit quietly or play nicely with whoever was there, but once we were about ten, Mum insisted on us helping to prepare the food because it was a way of showing off what she had taught us, and what good daughters-in-law we were going to make.

CHAPTER 2

I came home from my school, St Chad's Infants, one day to find Mum and Ginda in the living-room folding yards of fabric into a big trunk. There were several different pieces in strong, rich colours, some brightly patterned and some covered in embroidery. I'd never seen anything so pretty in our house in my life.

'What's all this for?' I said, reaching out to touch a piece. Mum slapped my hand away. 'It's for Ginda's wedding. She'll be taking it to her new family. It's for her suits.'

'Ginda's getting married? When? Who to?' I looked between the two of them, trying to gauge the mood. Mum looked impassive, you'd think she hadn't heard me. She went on folding fabric, smoothing out the creases until her pile had a perfect surface.

'Who are you marrying, Gin, tell us,' I said.

'His name is Shinda. His picture is on the table over there,' she said, jerking her thumb over her shoulder.

I picked it up. It showed a man a few years older than Ginda, quite good-looking, neatly dressed. 'What's he like?' I said.

'I don't know, I haven't met him, have I, stupid?' she said, and set her mouth firm shut.

That's all the discussion there was. I'd grown up knowing that Ginda would be getting married because it's what all the girls we knew did, but I hadn't expected it to happen so soon. She was only sixteen.

A few weeks later Mum came home from work and said Ginda had gone to India that morning. She didn't say how long she would be gone for and we didn't ask. She was away a month or two and when she came back she was by herself but she was married. That was that. The only word I ever heard about it was one night in our bedroom. The picture I'd first seen of Ginda's husband was lying on our chest of drawers and I picked it up to look at it.

'He doesn't look like that anyway,' she said.

'What do you mean?'

'When I flew out for the wedding he came to meet me at the airport but I didn't recognize him. He doesn't look like that picture at all; I reckon it was doctored.' She rolled over so all I could see was her back and made out she was going to sleep; it was her disappointment and she wasn't going to share it.

Once she was back she went on looking after us like she had before, and she went to work in Reckitt and Coleman's shampoo factory like she had before. Nothing changed for a year or so but then her husband got his papers through and moved to England and she moved out to live with

22

him at his sister's house. That's when I really missed her. All my life she'd looked after me. She could ladle curry out of the saucepan without spilling it, she did our plaits and when Lucy, Robina and I argued, she sorted it out. Sometimes she'd even intervene when Mum was hitting us. That was really brave. She'd reach out and pull me in behind her and in her most soothing, placatory voice she'd say to Mum, 'I think she's learnt her lesson, she'll be a good girl now.' When Ginda left I was eight and I knew I was going to have to fend for myself.

She only went to live ten minutes from us in Depot Street but I didn't see much of her after that except sometimes at weddings. She'd be standing there flanked by her sisters-in-law, all of them queening it in their saris and their jewellery with their eyes darting round like magpies as they checked out all the other women's outfits. She was too engrossed in doing that to talk much to us, but even so I noticed that beneath all her make-up she looked quite down.

Mum and Dad would visit her occasionally on Sundays but it wasn't a regular thing. Ginda was part of her in-laws' family now, that's where her life was and it wouldn't have been right for them to interfere.

It was the same when Yasmin got married. When I was little I thought she might marry the pop man. He used to do deliveries round our street on Sundays and me and Robina thought Yasmin was sweet on him. She'd smooth down her suit and pat her hair when she heard him ring the doorbell and when she answered it she'd lean up against the door frame, all downcast eyes and a coy little smile. But I soon realized that wasn't going to happen. When Yasmin turned sixteen a picture appeared, a trunk got filled, she went away to India for a while then came home married. Her husband was the brother of my eldest sister Prakash's husband and Mum was really pleased about that because it was good to keep things in the family.

Yasmin had the same as Ginda, a ceremony that clinched the deal my parents made so that she could have a proper legal wedding once she'd called her husband over to England. When she came back she still made eyes at the pop man, even though she was supposed to be convincing the immigration officer that she was madly in love with this husband she'd barely met. It took a few months for his papers to come through and then once he'd arrived here she went off to London to stay with Prakash.

By the time I reached my teens I had three sisters married and Robina's husband was already being discussed. If I'd asked Prakash or Ginda or Yasmin if they were happy they would have said yes. That's what was expected of them; if the truth was any different they knew to keep it to themselves. But I didn't like what I saw of their marriages.

You couldn't tell much until the time came when they and their husbands moved into their own houses and, for the first time, they had access to a telephone without all the in-laws listening. They never came round to Dale Road much but they all used to ring. Often, if Lucy, Robina or I answered, whichever one it was would say 'Put Mum on, will you?'

She wouldn't want to chat to us.

'That's what marriage is like . . .'

'Because it's your duty . . .'

'Don't you dare to disgrace us . . .'

'Never mind your father, he would say the same . . .'

That's what the conversation sounded like at our end and when Mum put the phone down she'd be frowning and shaking her head. 'How's Ginda then?' I asked after one of those calls, but Mum just walked past me as if she hadn't heard.

Every few months, Mum would decide it was time to pay a visit and, until we were old enough to be left alone, we had to go with her. Memories of those visits stretch right back into my childhood and none of them are happy memories.

Each one followed the same pattern. Mum chivvied us all into the back of Dad's car. It was his pride and joy, a Ford Cortina. I can still remember how, on hot days, the plastic seating used to stick to my legs. None of us spoke on the drive over and there would be a gathering sense of gloom. The husband would open the front door. He never said anything, just stood back and ushered us all in. My sister – whichever one it was

– would be in the living-room, perched on the settee with her baby on her lap. The husband and Dad disappeared into the other room and Mum sat down opposite my sister while the rest of us sat cross-legged by the wall. I knew what was coming and I didn't want to hear it. I wished we could go and play in another room but I was afraid to ask; I knew better than to draw attention to myself at a time like this.

'What's all this about then?' Mum said, sounding stern rather than sympathetic.

My sisters never needed encouragement. 'I can't stand it any longer. He is a difficult man.' The complaints would come, of various incidents and conflicts. 'Baby was crying while we were eating, I wanted to go to him, but he wouldn't let me. Yesterday he shouted at me because he said his dinner wasn't hot. What can I do? Every day there's something. Why should I put up with it?'

'Because you are his wife,' said Mum, and by now there would be a sharp, don't-mess-with-me edge to her voice. She never shouted on these occasions but when she brought out that tone we knew exactly who was boss. 'It is your duty to look after your husband and to please him.'

'But he gets so angry.'

'This is his house, he can behave as he wishes. Stop that crying, crying does no good. You must learn how to calm him.'

'But I don't see why . . .'

'It is not your duty to see. It is your duty to have

a respectable marriage and to uphold the good name of your family. That is the very least that your father and I expect. Do you understand that?'

It was always hot and stuffy in those rooms, the babies were heavy and my legs would ache from sitting cross-legged but I never dared fidget. I jiggled the babies if they got fractious. Lucy pulled faces at them trying to make them smile.

Mum was more than a match for her daughters. They soon stopped trying to make themselves heard and sank back into the corner of the settee, twisting their handkerchiefs in their laps as tears rolled down their cheeks.

Then Mum called the men in. She pushed the son-in-law over to sit by his wife, and told Dad to sit down next to her. Dad never said anything on these occasions, only sometimes he nodded his head as if in agreement. Perhaps he was wishing he could escape to the Byron. A couple of times he would get out his cigarette pack and make as if to light one, but then he would look at Mum and put it back again. She didn't let him smoke indoors.

When Mum turned her attention to the husband, her tone was gentler and more wheedling. 'You can see she is trying, but it is hard for her away from her family. Perhaps you could try to be more patient with her. She has given you a lovely boy and if you are blessed perhaps there will soon be another. You must think of your family now. No good will come to your son if his mother is always crying.'

The sons-in-law never looked at her while she was speaking; they kept their heads bowed down so they missed her obsequious smiles. It wasn't until Mum had finished talking that any of them ever met her gaze and then even I could tell their eyes were insolent. You could see the corners of their mouths twitching as they said, 'Yes, *Bibi-ji.*' *Bibi* means mother and *ji* is something you add to the name of anyone above you. It's a mark of respect, but my brothers-in-law didn't sound respectful. They weren't afraid of Mum. She'd said what she'd come to say and they knew she'd never take it any further for fear of creating a wrinkle in our family's reputation.

We were all quiet on the way home. The only sound in the car was Dad muttering to himself. If you were sitting behind him you could see his head moving about as though he was having a conversation with himself, going through everything that had happened. I don't think he was happy with those meetings, but he'd never interfere with what Mum said.

She'd always sit still in the car looking straight ahead of her. It wasn't until we were turning into our road that she used to twist round in her seat so she was facing us. 'There's no need to talk of this with anybody. Not even your aunties. It is a private matter for our family. Do you understand that? I won't have people talking about us, I won't have you giving people reason to gossip in the *gurdwara.*'

CHAPTER 3

The year that Ginda got married we moved house. Dale Road was just round the corner from Northumberland Street, but it was a step up. The new house had three bedrooms, a proper bathroom and an inside toilet. It was luxury for us. It was so close to our old house that we carried most of our stuff round by hand. Some of Dad's friends from the factory helped with the furniture and I remember Mum walking down the street with a big case balanced on her head and me, Lucy, Robina and Yasmin all trailing along behind her carrying bits and pieces. Lots of our neighbours came out of doors to watch and it felt a bit like a procession.

We four girls were still sharing a room but Balbir had his own room again in Dale Road. He was doing an apprenticeship in engineering by then but that didn't stop him going out at nights. He used to come home late and put his music on really loud. Bob Marley was what he liked: 'No Woman No Cry', 'I Shot the Sheriff', 'Satisfy My Soul', 'Get Up, Stand Up' . . . Night after night those songs blasted round the house waking us up.

'Shut up, Balbir. Turn it down. We're trying to sleep,' we shouted from the bedroom but he couldn't hear us above the racket. It was Mum who heard us and she came into our room with a face like thunder as though we were the noisy ones.

'Stop shouting!' she'd say. 'Be quiet and go to sleep.'

'But Mum. It's impossible to sleep with Balbir's music. It's him, tell him to stop.'

'You leave your brother out of this. I'm telling you, shut up and go to sleep.'

One night I got so cross I decided to sort him out myself. I kicked back the blanket and stamped down the passage. There he was, bedroom door wide open, playing air guitar and caterwauling along with the lyrics. He looked so ridiculous I almost laughed.

'Can't you think of other people for a change, we've got school in the morning,' I shouted above his screeching. He didn't even stop twanging his pretend guitar, just aimed a kick in my direction. It wasn't hard, but dodging to avoid it I fell back through the door and landed practically on top of Mum, who was coming up the stairs. She steadied me and then gave me a shove back towards our bedroom.

'Get back to bed, young lady. You've no business here,' she said.

Next morning when we were getting ready I thought Robina was taking too long in the bath-room. I was rattling the door handle and calling through to her to hurry up when Mum appeared behind me, making shushing noises.

'Keep your voice down, your brother is sleeping. Have a bit of consideration, he's a working man now, bringing home money. He needs his sleep.'

When I was ten or eleven Balbir started going out with Dawn, who lived just round the corner from us on Darby Street. Dawn's dad was Asian but her mum was a white woman and our mum didn't like that; she called Dawn a half-caste. She was always going round to Dawn's house and hammering on the door, demanding to know if Balbir was in there. Sometimes she'd take me with her so I could shout the words in English. Once she made me say that something terrible would happen if Dawn didn't stop seeing Balbir but she didn't take a blind bit of notice. Nor did Balbir. He knew Mum would never really go against him.

After one of those trips I asked her why she didn't *make* Balbir stop seeing Dawn and stay at home. 'You wouldn't let my sisters do what he does, why is he different?' I didn't mean to be cheeky, I wanted an answer, but that's not how she saw it.

'Insolent child.' She stooped to take off her shoe and, grabbing my tunic so I couldn't slip away from her, started beating me with it. She didn't mind where the blows landed – legs, back, head – I'm not sure she even noticed, she was so worked up with her shouting. 'Don't question me, of all

31

my daughters you alone are difficult, always thinking you know best . . .'

One new thing Dad had in Dale Road was a shed. It was part of the house really, a sort of add-on to the kitchen, but we always called it Dad's shed because it was where he kept his gardening tools and where he stored the onions and potatoes that he'd grown. We used to climb on top of the shed when we were playing *Charlie's Angels*, and sometimes I'd sit up on the roof by myself and pretend I was guarding Dad's stuff. I was always looking for ways to make myself special to Dad. Out of all of us Balbir was the important one because he was the only boy and that's how it goes in Asian families; I knew that but I still liked to think the bond between me and Dad was different. We had a secret anyway.

It happened one night when I woke up so thirsty that I went downstairs to get a drink of water. I was treading carefully on the stairs so I didn't make them creak when I heard the sound of voices, men's voices whispering and laughing softly. It was coming from the shed. Usually it smelt dusty and dry but that night as I stepped into the kitchen I could smell something different, something sickly sweet and horrible. It was a smell I thought I recognized.

Suddenly the shed door opened and Dad came into the kitchen. He was carrying a couple of empty milk bottles and talking over his shoulder to his friends as he headed for the sink to fill them from the tap. When he caught sight of me he whipped round, quick as a flash. He had a really guilty expression on his face and he leant over to push the shed door shut before saying gently, 'Go back to bed, *putt*, it's late, you need to sleep.'

'What are you doing, Dad? What's that smell? Who's in the shed?'

'It's nothing for you. Don't worry about it, go back to bed.' He was trying to block my path with his body, but I was peering round him. The shed door had swung open and I could see two of Dad's friends, men I referred to as 'uncle', standing in the dim light.

'What are you doing, Dad? What are my uncles doing here?'

He sighed, then smiled. 'Okay, come and see. We are making Desi.'

The concrete floor of the shed was cold beneath my bare feet; I shivered. The tiny space was filled with acrid steam which made my eyes smart. I pinched my nose to block the smell. One of Mum's big saucepans was balanced on a gas canister and the liquid inside it was bubbling like anything. There were packets and bags and spoons on the floor beside it and, lined up against the wall, a row of empty bottles. Suddenly I realised what the smell was: aniseed. A couple of years back, attracted by the colour, I'd bought little red balls of it from the sweet shop. They were revolting.

'This is Asian alcohol, good strong stuff,' Dad

said, and he and the other men laughed. He dipped a ladle into the saucepan and filled a small glass with the clear liquid. 'Watch this,' he said, striking a match and wafting it across the top of the glass. To my amazement it caught light. The greeny-blue flame rose and danced, casting flickering shadows on our faces. Then it sputtered and died. Once it was out Dad and my uncles passed the glass round and they all had a taste.

'Can I try it, Dad?' I said, and the men laughed again.

'No, child, Desi is not for little girls. Now you've seen it, Jasvinder, go back to bed!'

When the time came to leave Dale Primary I went to join Robina and Yasmin at Littleover School. It was too far to walk there so when Dad came back from the night shift he used to stay up, drinking tea and reading his paper, until it was time to give us all a lift. I can remember him standing at the bottom of the stairs and shouting up to us: 'Lucy! Jasvinder! Neddy!' – that's what we called Robina when she was young. 'Come on, it's time to get up. Wash your face, brush your teeth and come. Quick!'

He'd stand there, shouting for us until we came down like a swarm of bees, grabbing a couple of biscuits for our breakfast, looking for our school books, fighting about whose turn it was in the front of the car.

It was about two miles from our house to Littleover

and Dad always took the same route. He went along Dale Road, then Cavendish and after the round-about at the end, he turned into a great long road called Warwick Avenue. We were still in the Asian area, but this was the smart bit.

Warwick Avenue is wide, it has trees planted on both sides and it is lined with huge old Victorian houses, beautiful houses with front gardens and off-street parking. I used to crane out of the window and imagine myself living there. I'd see myself getting out of bed – my own bed – onto a thick pile carpet, or watching the telly sitting on a big soft sofa, or opening the front door and step-ping out onto my own green lawn.

'One day I'm going to buy a house on this road, you know, Dad,' I said.

I was sitting next to him in the front and he turned to me and smiled indulgently. 'Course you are, *putt*, one day.'

'I am, Dad. Believe me, I will one day.'

'Oh yeah.' 'Very likely.' 'Buy two, why don't you?' said my sisters in a sarcastic chorus from the back.

CHAPTER 4

When I was thirteen I got my first job with the newsagent at the bottom of Northumberland Street. I was paid £5.25 a week for delivering the papers to about eight streets round us. The bag was heavy and my shoulder used to ache but I loved doing it. It wasn't for the money. I used to give that to Mum. She never said I had to, but I knew that was what she expected: I'd seen my sisters saving money to bring their husbands over. I'd say, 'Here you are, Mum,' and she would count it carefully and sometimes she'd pat me on the head before putting the coins in the jar behind the cooker.

I loved the freedom. The paper round was the only time I was allowed out on my own. If you were sent to the corner shop to buy something you had to get there and back within ten minutes. After school we had to come straight home. Mum never came to school – she never went to parents' evenings or talked to teachers – but she knew exactly how far away it was and if I walked through the door fifteen minutes later than I should have done I was for it. If she wasn't there to see for herself my sisters always told her. It was the same for all of us. If an aunty saw you dawdling in the street or talking to a friend she'd tell Mum. The paper round was like a liberation. In the winter I had to hurry to keep warm but on sunny summer Saturdays I'd saunter up and down those streets taking the longest route I could. I looked at the white girls hanging around in little groups, leaning up against the lampposts, showing off their tight jeans. I longed to have a pair.

'What are you thinking of? Why would you want to go round showing off your bum? Have you no shame, girl?' Mum said when I asked her.

Working was part of our lives once we reached adolescence. One summer holidays Mum got me a job in a pickling factory. She said not to say how old I was but the supervisor was a friend of hers and I don't think he minded me being under age. It was only for a couple of weeks anyway. I can't remember much about it except the mind-numbing boredom of the work and the way the smell of pickles clung to your clothes and your hair. I tried to train myself to breathe through my mouth until I could get home and wash myself.

The only good thing about that job was Avtar; she was the girl next to me on the line and once I'd got my part of the production process off pat we could talk while we worked. Avtar was a free spirit and she made me laugh. She stayed at the factory after I left but we kept in touch and, as it turned out, knowing her would later change my life.

In the meantime I got another job, in Presto, which was about ten minutes' walk from our house. I did two evenings a week, sitting on the checkout or filling the shelves. Over my clothes I had to wear a pale blue nylon pinafore with Presto embroidered on it and I got paid £12.50 a week but I told Mum it was £11.50 and kept the extra £1 a week for myself. I had to unseal my wage packet to get the money out and at first my hands used to shake, I was so scared of tearing it, but I soon became quite clever at it and Mum never guessed. I wanted the money to pay to have my hair cut; it took me almost three months to save up enough.

I was fourteen and a half but I'd never had my hair cut. Ever. Mum or Ginda occasionally trimmed the split ends but that was all and by the time I was fourteen my hair hung down below my bottom which was just how Mum wanted it. Short hair was for white girls with their fast western ways. Good Punjabi girls wore their hair in plaits.

That spring the fashion was for wild curls. In the dinner break at school my white friend Caroline and I used to sit with our backs against the fence and study the pictures in her copies of *Jackie* and *Just Seventeen*. Caroline had straight hair like me but she said her mum was going to let her have a perm. I knew Mum would never let me; I wouldn't even dare to mention it.

There was a hairdresser called Rafferty's just

near Presto and its window was full of pictures of all the different hairstyles you could have. I used to stop on the way to and from work and gaze at the picture of the girl with curled hair. It was cut just above her shoulders, tumbling this way and that, and I thought she looked fabulous. I'd stare in at the window and dream of looking just like she did. One afternoon I set off for work ten minutes early and, having checked that no one Mum knew was passing, I plucked up the courage to go in.

The woman at the desk was talking on the phone and she didn't look up. I stood there waiting, glancing out the window every few seconds to check no one had seen me come inside. Eventually she finished her call and said, 'Yes?'

'How much would it cost to have my hair done like this?' I asked, moving over to the window and pointing at 'my' picture. She came out from behind the desk, went over to the window, and stuck her head round so she could see which one it was. Then she consulted a list of prices on the desk. It felt like she took ten minutes but it can't have been long.

'Cut and perm costs nine pounds fifty. Do you want an appointment?'

'Can I come next Saturday?'

'Morning or afternoon?'

'Either. After ten o'clock.'

'Twelve-thirty, then. Name?' she said, and when I'd spelt it out for her she closed her book. I ran all the way to Presto and my heart was pumping fast.

Saturday morning came and I was up early, anxious to check that Mum and Dad were going out. They were supposed to be visiting Aunty Rajni in Stoke, but I was fretting that they'd change their minds. It seemed to take Mum ages to get ready, fussing about the pot of dhal she was taking, losing her glasses in her big flowery bag. Dad stood in the doorway smoking a cigarette and reading the paper. When they finally climbed into the old Ford Cortina and drove away I was so relieved I felt light-headed.

A couple of hours later I ran down the stairs. Robina had gone out to her Saturday job. She'd already been to India for her marriage and now, while she finished school, she was saving hard to bring her husband over. It was just Lucy in the living-room; she'd been in there since *Tiswas* came on the telly.

'I'm going out,' I called, without slowing my pace, and the door slammed shut behind me before she could ask where.

Everything in Rafferty's was new to me. The beige nylon gown they put you in. The adjustable chair. The enormous mirror right in front of you. Rod Stewart's 'Do Ya Think I'm Sexy' was blaring out and everyone seemed to be chatting; I began to relax and enjoy myself. I'd shaken my plait out just before I left Dale Road and now one of the hairdressers was pulling her comb through my hair, running it right through from top to bottom.

'Gorgeous thick hair you've got, love. Just a trim, is it?' she asked.

'No. I want it like that picture in the window. The one in the middle.'

She dropped my hair and, just as the receptionist had, walked over to the window and peered at the picture. Watching her as she headed back towards me, I could see she looked surprised.

'You want it permed?'

I nodded.

'Not many . . .' she faltered before closing her mouth on the word Pakis, and after a second went on, 'girls like you do that. Seems a shame when you've got this lovely long hair.'

'It's what I want,' I said firmly.

'Here we go then,' she said. 'First we've got to lose at least half of it.'

I watched, fascinated, as she pinned up hanks of hair and then got her scissors out. Within seconds lengths of hair lay coiled round my chair like fat black cobras. I didn't feel a second's regret. I was revelling in how cool and light my head felt. Abba's 'Mamma Mia' was playing now and it was all I could do to stop dancing in my seat.

My hairdresser was talking all the time, not to me, but to another woman working next to her. They were discussing a nightclub they were both going to that night. But it didn't seem to slow her down. Her scissors moved through my hair like

41

quicksilver, snipping this way and that. Once the length was right she drenched my hair in a solution which smelt foul and caught the back of my throat; then she went to work with her rollers. When she was done it looked like I had pink hedgehogs all over my head. That was the only time I wondered what I'd let myself in for.

But I needn't have worried. When the hairdresser finally put her brush down and stood back to admire her handiwork I couldn't stop myself; I grinned at my reflection with delight. My hair stopped just above my shoulders; she must have cut off eighteen inches, and it was soft curls everywhere. I loved it.

I tried to sneak back into Dale Road but Lucy saw me. She stopped dead in her tracks and her mouth dropped open.

'You're gonna get it when Mum sees you,' she said, her eyes round as gobstoppers. 'Robina, come and look, Jas has cut her hair off and it's gone all curly.'

I enjoyed the reaction but I knew she was right. Mum would be furious. The thought of her rage almost took the pleasure out of looking at my new reflection in the mirror. I decided I had to keep it from her. When she and Dad came home from Aunty Rajni's I had my head wrapped up in a towel, as if I'd just had a bath and washed my hair.

'Night, Mum,' I called, all innocent as I went up early to bed.

For the next three days I kept out of her way and made sure that, whenever I was in the house, I had a towel on my head. My heart used to beat that bit faster when I heard Mum's footsteps approaching, and I could feel the tension growing in Lucy and Robina as they waited for the blow-up. It came on day four. I went into the kitchen to fetch myself a drink and I could tell from the way Mum looked at me that she was suspicious. As I walked past her to the sink she turned from the cooker and twitched the towel off my head.

For a second we stood staring at each other. It was as if Mum was frozen; her face was like a mask of horror. Then she snapped out of it, grabbed my arm and launched herself at me like a crazy person. Her first blow hit me on the head; I lurched backwards and hit the counter, knocking a saucepan that was waiting to be washed. It fell to the floor with a clatter and its lid spun off and rolled round the kitchen floor with a clanging that resounded with the ringing in my head. Mum was raining blows down on me and shouting, 'What have you done, girl? Again you have shamed us. What were you thinking of? You think you are clever with your western ways but no decent man will want you now. Will you not be happy until you have dragged us all down into the gutter.' I was shielding my face with the arm she wasn't holding and trying to twist away from her, but with each question she landed a wallop, harder and harder as she worked herself up.

I tried to interrupt, to reason with her. 'Mum, it's only a haircut. It'll grow out again. Why does it matter?'

But I could hardly make myself heard above her shouting, incoherent now her voice was broken with accusatory sobs. 'Do you want to make yourself look cheap like the white girls? Do you want them talking about you in the *gurdwara*? Was it your plan to bring shame on your family?'

She was breathing heavily, a big woman tired by her exertions. Unconsciously, she let go of my arm to sweep her hair back off her face; I heard the deep intake of breath as she prepared to resume her tirade but I didn't stay to hear the rest. Seizing my opportunity, I darted beneath her raised arm and fled the kitchen, squeezing past Robina and Lucy, who were standing wide-eyed in the doorway. As I ran upstairs I could hear Mum wailing still. 'I am burdened with seven daughters, why must this one bring nothing but trouble? Why must I suffer this? What can I do with this girl?'

Two days later I was doing my shift in Presto, restocking the shelves with beans, when a figure suddenly strode down the aisle, grabbed the back of my hair and started shouting at me.

'What is this, you foolish girl? What have you done? Are you trying to disgrace us all?'

It was my sister Prakash, come all the way from London to inspect my haircut. I couldn't believe it. I was mortified but I was also scared. We were all scared of Prakash.

'Get off me,' I hissed, glancing round to see if anyone was watching us. 'Be quiet. Please. You can't shout at me in here.'

'I can teach you to have some respect. You'll see, young lady,' she said and, to my relief, she turned on her heel and stalked out.

She was there at Dale Road when I got back. Mum called out immediately.

'Come in here, Jasvinder. I want to tell you something.'

I stood in the doorway, hesitant. She and Prakash were looking very stern. 'When your sister goes back to London tomorrow morning you will go with her,' Mum said. 'Here you are dishonouring your family, picking up western ways. I can't control you and Prakash needs some help in the house. You can go and learn what it is to be a dutiful daughter.'

Prakash, sitting beside her, nodded her head and looked smug. The prospect of living with her – and worse still her drunken husband – was terrible.

'How long will I go for, Mum?'

'We'll see.'

'But I'll be back in time for school, yeah?'

She didn't answer. I felt my chest tighten with a mixture of panic and anger. School was my link with the wider world, my escape.

'You'll be in trouble if you keep me off school.

45

You're not allowed to, that's the law in England. Remember what the truant officer said last time you did.'

But she and Prakash had turned away. The punishment meted out, they had turned their attention to something else.

It must have been about three months I stayed with Prakash, long enough for my perm to fall out and my hair to grow back long enough to plait. Mum wanted me decent before I could be seen again in Derby. It was an awful time. The days were monotonous and each one felt endless. My big sister seemed to enjoy the task of teaching me respect. As soon as I got there she took away my one western skirt – it was well below the knee – and blouse and made me always wear Indian suits, dreadful things she'd made herself. But it didn't matter what I wore because I wasn't allowed to go anywhere except a tiny little park near the house where I sometimes took the children. They were my salvation. Her three boys Ranjit, Manjit and Baljit were all under twelve then and I enjoyed playing with them, when I was allowed to do so.

Most of my time was spent helping Prakash with her job, which was sewing ties. When I think of Prakash I think of her sitting at her sewing machine, day and night. She sewed the ties inside out and my job was to turn them right way round again, using a long stick. Then I had to iron them. The children had to help with the turning too when they came home from school, and if they didn't work fast enough Prakash would get angry.

As well as helping with the ties I had to do household chores, cooking and cleaning, cleaning and cooking. Prakash never seemed to run out of jobs for me. The evenings and the weekends were the worst because then her husband, Bila, was there, throwing his weight about, stinking of whisky. His eyes were yellow, which I used to tell myself meant he was a devil. I later learnt it was a symptom of the liver poisoning that finally killed him. He shouted at Prakash and shoved or slapped her if she didn't anticipate his every need. He was a bully and I hated him.

It was October and half the school term had gone by before Mum and Dad appeared at the house. I was so pleased to see Dad that I rushed across the room to hug him. He didn't know what to do. He stood there with his arms dangling by his sides, but he was laughing as he said very gently, 'All right, *putt*, all right.' Mum was strict as ever. At first I didn't know if she was going to let me come home but after she'd been there a bit she said, 'Have you learnt your lesson? Are you going to behave if we take you back to Derby? If you don't you'll be coming straight back.' That's when I knew my punishment was over.

CHAPTER 5

A few months after Mum brought me home from Prakash's house the subject of my marriage came up. I was in the living-room doing my homework when she showed me a picture, ever so casually. 'What do you think of him?' she said. 'Do you think he's nice? He's the man you're going to marry.' I must have known this moment would come but I still felt as if I had been slapped. I didn't want to look at the picture, in my head I didn't want to go there, but I couldn't stop myself taking a quick glance. She was pointing out a man standing in a group and my first thought was, no way am I marrying him, *he's shorter than me*. I just looked at Mum. Then she started laughing and put the picture away so I thought perhaps she was joking and I needn't take it seriously.

I tried to put it to the back of my mind and get on with my life, but every so often Mum would mention it. At first she was always light-hearted and jokey, but over the weeks she became more insistent. She kept saying I should be happy that she had found me such a good husband and that it was my duty to marry him. As the weeks went by I got more and more frightened. I kept thinking of my sisters and the bruises I'd seen on them; I remembered them sobbing as they told my parents how their husbands abused them; I remembered Mum saying, 'This is how men are, it is your duty to look after him.' I used to lie awake and dread the thought of my husband beating me, and Mum and Dad refusing to help. I felt as if my life were sliding out of my control. When I said, 'Mum, I want to finish school and go to university,' she just laughed.

At break times at school I'd watch the white girls. It was a style thing then for them to hitch their uniforms up so they were really short. I used to watch them, standing in groups with the boys, chatting and laughing, sometimes mock wrestling; occasionally a cheeky couple would even kiss. For them it was totally normal, but my mum would have killed me if she saw me doing that.

My white friends had started talking about going to college or university. When they said, 'Is it true you have to get married when you're really young?' I'd just say no. I used to wonder if other Asian girls in my class were going through the same thing as me, but I never dared ask them because I'd been so indoctrinated not to talk outside the family. Sometimes I used to fantasize about telling a teacher and asking them to help, but it would have flown in the face of everything Mum ever taught me. My fear of being judged was quite deeply ingrained by then.

Even if I had been brave enough to tell a teacher, I didn't think they'd understand. Robina stayed in India six months when she went to have her marriage and when she came back the teachers never even asked her where she'd been or why, they just put her down a year because she'd missed so much school work. Anyway I was ashamed to tell anyone that my mum was arranging my marriage while I was still at school. And I was afraid of what my family would do to me, and what the rest of the community would say about them if I did.

No matter that I was so reluctant, the arrangements for my wedding were soon well under way. The photograph of the man I was supposed to marry was on the mantelpiece, leering down at me when I came home from school. I'd studied it more closely by then: he was ugly as well as short, he looked much older than me and he had a stupid haircut. I still didn't know his name, no one ever bothered to tell me that. More and more often, I'd come back and find that Mum had been out shopping. Gradually the chest that would go with me to my husband's family was being filled up. Mum even bought my wedding dress without me, a red glittery thing that I refused to look at. She couldn't care less that I didn't want to get married; she had already married five daughters and she didn't see why I should be any different. Ginda and Yasmin backed her up; they used to say, '*Teri fol laga ya*,' which means, 'Why are you any different, have you got flowers attached to you?'

Even Robina was on their side. 'Just do it. It's what we've all done,' she said. She was keen on the match because her husband, Navtej Sanghera, was friends with the man I was supposed to marry and came from the same part of India. Since her application for Navtej to come to England had been rejected, he'd moved to Germany and she was joining him in Frankfurt as soon as she had saved some money to take with her. 'Your husband is going to Frankfurt too, Navtej told me. If you get married there we will be together,' she said.

She sounded light-hearted but my mind flashed back to a night not long before she left to meet her husband. She'd gone missing. At first Mum thought she'd slipped out to meet a friend and she was angry. But about ten o'clock Dad went out into the garden for a cigarette and he found Robina there, hiding behind the shed. He called Mum out and the three of them stood in a huddle. I could hear Robina sobbing and a couple of times she cried out 'Please'. Eventually they all came in looking grim and later on, when we were in bed, Robina whispered that she'd been hiding because she was scared of getting married.

Dad didn't say much about my marriage. He was the only one who might have persuaded me to go through with it because I loved him and I believed he loved me. But he left it up to Mum.

Sometimes when he'd had a drink – he was always more talkative when he came back from the Byron – he'd stroke my cheek and say, 'Come on, *putt*. Don't try to fight this, it's what we all do.' But it wasn't enough. He didn't try hard enough.

Mum more than made up for it. She was always one for superstitions, things like if you sneeze before leaving the house you have to go back in and eat something sweet. Now she got it into her head that someone had put a spell on me.

'I'm telling you, Chanan, the child is possessed. Someone has cursed her and my suspicion falls on that old man who sits on the corner by the *gurdwara*. You've seen him? Straggling beard and unwashed clothes. Well, what is he doing there if not causing trouble?'

I was doing my homework – it was maths and we were working on Venn diagrams, I can remember that because I liked the clear simplicity of them. I got up from the table and went to the kitchen door to listen. I peeped round in time to see Dad's head start its little nodding dance. He wanted to show Mum that he was listening, weighing up the situation. She had her back to me, stood there in front of him, hands on her hips as she continued.

'Her behaviour is not normal. Why would she be so difficult if she were not possessed? She needs ridding of those demons and I think I've found someone to do it.' Suddenly she dropped her voice and bent forward to whisper conspiratorially. I strained to hear but I could only catch the odd word, 'Hindu', 'demons', 'Thursday'. I was craning forward at the door but I jumped back as she straightened up and said in her normal voice, 'This is between the two of us, Chanan, I'm not going to tell the other girls.'

She didn't mention anything to me, but the following Thursday when I got home from school she was ready waiting by the door, with a head-scarf that I'd never seen before wrapped close around her head. I'd barely had time to put my bag down when she handed me a scarf, helped me draw it round my face and hustled me back out.

'Where are we going, Mum?' I said as she linked her arm through mine and hurried me down the pavement. Her eyes were glued to the ground and she didn't lift them or turn towards me as she said, 'You'll know soon enough. Quick now, and don't look about.' We stopped at a Hindu temple about twenty minutes' walk from our house. Mum wouldn't have risked being seen in our area.

The Hindu priest who was supposedly going to cast out my demons was really old and he had this great long beard; he was wearing a skirt thing and a baggy top. He asked Mum my date and time of birth and all my likes and dislikes and then he started wringing his hands and saying, 'We must calm this troubled spirit.'

I just sat there dumbly as he ranted on, spouting off at me in Punjabi. 'This is your fate and if you ignore it your family will suffer and you will meet with terrible misfortune. Ignore your duty at your peril.' Mum had obviously filled him in on the whole situation beforehand.

Before we left, he gave me this dark green bottle of what he called medicine and said I had to drink some twice a day. It was supposed to bring me to my senses. Any fool could tell it was only sugared water, but it made Mum happy if I drank it so I did.

She went about her preparations with new enthusiasm. I'd come home from school and find her refolding my fabrics, checking that each crease was perfect. She started making a new suit for herself so I guessed that she'd be coming with me. Watching her felt so strange, like looking at my life through the wrong end of a telescope. She was planning my wedding but the plans were moving independently of me. I tried to ignore them, to blank them out. I had to control myself or the fear trembling in my belly would rise up and block my throat.

One night it all got too much. I came into the living-room and Mum was there with Ginda and one of my aunties and they were all standing over the chest, admiring the wedding fabrics. Suddenly it seemed so real and close that I knew I had to do something. I said, 'Mum, I'm not getting married. I'm going to finish school and go to college.'

Mum was so angry that I could speak to her like that in front of an outsider – disrespectful and

54

blabbing about the troubles in our family – that she picked up her heavy sewing scissors and whacked me really hard on the arm. She was screaming and crying and saying to my auntie, 'Look what I have to put up with; I have to carry the burden of seven daughters and this one has no shame,' and my auntie was crying as well and saying, 'You must be a good girl and do this for your family, look how you are upsetting your mother,' and I started crying and I stormed out, slamming the door.

The next night I was stopping at Ginda's. Mum used to send me there occasionally: 'Go and stay with your sister, and while you are there see if you can find some sense!' When I was younger I used to like going. I'd always enjoyed having Gin all to myself, but nowadays there were awkward silences between us. She wouldn't talk about my marriage. What was the point? As far as Gin was concerned it was inevitable and there was nothing to discuss.

I felt she had abandoned me. Gin virtually brought me up. She used to bath me when I was little. She reassured me when I got my first period and sorted me out; Mum had never mentioned it. She'd told me what little I knew about the facts of life. Now, it seemed, she was too caught up in her duty and the community and the family's reputation to care about me. I went upstairs that night feeling really upset and angry. I felt I was screaming my lungs out trapped in a soundproofed box.

In Ginda's bathroom there was a shelf above the bath where she kept her shampoo and face cream, stuff like that. There was a bottle of paracetamol on it and that night, on impulse, I picked it up and unscrewed the lid. A second or two passed and then I shook a couple of tablets into my hand, and a couple more, and a couple more after that. How many were there in the end. Eight? Ten? I don't know. I looked down into my palm and instead of little white pills what I saw was an image of Mum, crying and beating her breast. I shoved the pills into my mouth and then stuck my head under the tap and took a great draught of water; and another. Then I left the bathroom and went and got into bed.

I lay there for a while monitoring myself for any little symptom. After about ten minutes I started feeling sick and frightened. I got out of bed and crept downstairs to the living-room where Gin was watching telly.

'Gin?' I whispered.

She cocked her head towards me without taking her eyes off the screen.

'Gin, I think I've taken too many paracetamol. I don't feel good.'

She whipped round. 'What do you mean, stupid girl. How many have you taken? Is the bottle empty?' She leapt up, grabbed me by the shoulders and peered into my face as if the appearance of my eyes and skin might give her the answer. 'You *stupid* girl, I must go for help,' she said and, letting go of me, she hurried from the room.

I could hear her hammering on her neighbour's door then a murmured conversation and, minutes later, she reappeared with a woman called Eileen. I knew her, she was Gin's childminder and I liked her; she'd lived in London and she always had stories to tell. Once, when Gin wasn't listening, she'd told me she didn't see why I should marry someone I didn't know. She had her slippers on and a pink chiffon scarf which was covering a head full of rollers. I expected she'd be angry about having her evening disrupted but from the one shamefaced glance I shot her I could tell she was concerned.

'Check the pill bottle, it should be in the bathroom. I'll put the kettle on,' said Ginda. Eileen was quite lame. She hauled herself up the stairs laboriously and by the time she reappeared with the bottle – which was still about half full – Ginda was pouring me a cup of black coffee. She told me to keep standing up while I drank it. In the next hour or so she made me drink three cups of coffee and she and Eileen kept me moving round the living-room. It was well after midnight before they let me go to bed. As I headed for the stairs Ginda sighed and said, 'Nothing is going to change, Jas. Grow up and face facts.'

CHAPTER 6

The best thing in my life at that time was Avtar. We'd stayed in touch and one Saturday I bumped into her while I was running an errand for Mum. We exchanged pleasantries for a bit, but then she suddenly dropped her voice and said very quietly, 'Are you having an arranged marriage?' I was so surprised that I dropped my guard; I looked right back at her and nodded. And she said, just as quietly, 'So am I.'

I saw her quite often after that. Avtar seemed to accept her marriage in a way I just couldn't. 'Mine's quite good-looking,' she shrugged. 'Anyway, Jas,' she gripped my arm and spoke through her giggles, 'I'm going to enjoy my life until I'm shipped off to India. You know that boy who lives in Violet Street . . . ?'

That was Avtar for you: happy-go-lucky, cheeky, much more daring than me. Her parents were just as strict as mine but sometimes, somehow, she slipped their control. She had three sisters and five brothers and the brothers guarded her honour all right. They gave her a really hard time when they heard that she'd walked home with a boy, or if she went out in a low-cut blouse. But they were busy with their own lives; as long as Avtar went about her business quietly she often got away with it.

If my mum had known this she would never have let me be friends with her, but she didn't so all she had to worry about was the fact that Avtar's family were a much lower caste than us. They were *chamar*. Mum had never let us have *chamar* friends. Years before I'd challenged her on that. I asked her why, if our *chamar* neighbour went to the same *gurdwara* as us, I wasn't allowed to play out with her kids. Mum beat me for that, but I never got an explanation.

I don't know why she condoned my friendship with Avtar. Perhaps it was because she had strict parents and protective brothers. But she did condone it, she even let me visit Avtar after school. I had to get permission to go; I had to say when I would be going and when I'd be back and, having said, I would never dare be even five minutes late. I wouldn't risk losing that freedom.

Avtar's parents both worked and all her brothers had jobs so we were often alone in her house. We'd watch TV programmes all through instead of quickly flipping channels if a couple started kissing like we always did in our house. We listened to music, secretly rifling through her brothers' record collections. We talked and talked.

One day we went into the living-room and one of her brothers was there, sprawled on the sofa balancing a cup of coffee on his chest. He didn't move at first, just looked at me so long and hard I felt myself start blushing. Then he swung his legs round, stood up and gave me a lazy smile.

'Hi, I'm Jassey. Make yourself at home, I'm just leaving,' he said.

Once he was gone Avtar looked at me. Her eyes were stretched really wide and they were full of mischief as she burst out laughing. 'That's my good-looking brother. No need to ask what you thought of him: you should have seen your face!'

What happened next was really due to Avtar. She encouraged it: 'He was asking about you, Jas, I think he really likes you.' She engineered it: 'Look after Jas for me, will you, Jassey, while I make the tea.' She organized our meetings and acted as our alibi. But that came later; in those early days just being alone with Jassey while Avtar was in the kitchen felt like the most exciting thing I'd ever done. I'd never been alone with a male who wasn't Dad or Balbir. I'd never had a conversation with a boy, not even at school. But Jassey made it so easy; he was relaxed and friendly and he seemed interested in what I had to say. I felt we could talk for hours.

I started going round to Avtar's as often as I could. Mum and Dad knew where I was and they'd said I could go there, so I told myself that I wasn't deceiving them. I felt safe with Jassey. He was older than me, twenty-one when we met. He worked for an engineering firm in Derby but he was also a very keen boxer, semi-professional Avtar said. I surprised myself by telling him what I was going through at home and he surprised me by not laughing it off or telling me to accept it. He was a good listener and he was very sympathetic. I'd never before had anyone pay me so much attention.

As I was about to leave one evening about four weeks after we'd met he suddenly said, 'Will you go out with me?'

Without giving it a second's thought I said 'yes'. I could feel this big grin spreading over my face, and my cheeks flushed hot with pleasure. He looked pleased too, his face lit up. We were standing by the front door and he had his hand on the latch, barring my way.

'Avtar will tell you where to meet me,' he said, and then, leaning forward suddenly, he dropped a quick hot kiss on my lips. I was stunned; we stood there looking at each other for a second and then he swung the door open and gave me a gentle push, under the arch of his arm out onto the pavement. 'Bye then,' he said.

The next day Avtar was all giggles and innuendo. 'I'll call for you at six-thirty Friday,' she said. 'We'll pretend we're going round to mine but when we get to the top of my road Jassey will pick you up in his car.'

'But I'm at Presto Friday evenings.'

'Tell them you're not feeling well and you can't make it.'

'Mum will want to know where my money is.'

'You don't get much, do you? Jassey'll give it to you. He gets paid loads.'

She sounded so convinced I didn't argue. It was like I was in a bubble of excitement bouncing along at one remove from real life. When I was getting ready to go out on Friday Lucy came into our room and sat down on our bed.

'Why are you putting on make-up? You're only going to Presto.'

I pretended to be absorbed with my mascara and didn't answer.

'You're not going to Presto, are you? You've got your best trousers on. *And* that's your favourite blouse. Where are you going? What are you doing, Jas?'

I didn't even look round, but I could feel her gaze as she scrutinized my clothes.

'You're meeting someone, aren't you? I bet you are! Who is it?'

I'd finished doing my mascara. I put the brush down and turned to face her.

'Okay, you're right, I'm meeting someone. Just don't ask any more, okay?'

And she didn't. We both knew it was for the best. If you don't know, you can't get into trouble for not telling. If you don't know, when you're asked you can't say, even if they try to beat it out of you.

That first evening with Jassey was magical. It was just like Avtar said. She called for me. We set off for her house and at the top of her road there was Jassey waiting in a purple Escort. He'd rolled the passenger seat right back, so when I got in and lay back no one could see me. He knew to do that, I didn't have to ask him; in the Asian community lots of girls and boys have to hide their romance.

He drove for about fifteen minutes, right out of the Asian area and over to Markeaton Park, where I'd only been once or twice before, on family outings. We got out of the car and he put his arm round my shoulders and we walked away from the paths and through a wooded bit where the greenish-grey light coming through the leaves made everything look mysterious. I shivered and Jassey pulled me closer to him. There were so few people about that we could hear the racket the birds made as they settled in the trees. The ground was wet and our feet left silvery trails in the grass. I felt so full of happiness that I could hardly breathe.

On the way back we stopped at the children's play area and Jassey pushed me on the swings, higher and higher until, through my laughter, I was shouting at him to stop. He waited for the swing to slow down a bit, then he grabbed the chains and pulled it to a halt and, while I was still sitting there catching my breath, he nipped round the front and bending right down he kissed me, this time properly. I thought I was going to melt.

I had to be home at 10 p.m. We'd agreed I'd

walk back by myself from Jassey's road because it wasn't safe for him to come anywhere near my house. I'd been worrying what I'd tell Mum about my wages, but Avtar must have talked to him because just before we said goodbye he dug in his pockets and counted out £6.25. 'There, that should keep your mum happy.' Then, very quickly because we were back in the Asian area, he cupped my face with both his hands and kissed me goodnight.

That was the first of several visits to Markeaton Park that summer. It was our favourite place to go because we felt safe there, away from the eyes of the Asian community. In Markeaton Park Jassey first said 'I love you' and I said 'I love you too'. I don't know if I meant it. I certainly wasn't thinking 'I want to spend the rest of my life with this man and have his babies', but I didn't want to stop seeing him. I wanted to be with him more than anything at that moment. I was fifteen and I had a boyfriend and in the hours I spent with him I could forget about my duty and my family's honour and my future with the man whose picture leered down from our mantelpiece. I think those times with Jassey are the closest I have ever come to carefree.

I was so happy I got careless. There is a pond in the middle of Markeaton Park which, at its narrowest point, has stepping stones right across it. One evening just around dusk Jassey set out to cross them. He rolled his jeans up to his knees and stepped out very slowly and carefully with his arms outstretched for balance. When he got to the middle he swivelled round on the stone he was on and called to me to join him.

I was laughing as I stood at the brink, but I took my first step and shrieked when I felt how mossy and slippery it was.

'Come on, I dare you. It's easy,' Jassey said, holding out an arm for encouragement.

I took the first three at snail's pace, feeling about for a sure footing before shifting my weight. But when I reached the fourth stone I stretched out to reach Jassey and that was that.

Splash!

The water wasn't so very cold, but it was murky and full of weed. I came up with green slime trickling down my face. Jassey was laughing and so was I, laughing and struggling to keep my balance as I splashed water at him. It wasn't until I'd squelched my way to the side and Jassey pulled me out that it dawned on me.

'If Mum sees me like this she'll find out about us.'

My hair was dripping and my clothes were plastered to me. Looking down at the muddy puddle forming on the grass beneath me, I was caught between laughter and tears. Jassey was struggling to keep a straight face as he pulled a piece of weed out of my hair.

'Here, take your top off and put this on.' He was holding out his jumper.

'I can't, I'll never be able to explain that.'

'You'll just have to run in quick and hope no one sees you.'

'Look at the time, we're going to be late, Jassey. Quick, we can't stay here any longer.'

That night he dropped me closer to home than usual. It was taking a risk, but I couldn't walk too far through the streets dripping wet. I bolted down Dale Road until I got to our house. Away from Jassey I didn't see anything funny in my situation and I could feel my heart bumping in my chest. Very gingerly I tried the front door handle, praying it wouldn't squeak. If it was locked I was really sunk; thank God it wasn't. Holding my breath I eased the door open and slipped inside, ducking down so I couldn't be seen through the frosted glass panel in our inner door. I could hear the telly in the living-room. Prayed that Mum was watching it. I leant back against the wall, plucking up my courage to take the next step. The stairs were just opposite the door and I decided to make a run for them. Three, two, one, I did it. I didn't even bother to shut the door behind me.

'Is that you, Jasvinder?' Mum's voice reached me as I hit the first step.

'Yes, Mum. I need the toilet,' I called back, taking the stairs two at a time. I rushed into the bath-room, locked the door, tore off my clothes and turned the bath taps on. I felt weak with relief.

CHAPTER 7

It was inevitable that Mum would find out about Jassey but I never dreamt it would be me that told her. I did it because I was desperate and I couldn't think of any other way to save myself. It was on a Saturday afternoon and some of my aunties had come round for a visit. 'My daughter will get the tea for us, won't you, Jasvinder? She makes excellent tea, I feel confident that she is going to be a very good wife. Remember to use plenty of fennel, Jasvinder,' Mum said.

She was all puffed up and important as I passed the tray round the group of gossiping women, moving carefully between my elders and betters, smiling and respectful, eyes downcast as I'd been taught.

'Jasvinder will be going to Germany to make her marriage soon. A very good match has been made. We are pleased,' Mum said, fetching the photograph from the mantelpiece and placing it in greedy, outstretched hands. It was dog-eared now that so many of my aunties had fingered it, twisting it this way and that as they assessed my catch. 'Look how nicely he smiles, Jasvinder,' my auntie

Dhanna said. 'Not long now and you will be smiling for him too.'

Soon. Mum had said soon; but how soon? When? I wanted to scream out 'I won't do it. You can't make me. I won't go.' But I didn't. I sat there as expected, impassive, dutiful and quiet.

My mind was in turmoil. The holidays were only days away and that made me very nervous. Every year a couple of Asian girls would disappear from Littleover during the holidays. It was easier if they went then, when the teachers weren't expecting them, weren't making accusatory 'absent' marks in the big black register each day.

'Four saris in her chest. Such an expense, but now there is only Lucy left for me to think about.' Mum was showing off. For years she had felt herself pitied and patronized: 'Seven daughters? Oh my, Jagir, what a fate!' But this afternoon she was the queen, surrounded by admiring courtiers, all nodding their appreciation at her cleverness in marrying off six girls.

I had a vision of myself clinging to my bed, refusing to leave the house. Then the ghost of a whisper came back to me, something I'd overheard Robina discussing with a friend. I only caught snatches: '. . . sleeping pills . . . carried onto the plane . . . woke up in a taxi . . .' but I knew what they meant. I felt a prickle of sweat forming on my upper lip. Mum wouldn't dare to drug me. Surely Dad wouldn't let them do that.

'Yes, Ginda has a daughter but also a son, Sukdev,

we call him David. And Yasmin already has two fine boys and Prakash, you know, my daughter in London . . .' Mum was in her element. I'd never before heard her sounding so proud – or so fond – of us. I think that's what made me tell her. Either that or I had lost my wits through fear.

I waited until the aunties had gone and then, on my best behaviour, I carried the tea things through to the kitchen and washed them all up. When everything was put away I went to where Mum was doing in the living-room and touched her gently on the shoulder.

'Mum?'

Behind her glasses she blinked herself awake.

'Mum. You know my marriage? Well, the thing is this. I can't go through with it.'

Mum was wide awake now, sitting bolt upright in her chair.

'You see it's like this, Mum.' I swallowed hard. 'I can't go away. I've got a boyfriend. I'm seeing someone here.'

Why did I do it? What was I thinking? Did I, even for a second, imagine Mum would say, 'Oh, fine. Stay here and marry an untouchable whose family means nothing to us.'

The effect on her was instantaneous. Grabbing my arm she pulled herself off the sofa-bed and started yelling even before she'd found her feet. She took a couple of swipes at me but then changed tack and started beating herself, tearing at her hair and clothes. She was calling out for

Dad, for Ginda and Yasmin, for anyone who would listen. Robina, Lucy and Dad came running.

'Oh, the shame! What is this girl doing to me? She will kill me.' She clutched at her heart and steadied herself against a chair. 'All my life I have struggled to bring up seven daughters – seven daughters – and this one will not rest until she sees me dead. Ayee! I can hear them now, talking in the *gurdwara*.' She covered her ears and bent her head against the imagined gossip. 'Have you heard this now, Chanan? My daughter, *my daughter*, has a boyfriend. You have ruined yourself, girl. What will become of you? What will become of me? You have brought dishonour on us all.'

She went on and on until, having spent all her energy, she collapsed back onto the sofa-bed. I had sunk to my knees, sobbing, at the beginning of her onslaught but now, thinking to make my escape while she was exhausted, I stood up and slowly – very slowly – began to edge towards the door. Her hair had fallen from her bun and it was hanging wild about her face, but she spotted me and was on her feet again in seconds. She grabbed me by the hair on the back of my head, thrust her face into mine and screamed, 'You will stay in your room. Go there now. Don't think of coming out. I should never have trusted you. You will not go anywhere on your own.

'Chanan!' She jerked her head to indicate that Dad should follow me and, raising a shaking hand, mimed the turning of a key in a lock.

Dad followed me up the stairs. I was emotionally drained, almost too tired to speak, but as we reached the bedroom door I tried one last entreaty. I didn't quite dare to lean against him, but I yearned towards him as I said, 'Dad, please, don't let her make me marry him.'

He stood there looking sadly at me, then he gave a weary sigh and, dropping his eyes so he didn't have to see the plea in mine, he shook his head. I heard the key turn in the lock as I flung myself face down on my bed.

For the next three days that room was my prison. The first evening I was in there I heard Dad screwing a bolt onto the outside of the door. If I wanted to go to the toilet I had to shout out and whoever came to open the door would stand outside the bathroom. Lucy brought me food a couple of times a day but she never said much. She was angry with me and I knew why. I'd heard Mum shouting at her: 'Who is he? Where did she meet him? Don't try to protect that prostitute.' 'They've been to see Avtar,' she said on the second evening. She'd brought me up a bowl of dhal but the way she thrust it at me made it clear she wasn't planning to stop for a chat.

'What did she . . . ?'

'Nothing.' Her hand on the door handle, Lucy cut me off. 'But Mum told her parents that she wasn't welcome here anyway. She said Avtar was to stay away from you and so were her brothers.'

'Did they . . . ?' Lucy closed the door on my

question. I wanted to know if they had beaten Avtar. I hadn't thought about her until that moment. I'd barely thought of Jassey. My head ached from crying and my brain felt numb. In all the hours I'd lain on my bed I'd been tormented by a vision of me and the man in the photograph sitting side by side on a settee while Mum lectured us about honour. In my mind's eye my face was bruised and there were tears pouring down my cheeks.

I was so absorbed by this image that at first I didn't register the rattle on the window. When it came again I looked up and was quick enough to see a trickle of tiny stones slide down the glass. Two steps and I was there looking out. If I peered right round to the left I could see the street and there was Jassey's Escort right opposite the house. How did he dare? Where was he?

Suddenly the driver door opened and Jassey climbed out and walked along the pavement to stand beneath the lamppost just down from our house. He waved and my heart lurched at the sight of his slow familiar smile. Standing in the dim street light he started acting out a little charade. I tucked myself in behind the flimsy curtain and watched. His arms encircled the air in front of him and he planted a kiss on the imaginary person he was hugging. He pointed up to me and then down into the empty space in front of him. He tilted his head towards me and, with a clenched fist, bumped out the rhythm of his heart. If I ever really loved Jassey I think it was at that moment.

Then his mime changed. He pointed up to me, then to himself and then made out he was running. Given that his left hand was held out beside him, clenching thin air, I reckoned that I was supposed to be running with him. My smile faded as slowly it dawned on me what he was suggesting. Involuntarily I turned to look back into my bedroom, my *own* bedroom, a privilege my older sisters' marriages had bestowed on me. The curtain caught on my shoulder and the light from the street flooded in, illuminating the Magnum poster that I'd fixed above my bed with Blu-tack.

For a moment I stood there surveying the silhouettes of everything in that room that was familiar to me. The tangle of clothes that never quite got put away. The jumble of make-up spilling out across the chest of drawers. The narrow bed with its lumpy mattress and candlewick bedspread, mine alone and a haven after all those years of bed being a battlefield of arms and legs. The street light lit up the flowery wallpaper, the flowery carpet. I thought about how pleased and proud Mum was when we got them, 'the very latest design'. This was my bedroom and in all the time I had spent dreading my arranged marriage I had never actually envisaged leaving it.

I turned back to the street where Jassey, head on one side, was looking at me quizzically. I smiled and shrugged my shoulders. It seemed impossible.

Where would we go? What we would do? Who would I be without my family?

Those were the questions that ran through my mind in the days that followed. On the third day, after Mum had given me a long lecture about doing my duty, the bedroom door was left unlocked, but not the front and back doors. I wasn't allowed to use the phone and I wasn't allowed out of the house unless someone was with me. I spent hours sitting by the window, wondering about my future and waiting for Jassey to drive past. He kept coming. It wasn't always safe for him to stop but he'd drive past slowly enough to clock that I was watching. I began to think he was the only person in the world that cared about me.

The Saturday after I'd first been locked up, Mum said I was to come into town with her and Robina. Everyone was out and she didn't want me alone in the house. I thought I'd relish being out and about but it felt humiliating being sandwiched between my mum and my sister, walking at their pace, not being allowed to stop when I wanted to.

They had a couple of things to buy, and as we made our way up the street I became aware of a strange person shadowing us. At first I wasn't sure if it was a man or a woman. It was wearing women's clothes but the hair was obviously a wig and the lipstick, well, whoever applied it must have had their eyes shut.

My first instinct was to nudge Robina and have a giggle, but something stopped me. We got to

Bacon's where she was planning to buy some shoes and, while she and Mum discussed styles, they both relaxed their watch on me. That's when the person brushed against me. She – or he, I still hadn't decided – pretended they were moving towards the racks of shoes; they passed too close and I twitched away. I thought I felt a hand touch mine. A couple of seconds later it happened again but this time I moved so I could see the person's face.

It was Jassey!

My mouth dropped open in astonishment and I was about to say something but he frowned and shook his head almost imperceptibly. Again I felt the nudging hand but this time I met it and my fingers closed on a folded piece of paper which I quickly tucked into my pocket. Mum and Robina seemed to spend hours choosing shoes after that, then Mum wanted some spices and Robina needed something at the chemist. The shopping trip seemed to drag on for ever.

Eventually we got home and, with the note burning a hole in my pocket, I went straight upstairs to the bedroom.

I want to help you. We could go away together. I will look after you. Look out for me at 11 tonight J xxx

That's what the note said. I sat there for ages looking at it. I heard Mum rattling pots and pans in the kitchen. Somewhere downstairs Lucy and

Robina were having an argument. Dad came in from the pub and turned on the telly. If I went, would it finally make them understand?

I had to talk to Jassey but that seemed impossible when there was always someone watching me. Suddenly it struck me that there was a way to buy back my freedom. I considered it for a couple of seconds and then stood up and went downstairs.

I stopped in the kitchen doorway. Mum was at the stove.

'Mum, I've changed my mind, I will get married.'

She whipped round. Her face was stern but her voice was gentle as she said, 'What did you say, child?'

'I will get married, I will go through with it. I'll do it for you and Dad.'

'Good. At last you've come to your senses,' she said, nodding approvingly. As she turned again to her cooking pot I thought I saw a change in her bearing, her shoulders seemed to relax.

My announcement worked just as anticipated. The front and back doors were still locked but I wasn't so closely watched. The atmosphere changed. People were pleased with me, aunties who had lectured me came round and patted me and pinched my cheek. I forced myself to smile. Mum hummed as she smoothed and refolded the fabrics in my chest. The air was sticky with the smell of sweets, dozens of them being baked for me to take with me to my new relations. Their cloying scent hit the fear still settled on my stomach and made me nauseous.

My freedom was still very limited. I lived for the moments when I could ring Jassey. He never dared ring me. Our conversations were brief and urgent. I was scared. Mum hadn't said anything about dates but I could tell from the way preparations were going that they would be sending me away any day. I overheard her on the phone discussing flights to Frankfurt for me, her and Ginda. I couldn't think straight but Jassey seemed so confident.

'You can't marry a stranger,' he said. 'I'll look after you. We'll be fine.'

We made plans. I hid a small suitcase under my bed and gradually I packed it. I had to be careful no one noticed what went missing. All I took was a few clothes, a photograph of my dad and a photograph of Ginda's eldest, David, because I loved him very much. At the last minute I put in a panda bear that Robina had made at school in needlework. She'd given it to me several birthdays back and now it had a half-torn ear and an eye hanging off, but it was precious to me.

We'd worked out how to get the case out of the house. I couldn't just carry it out the front door because even if Mum and Dad didn't see me, one of the nosy neighbours in our terrace would. The night we'd agreed to do it I stayed awake until 2 a.m. I was so worn out with worry it was hard for me. I kept dropping off then jerking back awake. When the time came I tiptoed along to the bathroom, keeping as close as possible to the walls so the floorboards didn't creak. I'd pulled the sheet off my bed and now I knotted it really tightly to the handle of the case. My heart was beating so hard I could almost hear it.

I flushed the toilet to disguise the noise of the sash window scraping open then I ran the tap as, standing on the seat, I gingerly lowered the case down into the garden. The sheet wasn't quite long enough and I suffered agonies of indecision before deciding I would have to let it drop. It landed with a dull thud. My mouth was dry and the blood was pounding in my ears. I stood there frozen as I waited to hear Mum stamping out of her bedroom, come to see what was happening. A couple of minutes passed and nothing broke the silence. I sank down onto the toilet seat and sat there with my head in my hands until my pulse slowed down.

Next morning I woke with a start at eight o'clock. Mum would have gone to work and I could hear Dad in the bathroom. I hurried downstairs, through the shed and into the garden. The case was gone. Having checked no one was watching from an upstairs window I looked behind the stack of empty seed trays piled up by the back gate. My sheet was there, neatly folded. As I picked it up I felt the crackle of a piece of paper beneath the top fold. It was a scrap torn from a paper bag.

3 a.m. WE DID IT! J xxx

CHAPTER 8

I spent the next few days in limbo feeling as if all my drive and energy had been sapped. I was ready to go but I couldn't imagine going. This was my home. It was what I knew and who I was. I looked in the mirror and fancied that I saw myself dissolving.

Then something happened to snap me out of my torpor. I was woken one morning by the sound of the front door slamming. I looked at my watch: it was late. Mum would have been at work for hours, Dad would be asleep after his night shift; it must have been Lucy going out. From where I lay I could hear her footsteps hurrying down the pavement. Something – instinct, intuition, call it what you like – made me want to see if she had remembered to lock the door behind her. Perhaps it was just hope. I climbed out of bed, went downstairs and gingerly tried the handle. The door opened. I closed it again instantly, and as quietly as I could. I knew I had to seize this opportunity.

Upstairs, I tore a page out of one of my school exercise books and sat down to write Mum and Dad a note. There were so many thoughts crashing round inside my head that I struggled to find the words to describe why I was going, how I felt. I kept crossing bits out and starting again: I wrote three or four versions but in the end what I left on my pillow was this.

Dear Mum and Dad,

When you read this I will have gone but I can't say where. I've tried to explain things to you but you won't listen so I can't stay here any more. I'm too young to get married. I want to go to college and make you proud of me. I want to have a life.

Don't worry about me because I'm going to be okay. I love you both very much and hope I will see you again soon.

Your loving daughter, Jasvinder.

Once it was done I wanted to go straight away. I had nothing to pack. I told myself to wait a while. Jassey was at work and he didn't know I was coming. It would be better to wait until the working day was over, but I was terrified that Lucy would come back. I sat down in front of the telly and tried to concentrate but I found myself looking at my watch every five minutes. I drank two cups of coffee. The house seemed deathly quiet. Even the street outside seemed dead and empty. At about twelve o'clock I couldn't stand it any longer. I got up and ran.

I ran as if the hounds of hell were after me, up

Dale Road, Normanton Road, into the centre of town and out again. I was so scared of getting caught, it was not until I was well clear of the Asian area that I slowed my pace a bit; I was hot and I needed to catch my breath.

With only the vaguest idea where Jassey's workplace was I got lost several times but I wasn't bothered. Outside the Asian area I felt anonymous. When I asked directions I was careful to ask white people and I was glad to see I didn't spark their interest, they barely noticed me. Eventually I found the engineering works, tucked under a bridge on the outskirts of Derby. There were a good two hours to go before Jassey's shift was over, so I sat down on a wall to wait for him. I sat there willing the hours to pass. My heart was racing, but time seemed to have slowed to a crawl, eking out each minute between the ending of my old life and the beginning of my new one.

Jassey was absolutely shocked when he came out and found me there. I was too caught up in my own feelings to give him credit for that and I babbled on, oblivious to his incomprehension. When I paused for breath he said, 'We can't go now. We're not ready.'

'But we've got to go. Don't you understand? I might not be able to get out of the house again.'

He stood there, twisting his overalls in his hands, looking really worried.

'But Jas, what about work? I haven't told them. I can't just . . .'

'You said you'd help me. You said you loved me. Well, now's the time. I'm telling you Jassey, it's not safe for me to stay here any longer.'

He came round quite quickly although it can't have been easy for him. His workmates were streaming past, calling out and teasing him for talking to me. Once he'd made his mind up he said he'd need about an hour to go back to his house, pack his stuff and get mine. He said I was to stay there and wait for him.

That was the longest hour. The sun went in and as the streets emptied I felt conspicuous and cold. Eventually the purple Escort pulled up beside me. Jassey was looking hassled but he managed a smile. His mum had seen him carrying cases out of the house and asked where he was going. 'I just told her I'd be back later.' He hadn't even had time to leave a note for her. At that moment I was too self-absorbed to think what that must have meant to him.

My heart was racing. It was six o'clock: Mum would be getting home soon and people would realize I was missing. Then they'd start looking for me. I was scrunched up in my seat, trying to see out of the car window without being seen myself.

'Where are we going to go then?' Jassey said.

I gawped at him. We'd never even thought about that. He picked a map book off the back seat and opened it at the page with Derby on it. 'Here,' he said. 'Close your eyes and point. Wherever your finger lands, that's where we'll go.'

So I did. My finger landed on Newcastle. It meant nothing to me; I'd never been; I didn't know anybody there. Jassey said he'd been once, to visit an auntie, years before. It took us about four hours to drive there and we hardly talked at all. What I had done was beginning to sink in, and my stomach was churning with a mixture of relief and terror. The fact that I had actually managed to escape made me feel elated, but at the same time I was convinced that at any moment someone would catch up with us and drag me home again. Just outside Derby a police car passed us with its siren screaming and I sank down into the footwell of my seat and remained crouched there for the rest of the journey.

Jassey was scared too, and very worried about what we'd done. During all our preparations I don't think he'd really considered things properly. I was so young, so naive, although I don't think he saw me like that. He never took advantage of me, or made me do anything I didn't want to do. As far as he was concerned, he'd fallen in love with me and I was in trouble and he wanted to help.

It might sound very romantic but Jassey and I were not Romeo and Juliet. I wanted to teach Mum a lesson. I wanted her to say, 'Oh, all right then, come home, you don't have to get married. Finish school. Go to college. Do all the stuff the other kids are doing.' I must have been mad.

We stopped once on the way and got a cup of

tea and some chips, and it was after ten o'clock by the time we reached Newcastle. We'd agreed that we'd sleep in the car to save money until we could find a room to rent, so Jassey found a public car park and we pulled our jackets over us and tried to get comfortable. I can remember biting really hard on my collar so that Jassey wouldn't hear me crying but he did anyway, and for what felt like ages he sat up, stroking my hair.

The next morning I woke up feeling cold and stiff, with all my worries sitting like a rock on my stomach. It felt so strange not having to watch the clock; I'd been used to having every minute monitored, now time stretched ahead of me like a vast blank canvas. We washed our faces in the public toilet in the middle of the car park and got some more tea in a café and then tried to sort ourselves out. We needed somewhere to stay and a job for Jassey, so we trailed up and down the streets looking at the ads in newsagent windows.

Finally we just sat in the car. We were so scared of being seen. Although I kept telling myself I was really glad I'd escaped, I couldn't help imagining what it would be like if I was still at home. I blanked out the chest full of bridal fabrics and that picture on the mantelpiece and just saw me and Lucy watching telly in the living-room, Mum in the kitchen chopping vegetables for the curry, and Dad sitting opposite her at the kitchen table sipping his tea before the night shift. It was all so warm and familiar it made me ache with longing. I grabbed hold of Jassey's hand and squeezed it really tight.

We were desperate to save our money, but living in the car was so grim that after a couple of days we checked into the Heron Hotel. A really lovely old couple ran it. They invited us to watch telly with them in their lounge and gave us tea and biscuits and they asked us so many questions – not prying, just friendly – that we ended up telling them our story. After that they let us stop another night without paying.

It must have been on about day four that we came across a shopkeeper who said he had a place that we could stay in. It was very dingy: one room three floors above his shop, with a shared kitchen and bathroom one flight down.

There were cigarette burns in the carpet and the only furniture apart from the bed was a chest of drawers and two hard chairs. The bed looked quite clean but the mattress was really thin. The kitchen stank of old grease, only one ring worked on the cooker and there was a pane missing in the bath-room window so it was permanently freezing. I felt my stomach lurch as Jassey said we'd take it. Home, in comparison, was a five-star hotel.

I thought that often in the months that followed, months when it got so cold that we could make jelly and leave it on the windowsill to set overnight. I was from a working-class family, no doubt about that, but until Jassey and I moved to Newcastle

I'd never felt poor. At home we'd always had hot water and clean clothes and enough to eat. Now, especially in the weeks when Jassey couldn't get much work, we often only ate one meal a day; sometimes we couldn't afford anything more than a bag of chips. I got used to bathing in the luke-warm trickle of water that the decrepit Ascot boiler spat out, but there was never enough of it to wash our clothes so we used to save up our fifty-pence pieces and take them to the launderette every two or three weeks. I'd brought very few clothes with me and those I had soon looked worn and grey but there was no money for anything new. I was beyond caring about my appearance anyway, and for the first weeks, before I felt confident enough to go out and start looking for work, I never went anywhere that it mattered what I looked like. The area we were living in was rough. The all-seeing eye of 'the community' used to drive me mad in Derby but at least I never feared coming to phys-ical harm on the streets. In our squalid area of Newcastle even Jassey's old Escort was a target for thieves and it was broken into twice. I never walked outside alone at night.

We tried to keep ourselves to ourselves and avoid the Asian areas but even so Jassey managed to pick up snippets of information; there was talk about us on the Asian grapevine. He learnt that my mum and dad had been round to his place and demanded to know where I was. Avtar was beaten until she finally persuaded her parents that she didn't know anything about our whereabouts. When I heard this I was glad we hadn't told anybody or implicated any of our siblings in our 'crime'. For years that's how I saw our escape; I felt I was the baddy and my family were the goodies and that didn't feel nice.

We heard a rumour that my mum and dad had hired a private detective and about ten days after our flight from Derby the police caught up with us. Early in the morning – before Jassey had set off on his daily search for work – there was a knock on the door. It was such a strong, authoritative rat-tat-tat that we guessed at once that it was the police. I was sitting on the bed and Jassey gestured that I should stay there as he went to open the door.

'Jaswant Rattu?'

From my position out of sight of the door, I could see Jassey nodding his head.

'I have reason to believe that you have abducted and are now harbouring a young lady, Jasvinder Kaur Kang. She went missing from her home in Derby ten days ago and has not contacted her family since. They are very concerned for her safety. Can I come in so we could discuss this?'

As Jassey stood back to let the policeman cross the threshold, I rushed forward, tears pouring down my face, and blocked his way.

'It's not like that.' I scrubbed at my tears with my sleeve. 'Jassey didn't abduct me, he rescued me, I asked him to take me, he was trying to help me because my parents are trying to force me into a marriage, he's never hurt me, it's them who . . .'

'Slow down, Miss, slow down and then we can get this sorted out. Now, if you wouldn't mind me coming in?'

I drew back to stand beside Jassey and as the policeman stepped inside I saw him run an appraising eye around our dingy room with its unmade bed. Our bed. I wanted to hide that from him. What we did together there was so beautiful and magical and mind-blowing that I couldn't stand to have it held up for scrutiny.

The policeman was tall and heavily built. He took off his helmet and I could see that his hair was greying and he had a fatherly air about him.

'May I?' He gestured to one of our two chairs. Jassey took the other and I sat back down on the bed.

'Now, if you'd like to tell me the whole story, but go slowly please so I can get it straight.'

So I did, I told him everything, starting with the fact that the plane ticket had been bought and how if Jassey hadn't rescued me – I made out he was the saviour in the whole situation – I would have been forced to go to Germany to get married. I explained that I didn't want to get married, let alone to someone I didn't know, because I wanted to finish school and go to college. I told him that Mum and Dad wouldn't listen to me no matter how much I begged them to, and I even told him about Prakash and Ginda and how their husbands

88

beat them. Then I swore blind that Jassey hadn't put me up to anything I hadn't wanted to do and pointed out that I'd be sixteen in just a few weeks.

All the time I was talking the policeman sat there listening; occasionally he looked surprised or nodded his head. He was so quiet and kind and it was such a relief to pour it all out.

'I've seen this before,' he said, when finally I'd finished. 'I understand your position, Miss, and I understand why you did what you did, so don't worry: I'm not going to tell your parents where you are. What I will do is tell them that you've contacted the police and that you are safe. And I think it would be a good idea, Miss, if some time soon you would ring them and tell them that yourself. All right then?' He gave an encouraging smile. 'Good luck to you both,' he said, as he stood up and left.

I wish I could remember that man's name because I owe him a debt of gratitude. If he'd taken me home I'm sure I would have been on the next plane out to Germany and the rest of my life would have turned out very differently.

CHAPTER 9

I longed to make that call home but for weeks
I didn't have the courage. Time – acres of
empty, unmonitored time – stretched out,
leaving Derby further and further behind, and I
yearned to do something that would close the gap.
It was the comfortable familiarity of it all that I
missed. I wanted to walk down our street and
know the people that I saw; I wanted to go into
our corner shop and put my hand on the groceries
on my list without having to think twice; I wanted
to stand in the playground at Littleover, laughing
with my friends. If you'd told me the previous
term that I'd mind leaving school I'd have laughed,
but . . . I kept thinking of the English teacher
who'd handed back my essay saying, 'Very good,
Jasvinder. You're showing promise.' What good was
promise now?

   Images of home teased me, dancing in and out
of my mind. I'd see Mum sitting on the floor in
the living-room peeling onions. Dad standing on
the back doorstep, his hand cupped around a cigarette. I can't believe I'm writing this, but I almost
missed Mum's nagging: 'A bag of flour and a white

loaf and straight back, mind, no loitering or skipping off.' In those days she always knew where I was.

I knew I'd call home eventually and in my mind I ran through the conversation I'd be having many times: Mum answering the phone, calling across to Dad, 'It's Jasvinder. She's safe!' Everybody crying, telling me I was forgiven and that everything was going to be all right.

I couldn't have been more wrong.

Mum's harsh words cut me to the quick – even today I wince at the sharp pain their memory brings – but almost as bad was the fact that she didn't even ask where I was. She hung up on me without even trying to find that out. It was like she was already being as good as her word:

'In our eyes you're dead.'

Deep down inside I couldn't really believe Mum had meant that. I couldn't accept I meant so little to her. I wrote to her, hoping words could bridge the gulf that had opened up between us.

Dear Mum and Dad,

I hope you are well. I am well but I miss you very much. I wish I could see you, or even talk to you. I think of you a lot.

I'm sorry I made you cross by running away and I hope you can forgive me, but you know why I left. I didn't want to leave you, but I didn't want to marry that man either. I'm too young to get married. My teacher at school

said I could do A levels. I want to make some-
thing of my life.

Please forgive me, I'd like to come home. I
miss you very much. I love you both and I
wish I could be with you. I hope I will be, some
day soon. Please tell my nephew David that I
love him.

Your loving daughter, Jasvinder.

I sent that letter and then I kept ringing, more and more often, but every time it was the same. If Mum or Dad answered, they'd just put the phone down. I felt I'd been kicked every time Dad did that.

Once I rang and Lucy hissed, 'Do you realize what you've done to us? How difficult it is for Gin at her house? Do you know what they're saying in the *gurdwara*, that people spit at Mum in the street?' And then she hung up.

I'd thought my sisters would support me but I was wrong. I don't know if the things they said were true. All I knew was that my whole family was rejecting me and they were saying this is *your* fault; this is because of what *you've* done.

Poor Jassey. When I could force myself to focus on our situation, it looked impossibly bleak. There we were in a strange city, cut off from all the people we knew and loved. Jassey had given up his secure job and income for my sake, and there didn't seem much work to be had in Newcastle, not for Asian people anyway. He'd been my knight in shining armour; he'd done it because he loved me, and that made me feel bad too, because although I loved his kindness and his sweet funny ways, in my heart of hearts I knew I'd never really loved him.

I'd made my bed and I had to lie in it. We had somewhere to live. Once we'd signed on for benefits we found somewhere a bit nicer, somewhere that was clean at least, but we still didn't feel settled. When I turned sixteen I started to look for work, but my heart wasn't really in it; most days I just sat on our bed wrapped up in my thoughts. With every day that passed I got more and more depressed. I'd lost my dad, my mum, my sisters, my brother, my nephews, my nieces, all those aunties who had so annoyed me with their busybody ways, my friends, Avtar . . . everybody. The only reminder I had of home was my two photographs and Robina's little cloth panda. I used to cry myself to sleep and I would wake up crying in the morning and the panda would be drenched with tears. My cheeks were red and raw. My skin flared up with all the anxiety and in the afternoons when Jassey came home we used to trawl the health shops looking for herbal remedies. Sometimes my homesickness and guilt and fear and loneliness would chase each other round my mind so furiously that I felt possessed. I'd peer into the mirror trying to see if the turmoil inside me was visible on my face. Sometimes I didn't recognize the blank face of the person staring back at me. I felt so isolated I didn't know who I was any more.

When it got really bad, Jassey put me in the car at five in the morning and drove me down to Derby just so I could see and smell the place where I'd grown up. He drove past my house then parked a small distance away so I could see my dad walking home from work. I watched him trudge along, his thermos and his newspaper – the Asian paper, he never learnt to read English – tucked under one arm. His feet dragged slightly and my heart bled. He looked much older than I remembered. I had to stop myself leaping out and chasing after him; once I gripped the edge of my seat so hard I broke my nails. I longed to talk to him but I knew if Mum found out she'd be furious and I didn't want to get him into trouble.

Sometimes we parked outside Dale primary school where my nephews and nieces then went and I pressed myself against the playground fence and watched them with their friends. I reached my hands out as if to touch them. It comforted me to see them looking so carefree. At least *they* weren't old enough to hate me.

Those visits were a bit like watching a soppy movie. For a couple of hours I could step out of my reality and pretend I was part of someone else's. Sometimes, driving through those streets I had known all my life, I could almost feel happy; the look of relief on Jassey's face when that happened made me realize what a burden he was carrying. He was endlessly supportive. But I was always crying again before we got back to Newcastle. My family had washed their hands of me, they were completely out of my reach, but I couldn't stop loving them.

It didn't help that Jassey was back in touch with his family. He waited a few weeks, until we were sure that they weren't going to send anybody after us, and then he rang home. His mum was really pleased to hear from him, she said she'd been worried sick about what my family might do to him. She wanted to know if he'd got work and where he was living, if I was cooking for him properly. I don't think she asked anything else about me, but she accepted our situation and she didn't blame Jassey for what he'd done, not on the phone at least. After the first few months we even saw them sometimes and the fact that he still had his family rubbed salt in the wound left where mine had severed our connection. He was still their son but I was no one's daughter.

'What does that make me? Who am I?' I used to wail to Jassey.

'You're my sweetheart,' he'd say, and hold me close. I leant on him so heavily during that first year in Newcastle. He bore the brunt of all my moods and feelings. Sometimes I had good days but the slightest thing – even the thought of my nephew's birthday – would lay me so low that I couldn't face the world outside our door.

It was to cheer me up that Jassey first suggested

we drive to Whitley Bay. It was a Saturday morning four or five months after we'd run away and I was sitting on our bed, too apathetic even to get dressed. Normally Jassey would have tried to coax me out of my mood, clowning around until he made me smile, but that morning he simply said, 'Come on, get up, we're going to the seaside.'

I'd never been before. It was less than an hour's drive from our flat. Jassey kept singing a Cliff Richard song, 'We're All Going on a Summer Holiday', and it did feel a bit like we were going on holiday. For the first time in months we were having a break from the grind of trying to build our life together.

We found a car park and walked past the amusement arcade to get to the beach. I will never forget my first sight of it, ever. I stood there on the promenade looking at this vast expanse of sand and beyond it sea, sea, sea right out to the horizon and I just thought 'Wow'. I couldn't believe that I had lived in England all my life and never before seen this extraordinary phenomenon. There was so much more of it than I had ever considered possible. I stood there and I could feel the boundaries of my world expanding: if this exists, I thought, what else is there I haven't seen?

Jassey grabbed my hand and pulled me down onto the beach. The silvery sand felt so heavy underfoot; I sank a bit with every step and it poured over the edges of my shoes. I stooped to pick up handfuls of the stuff and found it was nothing, it just flowed through my fingers and was gone, caught in the wind and carried off to infinity.

'Let's paddle,' said Jassey, who was already rolling his jeans up. We kicked off our shoes and socks and raced down to the water's edge. The dry sand scratched and crunched between my toes, but when we crossed the scummy line marking the retreating tide, I was astonished to find it transformed into a hard, cold surface. Holding hands and laughing we stood on the brink and then shrieked as a wave rolled in, soaking our trouser legs.

'It's freezing,' I yelled, dancing in the foam. We dodged the waves until our toes went numb and then, collecting our shoes, started walking down the beach towards the lighthouse at the end of it. It was a beautiful day, cold, but the sun was bright and for the first time in months we behaved like the young lovers we were supposed to be. Jassey flicked some seaweed at me and I screamed and ran away but then as I pulled the slimy strands out of my hair I saw all the little bubbles it was made of and discovered you could pop them. We skirted the water's edge trying to stay just far in enough to stop the waves swallowing our footprints. We hopped as far as we could, kidding ourselves that anyone who came after us would think they were following one-legged people. We found a sharp-edged stone and used it to write our names in the sand. We wrote, so big that all the world could see: 'I love you Jas', and 'I love you Jassey' and a heart with an arrow through it.

Eventually we came to a rocky outcrop near the lighthouse and, moving carefully on our cold, bare feet, found a smooth bit to sit on. For a while we were quiet, looking out across the sea, its iron-grey surface corrugated by white-fringed ripples. The seagulls screeched as they swooped and dived, and I gave myself up to the smell and the sound and the feel of the wind whipping over us. But Jassey was never quiet for long. Standing up, he gave an elaborate bow and said very solemnly:

'You are my sweetheart and I love you so much and to show you just how much I am going to drink sea water out of your shoe.'

He picked up my shoe, dipped it into a nearby rock pool and did as he had promised. At least he took one gulp and swallowed but then he gagged and spluttered and used the excuse of giving another bow to spill the rest. I laughed and laughed and as he came and sat beside me, folding his arms around me, I realized that, for the first time since we'd left home, I felt really happy.

Eventually we walked back along the beach and bought fish and chips and sat on a wall eating them. It wasn't until I was full and contented, licking the vinegar off my fingers, that I realized that in all the time we'd been at Whitley Bay I'd never once thought about Mum, Dad or my sisters. It struck me as strange then that I didn't know if Mum and Dad had ever seen the sea, except from the ship that brought them over. I could imagine Dad enjoying himself here, standing with his hands in his trouser pockets, smoking a cigarette and looking out to the horizon, but I'm not sure Mum would have liked it.

I wrote about that day in our diary. It was something we'd decided to keep together; Jassey said that one day we'd give it to our children. We were supposed to take it in turns to write but Jassey never seemed to find the time and I teased him about it. I wrote:

> *It's me again because he's too lazy to write our diary. Today my sweet took me to the seaside and told me he loved me and drank sea water out of my shoe.*

Then a couple of days later Jassey picked it up and wrote:

> *Sweet is nagging me again to write in this book. What she doesn't understand is that I work to feed her and clothe her and she has such a big appetite. But I love her dearly, she is my life.*

CHAPTER 10

We must have stayed in Newcastle about twelve months but that time is a blur to me. My days were long and purposeless and they all seemed the same. We never felt settled; I never stopped feeling like a fugitive. We were scared to tell the truth about who we were and what we were doing so it was hard to make friends. We felt so far from Derby, the city where our hearts were stranded. I felt that most keenly at holiday times. During *Diwali* I thought my heart would break. We were irresistibly drawn to the Asian area where we belonged. The pavements were clustered with people out visiting and parading their new clothes. Candles flickered in the windows of all the houses round us. At home Mum used to put candles in every room, even our bedroom, and for that one night it would be like living in a twinkling fairyland. She'd cook samosas and their hot, spicy smell would fill the house as she dropped them one after another into the bubbling oil. She let us eat loads.

Those memories were so vivid and so painful. *Diwali* is a special family time, and Jassey and I were on our own, hundreds of miles from home. We were lonely and, without our families, we were lost. That was the same for both of us. We'd been brought up by strict controlling parents who directed our lives and supported us along the routes they'd chosen for us. On our own we were rudderless. Until we ran away we'd always done what was expected of us; torn from that expectation we were aimless and uncertain. We were drifting on a frightening and uncharted sea of possibility.

One problem was that Jassey couldn't find regular work. Engineering was what he knew and there were engineering works in Newcastle but they didn't seem keen to employ anybody Asian. He did what he could get so we could survive – factory work, waiting, security – but he longed for something better.

That longing took us to Leeds. I don't know why we chose Leeds, it could have been London, or Huddersfield, or Manchester. Anywhere really. We just felt that if we moved on things might fall into place. We sold Jassey's Escort to raise some money and in its place we bought an ancient Toyota which was good on fuel. Having piled it high with our worldly possessions we set off. Leaving Newcastle didn't mean any more to me than leaving the bedsit in which I'd spent day after miserable day, week after week. I never, ever thought I'd miss it; I'd spent so long considering that dingy room to be my prison but it was a palace compared to the first place we found in Leeds.

We were back at square one, traipsing up and down scruffy streets scouring each newsagent's window for a card advertising a room we could afford. We had so little money and we couldn't claim benefits without an address so on the first day Jassey accepted a place that, under any other circumstances, I wouldn't choose to house a dog in.

The man who showed it to us, with his great beer belly hanging over his trousers, behaved as if he was showing us the Hilton. Then he flicked the ash from his cigarette onto the floor, and when I watched him use the toe of his shoe to grind it in I understood how the carpet had come to look so grimy. You could hardly see the pattern on it and it felt sticky underfoot. The whole place smelt: a mixture of stale cigarettes and something I felt sure was urine.

We were too embarrassed to inspect the bed closely until we had handed over a week's rent in exchange for the key, but as soon as our new landlord shut the door behind him we raced over to it. It was infested. When you pulled back the greying bedcover you could see the creepy crawlies with the naked eye.

'We won't get in, we'll sleep on top of it,' said Jassey, quickly jerking back the cover so the horrible things were out of sight. 'In fact, you can sleep on top of me, then you won't have to touch it.'

That's what we tried to do. If it hadn't been so

grim, it would have been funny. We got ready for bed by putting on our coats then Jassey lay flat on his back and I lay down on top of him. The fact that we managed to fall asleep like that shows how tired we were but, of course, I kept rolling off Jassey onto the filthy mattress and climbing back on again woke us both up. In the morning we were exhausted and Jassey was covered in bites that had him scratching like a monkey.

We were out of there by half past seven. Our rent included use of a kitchen but one peep round its door was enough to persuade us we didn't want to go in any further. From where we stood we could see mouse-droppings all over the counter. Just round the corner from our room was a greasy spoon café where Jassey said we could have breakfast. Its door was shut against the cool morning air and the windows were all steamed up on the inside. We pushed our way in and were immediately enveloped by a fug of comforting smells: beans and toast and frying bacon. Jassey ordered two mugs of tea and one plate of toast to share.

'But I'm hungry, can't we have a fry-up?'

'We can't afford it, sweet, you know that. We've only got forty pounds to last us until I can find work or we can pick up our benefits.'

'All I know is that you're always saying we can't afford things. If we're hungry we should eat. You're just tight-fisted, that's your trouble.' My stomach had started to rumble at the sight of laden plates of eggs and bacon being whisked past our table and it was making me bad-tempered. Jassey looked so crestfallen that I immediately felt guilty and ashamed. I leant across the table and kissed him.

'I'm sorry, sweet, I didn't mean it. I know you are trying to make things work for us and I'm grateful, I really am. Maybe Leeds is going to be a better place for us.'

We lingered over those mugs of tea as long as possible. We were determined not to spend a second longer than we had to in our filthy, grotty room and the day stretched ahead of us, long and empty. Our priority was finding somewhere decent to live and by lunchtime we must have read every single 'To Let' card in ten newsagents' windows. I felt as if I'd been trudging up and down the network of narrow streets for ever and still there was nothing in our price range, nothing we could even ask about.

We needed a break to lift our flagging spirits and Jassey suggested we go and look at Roundhay Park. We thought we'd walk round it but when we got there we just threw ourselves down on the grass and lay there side by side holding hands. For a while we watched the white clouds scudding through the brilliant blue sky above us but gradually the warmth of the spring sunshine soothed us to sleep. It was gone four o'clock by the time I woke up again. Jassey was still fast asleep and I tickled his nose with a blade of grass until he jerked awake sneezing. The sun had gone in and I felt slightly damp and cold but my mood was definitely lighter.

Roundhay Park became an oasis to us in the next few days. We went there every afternoon when our search for somewhere to live became too depressing and we'd spin out the hours wandering through its many acres. We walked for miles; there were woods carpeted with bluebells, the ruins of the old castle to explore and Waterloo lake where we sat and watched the swans and herons. One day when we've got money, I told myself, I'll come back here with bread and feed them.

On about the fifth day we sat on a bench quite near the entrance and shared a take-away burger for our lunch. When we'd finished Jassey got up to get rid of the greasy wrapping and there, right at the top of the bin, was a copy of that day's *Yorkshire Post*, which someone had dumped. He fished it out and while he was reading the news, I opened the classifieds and began browsing the flats to let section. I wasn't expecting to find anything we could afford, I was only doing it to pass the time, but one particular flat jumped out at me. I nudged Jassey.

'Listen to this, this sounds great.' I marked the ad with my finger and started reading. 'Two bed flat with verandah, Roundhay. Separate lounge. Kitchen. Bathroom. £30 per week.'

I turned to Jassey expectantly but he didn't even look up from the page he was reading. 'Forget it,' he said. 'We can't afford it. It's way out of our price range.'

'But can't we just go and look? It's somewhere

105

near here; just where we want to be. They don't know we can't afford it, and anyway there's nothing to stop us looking. It would give us something to do.' I jumped up and started trying to drag Jassey to his feet. 'Come on, sweet, please. It'd be better than sitting here all afternoon.' Jassey sighed and smiled at me; it hadn't been difficult to persuade him.

We found a phone box; Jassey rang the number in the ad and arranged for us to go round at four o'clock that afternoon. The address was Newton Court, Roundhay. We drove over there in good time and found it easily. The flat was one of four in a big white house with an open verandah which led off the kitchen and ran round the front of the building. Someone had put chairs out so you could sit overlooking the garden.

The door was opened by a young man, about the same age as Jassey. He introduced himself as Anil. He had thick slicked-back hair and flashy clothes and we later found out he was half-Asian, half-Iranian. He was really friendly as he showed us the flat and it was gorgeous. There wasn't much furniture but the lounge had a settee and a small round table and chairs to sit on and, although one room only had a mattress on the floor, the bed in the bigger bedroom looked newish. The whole place was fresh and clean and I loved it. We had a look round and then he offered us a cup of tea and explained that he was in the import business; dealing mostly in fabrics but sometimes carpets.

He and Jassey were getting on really well; for so long we'd had no one but ourselves to talk to. I could hear Jassey telling him about us leaving Derby and wanting to make a home for ourselves, but I couldn't concentrate on the conversation because my whole mind was thinking, 'Somehow we've got to live here.'

Eventually Anil said, 'So, what do you think of the place? Do you want to take it?'

Normally I would have let Jassey do the talking but this time I butted in immediately. 'It's nice but it's a bit expensive. Is there any chance that you might drop the rent a bit?'

He looked really surprised. It could have been partly because I'd been so forward; up until that point I hadn't really said much. He thought for a bit and then he said, 'Look, like I told you, I'm in the import business and I'm away a lot but I need a room in Leeds sometimes, maybe four or five nights a month. If you don't mind me using that second bedroom when I need it we could call it twenty-five pounds a week. How would that suit you?' Jassey and I just sat there, grinning like idiots.

That flat brought me back to life a bit. It wasn't in an Asian area and that felt liberating. When I thought about it, I realized that it was a long time since we'd felt the need to lose ourselves in a crowd or be invisible. The rumours Jassey heard about people trying to track us down when we were first in Newcastle had dried up months and months ago, which was a relief, obviously. But it hurt having to accept that my family didn't even care enough to look for me.

Still, having a decent place to live made all the difference and I began to feel some energy flowing back into me. I started cooking meals for us and it made me feel like I had a bit of control over my life. I cooked Asian food because the taste and smell of it was always comforting. I liked the line of spice jars on the wall by the cooker. We got on really well with the owner of the flat and it felt – for the first time since we'd run away – as if we weren't completely isolated. Work was still a problem though and Jassey signed on for benefits.

I was still calling home regularly at that point. I never stopped craving any tiny crumb of contact. I know now how hard you have to stamp on hope before you can crush it altogether. The calls became almost formulaic. Lucy answered after two or three rings and her 'hello' was pleased and welcoming, as though she was expecting a call from a friend. When she heard it was me she muttered something disappointed or exasperated like, 'Oh it's you,' or, 'Won't you ever learn' before ramming the phone back on the hook. Mum and Dad took longer to answer. I used to imagine Mum heaving herself off the floor and walking heavily towards the phone. They never said anything in greeting, just waited silently for me to announce myself. I'd know if it was Mum because she put the phone down really quickly, but if it was Dad it took longer, and sometimes before the click I'd hear a heavy sigh. The one thing I regretted about having our own phone was being stuck in the same room with it when the line to my family went dead. At least when I was calling from a phone box I could walk away, distance myself from the rejection and clear my head.

One night something different happened. Lucy answered and she didn't hang up. I was so surprised I faltered.

'Lucy? Is that you? Have I got the right number?'

'I can't talk now, call back tomorrow morning,' was all she said.

I was in a fever of anticipation. It was almost two years since I had spoken to anyone in my family, I'd had no contact and no news. If anything terrible had happened would it have reached me on the Asian grapevine? I hoped and believed so but I had no way of being sure and now I was terrified that Lucy had only agreed to talk to me so she could break bad news. I rang again about half past nine next morning. My heart was racing but Lucy sounded calm.

'How have you been?' she said as though we'd been chatting only a month ago.

'Yeah, fine. How are you? How's Mum and Dad?'

'They're all right. Where are you living then?'

'In a flat, in Leeds.' It was so good to hear her talk without criticism in her voice that tears were running down my cheeks and splashing on my jumper. She didn't ask much more about us, but she answered my questions. David, my little nephew, he was fine. Yasmin had given birth to a boy, and so had Robina, but she was back home because her marriage hadn't worked out. Lucy sounded quite matter-of-fact about that, but I was horrified. Poor Robina! She must have been so unhappy and I wasn't even there for her. 'How is she?' I asked but Lucy had moved on, she was telling me about Prakash, who was a widow now since Bila died of drink. Then, suddenly, she said, 'There's someone at the door, I've got to go,' and before I could say anything else she put the phone down.

I sat there for ages going over our conversation in my mind. Lucy's manner made it clear that it was all old news, but to me it was like being hit with a cannon ball of information. So much had happened I needed time to sort it all out. My main thoughts were with Robina and I was trying to get straight what Lucy said. It was something about Navtej not coming to Britain but moving on to Canada and marrying someone else. But what about his baby? My fingers itched to dial the number again but I didn't dare to. I didn't want to risk upsetting her. Having been in isolation for so long, having any news at all meant so much to me and I was just so grateful for it. I felt like my family had been dead and were now brought back to life again. I decided I'd wait to see if Lucy would speak to me again in a couple of weeks.

For the first six months in Leeds Jassey did casual jobs here and there and then we decided to try and make a go of a market stall. We'd spent long enough mooching round markets killing time and Jassey always liked the atmosphere, the hustle and bustle, the constant change and challenge. He liked the easygoing, good humour of the stall-holders too and we became quite friendly with a couple of them. They encouraged us to try it.

Jassey was always a wizard with money and now he managed, somehow, to save and scrape together £50 to get us started. He found out where the warehouses were and what they had to offer and we invested in small, battery-operated goods, things like watches, torches and alarm clocks. It cost £5 a day to take a pitch in Kirkgate market and at first we just did Fridays and Saturdays.

We watched the other stallholders carefully and learnt all their tricks, like how to make £20 worth of stock look like a million dollars. We used to drape an expensive-looking bit of cloth over the stall and then cover it with boxes. It didn't matter if the boxes were empty, they were just there to make it look as if your stall was laden. Then you put your best bits and pieces at the back, because it meant that to see them properly people had to lean right into the stall to see what was what. Once you got them doing that you were halfway to selling something.

I began to realize that right at the start when people approached the stall, they wanted to be left alone. If you made the first move too soon you frightened them off, so I'd always pretend to be busy, re-arranging stuff or chatting to my neighbour. It wasn't until a customer actually touched something that I'd engage with them. I might say something about the different styles available, or I'd tell them about any special features, luminous hands on a watch for instance. If they showed interest in any one thing for more than a few seconds I'd begin to put the pressure on. I'd tell them that particular thing had been selling like hot cakes all morning and I only had two of them left, even if I still had hundreds piled up beneath the stall. Or I'd say that, since it was the last one, they could have it for a knock-down price. We'd buy digital watches for 25 pence and sell them for £1.50; on a Saturday you could sell 100 of them. It was easy.

I found I had a natural gift for selling. I surprised myself by how good I was, and I liked the human contact. All the time we were in Newcastle Jassey had been my only link with the outside world and I'd felt frozen inside. Now in the hurly-burly of the markets I began to thaw out. There were people to say hello to when you arrived to set up, stamping your feet and banging your hands together against the morning chill. Customers became familiar and they'd stop to chat. There was always someone to have a laugh and a cup of tea with. There was life and I felt I was on the fringes of it, plucking up the courage to jump in.

For the first time since leaving Derby I thought Jassey and I might make something of our life together. We made a good team and we soon started doing the indoor market at Kirkgate as well as the outdoor markets. By the time we were working regularly several days a week we had stopped worrying about having enough money to eat properly and begun to set ourselves targets: we bought ourselves a take-away meal, we went out for a drink, we took out hire purchase on a television.

My family's rejection of me had made me feel totally worthless but now I found I could do something, and the day we brought our television home I felt so elated I really wanted to share that with them. I kidded myself that my parents would be pleased for us; certainly Dad would. If only Dad would answer the phone, I thought, everything would be all right.

I was determined to ring and tell them my news before they hung up on me. I planned exactly what I was going to say and when I'd dialled the number and the phone started ringing I took a deep breath in readiness.

It was Mum who answered but, after a second's hesitation, I plunged in anyway.

'It's me, Mum. It's going well for us, we've got a market stall and we've saved enough to . . .'

The line went dead before I got the sentence out. I'd long since lost count of how many times that had happened, but it still knocked me back. My face felt hot, flooded with shame, hurt and humiliation. That's when I understood that my success would never please them. As far as they were concerned I was an outcast and outcasts belong in the gutter. 'Without us you'll end up in the streets,' is what Mum had threatened when I first called home and now I saw that was what she wanted. The thought that I could survive – let alone thrive – outside the protective, prohibitive scaffolding that had encased her and Dad all their lives was anathema to them. I should have understood that.

CHAPTER 11

We stayed in Leeds almost a year and then, out of the blue, Anil announced that he was selling the flat and moving away from the city. It was a blow but by that time Jassey had set his heart and mind on building a business and he wanted more space to store all our stock. He decided we should branch out in Bradford, not much more than twenty minutes' drive away.

Our new address was White's View, Bradford. It was a second-floor flat in a row of back-to-back houses, on a narrow street which ran all the way up a steep hill. I'd never before seen anything like those houses. They were built so close together that there was no room for any gardens at the back, and at the front it looked as if they were all tied to one another with a cat's cradle. Those were the washing lines, bits of string running between the upstairs windows and fixed to a pulley so that all the women could easily hang their washing out or bring it in again. I found the sight of them quite cosy, but I couldn't help thinking that Mum wouldn't have approved of the arrangement. She wouldn't have wanted strangers seeing Dad's vests, let alone her bits and pieces!

The fact that I could think about Mum in an almost light-hearted way shows the frame of mind I was in when we first arrived in Bradford. The year in Leeds had been good for us and I was feeling much stronger, less reliant on Jassey carrying me through each day. White's View changed that. The flat was small and poky and it was infested with mice, but those weren't the things that mattered. The problem was that White's View was right in the heart of the Asian area and I hadn't banked on what being back in that situation would do to me.

'Are you new here?' said an elderly woman standing beside me as I queued to pay for milk in the shop at the end of our road.

Before I had time to think, years of Mum's discipline rose up in me and, keeping my eyes respectfully on the ground, I answered, 'Yes, Auntie-ji. I've been here one week.'

'Where have you come from?'

'Leeds,' I murmured.

'Is that where your parents live?' she asked. Silence fell and transactions ceased as the shop-keeper and his customers tuned in to my answer. Unabashed by my reluctance, unembarrassed by her own directness, my inquisitor pressed on until she found out my family's whereabouts, my father's name and that of the village he had come from in the Punjab.

'I have an uncle in the Punjab,' she said, turning her back on me at last to buy her milk.

Everywhere I went in my new surroundings it was the same: questions from strangers who wanted to place me and possess me and suck me into the vortex that swirls around any place where Asians congregate. The questing, inquisitive undercurrents that had tugged at me throughout my childhood were every bit as forceful here in Bradford. I was scared their greedy embrace would reach back to Derby and discover the truth about us, so I started telling lies about my parents. As the lies multiplied I struggled to remember what I'd said to whom; and once again I became uncertain who I was.

All my life I'd hated the suffocating feeling that comes from being constantly watched and judged and now, in a city of curious strangers, it grew stronger. But even as I shrank from scrutiny my heart twisted with envy as homesickness took hold again. Each morning I would stand at our bedroom window looking down on the groups of head-scarfed women going about their business – sisters, daughters, mothers, aunties, nieces – and I would ache with loneliness.

It set me right back. I could feel myself slipping towards the dismal days in Newcastle when, I would say in retrospect, I was suffering from depression. In those days I was in and out of GP surgeries with backaches and headaches and skin complaints but if anyone ever asked me how I was feeling in myself I said 'fine'. That's what I'd been taught to do. Physical ailments were one thing, no shame in that, but your state of mind was something you kept firmly to yourself.

If I'd been going to tell the truth at any time during those long, miserable months, I'd have said my mind was like a quagmire. All Jassey's efforts to cheer me drowned in its murky depths. I was still convinced I was the one who had done something wrong and sinned against my family. Guilt hung over me like a big black cloud. Because of me people were spitting at my mum in the street. She was a battle-axe but she was who I'd grown up with, what I knew, and the thought that I'd brought shame on her made my guts shrivel. I felt really small.

The truth was I needed her. I'd been challenging Mum since right back when I was tiny but when I won, when I escaped and got my freedom, I didn't know what to do with it. She and my sisters were the only role models I'd ever had; I didn't know how to lead a life outside the confines of the community that had always cocooned me. Being in White's View reminded me of that. I was surrounded by women leading the life that I'd rejected. Standing alone at my window, watching their busy, bustling lives, I sometimes wondered why.

Two years before in Newcastle, with Jassey doing odd-jobs and me stuck in our bedsit measuring each day in empty, endless hours, I'd had no answer.

Now, thanks to our market stalls, I'd found a purpose. All the hard work we'd done in Leeds had driven depression's black dog from my shoulder, and now in Bradford the need to keep working kept me from brooding and stopped me sliding backwards. Jassey and I had built a business. We'd started with nothing but determination and the stamina to work long hours and we'd made something successful.

We were so successful by the time we got to Bradford that Jassey decided he could run the markets single-handed. His next target for us was to buy a house and he said we needed a second income; he wanted me to get a job. He was still the one making all the decisions, so I went along with it. I got a job in Argos. It was nothing exciting, not as much fun as working in the market, but I accepted it because Jassey said it would help to build our future. And on cold wet days I was glad to be inside.

It was not long after we moved to Bradford that Jassey's parents first visited us. While we were in Leeds Jassey had popped back to see them every now and again and although I was happy for him, the injustice in the different ways our families treated us rankled. His family were totally accepting of our situation. They were kind to me and welcoming. They teased me about being their *jatti-nor*, which means their higher caste daughter-in-law, and although there was no malice in it, it stung because I knew most of Mum's problem with Jassey was his being *chamar*. I found it a strain putting on a show of happiness, and I used to be glad when their visits were over.

It was some small consolation that I was talking quite regularly to Lucy by then. Our conversations were usually brief, but at least I had news of my family. She told me when her marriage was arranged. She'd been promised to the man I stood up; it was a face-saving arrangement but she didn't seem to mind. She sounded so grown-up.

Having that little bit of contact made me crave more; I plucked up the courage to ask Lucy if she would meet me somewhere and, to my amazement, she agreed. She said I should come to Derby and I suggested Markeaton Park, our old hiding place. She said she would meet us there on Saturday afternoon.

She was waiting in the car park and my heart leapt when I saw her. I jumped out of the car and hugged her so tight that eventually she pushed me off. It was only then that I took in her appearance. She'd been hovering on the edge of adolescence when I left Derby, still proud of her long, thick plait, hoping Mum wouldn't hear if she played kiss-chase in the playground, happy to wear her Indian suits at home. Now she was wearing a really fashionable western skirt and a fitted blouse and she'd had her hair cut, in a short, sleek bob. I was amazed that Mum had let her out of the house dressed like that. And I soon found out that her appearance was just the start of it.

She climbed into the car with us – we weren't bothered about being seen any more but she didn't want to get caught with us – and started telling us about her life. She seemed much more confident than I'd remembered. While she was waiting for her marriage to happen she had so much freedom. She was allowed to go out with friends, she was going to the pub, she was even going to nightclubs. She was doing things that I and my other sisters had never even dreamt of. I should have been happy for her, but I was shattered. I'd had to give up my whole life – my family, my friends, my education, everything – for the sake of my freedom and now it seemed Lucy had been handed hers on a plate. I felt it made a mockery of everything I'd been through. I sat beside her on the back seat of the car nodding and smiling but all the time she was talking I was thinking 'I should have stayed, I needn't have done this'.

But there was no going back. Lucy made it clear that, as far as Mum and Dad were concerned, I wouldn't be welcome. She was adamant that she didn't want to discuss it and I didn't want to spoil the time I had with her by pushing it, so an awful lot of what was on my mind got left unsaid. She spent about an hour with us and then she got out of the car and went back to the world that used to be mine. What little peace of mind I had went with her.

Later, back in the flat, I talked it through with Jassey. As always he was calm and sensible.

'It's *because* you ran away that Lucy has that freedom. Don't you see, your mum must be terrified she'll lose another daughter.' A corner of my rational mind knew that must be true, that I must have paved the way for her, but it was swamped by a swirling mass of guilt, regret and misery.

'Could I have compromised?'

'Might things have changed anyway?'

'If I'd stayed, could I have had a proper life?'

Those were the thoughts that chased each other round my mind until I longed to force my fists through my skull and batter them into silence.

I went on seeing Lucy. She came to Bradford too, looking stunning in high heels and a red suit with a fish-tail skirt. She'd cropped her hair and had it dyed; I felt so drab in comparison. The first time she visited I felt uncomfortable as I watched her running her eyes around our tiny flat. I thought she must be thinking, 'Well, you've got what you deserve,' but she didn't say anything. On her second visit she brought Robina with her and Sunny, my nephew. He was about three and you could see Robina doted on him. When she looked at him her eyes were so full of pride and love that she seemed radiant despite all she'd been through.

She had so much to tell me. It was a beautiful bright day and we put Sunny in his pushchair and wheeled him over to our local park. It was time for his rest and he lay there, sucking on his dummy, while we sat on a bench and Robina talked and talked until she'd told me everything. I felt as close to her that afternoon as I had been when we were at school together.

At last I got the full story of her marriage break-down. She'd never managed to get Navtej into England. They left Germany and went to try their luck in Canada where Navtej had family. But things hadn't worked out as they hoped so she came home. There was no need for a divorce because their ceremony in India had sealed the arranged marriage without being legally binding. She'd arrived back in Derby more than a year ago.

'Mum and Dad have been very good about it, they let me come home, and that's where we've been living. It's been nice having the support with Sunny, it's right for him to be near his family, his real aunties, Ginda-*masi*, Yasmin-*masi*, all the cousins.' There wasn't a trace of self-pity in her voice, she sounded quite happy with her life, and I soon found out why.

'I've met someone else, Jas, and he's asked me to marry him.'

'You *met* him? It's not arranged then? *Robina!* What do Mum and Dad think?'

'They're all right, they've accepted it.' She was looking down into her lap just like a blushing bride but I think she was embarrassed about what she had to say to me. 'He's a *jatt* like us, Jas, he's from

123

a good family. They're happy for me, they're even going to pay for the wedding.'

I was dumbfounded. Mum and Dad happy about a *love match*? Had they changed completely? Why were things so much easier for my sisters than they'd been for me? The child in me wanted to shout out, 'That's not *fair*!' but I controlled myself. I managed to say, 'So when's the wedding going to be then?'

'We're not sure yet. He's in prison at the moment.' She looked up and smiled reassuringly at me. 'It was nothing serious. But he's coming out at the end of next month and then we'll fix it.'

She was busy with her wedding preparations and then with her new husband so in the next few months it was Lucy I was most in contact with. She told me about Robina's wedding when it happened. They'd done the whole thing: there was a big ceremony, they poured oil on the doorstep of Mum and Dad's house before Robina went back into it, all the women had cried when they said goodbye to her. It was a proper Sikh wedding and all the family were there, except me. Even Robina had made it clear she didn't want me there.

It was Lucy too who told me when Dad got ill. He developed jaundice and was taken into hospital. I kept fretting about what could have caused it. 'The doctors say all the worry and stress hasn't helped him. Mum says he's been getting old and sick from the moment you ran away,' said Lucy, shrugging her shoulders.

He was in the hospital for weeks and I used to lie awake at night wondering and worrying about him, asking myself if his illness really was my fault. 'Why don't you go and see him?' said Jassey. By then he was driving down to Derby quite regularly to see his family and I could easily have gone with him. I did go once, but we got as far as the hospital car park and I lost my nerve. How would I react if Dad was hostile towards me? What would I do if Mum was already in there with him? I sat there for an hour with the flowers I'd bought him wilting in my lap. In the end I didn't see him. I couldn't do it; I just wasn't brave enough.

CHAPTER 12

When I was eighteen I fell pregnant. I was taking the pill but it happened anyway. I was still so naive that I didn't recognize the signs; I'd gone to the doctor because I felt so tired and sick and he confirmed it for me. 'Not married?' Dr Bazu was writing notes and his turban obscured his face but I could imagine the look of disapproval, hear the tut-tutting he would later do with his wife.

'Where was it you said your parents were living?'

'I didn't, but it's not near here.' The appointment was drawing to a close and I stood up quickly. 'Thanks for your time,' I said and left without giving him the chance to pry any further.

Jassey was thrilled. When I told him he went running round the room, jumping in the air like a little kid. For the whole of that evening his face was one big cheesy grin; I don't think I'd ever seen him look so happy. Before I told him I hadn't known what to think. Cut off from my family, creating a family of my own seemed inconceivable, but Jassey wasn't having any of that.

'You'll marry me now, won't you, sweet?' He

was down on one knee, holding my hand. 'Our baby is going to need a respectable mum and dad; we'll be a proper family and I will look after you both.'

It was what he'd always wanted; he'd asked me to marry him several times before and now I had a strong feeling that I owed it to him. He was a good, kind man with my best interests at heart and I knew he would never hurt me. Besides, what was the alternative? I felt, ironically, as if this was my arranged marriage and I had to make it work. I also believed that if I had any chance of redeeming myself in my family's eyes it would be by becoming respectable. If I had a successful husband, a baby and a nice house, perhaps they would like me again. They might even have me back.

Robina helped me prepare for the wedding. I guess she thought she'd get away with it as long as she kept her involvement secret from Mum and Dad. All my life she had been my role model, and now she stepped in to play the part of mother. We went round all the shops together, looking for a wedding sari. There are so many Asian shops in Bradford it took hours, but Robina never stopped being light-hearted and merry. She was determined to make it a special day for me and it was special. For the first time in years someone from my family was playing a part in my life.

Robina was determined I shouldn't miss out on all the most important parts of the ritual, and she bought me a maroon wedding sari, embroidered with so much gold that it weighed a ton. When I first tried it on I couldn't believe anyone could wear it for more than half an hour.

Then, when the day came, she was there in time to dress me. She shooed Jassey out of the flat and sat me down in the bedroom so she could do my make-up. She plastered on foundation, followed by bright red lipstick and the *bindi* on my forehead. I hadn't worn make-up since I was fifteen and when I looked in the mirror it didn't feel like me at all.

She also covered me in golden jewellery. We couldn't afford to buy any, so she'd lent me hers: bracelets, necklaces and the special gold chain that runs round your head and across your face to your nose. She treated me exactly as my mum should have done and made me look every inch the Asian bride.

For a split second as I stood there in my fineries, I felt proud of my heritage: the lavish drama of my costume, all that gold honouring a tradition that stretched back down the centuries, the *bindi* denoting the caste of which Mum and Dad were so proud. But the feeling didn't last. Because I was an outcast it was all empty symbolism. I hadn't done the proper Asian thing so I couldn't have a proper Asian wedding. Robina was trying to make it all real for me, but inside I just felt terribly small and sad. I wasn't going to be shown off to hundreds of people; there wasn't going to be a big family gathering; I wasn't even going to be seen by my own mum and dad. My wedding was just an hour in a registry office with Lucy and Robina and Jassey's family. Afterwards we went back to the flat and ate some food that my sisters had made. No one stayed long. In their absence Mum and Dad took up more of the room than they ever would have done in person and it made us all feel awkward. Jassey and I were back at work the following day.

I went on working at Argos and helping Jassey in the markets until I was five months pregnant. By then Jassey was doing so well that we didn't have such a pressing need for money, and I was tired, weighed down by constant yearning for my mum. We'd never been close. I'd managed to survive three and a half years without even talking to her but now, with the baby growing inside me, my need for her was sharpened. I wanted her to pat my swollen belly, I wanted her to be there telling me to get enough rest and eat right, I wanted her to show me what it means to be a mum.

It was left to Jassey's mum to do that. Jassey was working so hard he had no time to look after me, so he sent me down to stay with her a month before my due date. We decided we wanted the baby born in Derby where we belonged.

I was fat and bovine by the time I got there. Jassey's mum was kind and solicitous and I was placid and passive, accepting her care. Avtar had married and was waiting for her husband to arrive from India. I had seen her several times in the years since we left Derby but the pert schoolgirl I'd known had been replaced by a respectable woman and we couldn't seem to find the friendship we'd once so enjoyed. Strangely, staying in Derby barely fifteen minutes' walk from Dale Road, I felt even more cut off from my family than I had in Bradford. I didn't even fantasize about creeping round to try and catch a glimpse of Dad as I might have done a few months back. Without the stimulus of work to bolster me, my thoughts began to spiral. I felt like I was going through the motions of a life I hadn't chosen. I was an outcast and I was having a baby; those were the facts and nothing I could do would change them.

Jassey made it down from Bradford in time to see Lisa born. I was glad to have him there to prove I was a respectable married woman, because I was much the youngest on the ward and the midwives scared me with their disapproving frowns. He held my hand and they gave me an epidural and the whole thing passed in a bit of a blur. His mum was the first one to come and see us. She patted my cheek and said, 'Never mind, dear, next time it will be a boy.'

To me it didn't matter. I loved Lisa from the second they placed her perfect, blood-streaked body in my arms. In those precious, shell-shocked moments after the birth Jassey stood there with his arms encircling me and this brand new life we had created and the tears poured down his face. 'Why would I want a son when I've got this beautiful creature?' he said, much later, after his mum had left.

Robina came to see me. She brought Sunny with her and the prettiest pink baby dress you've ever seen. Sunny was fascinated by Lisa. He sat on Robina's knee, holding the edge of the bassinette and blowing kisses to her.

'I've told Mum about the baby and I think she's going to come and see her. She said she might. I'll talk to her again when I get home.' Robina's face was all encouragement and enthusiasm but the reunion between me and Mum – although it did happen – wasn't what she'd hoped for.

She came the next day. I watched her walking down the ward towards me and my first thought was that in the years since I'd seen her she hadn't changed a bit. She was encased in a fur coat and her bearing was formidable, tall, stout and proud. Her lips were pursed and her face was stern and, short of going backwards, she couldn't have seemed more reluctant. Robina kept looking over her shoulder to make sure she was still following. When they finally reached me Robina indicated the chair by my bed, so Mum could sit right by me and see Lisa in her bassinette. Mum ignored that. She stood there, stiff as a post, clutching her bag close as if she was scared of touching something dirty.

'Hi, Mum,' I said. We'd never been a physical family but I was aching for her touch. I clenched my fingers round the sheets in an effort to control myself. 'This is Lisa.' As luck would have it my baby, Mum's grandchild, was wide awake. I'd put her in the pink dress Robina brought and smoothed the shock of black hair that she'd been born with and she was lying there, tiny and innocent with her brown unblinking gaze.

Mum glanced into the bassinette for as long as it took to ascertain there was a baby in there. Me she acknowledged with the curt nod she might give a little-known acquaintance in the *gurdwara*. Then, without having said a word, she turned her attention to the comings and goings in the rest of the ward. Robina tried valiantly to keep some sort of conversation going but we both knew it was impossible and long before the visiting hour was over she escorted Mum out. As I watched them walk back down the ward I thought my heart would break. The last time I spoke to Mum she said I was dead in her eyes and now she'd proved she meant it.

About two weeks after Lisa was born Jassey took me back to Bradford. I hadn't heard from Mum again. Her indifference had set me right back and if I hadn't had Lisa to look after I don't know what would have happened to me. She was an easy, sunny baby; in her first few weeks she slept a lot and made few demands. She started smiling and there were days when her gummy smile and the funny little cries she made were the only things that anchored me to life.

I don't know where the days went to. I kept the curtains drawn. If I looked outside the streets seemed to be filled with women moving in happy gaggles. I'd see a couple of head-scarfed sisters, backs bent in symmetry as they heaved their pushchairs up our hill. There was a group of young girls that used to pass by, all linked arms and swinging plaits. A girl about my age used to walk alongside while an older woman – I was sure it was her mother – carried her baby. They were forever leaning over to wrap the shawl a little closer round its tiny head. I felt like a freakish monster in my isolation.

Sometimes I couldn't find it in myself to get up all day and Lisa would happily lie there beside me on the bed. She'd grip one of my fingers with her tiny, determined little fist and her brown eyes would fix on my face, following my every move with fascination. During those long hours alone with her I thought a lot about mother love. The moment the midwife placed Lisa in my arms the depression that had been blanketing my emotions was pierced by something so fierce it was almost painful. I felt tremulous, proud, passionate, tender, fearful, joyous . . . Had Mum ever felt like that about me? I wondered. And if so, where had those feelings gone to? Had they died or were they hidden some-where, stifled beneath her protective cloak of honour? As I nursed Lisa, cradling her fragile body close, I vowed I would never allow anything to dull my feelings for her.

Jassey would come home from work and find us lying there. Sometimes I'd still be in my pyjamas. He'd sweep Lisa up into his arms and demand to hear every detail of what we had been doing. He used to look after her while I had a bath or he would urge me to get dressed and we'd all go out and get some food in. I ate all day – comfort food I barely tasted – and the weight piled on, but despite my greed, I couldn't get to the shops without Jassey, even the corner shop which was no more than fifty steps from out front door. I was scared to go out alone; even when I was with him I kept my eyes on the ground and clung to his arm as if for protection. I'd lost all my confidence.

Was that hormonal? Was it post-natal depression that brought me so low? Nobody suggested it, but then I never gave them the opportunity to do so. I made the appointments that Lisa needed – vaccinations and so on – but when I saw the midwives I made sure I kept my feelings to myself. Perhaps professionals could have helped me. Medication might have numbed the pain but it couldn't change the glaring fact that my own mum had shut the door on me. Before her visit to the hospital I had hope. I'd left home an errant schoolgirl but now I was a married woman with a thriving business and a beautiful baby. Was there nothing she could find to like in that?

Once again, Jassey did his best for me. He was always trying to cheer me up; he'd pull funny faces at me to make me smile, he bought me flowers. It was he who suggested I take up aerobics when I complained about being so fat.

He understood how the loss of my family tormented me and, although we didn't talk about it any more – what else was there to say? – he did his best to fill the roles of mother, father and friend as well as husband. He tried to be all that he could to me. It wasn't his fault that it wasn't enough.

It makes me smile to remember the only thing he gave up on, teaching me to drive. He didn't want me straining to push Lisa up and down the hills of Bradford and so he started giving me lessons: 'Clutch, clutch,' he screamed as I hiccoughed my way up a hill. The car stalled and I jammed on the handbrake. 'Fine! You drive if you know so much about it,' I said, leaping out of my seat and slamming the driver's door behind me. I didn't look back as I stamped down the hill, but I could hear the line of cars behind him blaring their horns in anger.

Even that he forgave me. He drove round until he found me and then, right there on the pavement, he hugged me and told me that it didn't matter.

'You and Lisa are my pride and joy.' He was always saying that; he even wrote it in our diary.

He was my rock and my support and, if he could, he would have carried me for ever. But as his business grew, so did the demands it made on him. He was leaving home at 4 a.m. to set up his stalls and sometimes, when he was collecting stock, he wasn't back before midnight. When he did get home early he'd shovel down his dinner and then start on his paperwork. He'd always been so quick with numbers, but now he seemed to find it hard. I'd hear him cursing when he couldn't make the figures add up right. Once I found him asleep with his head on the table and a screwed up piece of paper balled in one hand. He'd always been well-organized, but now he was forgetful, almost careless: he couldn't remember where he'd left his car keys, he got stranded on the motorway when his van ran out of petrol.

One evening when Lisa was about twelve months old he came back from work and, as he always did, came straight to find us. I was feeding Lisa in the kitchen. He kissed the top of my head, tickled Lisa's neck and then, as he put the kettle on, he said, 'You have to pull yourself together, sweet. There's too much for me to do now. I need your help.'

I looked up from spooning rice into Lisa's baby-bird mouth and I saw Jassey, really saw him, for the first time in weeks. It was a Sunday and he'd left for the market at 4 a.m. Now, under the harsh electric light, he looked exhausted. There were dark rings under his eyes and he needed a shave. His clothes were baggy on him and I realized, with a jolt of surprise, that he must have lost weight.

136

The guilt that was always there, lapping at my conscience, rose up and flooded my face.

My friend Lizzie who I'd met at Kirkgate market became Lisa's childminder and Lisa settled with her very well. I went back to the markets and joined Jassey working seven days a week, moving between sites. With me back in the business he could take on twice as many stalls and we agreed that I should look after the outdoor markets in Leeds while he focused on sites in Morley and Bradford. It was two years since I'd set out a stall, but all the old tricks came back to me. The patter flowed easily, I recognized my regular customers and always had a friendly word for them, I never got the change muddled. I was a good saleswoman and rediscovering that seemed to spring-clean my mind. Work, as usual, was a panacea. Jassey and I were making a success of our business and contributing to that success boosted my spirits.

But as the deadening cloud of depression lifted I found myself staring into the face of an uncomfortable truth. Jassey was so busy working for our future that he didn't seem to register the cracks in our present, but to me they were growing ever wider. In the months following Lisa's birth the emotional closeness that had carried us through my darkest days began to dwindle. We still had fun together, but it was largely through Lisa. What little free time we had was devoted to her. We took her to the park and, taking one hand each, we'd swing her high into the air with her feet kicking up through the autumn leaves and her little voice shouting with laughter. We spent Sunday afternoons at the zoo and basked in the saucer-eyed wonderment with which she viewed the elephant. We took her swimming and were dizzy with pride when she splashed her plump sausage legs.

Those moments glued us together and beyond our mutual absorption in Lisa it was still true to say that I relied on Jassey and he looked after me, but more and more our relationship seemed to me like a business partnership. I felt I was trapped in the sort of empty marriage I had fled Derby to escape.

Jassey didn't notice because our life was working out just as he wanted it. We had a decent car and a van and, within eighteen months of Lisa's birth, we had bought our first house. It was on the outskirts of Bradford, away from the Asian area. In White's View I'd never got over the feeling of being watched and judged; each time I went out I imagined that people held their daughters close, not wanting them tainted by that shameless woman who disgraced her own family.

The house we bought was something to be proud of. It was semi-detached with a big garden and a garage with a bright red door; it even had a driveway. I remember the day we moved in Jassey carried Lisa round the house, showing her all the rooms, talking to her about the life we were going to lead there. I followed in their wake, keenly aware that the enthusiasm I should have felt was being drowned by guilt. Jassey had built for me the life that every Asian woman dreams of but deep down inside I didn't want it. For all we'd been through together, all I owed Jassey, I still couldn't love him. He'd worked so hard to buy me a home and now, try as I might, I couldn't drag my heart through its door.

CHAPTER 13

I don't know what made Mum decide to start speaking to me but one day, out of the blue, she did. It was only her and Dad left at home by then. Robina was living in Leicester with her new husband, and Lucy had gone to Germany to join the man she'd been married to, so Mum no longer had to brandish her honour in front of them. My brother Balbir had gone too. He was living with Dawn, the half-white woman he'd taken up with before I left home. 'Mum's not happy with it, but she'd never say so,' Robina told me on the phone. 'She still rushes round after him when he goes home, still treats him like a king.' The injustice of this twisted my guts into tight knots of anger, but even then I couldn't quash my longing for acceptance. I went on ringing and one day Mum said, 'Hello.'

'Mum, is that you?' I said, determined to keep the wobble from my voice.

'Yes.'

'How are you?'

'All right.'

'How's Dad?'

'All right.'

'Has he gone to work?'

'Yes.'

'Have you been at work?'

'Yes.'

'Does my auntie . . .'

She cut me short – 'The doorbell's ringing. I have to go now' – and put the phone down.

We spoke quite often after that. It was always me that did the ringing, and all she ever said was 'yes', 'no', 'yes', with the occasional weary sigh in between. She never volunteered anything, never asked about me or Jassey or even her grand-daughter, Lisa, but she was there at the other end of the line and she didn't hang up and she wasn't abusive. I was supposed to be grateful for that, it was supposed to be enough and in a funny way it was because I had no choice. For so long I'd had nothing and at least this was something, some tiny scrap of recognition that she was my mother. That's what I longed for. I wanted her to acknowledge that we belonged to one another, I wanted her to see that casting me out was wrong, I wanted, more than anything, to feel her affection. I wanted to be loved unconditionally like I loved Lisa.

It didn't happen. Those brief, staccato calls – moments of elation followed by hours lost in disappointment and regret – did nothing to bring us together. Slowly it dawned on me that every monosyllable Mum reluctantly let fall was like a nail in the coffin of my love for her. Where her total silence had taunted and encouraged my longing, the mealy-mouthed conversations we now endured were killing it. Within months of first speaking to her I had given up hoping she would ask after Lisa. I'd admitted to myself that she didn't care where I lived. I was beginning to accept the fact that you can't make someone love you. That's when I started telling myself that I had to change my expectations of Mum.

I don't think I would have managed to do that had Lucy not turned up on my doorstep. In the previous year she had rung from time to time and she never sounded happy. Her marriage wasn't working out. She had no more reason for complaint than Prakash, Ginda or Yasmin, but she'd led a different life from them before she married. She'd had all that freedom, all that going out, and she wasn't as subservient as they were. She didn't even want to accept being stuck in a foreign land all alone except for a husband whom she barely knew and didn't like. It struck me as ironic. She'd conformed, she'd upheld the family honour, but now she felt as lonely and miserable as I'd been.

She'd told Mum and Dad but, of course, they weren't having any of her miseries.

'Stupid girl. Of course you can't come home. Do you not think we have been shamed enough already.' That's what Mum said.

Even though I'd spoken to her about a fortnight before, I was surprised by the state Lucy was in when she arrived with us in Bradford. She didn't give us any warning. It was early evening and Jassey and I were playing in the garden with Lisa when we heard the doorbell ring, long and loud. I went to answer it and there was Lucy on the doorstep, with a suitcase, sobbing. It was some time before she calmed down enough to talk to us, and even then she was edgy and nervous. The phone rang once and you'd think it was a gunshot the way she jumped. She'd run away without her husband knowing. All the way from Germany. It must have taken her months to save the fare.

She sat, nursing her cup of tea in trembling hands and looking completely woebegone. The sassy confidence I'd noticed in Markeaton Park had drained right out of her.

'What am I going to do, Jas?' she asked, and her voice was small and frightened. 'Where am I going to live? I can't go back.'

I had no idea what to say to her. I couldn't remember any women – except widows – living on their own when I was growing up in Mum and Dad's community. I couldn't imagine how I'd have lived through the last six years if I hadn't had Jassey. What place was there for a woman who had left her husband? I thought for ages but in the end, all I could suggest to Lucy was that Mum might have her back.

I couldn't have been more mistaken. I rang Mum later that evening while Jassey was putting Lisa to bed, and she wasn't interested.

'Send her back to Germany at once,' she said. 'She has no business here.'

'But Mum, don't you see, she's unhappy,' I pleaded. 'If you could see how upset she is you'd think differently.'

'Don't tell me what I think. Her place is with her husband. She knows that. Send her back.'

'I can't do that, Mum. She won't have it. She says she'd rather go on the streets than go back.'

'As you wish.' I could hear Mum losing patience with the conversation. 'But if you want to have any place at all in this family I am telling you to send her back. If you don't do that, I'll have nothing more to do with you. You will both be dead in my eyes.'

She hung up and I was left, the receiver dangling useless in my hand, trying to make sense of what she'd said to me. I was back in the wrong. How had that happened? Lucy had left her husband and somehow, in Mum's skewed logic, it was my fault. She'd said I had to choose between her and Lucy. Was her punishment of me never going to stop?

I looked at Lucy. She was exhausted, both physically and emotionally. She was slumped at the table resting her head on her folded arms, like we had to do at St Chad's Infants when we were naughty. Now she sat up and, with her elbows still on the table, she put her chin in her cupped hands and looked at me questioningly. I didn't need to say anything, she could tell by my face.

144

'She won't have me, will she, Jas? She doesn't want me.'

Her voice was flat and expressionless and, as I shook my head in answer, hers sank back down onto her forearms and she started quietly sobbing. I moved round the table and, gripping her by the shoulders, swung her round to face me.

'You can stop here, if you like, Lucy. You can stay with me and Jassey, help us in the markets. It'd be nice for us to have some family, nice for Lisa to have her *masi* about.'

I meant what I said. I had to because Lucy had no alternative. She had nowhere else to go and no money to get herself back to Germany even if she could have been persuaded to return to her husband. She had no choice and, as I saw it, neither did I. How could I – having suffered six years of rejection from those who were supposed to love and protect me – turn her out?

Even as she was thanking me, a needling inner voice insisted I was ruining any chance I might have had of seeing Dad again. It told me I was making sure Lisa never got to know her grandparents. The voice was right, I knew that. But I shut my ears to it and went upstairs to sort out Lucy's bed.

Lucy's coming to live with us stirred up my life. I was banished by Mum again, as she'd threatened, and Robina went very quiet as well, which really hurt. But at least I had an ally who knew

145

what I was going through. That was consolation, and so was having someone from my family with me all the time. I could see my own sister and it didn't have to be a secret!

When I said she could stop with us I had imagined myself looking after Lucy, caring for my little sister, but as she recovered from the shock of what she'd done and Mum's reaction to it, living with her began to be more like living with a flatmate or a friend. She was fresh and vibrant, she wore different clothes, she was used to going out, she was determined to have fun.

'Who are you meeting?' I asked one Friday evening. I was bathing Lisa, and Lucy was using the bathroom mirror to put her make-up on, getting ready to go out to the pub.

'People from the market, you know . . .' And she reeled off a list of names of people whom I'd smiled at but never said more to than 'How's it going? All right?'

'You should come, Jas. You'd enjoy it. Ask Jassey if he'll babysit, just this once. Come on, it would do you good to go out.'

She was persuasive and I was tempted. Going out had played no part in my life with Jassey, we were always so busy saving for something, striving to prove to ourselves and our families that we could make it without their help. I lifted Lisa out of the bath and onto my lap and together we sat there, watching Lucy paint her lips dark red. I couldn't remember how long it was since I'd worn make-up, since I'd made an effort to make myself look good.

One night, a couple of weeks after that, I did go with her. Jassey was fine about it. He said he was happy to be with Lisa and he didn't want to come; he was pleased to see me having fun with Lucy. I remember rummaging through my clothes trying to find something to wear and thinking everything I owned seemed drab and workaday; in the end Lucy lent me a scarlet blouse with a ruffled front and great big shoulders. She made me put on make-up and showed me how to blow-dry my hair.

'You look beautiful, sweetheart. Enjoy yourself,' Jassey said when I went to say goodbye to him. He was sitting watching telly with Lisa on his lap.

We went to a pub first. There were about ten people in the crowd Lucy had arranged to meet and I knew several of them by sight because they worked in the market. They were all very friendly, asked after Jassey and Lisa, said it was good to see me out from behind my stall. We piled onto a bench that ran around a table; it was hot and close and they were all talking and laughing really loudly. They were arguing about who was the better snooker player, Steve Davis or Jimmy White. I didn't know but it didn't matter. I sat there drinking my Bacardi and Coke and feeling flushed and happy. Late in the evening a girl got up to put the Pet Shop Boys' 'Always on My Mind' on the juke box and we all started swaying and singing along.

When the barman called last orders someone suggested we go on to a nightclub and I was ready for it. We spilled out of the pub and I remember the caress of the warm night air on my face. We linked arms and walked along the pavement and it struck me how strange it felt to be touching anyone who wasn't Jassey or Lisa. I wasn't telling any of Lucy's crowd but I'd never been to a nightclub before. I was twenty-two and for the first time ever I was going dancing. I could have danced down the street.

The nightclub was in a basement and as we walked down the stairs to it I could feel the pounding music through my feet. Loud! I'd never have believed it. Inside it was hot and crowded and exciting. Lights were bouncing off a huge silvery ball suspended above the dance floor which was crammed with people. Lucy grabbed my arm and we pushed our way in, dodging flailing arms, until we found a place for ourselves among all the sweaty bodies. And then we were part of it. The heat, the energy, the sheer physicality of arms, feet, legs, thrusting hips and heads thrown back. Nothing mattered to me then except the music and the movement of my body and the rhythm pulsing through it. 'Born in the USA', 'What's Love Got to Do with It', 'Let's Go Crazy'. We twisted and spun and stamped through the night.

I'd say now that my teenage years began in that nightclub. It was in there I had my first cigarette: Lucy smoked so I did, I thought everything she did was cool. From then on I went out with her most Friday nights and often on Saturdays too, falling into bed with just a couple of hours to go before I'd have to wake up and, bleary-eyed, help Jassey do the weekend markets.

There was always a gang of us; we went drinking, dancing, sometimes to the cinema. It was easy, innocent fun. Jassey always said he didn't mind me going. He never wanted to come and I felt bad about that, but he was insistent. 'You go. Go on, you've worked hard, you deserve it. We're happy here at home, aren't we, poppet?' And he kissed Lisa on the head.

In the next few weeks it was as if I danced the life back into me. On those nights out with Lucy I felt younger, brighter, more light-hearted than I had in years. The new optimism I'd found inside me began to affect me in everyday life. I'd spent so long hunched over my disgrace but now I began to open out and for the first time since fleeing Derby I found I could look the world around me in the face.

That's how I saw Surjit.

He was a market-trader too. He was six foot tall, with black hair and stylish clothes. He was the first man apart from Jassey who'd ever really looked at me, and his gaze was uncomfortably direct.

The first time we went for coffee (it was his suggestion, our stalls were very quiet that day), I told myself that he was only being friendly. The second time I let him hold my hand. The third time he persuaded me to stay on later and have a drink with him, and as we said goodnight he put his hand beneath my jumper and touched my breasts. I felt I'd been shot through with electricity. I half expected his fingerprints to be branded on to me, the mark of my shame.

How could I do that to Jassey? He made it easy for me by trusting me completely. As I told him the lies about where I was going I could hardly bear to look into his kind, innocent face. So much tied me to him: fondness, familiarity, gratitude, duty, mutual responsibility. What drew me to Surjit? I think it was the absence of responsibility. I felt I was having the carefree youth that I'd missed out on. It was like a drug.

Surjit made it easy for me too, at first. I made the rules about when we met and where and what time I had to be back. He respected the fact that I was married and he was very discreet. But after a couple of months that began to change. One night I went to get up and get dressed but he grabbed my wrist and pulled me back down again.

'Stay here tonight,' he said, and there was a harsh edge in his voice that I didn't understand. His grasp twisted and tightened.

'Let go, you're hurting me. You know I can't stay.' I was trying to read his expression but he'd turned his face away from me.

'Suit yourself,' he said, and dropped my wrist, and then he added, really quietly, 'slut'.

I went on seeing him but it was different, he

became increasingly possessive. The first time he frightened me we were in a pub. He'd gone to get drinks and while he was at the bar I was looking idly round. The place was packed, but I wasn't conscious of looking at anyone in particular. Surjit said I was though. He came back with the drinks and sat down beside me.

'Like the look of him, do you? You've been staring at him hard enough.'

'Who? What are you talking about? I haven't been looking at anyone.' I was taken aback.

He grabbed my face. He was cupping my chin and his fingers and thumb were pressing into my cheeks as he thrust his face into mine. I tried to pull away but he just pinched harder. 'You're my girl. Got that, *mine*. It's me you look at.'

I was scared of making a scene and even more scared of Surjit's expression, so I just nodded. There wasn't much to say after that. We finished our drinks as quickly as we could but then, as we were walking back down the street, he put his arm around me.

In the weeks that followed memories of the headiest days of our romance clouded my judgement. Surjit became more insistent, more of a bully. He was unpredictable. There was the odd shove, sly pinches that made me cry out with pain. I grew wary in his presence, tense and alert; if he moved suddenly I flinched. I wanted to end it but I didn't know how.

The first time he hit me – 'Tell me, I've got a right

to know, do you still sleep with him? *Tell me!*' – his palm was open and the mark of all four fingers was left on my cheek. It was still burning half an hour later when, forcing myself to keep my gaze steady, I told him we had Jassey's family staying, that I'd be too busy to see him the following week.

I couldn't believe how well he took it. 'Okay, babe,' was all he said before, very casually, he went and got a jacket from his bedroom. His insouciance unnerved me.

'What are you doing?'

'I'm walking you home, babe. If I'm not going to see you for a while there's things we need to get sorted. It's about time Jassey and I met. It's only fair a bloke knows who's been screwing his wife.'

'But you can't do that, please don't, you can't.' I was tugging at the sleeve of his denim jacket. An image of bewildered incomprehension on Jassey's loving face flashed into my mind.

'If you're going to leave me, I can do anything I bloody well like, babe. Got that?' he sneered.

That's how Surjit made me stay with him: he reduced our giddy effervescent happiness to a rank display of power. I'd lie beside him, rigid with resentment and self-loathing. I don't know who I despised more, him or myself. Jassey's tenderness taunted me each time I said goodbye to him. He still had no idea of my perfidy and I'd look into his gentle, brown eyes and pray to find a way to keep from hurting him. But of course it was too late.

In the end I told him. Surjit was becoming more violent and irrational. He smashed my windscreen, he followed me like a stalker; one day I found him hiding in the boot of my car. The open-handed slap had long since become the clenched fist and when, during one particularly vicious rage, he broke my nose, I knew I had to end it. I was terrified of him and I couldn't carry the deception any longer. I wanted to confess; I wanted to pay the price for my mad, selfish folly and feel the scourge of Jassey's rage.

I told him one evening when Lisa was in bed, Lucy was out and we were clearing up our meal. I said the words that made a mockery of all he'd done for me and my heart twisted as I watched the pain of betrayal flood his face. I didn't try to lessen my guilt. I said I'd been having an affair, it had got out of hand and now, much as I wanted to, I couldn't end it. Some instinct stopped me mentioning that Surjit hit me; I'd earlier explained away my broken nose by saying that I'd stood up clumsily and smashed my nose on the stall. I think Jassey would have gone quite mad if he knew someone had hurt me.

When I finished talking he was silent for a long time, staring straight ahead. I tried and failed to read the expression on his face. When eventually he spoke his voice was flat:

'Don't worry. I'll help you. I'll talk to him, we'll sort it out.'

'But aren't you angry? You're supposed to be

angry. I thought you'd shout.' The quiet emptiness in his voice was much more devastating than anger would have been. The tears were streaming down his face.

'I'm sorry, Jassey, I'm so sorry, I didn't want to hurt you. Tell me if you're angry, you've every right.'

'I'm not angry.' He stood up so abruptly that his chair clattered to the floor behind him. He kicked it viciously aside and began pacing the room. 'I'm not angry.' He stopped with his back to me, facing the wall, and was still for a few seconds before lashing out with his right foot. It left a dent in the wall, just above the skirting board. 'At least not with you,' he said and, without looking at me, he left the room.

We barely talked about it after that. If I'd wanted a cleansing confessional session it wasn't to be. Jassey never blamed me, never asked for details except what Surjit's name was and where he could be found. A couple of days after I'd told him he left Lucy and me in charge of the Bradford stall and went to where Surjit worked. Later he told me they'd had it out; it was just a verbal exchange, nothing violent. 'I've spoken to him, that's the important thing,' said Jassey. 'Now it will be all right.'

But it wasn't really. Surjit hung around for a while, trying to cause trouble. He'd turn up at the house, asking to see me. One Saturday morning he arrived and leant on the bell. I'd seen him walking up the path and I was cowering upstairs; it was Lucy who answered. She told me afterwards that he was looking wild-eyed and mad. When she opened the door, apparently, he took off his T-shirt. 'He'd shaved his chest hair off, and his whole chest was covered in blood and scratches. He'd tried to scratch "Jas" on it with a razor-blade. Can you believe it? I'm sorry, but you've got to laugh, Jas, talk about daft.' She was enjoying the re-telling of it.

'Then he opens his hand and he's got this fistful of pills.' Here Lucy rolled her eyes and moved into melodrama. 'He goes, "Get Jas down here to see me, or I'll take these." I said, "Hang on there a minute. I'll get you a glass of water."'

Lucy was chuckling away and I gave a wan smile, trying to share her amusement. She and Jassey were trying to protect me from Surjit and I was grateful to them for that. I was doing all I could to be the dutiful wife. I stopped going to the market in Leeds, there was too much gossip. Lucy looked after it while I stayed up in Bradford with Jassey. On the surface we behaved as if everything was fine but I knew that another small part of our relationship had died. Jassey was as caring and solicitous as ever but – and I'm not sure he even realized this – after I told him about Surjit there was something more muted and automatic about his affection. He became quieter and less zany. There were fewer jokes.

And me? I had to accept that I'd made a choice and it had been a very bad one; I'd tried to lead my own life and failed, just like Mum said I would. I felt I was staring into a void. Cursing myself for my ingratitude I looked around me, at the house in Bradford, our successful business, my loyal husband, my healthy, beautiful, enchanting daughter. I vowed to get on with my life.

CHAPTER 14

I found I could lose myself in exercise. I'd felt so vulnerable at the first aerobics class I went to, about six months after Lisa was born. My thighs were heavy and my belly was all loose and flabby and I felt hideous. Jassey had suggested I go: I agreed on the condition that he lend me one of his biggest T-shirts so I could cover myself up. He drove me to the class in a local community centre and practically pushed me through the door; I think he was so relieved at the prospect of a solution to one of my problems. He'd kissed me goodbye and said he and Lisa would be back to pick me up when the class was over.

I stuck to the back of the room in that first lesson and while I was waiting for the class to begin my eyes were glued to the floor. I was so scared I'd make a fool of myself. I'd loved netball at school but I'd never done anything remotely sporty since and I was sure everyone else would be lithe and beautiful and know all the steps. When the teacher arrived I was surprised by how friendly and enthusiastic she was. She had a tape recorder with her and she put a Madonna tape into it and started guiding us through a warm-up. I was so busy trying to follow the steps and keep in time that I forgot about feeling self-conscious and by the time 'Like a Virgin' came on and we were skipping on the spot, boxing the air in front of us, I was sweating and breathless but I was really enjoying myself. When the hour came to an end and we were doing our cool-down stretches I sneaked a look round the rest of the class and saw that not all of them were in great shape and there were several faces just as hot and red as mine.

'I'm coming again next week,' was the first thing I said to Jassey when he picked me up.

I tried to go regularly after that; I aimed for once a week but sometimes with the markets and Lisa to see to it was more like once a month. The exercise worked. Slowly but surely I lost all the post-baby fat and, what's more, I found that after each session my mood was lighter; I felt more in control of my life. I recognized the good it was doing me and at the time I was glad of it, but somehow, once Lucy was staying and I started going out, I forgot about aerobics and hardly ever went.

When the affair with Surjit ended I hoped that, once again, exercise might ease my mind and I took up the classes again. I went as often as I could. I even thought about training as a teacher myself and, when I asked the woman who took my classes how to go about it, she said I could begin by helping her out. If a lot of people turned up I'd go up to the front and do the demonstrations with her. She taught me a routine and, as I grew more confident, I asked some of the other regulars in her class if they would let me 'practise' on them. I'd book the hall and whoever turned up would get a free lesson while I got experience. I found that teaching really gave me a buzz.

It was at that time Robina got back in touch. She never explained her silence or said anything about Mum and Lucy, she just rang up one day and started chatting as if we could pick up exactly where she'd left off. And I didn't say anything to prevent that. I was still grasping at the smallest bit of contact my family offered. She was living in Leicester by then; she and Baldev had moved out of his mum and dad's and got their own place; they were doing factory work. Sunny was nearly six; growing up fast, Robina said, 'and full of mischief, morning, noon and night'.

Everything she told me suggested that she was fine, but something about the way she said it niggled at me. She was a bit too reticent for a woman who was leading exactly the life she wanted. (When she questioned me I knew how much misery lay behind my cheerful response, 'Fine, I'm fine', but I certainly wasn't going to add to my shame by telling Robina about Surjit.) There was one call when, right at the end, she went, 'Jas?' and then there was a long pause before she gasped, 'It's just . . . Oh, nothing. I've got to go because Sunny's calling.' She put the phone down so quickly I didn't have time to say goodbye, and afterwards I couldn't stop wondering what she had wanted to tell me.

The next time we spoke she sounded so flat I had to mention it.

'What do you mean? I'm fine,' she said, and changed the subject. We swapped news, mostly about Sunny and Lisa and the funny things they were doing but, try as she might, she couldn't make her voice sound normal. Her unhappiness vibrated through the telephone wire connecting us.

'I tell you what,' I said. 'Why don't I take a day off next week and come down to see you. I'd like to see your place and Sunny will have changed so much since I last saw him.' I had my brightest voice on, like it was going to be a big treat for both of us and, in truth, for me it was: I'd really missed Robina.

The house in Leicester was a flashy place; there was even a built-in bar in the through lounge. But I knew from the moment I walked in that something wasn't right. There was a smashed window in the lounge and the bathroom door had obviously been forced open.

Robina caught my eye, then hurriedly looked away. I'd left Lisa with Eileen so we could talk but Robina wasn't having any of it. She hustled me out of the door with: 'Come on, let's go shopping.'

When I next went it was worse; there were a couple of holes in the wall which must have been

160

made by kicking and there had been no attempt to cover them. I wasn't going to let it go a second time and I asked Robina, straight out, what was happening.

'He just gets angry sometimes,' she said. 'He kicks things.'

'He doesn't hit you, does he?'

'Oh, no, no, *no*,' she said.

The first time I knew for sure something was wrong was when I next went down to Leicester and she met me at the bus station. Sunny was standing beside her, holding her hand, his little hat covering his ears because it was cold. When I went to hug her, she flinched. 'Don't do that . . .'

'What –?'

She glanced down at Sunny and shook her head.

Baldev was at the house when we got there, so we still couldn't talk about it; I had to make conversation with him instead. I'd met him a couple of times before and he had been polite and charming but this time I couldn't wait for him to leave. When at last he did I said, 'What's going on?'

She hesitated. 'Nothing . . .' She flushed and added quickly, 'We just argue a lot.'

'What are you going to do?'

'There's nothing I can do.'

'Do Mum and Dad know?'

'Oh yes,' she sighed. 'I've told them . . .'

And they'd done nothing.

This didn't surprise me. They'd never done anything to help Ginda or Prakash. As far as my mum and dad were concerned, personal happiness wasn't important. What mattered to them was having a daughter who was dutiful and respectable and did nothing to disgrace the family name. 'Heavens, girl, that's what men are like. Why all the fuss?', that's what Mum would say.

'I can't leave him, if that's what you're thinking,' Robina said. She was making us coffee and I noticed she moved her arms really stiffly, as if she was in pain. I knew her reasoning: she was telling herself that she'd chosen Baldev and she had to prove to the community that she could make their union work as well as an arranged marriage.

'I couldn't do it to Mum and Dad, it would destroy them. They're only just now recovering from what happened when you ran away. Mum's just beginning to hold her head up in the *gurdwara*; people who've cut her for years are starting to talk to her. If I left Baldev now, the shame would kill them. And, anyway, what would happen to me? Who would want me after this? I'd be twice divorced. How would I ever get married again?'

'But you can't just put up with it,' I said. 'You *can* leave him. Come and live with me.'

'That's easy for you to say. You don't have to think of the others. When you ran away with Jassey, you didn't think about us.' Her voice was starting to rise. 'You didn't care about your duty, or your family. I'm not the same as you; I still have to put the family first.'

Her words really hurt me, but I tried not to show

162

it. I tried everything to get her to change her mind, but nothing I said seemed to make any difference. Finally I tried to persuade her to have a break, to bring Sunny and come and stay with us for a few days.

All she said was, 'I can't do that. Baldev would be upset and I don't want to hurt him.'

She wanted the marriage to work and she wanted the support of the family, people whose opinion she valued. I had to face the fact that, despite our companionship, what I thought didn't matter because I'd been disowned. The last thing I said to her as I was climbing back on the bus was, 'Go back and tell Mum how bad it is. Show her the bruises. If you won't tell her the truth for your own sake, do it for Sunny.'

A few days later she rang me, sounding much stronger. She'd spoken to Mum and this time, as far as Robina was concerned, Mum had been helpful. She was getting the community leader to come and talk to Robina, to help her sort things out. 'He'll know exactly what to do; he's so wise. That's what Mum said.'

I knew exactly who she meant and my heart sank. I remembered him coming round to Dale Road when I was little and Dad practically bowing as he poured him out a whisky. Like everyone in the community, Mum and Dad would call on him if they needed paperwork doing for a visa to India or something like that. He endorsed everything, and what he said went.

He really mattered to Mum and Dad but as far as I was concerned he was into all the things – caste, forced marriage, the importance of honour – which I think are wrong. I wanted to say that to Robina, but she wasn't in the mood to listen; if Mum had said Father Christmas was the man to talk to she'd have headed straight off to Lapland. She was staying at Mum and Dad's until the meeting and I said I'd meet her there just beforehand. I wanted to encourage her to tell the community leader everything; I was concerned that she'd be trying to save face by making light of it.

I didn't really think about it until I got to Dale Road, but Robina was taking a big risk allowing me to go there and we were both very nervous. When I arrived she checked the coast was clear before letting me in at the back. Then she locked the door and drew the curtains. It was seven years since I'd been in my parents' house and it felt very strange. It didn't feel like I was coming home; not at all. Everything was familiar: Dad's cup and saucer on the draining board, the worn linoleum, the picture of Siri Guru Granth Sahib on the wall, but I felt disconnected from it. I didn't have time for reminiscences anyway because my focus was on Robina. She looked worn out and sad and a bruise was ripening on her face beneath her make-up.

We'd hardly had time to talk at all when the door-bell rang. She panicked, I panicked; there would be trouble for both of us if I was found there. She got me by my arms, shoved me into the pantry under the stairs and slammed the door shut. It was quite cold and full of the smell of food and spices, sharp pungent smells that brought the memories flooding back to me. We used to hide in there when we played hide-and-seek. Now I crouched down, trying to stay hidden. There was all sorts of junk on the floor, shoes and suitcases and stuff, and it was hard to find a steady footing.

I heard Robina let the community leader in. I could picture him strutting like a peacock, filled with self-importance, his big stomach swelling beneath his suit and tie. He got straight to the point; he wouldn't waste pleasantries on a hapless young woman.

'Well, here I am. Tell me what's wrong.' I could easily hear him through the wall. He was speaking loudly and clearly in very good English.

Robina started talking very fast and she soon burst into tears. To my surprise she was being quite open. 'I'm scared of him.'

'Why?'

'He gets so angry.'

I heard his voice again, talking now in Punjabi. 'These things happen. When men get angry, you have to be calmer. When a pan of milk is boiling up, it's a woman's job to settle it down again.'

'But I'm scared of him. What if he hurts me? Should I not leave him, for the sake of my little boy?'

'No! For the sake of your little boy and for the

sake of your family you must stay with your husband. And for your own sake too. Where would you sit without your husband? Stop snivelling and go back to him. You know what happened when your sister ran away from home. You saw how that nearly destroyed your parents.'

I almost lost my balance when I heard that. I wanted to jump out of the pantry and slap that smug, self-righteous creature. I hated him for dragging me into it, for using me as a weapon against Robina.

'If you leave your husband, it will kill your parents – just when they are starting to get back their respect. Think about your family name. Do you want to bring more shame on your family?'

Robina went very quiet. All she'd wanted was for the rows to stop and to have some reassurance that she would be supported by her family. What she was getting was reinforcement of all her worst fears from a man of stature, a man who was speaking for the people she loved, and the whole community where Mum and Dad had to live. How could she not listen?

I was having to strain harder to hear now, because the community leader had dropped his voice and was talking more quickly. I heard him advise her again to go back to Leicester. I couldn't hear anything from Robina. Then they began to move towards the front door. It was easy to distinguish the sounds of their footsteps: her slow, sad shuffle, his confident and heavy tread.

I crept out of the pantry, expecting to talk the whole thing through, but Robina was running around like a demented person, getting her things together.

'What are you doing?' I said.

'I'm going back.'

'You can't go back.'

'You heard him. I have to.' She was crying her eyes out. I stood at the foot of the stairs watching her tears splash onto the little bag she was packing. I wanted to hold her, to draw her to me and keep her safe, but I knew she wouldn't have it.

'You will call me, won't you, if you need anything?'

'Yeah, I will.' She tried to smile through her tears. 'I better go now, I'll have to hurry if I'm going to get home before Baldev.'

She did call me, just a couple of days later. I was surprised to hear from her so soon, and even more surprised by what she had to say me. She asked me if I'd ring Navtej, Sunny's father.

'Of course I will, but why? What do you want me to say to him?'

'I've tried to ring him myself. You know he's still in Canada? I've got through a couple of times but when he answers and I hear his voice I just freeze up. I can't bring myself to speak to him. Will you do it for me, Jas?'

'I've said I will. But you still haven't told me what you want from him.'

'Nothing. I don't want anything from him, not in the way you think. But I'd like Sunny to know his dad; boys need their dads and it's so long since they've seen each other.'

CHAPTER 15

I liked doing the weekend markets. They were busy, but the customers were more relaxed and there was always the hint of a party in the atmosphere. Jassey and I had friends among the other stallholders and before the rush started we'd stand round chatting and warming our hands round mugs of coffee. Some of them had children the same age as our Lisa and on Saturdays and Sundays she'd come along with us and she and the other kids would run around amongst the stalls.

On the Sunday after I'd spoken to Robina about Navtej we were at Cannon Mills just outside Bradford, when Lizzie ran up to our stall. Her hair was everywhere, her face was flushed and she was so breathless that it was a minute or two before she could speak. 'Your mum's rang,' she gasped. 'It's your sister, Robina . . .'

She didn't have to finish the sentence. Everything about her spoke of something terrible. I headed straight for the phone box. My hand was shaking as I dialled. Mum picked up almost at once.

'What's happened?'

She said, 'It's Robina . . . She died . . . She's dead.'

169

My brain refused to process this. *No* . . . Robina was my living, breathing, vibrant elder sister; she was part of me . . . We'd shared a bed, we'd walked to school together, she bought me clothes for my wedding, I'd seen her just a week ago. 'What do you mean, dead? How has she died, Mum?' The words came out mechanically. I was on autopilot.

There was a pause. I thought I heard a sob. 'She's committed suicide. She set herself on fire and died in hospital.'

The world seemed to stop.

My legs went weak and I felt completely hollow. Numb with shock, I stood there listening to this really weird, sub-human noise. Then I realized it was howling, and it was coming out of me. I steadied myself against the wall and said, 'Mum, I'm coming to Derby. Right now.'

'No.' She said it really loudly. 'Don't come to Derby. Don't come here; don't show your face here. You'll just make things worse.'

'Mum. Robina is dead. Are you not going to let me come to the house?'

'No. You will make it worse.' She hesitated. 'You can come when it's dark and nobody is here.'

I said, 'Mum, please . . .'

'No. I'm telling you, you'll make it worse.'

I went anyway. We packed up the stall, Lisa went back to Leeds with Lizzie and Jassey drove me down to Derby. Lucy came with us but no one said a word for the entire journey. Jason Donovan's

'Too Many Broken Hearts' was playing on the radio, over and over again. I hate that song now.

Could I have saved Robina? That's all I was thinking. Should I have guessed she was thinking of suicide? No one can answer that question, but the guilt still twists inside me.

When we got to my mum and dad's house the mourners were all there; I could hear the women wailing as I opened the front door. They were all in the living-room where there was a white cloth spread out on the floor and they were sitting on it, crying and beating themselves with their hands. There were about fifteen of them, including my sisters and some others that I thought I recognized but I'd been away so long I wasn't sure.

It was such a shock to suddenly be back amongst them that my head began to swim; for a few moments I thought I might faint. I leant against the door frame. I could feel the heat of Lucy's body pressed close beside me. The room was hot and stuffy and, since we'd stepped into it, completely quiet. All those eyes stared at us, no one said anything, and then, without even acknowledging us, our sisters – Prakash, Ginda and Yasmin – stood up, wrapped their white scarves around their heads, and walked out.

I was stunned.

Robina, our sister, our own flesh and blood, had died a horrible violent death, and they were still punishing me for something that had happened seven years ago.

With a shred of hope still in my heart, I looked at Mum. I wanted to go over and throw my arms around her, because Robina was dead and I needed her and I wanted her to need me. But she just sat there, cold as a stone.

I turned to face Lucy. Her face was a mask of shock and incomprehension. 'There's nothing for us here,' I said. She nodded and we left.

The funeral was in Leicester. I knew they didn't want me there but I went anyway. I was past caring by then. For the mourning beforehand we went to Baldev and Robina's house and the burnt smell made me gag as soon as the door opened. Seeing them all there made me so angry. The community leader, Mum, Dad: she'd asked them for help and they as good as turned their backs on her. They may as well have spat in her face. Now it was too late and they were parading their sorrow: a respectable emotion dressed up in a solemn expression and white mourning dress.

Upstairs in the bedroom there was a great charred mark on the carpet. I couldn't bear to look at it. Baldev stepped back as I approached him. 'Why didn't you stop her?' I asked.

Mum had told me it happened when he and Robina were arguing. She told me Robina said she was going to kill herself, then drenched herself with paraffin. Then she'd said again that she was going to set herself on fire.

'Why didn't you stop her?' I asked again.

'What could I have done? She lit the match and her suit caught on fire.'

By the time the ambulance arrived, she had suffered ninety per cent burns, but she was still conscious, that's what they told me. 'Please cover my face,' she'd whispered as she was carried across the pavement and into the ambulance. With her dying breath she tried to spare Mum and Dad's shame.

Her casket was laid out in the living-room. She was so disfigured that, against all tradition, it was closed. There was a photograph on top instead. Regardless of what anybody else thought I picked it up so I could have one long last look at my darling sister. Mum always taught us not to smile in photographs, but Robina was looking right into the camera and you could see the light of laughter in her eyes. She might have expected her family to cherish and protect that light, but they didn't. Mum, Dad, the community leader . . . between them they stamped it out.

CHAPTER 16

It didn't sit with me that Robina would take her own life and I was determined not to leave it there. The only person who knew the truth was Baldev and he would only say over and over again: 'I've told you, she said she was going to set herself on fire, but I didn't believe her. She lit the match and her suit caught the flame.' Robina may have made a cry for help but a kind word from someone, a consoling arm, would have stopped her. I was sure she never meant to die. My anger and grief made me want to see Baldev punished.

I thought about it for a bit and then I told Mum what I felt. I'd turned a corner in my head by then. Her rejection of me at the time of Robina's death changed things. I considered the game she'd been playing for so long, taunting me by withholding her affection and acceptance, and I thought, 'Why am I still playing a part in this? What more can I lose?' I realized then that in order for me to live, something inside me had to die. I still yearned to be part of my family, but I wasn't going to let it rule my life.

When I rang Mum my only thought was for

Robina. 'I want to find out what really happened that day. Will you come with me to a solicitor?'

She said she would. She barely hesitated before agreeing and I wondered afterwards if she was glad of a chance to right the wrong she'd done Robina. Jassey and I came in the car to get her and that was the first time that she met him. I'd longed for that meeting to happen but when it did – her sitting beside him as he drove though the streets of Derby – it didn't matter to me any more. It had come too late.

From the Yellow Pages I chose a solicitor, picked out because the company name wasn't Asian. Jassey waited in the corridor while we went inside. Mum sat beside me, both of us on hard chairs opposite this great big desk; me translating everything into Punjabi so she could understand it. When I asked her to confirm things – did Robina tell her what Baldev was like? – she said very meekly, 'Yes'.

She was so quiet and compliant that I couldn't believe she was the same hard, stubborn, mouthy woman I had known all my life. And it wasn't just when we were in the solicitor's office. It seemed to me that the day Robina died Mum turned into a mouse. Her only interest was in Sunny. She took him in; she even got herself made legal guardian because she was scared Navtej would come and take him. She and Dad devoted themselves to bringing him up. It can't have been easy for them; their life had slowed down by then and suddenly they were landed with a six-year-old kid. But they did their best and he became the light of my dad's life.

I asked the solicitor if he thought we had a case and he said possibly. In the next few weeks we gave him all the evidence we could. We went to the inquest; Jassey and I took Mum and Dad. One of Robina's neighbours had made a sworn statement saying she heard Baldev shout, 'You bitch, you bitch, what have you done this time?' shortly before he called out of the bedroom window, 'Fire, fire, get an ambulance.' She said she'd heard them rowing in the past.

The forensic scientist who went to the house saw signs of fighting. His statement said the available information suggested that 'a disturbance between Mr and Mrs Basi took place in the through lounge'. He saw a coffee table on its side and a broken wall plate lying on the floor. He also mentioned a hole 'apparently caused by kicking' by the side of the lounge door.

Baldev's statement said he had stayed out all day and come home to find Robina crying. Then they'd had a row. He said he used a bed quilt to smother the flames that were eating at my sister. Could he have been quicker with it, that's what I wanted to know. The pathologist's report said Robina had extensive third degree burns to ninety-five per cent of her body.

The coroner gave an open verdict. That upsets me to this day. No one was held accountable for

Robina's death. There was no evidence to suggest it wasn't suicide.

Mum never told the others – Prakash, Ginda, Yasmin and Balbir – what we did. After her death Robina was never spoken of at all. My guess is that Mum kept quiet about going to see the lawyer because she didn't want them to know she was talking to me. I accepted that. I was still playing by her rules so I didn't embarrass her. I knew she was afraid to let other people know she was talking to me, lest they should think she condoned my behaviour. She was afraid of the gossip in the *gurdwara* and among the neighbours, and afraid that my sisters would say, 'If you want to talk to her, don't talk to us.' She didn't want the family's good name tainted by my dishonour, and I accepted that because I had to; I'd rather see my mum and dad in secret than not at all.

It led to some absurd situations. Several times when I was visiting, one of my sisters would arrive and I'd have to rush upstairs and hide in a bedroom. Once Mum rang and asked me to come round because Sunny was sick. In her panic she rang Gin as well but she forgot about that until we heard the front door click shut and Gin call out 'Mum?'

'Go! Quick! Get out of here! Go!' Mum was shooing me out as if I was a chicken.

'But where? Where do you want me to go?'

'Anywhere! Out through the back door. Go out the back.'

I went out the back door and hid behind the outside toilet while I decided what to do next. I was scared Gin would see me through the living-room window if I went through our front gate, so I climbed the wall into our next-door neighbour's garden and went out that way. I jumped through hoops because I was scared that if I got found out I'd lose the little bit of Mum and Dad I had.

I cared about that but I didn't care if my family found out that I was house-hunting in Derby. Jassey and I had decided we weren't going to stay in exile any more. It was supposed to be a fresh start for us, away from all that had happened in Bradford and Leeds. The markets are a close community and Jassey felt humiliated by the other traders knowing about my affair with Surjit. Lucy wasn't living with us any more, she'd rented her own place in Leeds and I think Jassey hoped too that a move might rekindle our romance.

The house I eventually found was another step up for us. It was detached, with four bedrooms and two bathrooms. There was a great big living area divided by a real log fire and with patio doors out onto the garden. It even had a greenhouse where I grew tomatoes. We'd started with nothing and that house was what we achieved. No one helped us. No one gave us a thing. My sisters, Jassey's siblings, they would have had financial – as well as emotional – support from our families, but everything we did, we did alone. And compared to the rest of them we were well-off by the time we came back to Derby. 'Without us, you'll be rolling round in the gutter.' That's what Mum said when I was a sobbing teenager in Newcastle, and we'd proved her wrong.

She never acknowledged that, of course, never said she was impressed by what we had achieved, although she must have been. She came to the house two or three times, and Dad did too. In a strange way I think she felt she owed that to me, like it was payback for the way I'd tried to get justice for Robina. But those visits didn't mean much. We never got past 'how are you' or 'did you see that on television' and there were long, unbearable silences. Lisa was the only bridge between us, the little person in the middle who kept the conversation going. I was glad she was finally getting to know her grandparents but still, I was relieved when they stood up and said it was time to go home.

I found Dad's presence warming, just as I always had done, but he was still Mum's silent shadow and the relationship between her and me was very brittle. There were so many things I wanted to ask her: 'How could you have told me I was dead in your eyes?' 'How could you have turned Robina away?' 'How could you not have been there for me when I had Lisa?' Those questions were such a big part of me, but they were never mentioned, she just didn't want to go there. From my point of view they sat between us like a rock.

She let me go to her house though, me and Jassey. The irony was that, as time went on, those two got on better than me and Mum did. She saw he was a good man in the way he supported me through the business about Baldev, and once she got over the fact of his caste she liked him.

I bumped into Ginda on a couple of my visits to Mum and Dad's house. Her marriage was going through such a bad patch at the time that she was stopping there. The first time it happened I was in the living-room talking to her kids, Sereena and David, when she walked in. I immediately got up to leave because I thought that's what Mum would have wanted but, to my surprise, Ginda started talking to me.

'Nice house you and Jassey have got yourself now. I bet that cost a packet,' she said.

'Yeah, well . . .' I smiled and looked away. She hadn't spoken to me for so many years and I wasn't certain of the ground between us.

'You heard about me and your brother-in-law? Mum told you that I left him?'

Her tone had changed and I knew then that this was going to be about her not me. We talked for a bit and she was so full of miseries that I couldn't help but feel sorry for her. She'd done everything right: made the marriage Mum and Dad wanted and conformed to all the invisible but oppressive rules laid down by 'the community', but I could see now that it hadn't given her a special pass to happiness. She was part of our family in a way I'd never be but, beyond that, her life didn't look fantastic.

I listened to Ginda and heard her complaints and they took me back down the years to those terrible Sundays when I was little. I knew then without doubt that in running away from my arranged marriage I'd done the right thing. At least I got to make my own choices and decisions. Where on earth would I have been if I had stayed?

I was walking in town a few days later when a woman stepped out of a bus queue and touched my arm.

'I thought you were dead.' That's what she said as she stopped me.

I didn't recognize her at first, she was standing behind a pushchair with a crowd of small children at her feet; I guessed she was about forty. I must have looked blank, because she said, 'I'm Habiba. Habiba Ahmed. Remember?' Then she smiled, a big smile that showed a gap between her front teeth.

A memory flashed through my mind of me standing in the playground at Littleover School and watching a giggling Robina trying to measure that gap with a ruler. She and Habiba had been great friends although Robina was always a bit in awe of her because she was so clever, the sort that got her work read out in assembly. I looked down at the children, five of them, and up again into the tired, worn face of their mother.

'Habiba! Of course! Of course I recognize you. But I'm not dead. Whatever made you think . . .' Suddenly I realized her mistake. I put my hand on her arm. 'It was Robina who died.'

'No. I know that and I'm so sorry, so very sorry. Her death was a terrible thing.' She paused, embarrassed, but then pressed on. 'I thought you were dead also. I thought you died years ago, that's what they told us.'

It was on the tip of my tongue to say 'who told you?' but I decided against it. 'Dead in her mother's eyes!' 'Dead, I'm telling you.' I could imagine the whispers that slithered through the *gurdwara* after I ran away. I forced a laugh.

'No, here I am, alive and breathing. And how about you, Habiba? How are you? Did you go to college?'

'No, Jasvinder, I didn't.' She gave a sad little smile. 'I was fifteen when I married and then, you know how it is, we needed money to bring my husband over. Then he came and we had Aabid.' She ruffled the head of the tallest child, who was leaning against her. 'Then the others. I'm lucky, my husband is a good father.'

CHAPTER 17

I worked to make that house in Derby a home for us. I decorated the rooms in strong, vibrant colours, painting them myself because I liked doing it; the simple repetitive action soothed my mind and left me too tired to think. I found I loved gardening and I filled the garden with flowers, and even planted a few vegetables. We had all that we wanted but since moving back to Derby we were finding it hard to earn the money to support our new life. We'd made such a success of the markets in Leeds and Bradford and we'd just assumed it would be easy to carry that on in Derby, but it didn't happen. We had all the expertise, but by then the hunger . . . the drive . . . the partnership didn't exist between us. It soon became clear that there wasn't enough work for both of us, so I looked into setting myself up as an aerobics teacher. Another bond was broken.

We held it together, for Lisa's sake. She was at school by then and loving it. Come three o'clock I'd be waiting at the gate and she'd come running out, her cardigan dangling off her shoulders, full of all she'd done that day, waving some still damp picture. For all she knew, we were still a happy family. Most people, looking at us, would have thought so, but the fact was Jassey and I didn't even share a bedroom any more. We couldn't even pretend we had that between us.

We never argued but we didn't communicate either, we just co-existed, leading our separate lives in the house we'd worked so hard for. The way we were reminded me of how Mum and Dad had been: soldiering on alone together. Should that have been enough for me? Should I have been satisfied? Jassey was. He said so. 'Don't leave me sweet, please. We're all right like this. We can still share our life together.' That's what he pleaded.

Sometimes I'd look at Mum and think that Robina's death must have done her actual, physical damage because from the day it happened she dwindled. It wasn't just that she became this new cowed, quiet person; I watched her getting smaller. She lost so much weight it looked like she was shrinking. She'd been so dominant in that house and now it seemed somehow empty, as though a life force had been sucked out of it.

She'd always been a great one for ailments: a strange ache here, an unexplained twinge there, and the doctor's was like a Mecca for her. She loved going up there, and coming back home with a new diagnosis and a bottle of pills. But now she really did seem ill. As far back as I can remember, when my mum sat it was always on the floor by the fireplace – I can see her in my mind's eye now, sitting there, cross-legged, dealing with her vegetables. But there came a time when that seemed like too much effort for her. She preferred to sink back on the old worn sofa-bed. She'd sit there holding her mug of tea – she needed two hands to keep it steady by that time – and she seemed to have retreated into a world of her own. Dad hovered around the living-room, wanting to help, uncertain what to do, his brow furrowed with anxiety, his head nodding as he mumbled on in endless conversation with himself.

The GP thought it was gallstones Mum was suffering from and he sent her to the hospital to have them removed. That's when they told her she had bowel cancer. The doctor who confirmed the diagnosis said it was terminal.

I went to see her more and more often. It was a relief to be out of our house, anyway. I never went without ringing first, because I didn't want to embarrass her by arriving when my sisters were there, but it soon became apparent that I didn't need to worry. They weren't regular visitors. Sometimes she'd ring and ask me to come, if she needed a letter written, or she wanted help with a phone call, or with filling in a form. Other times I'd drop in and make her and Dad a cup of tea; I'd check the cupboards and, if necessary, I'd go up to the shop and get some food in for them.

It sounds callous, but it wasn't love of her that made me go there. I had special feelings for my dad, but it was a sense of duty that made me care for Mum; duty and the fact that after all those years I had what I wanted: I was allowed to see my parents, they agreed to have me in their home. I wouldn't have said I was back in the family, but I wasn't a complete outcast any more.

I don't know what Mum was feeling. She never said much. She accepted what I did for her, but I had no idea what was going on in her head. The only hint she ever gave me came one day when I was bathing her. I did that quite often because, although Dad was there to care for her, he was also quite frail and lifting Mum in and out was too much for him even though there was almost nothing of her by then.

I was glad to give her a bath, because the warm water seemed to soothe her. She'd want me to wash her hair but it nearly broke my heart to do that. She'd always been so proud of her long thick hair and so particular about dyeing it, but now it was grey and sparse and, when I washed it, great clumps came out and the limp strands twined round my fingers as I tried to hide them from her.

I used to make excuses not to wash her hair and then she'd lie back with her eyes shut and it was as if the heat of the room eased the tired, tense lines from her face. I'd let her soak there a while and then, when I started to worry she'd get cold, I'd help her out onto the mat. She was so light it was no trouble. Usually she didn't say much, but the day I have in mind she suddenly said, 'This is wrong. It should be the other way round.'

She said it very quietly and with real humility and I knew what she meant by it. It was her way of saying, 'I'm the mother, you're the daughter, I should be looking after you.' That's the only time I ever thought she might regret all that she'd done to me. I didn't answer her. I couldn't; I was too choked up. I pretended I hadn't heard as I stood her on the bathmat to get her dry. Then I dressed her in a pink flannel nightdress and Dad's old brown cardigan and took her downstairs to settle her in the armchair the hospital had provided. And all the time I was thinking, 'You've wasted so much time.'

The first thing I ever told Rajvinder was that I was going to see my mum. He worked in the garage where I used to fill my car with petrol and he was on the till the day I met him. I went up to the counter to pay and I was writing out my cheque, deep in thought, when I suddenly realized he was talking to me. I started.

'Sorry, I wasn't listening. What did you say?'

'Only asking where you're off to, dressed like that.' His voice was friendly and full of confidence.

'I'm off to work. I'm an aerobics teacher and I'm going to take a class.' I smiled as I passed him the cheque and something made me add: 'But first I'm going to see my mum, she's not been well.'

'Sorry about that,' he said, making it sound as if he really was sorry. 'I hope she's better soon.'

That was that really. I got back in the car and drove off but there was something about the memory of our encounter that I couldn't shake off. He had an infectious grin and the most fantastic eyes, that's what stuck with me. He had long, long eyelashes and his eyes were so sparkling and full of life. It was more than two years since my affair with Surjit had ended and in all that time I'd kept my head down, trying to stay strong and get my life in order. Even when I finally accepted that my marriage had no future I hadn't given a second's thought to meeting anybody else. Now I noticed, with a complicated mixture of excitement and distress, that I felt a tingle of anticipation.

I was back at the garage the following week. The same man was there and he remembered me. I tried not to show how pleased I was. He waved from his place behind the counter while I was filling the car and then, as soon as I went inside, he said, 'How's your mum, then? I hope she's a bit better.'

'Not really, but thanks for asking anyway. She keeps losing weight, and I know my dad's worried; he looks so tired and . . .' I stopped mid-sentence, suddenly unsure why I was blurting out all this to a stranger.

'That's a shame. I bet they're glad to have a daughter like you looking out for them,' he said. 'Is it far for you to go?'

We talked on for a bit in between his serving customers, easy, inconsequential conversation. He told me he was running the garage for his dad, who owned it. As I turned to leave he said, 'I'm Rajvinder Sanghera, by the way. Friends call me Raj.'

'Right.' I smiled. 'I'm Jasvinder Kaur, but everyone calls me Jas.'

Filling up with petrol became a highlight of my week. I wasn't thinking of romance, it was Raj's friendship I appreciated. There is no lonelier place to live than in a dying marriage. I was creeping round our house, struggling for breath in the emotional vacuum that surrounded us. Guilt tormented me, seeping through my mind, spreading itself like a foul slick of oil over all my moods and feelings. I was frightened of the future. If I stayed I felt sure I would wither and die, but I was terrified of leaving. Raj's friendliness, his interest in me and his concern all acted like a balm on the persistent ache inside me. I'd turn away from his till after five, ten, fifteen minutes' conversation and, walking back to my car, realize that I still had a smile on my face.

I told him the situation I was in with Jassey and he was very sympathetic. He said he understood my feeling torn apart because he was recently divorced himself. The more I learnt about him, the more I liked him. He was twenty-six, just a year older than me, and he seemed very sure of himself. He was charming and he had a lovely sense of humour which, at that time, I really valued; it felt so good to have someone to laugh with.

Mum's bed had been moved downstairs into the living-room by then. With that and the commode the hospital sent it looked just like a sickroom. Mum had a colostomy bag and she hated it. The first thing she said whenever I went in to see her, was 'Does it smell in here?' and I'd say 'No, Mum, it doesn't, don't worry about that'. But it did; the sour stench of sickness tainted the house and the lavender air freshener that she sprayed everywhere did nothing to disguise it. I'd arrive and find Dad wandering aimlessly from room to room; in the face of Mum's decay he seemed lost.

I should never have told them that my marriage was collapsing. Mum was too frail and sick, she didn't need the worry and nor did Dad. But after all the years of separation, secrecy and evasion I wanted them to know me – and accept me – as I was. I knew they were reluctant, but I made them listen.

'I don't love him, Mum. I've tried and tried to, but I don't.'

She struggled to lift herself off her pillows, angered into forgetting her failing body, eager to bring the dignity of height to her tirade against my folly. But her arms were too weak, they wouldn't hold her and she wouldn't let me help her. She turned her face from me and with all the contempt she could muster spat out, 'Love!'

Why did I expect her to understand me? She was Jagir Kaur, who, at the age of fifteen, had been made to marry her dead sister's husband, my father. She had worked hard, raised eight children and led her life according to the unspoken rules of the community she feared and treasured. What did she care for love?

I hadn't meant to tell her about Raj, but in the end I did because I needed something to refute her belief that I was mad to consider walking out on a good man like Jassey. I wasn't afraid of her any more but I still longed for her to respect the choices I made and the way I lived my life. She made no comment, I wasn't even sure she had taken it in, but a few days later when I was helping her to drink a cup of tea she pushed my hand away and said, 'I had a dream last night about the man you want to marry.'

'What man?' I said.

'The man you've been seeing. The man you are leaving your husband for.'

'I'm not leaving Jassey *for* anyone, Mum, I'm leaving him because . . .'

'I dreamt you married this man and he brought you nothing but unhappiness. I dreamt you got divorced.'

'Well, you can forget your dream. I'm not planning on marrying anyone.'

That was the truth. I tried to keep the anger out of my voice, but it's what I felt. My relationship with Raj had gone beyond friendship but marriage,

191

to him or anyone else, was the last thing on my mind. I thought Mum was just up to her old manipulative ways and I ignored her. I never for one moment thought she might be right.

CHAPTER 18

I didn't plan to take much with me when I left Jassey. I packed a single case with nothing more in it than a few clothes for me and Lisa. When the day came, I aimed to leave quickly.

It was about 6 p.m. one weekday. Once Lisa had finished her tea I took her by the hand and we walked out through the front door and I didn't look back. I remember the hot, sticky feel of her fingers crushed in mine and the confusion in her voice as she kept asking, 'Where are we going?' I ignored her question and held her hand too tight as I hurried her along, the suitcase banging against my legs as I tried to escape from the terrible sobbing behind us. I can bring the desperate misery of that sound to mind as if I heard it yesterday, and the memory of the pain I caused still makes me wince. Lisa's little face, pinched and frightened, trying to be brave as she said goodbye to her daddy. 'But can't he come with us, Mummy?' And Jassey, my knight in shining armour, broken. Ten years before he'd rescued me and now, in return, I'd left him weeping.

We went to Raj's house and as far as everyone

was concerned that confirmed me as the baddy. When he offered me a place to stay and said Lisa could come too, I knew I had no alternative. And once we got there it was easy to live with that decision because he did his best for us. We arrived, pale and shattered, and he was at his most disarming: gently solicitous but also very funny. He even managed to make Lisa giggle.

That's how he was in the weeks and months that followed and gradually, as he wrapped me round with his affection, I began to let go of my guilt and allow myself to fall in love with him. It's what I wanted. I craved affection and the safety of a relationship. For all my wilfulness I felt too vulnerable to survive alone. I yearned for a solid respectable marriage that would allow me to hold my head up high. I'd always despised the strict censoriousness of Mum and Dad's community, but in the years alone with Jassey I'd come to understand that it did afford a safe place in the world, a clear pattern, and I'd found nothing to replace that. I wanted to show the people I'd come back to live among that I wasn't worthless.

I never introduced Raj to Mum. It seemed bitterly ironic but, just as I'd found someone Mum and Dad could really have approved of – a *jatt*, like us, a dutiful Asian son running his father's business – they decided to acknowledge their *chamar* son-in-law. Mum thought the world of Jassey by then.

'You won't take the house from him, will you?'

194

That's what she kept saying once I'd left him. The first time it came up, I pointed out that I'd worked hard for the house too, it hadn't all been down to Jassey, but Mum ignored that. 'Please, Jasvinder, don't take it from him. Think of me, you know I'm dying, let me go to my grave knowing that my daughter has done the right thing. Please, for my sake, say you'll let that poor man keep the house.' She was so insistent that I soon agreed to what she wanted. Losing the security didn't bother me. I'd learnt how to make money; I was confident that I could work my way up again. What hurt was that, yet again, Mum couldn't find it inside herself to give me her backing.

Lisa took her dad's side too. At first she seemed quite happy stopping with me at Raj's. We did her room up nicely. He paid attention to her, he taught her how to ride a bike; one weekend the three of us went to EuroDisney. I'll never forget the look on Lisa's face when she saw Mickey Mouse.

But she never really settled. She often asked about Jassey. 'Does Dad have anyone to eat his dinner with?' or 'Do you think Dad has anyone to talk to?' She'd say those things looking up at me with her clear, brown-eyed gaze and, as I scrabbled for an answer, I hated myself for putting her in a position where she had to think like that. I wasn't surprised when, one night as I was putting her to bed, she said, 'Mummy, would it be all right if I went to live with Daddy for a bit? I would miss you. But you've got Raj to look after you and Daddy's got no one, he says he's lonely by himself.'

My heart lurched. I'd foreseen this moment and I'd been dreading it. I wanted to grab Lisa and clutch her to me, rest my cheek on her silky, sweet-smelling hair and feel the warm weight of her solid little body on my lap. I didn't though. Willing myself not to cry, fighting the lump that was forcing its way up my throat, I bent forward, smoothed her hair and kissed her on the cheek.

'Course you can, if that's what you really want. I'll talk to your dad about it in the morning.'

I rang Jassey and he was delighted. We agreed that, as a trial, she should stop with him for a week, starting the next Saturday when his usual access visit was due. When the time came to leave her there I wouldn't let myself hug her for any longer than usual; I didn't want her to know that letting her go was tearing me apart. But after I'd dropped her off the days dragged by; the week seemed to last for ever. I'd made Jassey promise to let me know if she was missing me, but I didn't hear a thing.

The following Friday at 5 p.m. – our normal handover time – I parked outside my old house and ran up the path to the door. I'd been half hoping to find Lisa waiting for me, her face pressed against a downstairs window, but she wasn't there. I rang the bell and waited but no one came. I tried again, leaning on it a little longer this time. Still no response. I made my way round the house, peering into any windows I could reach, and then I called into the back garden in case they were there. Nothing.

I checked my watch. It was quarter past five. Either I'd got the time wrong or Jassey had kept her out late. Annoyed, I got back in the car and settled down to wait. At six o'clock I went back to the house and rang the bell again, and this time I rapped on the door as well, I knew that was madness because they couldn't have gone back in without me seeing them, but I had to do something. That's what made me drive the few streets to the nearest phone box and dial Jassey's number. As I expected, there was no reply. I checked my watch again, trying to ignore the prickle of panic that was creeping over me.

When I told Raj he was all for not fussing, but I couldn't help it. I went back to check the house at eight and nine o'clock and then, really frightened, I rang Jassey's mum.

'But he's in India, he went three days ago.'

'So where's Lisa?'

'She's with him of course. He's taken her to meet her relatives.'

'Lisa! In India?' I could hear a sharp note of hysteria in my voice. 'When's she coming back? Why didn't Jassey tell me?'

My mother-in-law's voice was cool. 'Lisa is his daughter, Jasvinder. He can take her to meet her family if he wishes.'

★   ★   ★

197

It was almost three weeks before they came back and in all that time I didn't hear from them. I was beside myself with worry and confusion. I missed Lisa desperately and I found it so hard to believe that Jassey, who for years had done all he could to protect me, would now do something so unfair.

I went round the day they were due back in Derby but Jassey wouldn't let me take her home with me. 'She's not a parcel, Jas. We can't keep moving her about the place. She likes it here with me.'

They were standing in the doorway. Lisa was leaning up against him, wearing a little embroidered top that he must have bought in India. I noticed that her hair had grown and that, behind her big bottle glasses, she looked tired. I opened my mouth to argue or plead, I'm not sure which, but then I closed it again. She loved us both and I didn't want to fight in front of her. I knelt down and gave her a kiss and a hug and then, turning to leave, I said, 'Have it your own way, Jassey. I'm going to talk to a lawyer!'

When our case eventually came to court, Jassey got residence. The court said Lisa was used to living with her father and it would be unfair to unsettle her again. I was to be allowed access one night a week and on alternate weekends. Those words landed on me like hammer blows. I didn't speak to anyone as I left the court. I don't know how I got home; I must have driven but I've no recollection of the journey. I just remember sitting on the bed in the room that Raj and I had made nice for Lisa and holding the pillow up to my face so I could smell her smell. My arms ached to hold her. My mind was a kaleidoscopic mess of all the moments in her life I now wouldn't share. I visualized her woken by a nightmare, trying out make-up, getting her first period, falling in love . . . all the moments when a girl needs support and guidance from her mum, moments when I wasn't going to be there for her. I wept for my precious daughter and the way I'd let her down.

I cut myself off from Jassey after that; the only way I could cope with the situation was by switching off completely and, unless we had something to say about Lisa, we didn't talk at all. I knew he was going for all the sympathy he could get, and the word on the Asian grapevine was that he deserved sympathy because I'd abandoned him and left him to bring up our child alone. That infuriated me because he knew that I'd have given anything to have Lisa safe with me.

I stuck to the court order though. The only time I broke it was one night when Jassey left Lisa home alone. She rang me about nine o'clock. 'Daddy's gone out again,' is all she said. The telly was on in the background but I could still hear the little tremble in her voice. I told her I'd be there in fifteen minutes.

When I got to the house I knocked on the door, but she didn't come and open it. I knocked again and then I started walking round the house, calling out to her. She appeared at the living-room window, peeping cautiously round the edge of a curtain, but when she saw me relief washed the worry from her face. She let me in and we had a cuddle and then I told her I was going to take her home with me.

She was worried about that: worried that Jassey would be cross with her when he came back and found her gone, worried that the magistrate would be cross with me for taking her. 'She said I could only come to you on Tuesdays in the week and it's Thursday today,' she said, pulling away from me so she could look into my face. She looked so serious, so anxious, and it tugged at my heart that such a little girl should have to think like that, but I did my best to reassure her. I took her home and tucked her into bed and she quickly fell asleep.

It was about 11.30 p.m. when Jassey rang and there was panic in his voice. I hadn't left him a note telling him I'd got Lisa. It was a mean thing to do, I knew that, but I thought he deserved a shock for having left Lisa on her own. He came roaring round once he knew I'd got her. He was hammering on the door and screaming that he wanted Lisa, insisting that he was going to take her home immediately. He was making such a racket that I'm surprised he didn't wake the whole neighbourhood. Thank heavens Lisa didn't wake up.

'She's stopping here tonight, no question,' I said. I was standing at the front door with my arms folded as if I was physically guarding her. 'I'll bring her back after that if you agree never to leave her on her own again.'

He denied he'd done that. 'It was only for five minutes . . .', that was the sort of excuse he was making. But I wouldn't listen. Why should I? If he couldn't cope I would have had her more than gladly. He knew he only had to ask.

CHAPTER 19

The time came when Mum was so sick that she was in and out of hospital. I used to take her to appointments and as I helped her down the endless corridors and sat with her in airless waiting-rooms it struck me that, although she'd lived most of her life in England, she was still a stranger stranded in a foreign land. She'd have been totally lost on her own. I could see the panic growing in her if I left her alone for a second, to go to the toilet for instance, or to fetch us both a cup of tea.

My heart used to tilt as I watched her clinging to the shreds of her dignity in the face of the nurses' over-familiar cheeriness and the doctors' L-O-U-D, S-L-O-W E-X-P-L-A-N-A-T-I-O-N-S of the procedures she would have to undergo.

'She's not deaf, shouting at her isn't going to help. She doesn't speak English,' I said, struggling to control my anger as a well-meaning young doctor boomed into her face.

'I'm only trying to help her understand,' he said, rounding on me.

'That's not the way to do it. Would you understand

if I shouted at you slowly in Punjabi? Why don't you speak to me and I'll translate it for her.'

We were both exhausted at the end of those appointments. I'd drive her home and half carry her from the curb to her armchair. I'd do all I could to make her comfortable and then – it still hurts to admit this – if one of my older siblings was coming over I'd have to leave. Only Lucy was allowed to know about my visits. She was there sometimes. Mum and Dad let her come over when she wanted. They never let her move back in again, she had to fend for herself, but still, she was accepted more than I was. Her visits weren't kept secret. When Mum and Dad hustled me out of the house I'd drive home in tears, angry with myself for being so stupid as to care.

A few weeks before she died Mum was given a place in the local hospice. She was in constant pain by then and Dad couldn't look after her properly any more. At first she was put in a room with three other patients; it was a bright, airy room and the others were friendly but they had a problem with Mum's prayers. I had to sympathize. She was still in the habit of putting them on full-blast first thing in the morning and mumbling her own devotions along with the tape recorder. *Ik-cum-kar, ik-cum-kar* – I remembered the dawn chorus from my own childhood all too well.

The nurses were very kind. They suggested she should play them later or more quietly, preferably both, but the very thought of that made Mum look bewildered and miserable. She was an old lady, wedded to a routine she'd clung to for almost fifty years, and it seemed too cruel that she should lose that comfort in the last weeks of her life. I wanted to spare her that, so I asked the staff if they could move her, if there was any chance they might find her a little room to herself, and after a few days they did.

It was a tiny room, just big enough for a single bed, a bedside table and a high backed armchair. I used to have to bring a chair for myself from another room when I went to visit. I went as often as I could, always going early in the morning or late in the evening when I knew my sisters and brother wouldn't be there. Right to the end she couldn't admit to them that she was seeing me.

She was sitting in the armchair when I arrived one morning about a week before she died. The nurses had put her there, but they hadn't got her dressed, so she was still in her nightdress. It was blue with little flowers on it and long sleeves. She was slumped in her chair, just staring into space, and my first thought was how thin and frail she looked. It was hard to remember her as the strong, unbending woman who had so determinedly locked me out of her life. She wasn't strong any more, all her fight was gone.

Something happened when I arrived that morning. Her face lit up when she saw me in the doorway; for a few seconds the pain let go its vice-like grip and she was completely transformed by joy. She said '*Tu agai ya*...' 'You're here...' I was so surprised that I looked over my shoulder to see who was coming in behind me, but there wasn't anybody there. Her smile was for me.

I can put my hand on my heart and say that was the first time in my entire life I felt my mum was pleased to see me. It made me incredibly happy. I wanted to go over and hold her tight and tell her I loved her, but I knew that if she didn't respond I'd be really upset. So I just said, 'Yeah, I'm here, Mum.' And I got my chair and sat next to her, very casually.

I'd like to be able to say that I behaved differently, that I showed her all the love that she'd spent years rejecting, but I wasn't brave enough. The moment was too nice and I didn't want to lose it. There she was in her chair and the sun was shining through the window on her and she was genuinely pleased to see me. I'll have that picture in my mind for the rest of my life.

I kept going to see her during the few days that were left, and Mum started to show me a side of her that was human and compassionate, a side I'd never seen before. She'd always been so strict about her position, who she was and what she said, but now she knew she was dying she let her guard down. When I went there now, it was just her and me, and I could sit there, holding her hand.

I wanted to ask her all those same questions, 'Mum, what do you really feel about me, and how you treated me? Do you feel bad about Robina and what happened to her?' I know that sounds selfish because she was dying, but I still had these unanswered questions buzzing round my head. For years I'd been waiting and hoping for a proper reconciliation, and now time had cheated us. I couldn't ask her anything important. She was just a frail old lady preparing to die. But there was one change. In those last days I came to believe that she was proud of me. She didn't verbalize it, but I think she felt it. I hope she did.

The nurses warned me the day she was going to die. I'd been there about an hour and she'd been quiet and peaceful, but then she started trying to tell me something. Her voice was barely a whisper, so I bent down really close to her mouth and through her ragged breath I could just make out the words, 'Balbir, Ginda, go . . .' With her dying breath she was asking me to make way for my siblings but this time, knowing it would be the last time, I said, 'I'm not going, Mum,' and I think she was okay about it because she squeezed my hand and seemed to relax.

In the next hour or so they all arrived, Dad – looking utterly worn and dejected – Prakash, Ginda, Yasmin, Balbir, Lucy . . . We were all of us crammed into that tiny room, pressed together, peering at the fragile figure of our mum as, breath by painful breath, she let go of her life. I was closest to her, at the top of the bed, when she died. I was holding her hand and Balbir was hissing at me to let go of it and move over but I wouldn't. She knew what was happening and she was moaning, 'No, no . . .'

You could almost see the cancer travelling through her; her body twisted and twitched. Her mouth was so dry that I kept wetting her lips with a little sponge. Tears were pouring down my face. Everyone was crying, and every so often one of the sisters would call out, 'Mum . . .'

And then at the end she suddenly said, 'Robina, I'm coming to you,' and her hand went limp.

Later, when all the formalities had been dealt with, I drove myself home. The others didn't even say goodbye to me. I think they all went home with Dad. I've never felt so alone, before or since.

CHAPTER 20

I made it my business to keep my eye on Dad and Sunny after Mum died. Dad needed help with him. There he was in his retirement being mother, father and now both grandparents to that little kid. And Sunny was a handful. I did the school stuff, talking to the teachers and going to parents' evenings, but I also tried to visit them in Dale Road quite regularly. My life had a pattern by then. A couple of months after Mum died Raj and I got married, in a registry office without any fuss. He was working in the garage, I was teaching aerobics, it was easy to find the time to go to Dale Road but it was the same old thing: Dad couldn't admit that he was seeing me, I could never go there without ringing first. I still minded that. Try as I might, we never recovered our old closeness; he kept an invisible barrier between us, almost as if he was afraid.

I arrived at his house one day to find Sunny sulking in front of the telly and Dad fretting about money. 'He says he has to have this brand of trainers and I don't know how I can afford them, Jasvinder. You know, they cost forty pounds.'

'Don't buy them for him, Dad. He's a kid. He just needs something to wear playing football.'

'He says all his friends have this kind. And your mother would have bought them for him, I know that. She always made sure he had the best.'

Dad wanted the best for him too, he doted on that boy. I once found them play-wrestling in the living-room. I was so surprised; I'd never seen Dad doing anything so undignified in my life. 'You can't let the young ones win all the time,' he said, smiling to cover his embarrassment as, breathing heavily, he collapsed onto a chair.

I wonder if my siblings resented the fact that Dad was there for Sunny in a way he'd never been for us. I didn't mind, until he took Sunny back to his village, Kang Sabhu, to meet the family – something all the others had already done with Mum. I wasn't jealous but I wished that I could go. The stories Dad told me about that place were still so clear in my mind. All the time they were away I was wondering what Dad's reunion with his family would be like. He told me when he got back that everyone in the village came out to meet them, they had a great feast and endless celebrations. It took me weeks to pluck up the courage but one day, when we were sitting together drinking tea, I did blurt out the question.

'Will you take me with you to India one day, Dad? I want to meet Bachanu. I'd love to see the farm, all the places that you used to tell me about.'

Dad's hand trembled slightly as he lowered his

cup into its saucer, but he looked me straight in the eye as he said, 'Shame travels, Jasvinder. If you visited my family you would taint them with your disgrace. I will not be party to that.'

Going about my business I noticed a drop-in women's centre in the middle of town and it set me thinking about what I might do to help other women like my mum. I was haunted by the last weeks of her life. I kept having this vision of her in her hospital bed, fading away, stubbornly refusing to eat the food on offer because it wasn't Asian; surrounded by people talking too loudly in a language she'd heard for years but couldn't understand. All her years in Derby she'd buried herself in the Asian community and then, right at the end, she'd been plucked out of her little enclave and left like a snail without its shell, piti-fully vulnerable and exposed.

That stuck with me. It lodged in my mind with the same insistent tick as Robina's death had done. If Robina had only ignored the strictures of the community she relied on to protect her; if she could just have found the courage to reach out and embrace the culture of the country she was born in, she needn't have died. The tragedy of that possessed me. I could feel the sorrow and anger fermenting inside me, building an energy that propelled me towards action. I felt I owed it to Robina to do something constructive with my life and, more than that, I wanted to do something to change the world that had failed my family. A small part of me, fuelled by bitterness, also wanted to show Balbir and my sisters that I didn't need them. I'd felt so totally alone driving away from Mum's deathbed. If they didn't want me I would prove to them that I could tread my own path and still make something of myself.

On the way home from a class one day I stopped at the women's centre. It was in a big old Victorian building and the actual centre was one big room with two or three offices and a tiny little kitchen off it. It was all pretty shabby but the atmosphere was friendly. It was easy to feel relaxed.

I was buying myself a cup of tea when the woman standing beside me stirring sugar into her cup said, 'I haven't seen you here before. Were you after anything in particular?'

She was a white woman, large and jolly-looking, with something comforting about her. I explained that I'd come because I wanted to help other people. 'I wondered if you needed any volunteers?'

'Always,' she said, taking me by the elbow and steering me into a tiny, cluttered office where, having swept a chair clear of papers, she sat me down and asked me about myself. She was quite brief and businesslike and I just gave her the bare details before she said, 'At the moment we're badly in need of volunteers in our pregnancy testing centre. There's a slot on Saturday mornings if you'd be interested.'

I agreed to that. She said I'd be shadowing someone

else to start with but as soon as I was ready I could do the Saturday session on my own. She wrote my name down in the register of volunteers and then, before she said goodbye, she introduced herself as Trish.

The following Saturday I was back at the women's centre at 9 a.m. The actual process I had to learn was easy. You opened up the centre, got all the glass slides, droppers and pipettes organized and, by the time you were ready to start, there was usually a queue of women in the waiting-room. I sometimes saw as many as fifteen in one two-hour session. They'd come in, one by one, clutching their urine sample, and you had to ask the date of their last period. The test was easy, it just took a couple of minutes and we did it while they were sitting there. The interesting bit came when you had to cope with their reactions.

I remember one woman, I'd say she was about forty, and she was very quiet and still. I looked up at her as we waited to see if the 'positive' circle would appear on the slide and she was biting her lip; she looked so apprehensive. She was pregnant and when I told her so, she went bright red and tears spouted from her eyes. 'I don't believe it,' she kept saying.

I stretched out my hand to touch hers. 'I'm so sorry . . .' But she interrupted me.

'No, don't be sorry. I'm thrilled, really. It's just the shock. I've been trying for so long that I'd given up hope. I didn't tell my husband I was coming here today because I didn't want to disappoint him. Are you really *sure* it's positive?'

But of course there were women who were devastated. Young women who dreaded telling their parents. Married women appalled to find they were carrying babies conceived while their husbands were working away. Tired women exhausted by the prospect of a sixth or seventh pregnancy. We gave them all a confirmation slip to give to their doctor and we gave those who wanted it information about abortion. We supported them all, whatever their choices, and I could see they valued that support. It made me realize that there *were* women out there that I could help.

CHAPTER 21

The one thing an aerobics teacher has to do is smile. No matter what's going on in your life, however down you feel, when you step out in front of that class you plaster a smile on your face and you don't let it slip until the last woman has left at the end of your hour. I came to value that. With a false grin on my face I could almost convince myself that I was all right.

Raj and I were teaching some of my classes together by then. He'd trained as an aerobics teacher not long after we started our relationship. We must have looked like the golden couple in our big smiles and our sports gear. And we did have our moments. He could be funny, charming and attentive and when he was I loved him. I wanted so much to love him and I tried really hard to please him. But from the start of our marriage it wasn't easy.

I lay awake at night thinking about my future. I needed qualifications. I'd left school twelve years earlier with nothing, I was completely ill-equipped for independent life and I wanted to change that. The thought of studying again was scary, but I made up my mind to do it. I knew there was a college on Kedelston Road and on the way to work one day I parked outside it.

It was a big place, much bigger than I'd expected, with a sweeping lawn leading up to the main building. I didn't know how I was going to find what I wanted. There were students milling about, but they all looked so sure of themselves and confident that I didn't dare ask any of them. I pushed through the swing doors and kept going until I found a desk marked RECEPTION.

'Hello,' I said. 'I've come to enquire about doing my A levels here.'

There was a middle-aged woman sitting behind the desk and she smiled at me as she said, 'You're in the wrong place, I'm afraid, my dear. We don't do A levels here, this is a university.'

She said it kindly, but I felt such an idiot. I thought she would think me so above myself, so ignorant not even being able to recognize a university.

'I'm, I'm, I'm sorry,' I stammered. 'I thought . . .'

But I couldn't stay to get the words out. I turned and fled, running blindly back through the building, out of its swing doors and onto the grass where the air felt cool against my burning cheeks. I didn't stop running until I reached my car which I leapt into hoping it would swallow me up and hide my humiliation.

'Sorry, my dear, this is a *university*.' Those words rang in my ears until my exercise class started and the Madonna tape drowned them out.

I didn't give up though. I found Derby Tertiary College in Wilmorton in the phone book and discovered they held adult education classes in a special block at our local infant school. I signed up to do an A level in English language and literature. I didn't mention it to Raj until it was all sorted out, but when I did he said, 'That's a good idea. I think I'll do that too.'

Going back to school felt so strange. All that red brick, the lino on the floor, the funny mixed-up smell of chalk and polish. There were about ten in the class, different sorts of people but all of them like me, wanting to better themselves. We looked big and uncomfortable wedged in behind the wooden desks.

The first book we read was Maya Angelou's *I Know Why the Caged Bird Sings*. I loved reading that. To be honest with you, I'd hardly opened a book in the twelve years since I'd left school and I'd forgotten what it's like to lose yourself in someone else's world, to be so hungry to know what's on the next page that you can't get your eyes across the words quick enough. That woman's courage took my breath away. I could so identify with her feelings of abandonment and isolation it was like she was speaking right to me.

In the class discussions there was so much I wanted to say. Our teacher encouraged everyone to chip in. 'Let's think about Maya's sense of displacement. Does it make her vulnerable to Mr Freeman's sexual advances? Does anybody have a view on that? Anybody want to start the ball rolling?'

My hand shot up, and I jumped right in almost before the teacher had acknowledged me, but I'd hardly started when I heard this derisive snort. It was Raj, who was sitting right beside me. I stopped and looked at him. The teacher looked too. 'Wait your turn, Raj,' he said. 'Let Jasvinder finish.'

'Yeah, sure, sorry. It was just the way she said . . .' He was making out that he was having to suppress his laughter. 'The way she said . . . oh, never mind, forget it. You go on, sorry, Jas.'

I found it really hard to pick up my thread. My thoughts had got all muddled and I'd lost confidence in them anyway. I stammered out a couple of sentences and then shut up. I didn't put my hand up much after that.

But Raj couldn't kill the pleasure I found in reading. Books opened up a whole new world for me. I joined the local library and plundered the biography section as often as I could: I found inspiration reading other women's stories. Writing essays was the hard part, it was so long since I'd had to use my brain that way. Sometimes I struggled to marshal my jumble of thoughts into orderly paragraphs but I was determined to stick with it. At school it had sometimes seemed so pointless: my sisters had all left aged sixteen to get married and then go on to factory work. Why should I be any different? But now the fact that I was working towards a qualification, something that would empower me, made me feel strong. For the first time in my life I had a sense of purpose and it was strengthened when, one spring morning at the women's centre, with my period five days late, I did my own pregnancy test. As I sat there watching the slide develop I weighed the thrill of new life against my stormy marriage. I didn't know what to feel as I saw the thin blue line begin to emerge confirming that I was pregnant. As I watched it growing darker and stronger I still felt uncertain. Later, it was Raj's amazed, unaffected delight – 'We're going to have a baby? You're serious? That's wonderful!' – that made my mind up for me. Perhaps a new life would mean a new beginning for us.

In my last term of doing A levels the tutor talked to us about our options for the future. He asked if I'd thought of doing a degree and told me about an open day at the university. My aspirations hadn't climbed that high when I started the course, but he said it was possible, so with Raj and a couple of others, I went to have a look.

I was drawn to the Social Sciences building and I found the tutors there full of information and advice. They asked what I wanted the degree for, if I had a particular career in mind, and I told them a bit about my desire to help women. An idea had been slowly formulating in my mind to start a project for women with language and cultural barriers. They told me about various options including Cultural and Social Studies, which I liked the sound of because it gave you the chance to study lots of different subjects. The grades I'd need to get accepted seemed attainable and I decided to make that my goal. I was pleased to have something tangible to aim for.

When the results came Raj and I had both done well enough to go on to university. I remember clutching the slip of paper that had my results on and thinking 'Yes!' I'd got my foot on the ladder that was going to take me to a better place. That night I cooked lots of different dishes and we had an Asian feast; when it was all ready I put on a sari in honour of the occasion. Lisa was there and for once the three of us were happy. It was a real celebration.

I went on with my exercise classes right through my pregnancy, heaving my swollen belly through all the routines. Each week Raj and I did a couple of classes together and I was glad of the break our double act gave me. I'd lead a set of exercises, then slow down while he led one, and so it went. I made the bump work for me, though. 'If I can do it with a belly like this, you've no excuse! Come on!' It made the women laugh and try that little bit harder.

I was meant to take a class the day Maria was born. I waved at Raj as I drove off that morning and called through the window, 'See you later.' My first appointment was at the dentist's for a check-up. His rooms were up a couple of flights of stairs and I remember using the handrail to haul myself up. I was still eight weeks from my due date, but I felt hot and heavy as I flopped into his chair. The dentist has never held any terrors for me, and I was relaxed as he clipped on the paper bib, wound back the chair and started to probe my mouth. But suddenly my head started to swim, I felt really dizzy and the room began to blur. I lifted my hand to stop him and I remember struggling to sit up before it all became too difficult and I slid backwards into darkness.

Waking up again was very strange. The first thing I became aware of was the feel of foil against my skin; I was wrapped up like a turkey. I was lying on a trolley which was narrow and enclosed and I felt trapped. I was in pain. Something was covering my nose and mouth and I wanted it off me. I reached up to feel it, to remove it, and felt the sharp tug of an IVF line in my arm. I opened my eyes to find a bank of monitors winking and blinking beside me.

'Don't do that, leave the mask in place.' A nurse appeared beside me; her restraining hand was firm but gentle. 'It's oxygen, you need it. Your lung collapsed while you were on the operating table and you're in intensive care.' Her words drifted through the drugs being pumped into me and suddenly found my brain. Operating table? The fog cleared and I snapped out of it at once.

'Where's my baby? What's happened to my baby?'

The nurse was quick to reassure me. 'You've had a little girl. She's small but she's going to be fine. She's in paediatric ICU and she's in very good hands. That's the very best place for her at the moment.'

'Can I see her? I need to see her.'

The nurse was round and motherly. She bent forward and smoothed the hair from my forehead. 'Not just now. You need to rest. You gave us all a fright. We thought we'd lost you.'

For the next couple of days life drifted in and out of focus. My first clear memory is of someone putting Maria into my arms and telling me she was two days old. She was tiny. She'd weighed less than five pounds but the nurses said she was doing well. For a while she did better than me. I had had an abrupted placenta and lost so much blood they thought I wouldn't make it. The ambulance man who had brought me in came to see me on the ward and told me that on the way to hospital he stuck needles into my feet to try and get a reflex but I didn't have one. He looked really relieved to find me sitting up in bed. Even the dentist sent flowers and a card. He told me at my next appointment that I'd given him such a fright he went home and read up all his childbirth notes.

Raj was thrilled with the baby. He said he didn't mind not having a boy. His parents were disappointed though and they didn't like it that I'd chosen

Anna as her second name. His mum explained why: 'You know, Jasvinder, that an *ana* is an Indian coin? A coin so small it is almost worthless. Surely you can't name her after that.'

CHAPTER 22

Maria's birth came at a time of change for us. Raj's dad sold the garage and Raj had to sell his house so he could pay off his ex-wife. I came out of hospital with Maria and we spent just a couple of months there before we had to move out. Raj had arranged for us to move over to Nottingham to live with his parents. He said it would just be for a little while, until we found our own place, but I remember packing up my stuff with a sense of dread: I was about to become the dutiful Asian wife, trapped in her in-laws' house. Like any bride whose marriage had been arranged, I would be under constant scrutiny.

I did what I could to fit in and be what they wanted but that wasn't always easy. If I ever asked Raj to help me clear the table or do the washing-up his mother would exclaim: 'I won't have my son washing pots. Not in this house.' I didn't want to disrespect her, so I never spoke above my station. I was very quiet and submissive, I put on my Indian suits when I came indoors and kept to our room when I could. I felt it was them against me.

I was frightened of Raj by then, and I think his mum knew it. She certainly knew what was going on between us because she witnessed quite a lot of it. She was in the next-door room the night a row blew up about Lisa. I'd made Raj a curry using lots of chillies. I'd gone to real trouble with it because I was trying to please him. It was just for him and me, and we were sitting there eating it when he said, 'Is your daughter coming here tomorrow?'

He knew she was coming; I'd told him so the day before. I felt he was needling me deliberately, like he did when he and his mum talked about Lisa being an untouchable. Something inside me snapped. I dropped the meek, cowed voice I was used to using by then and sneered, 'Don't worry, I'll make sure Lisa is out of your way.'

He didn't like that. It surprised him. He stopped with his fork halfway to his mouth and stared at me, but I brazened it out and stared right back. 'What did you say?' he said, letting the fork fall back onto his plate and pushing his chair back. He stood up and leant over me, eyeballing me. My heart was fluttering in my chest like a trapped bird but I was determined not to let him know that. I eyeballed him back.

'You'll keep her out of my way, will you?' he said and, plunging a hand into the pot of curry sitting on the table, he pulled out a fistful and hurled it at the wall.

As the mess of food slid onto the floor Raj reached

for the pot again and I tried to grab it from him. I wanted to stop this before it got out of hand. There was a tug of war over the pot, then Raj suddenly let go. As though in slow motion the remaining curry emptied itself all over me, some of it flying up into my face and eyes. I heard myself gasp with the pain. I was so shocked that I just sat there, with the food dripping off me. I heard a hiss as Raj unscrewed the bottle of lemonade that had been on the table. For one confused moment I thought he was getting me a drink. But he poured it over me, all of it. It ran down my face through all the curry and, despite the shock, I can remember thinking what a weird taste it had as it trickled into my mouth.

I was coughing and spluttering, squeezing my eyes tight shut against the pain. Rats' tails of hair stuck to my face and my Indian suit was plastered tight across my body. When eventually I felt that it was safe to open my eyes, I realised that Raj was just standing there staring at me. I got a cloth from the sink and started clearing up. 'Don't bother doing that,' he said and his voice wasn't bullying any more. If anything, it was embarrassed.

I went on mopping up the mess and then his mum came in, in through the door that had been open all that time. There is no way that she hadn't heard everything and – if she was sitting in her usual chair – probably seen quite a bit too, but she was all bright innocence. 'Oh dear, what happened here?'

Fifteen minutes later when I had showered and put clean clothes on, Raj appeared at our bedroom door. 'You shouldn't have bothered to change,' he smiled. 'You looked quite sexy wet.'

Looking back, I can't believe I was so passive. He could be as kind as you like and for a long time I believed that the way I behaved affected that. I craved his kindness. I did all I could to earn it, I was so desperate to make a success of my second marriage. I thought I would never be able to hold up my head in Derby if my family knew I'd failed again.

When Raj was nice it was like the sun had come out and I felt I could do anything. I'd clung to my vision of a project for women with language and cultural barriers and he always backed me on that. I'd done my research and found there was nothing like it in Derby. Down at the women's centre I mentioned it to Trish.

'If I were you I'd do the Listening Skills Course at the Rape Crisis Centre over the road,' she advised me. 'If you are going to do any sort of befriending that would really help.' She took me into the office and rummaged about in a big grey filing cabinet until she found an application form. 'There's a new course starting in a couple of weeks' time. See if they'll take you on that.'

I had no idea what to expect when I turned up to the first session. The Rape Crisis centre was in an office building but the room we used had been made to seem cosy with soft lighting and candles. Cushions and low chairs had been arranged in a circle. Two trained counsellors were running the course, Sylvia, who was about my age, mid to late twenties, and Glenda, who I should think was ten years older. They were both lovely, calm, peaceful people. There were eight of us students, all sorts aged from twenty up to about fifty, but I was the only Asian woman there.

The first part of the course was about revelation and self-discovery. For two sessions I listened, fascinated, as the other women told horrific stories about their lives and the horrors were absorbed by the rest of the group. There were stories of rape, abuse, violence and depression all coming out of women who looked so together, so on top of their lives. I couldn't believe they were spilling their shame to a group of strangers. I could see by the way their bodies relaxed when they'd finished speaking that it was like letting out poison, but I couldn't do it myself. Such openness was completely alien to me. It was like a foreign language.

Then week three came and Glenda said she was going to divide us into pairs so we could take it in turns to be speaker and listener. It was an exercise in empathetic, active listening. I was to do it with Alicia and we were to speak from personal experience.

Alicia spoke first. We sat opposite each other and she was telling me all these terrible things that had been done to her when she was young. I was listening and practising all the things we'd been told about: empathy, repeating stuff back, being non-judgemental, providing reassurance. I was practising what we'd learnt but at the same time I was getting really sucked into her story. I'd never talked to anyone like this before. Because it was one to one it was just so intimate.

Then it was my turn. At that point in the course I hadn't told a single secret thing about myself. It had just been the barest bones: I was married, I had two daughters, one of them lived with my ex-husband, I taught keep-fit. I hadn't planned what I was going to say now, but suddenly I found myself talking about Robina. I'd never told anyone, even Raj didn't know the details, but I told Alicia everything: how Robina was forced to marry a stranger when she was fifteen, how she ended up on her own with a tiny baby, how her marriage was so unhappy, how Mum wouldn't help her, nor Dad, nor the community leader, how she felt so frightened and alone that finally she burnt herself to death. I even told her about Mum not wanting me at the mourning.

I was looking at Alicia's face all the time I was talking. I'd thought at first I'd feel ashamed but I wasn't, I felt I was vindicating Robina. Alicia wasn't doing the reassurance or the repeating back, she was just looking horrified, her face was sort of crumbling, and when finally I stopped talking she threw her arms around me and burst into tears. 'I understand, I understand,' she started, but I stopped her.

'You don't understand, don't say that.' I was crying now and having opened my heart all my pent-up grief and rage were spilling out of it onto poor Alicia. 'How could you understand what it's like to ask for help and have your mother turn her back on you. Your mother! The person you rely on to love you and protect you. Don't say you understand that because unless it's happened to you, you couldn't understand, you don't.'

That session marked a turning point for me. It violated so many of the premises on which my whole life had been built. Mum's insistence on preserving the family's good name and presenting a good face meant anything unpleasant had always been buried within the confines of our family. The concept of trusting an 'outsider' to listen sympathetically and not to judge you was never even mooted. Secrecy was a cornerstone of my childhood. Now I'd cracked that cornerstone and, to my amazement, the world was still turning just the same.

I'd told the truth about something bad that had happened, I'd exposed some of my deepest, ugliest feelings and they'd been accepted. I wasn't judged or criticized, made to feel ashamed or scorned. I was believed and – more important – I was valued. Those women's empathy showed me that my experience wasn't shameful or disgraceful. It was part of me and it made me who I was. I sat there that evening and it was as if my eyes had been opened. I looked back at my childhood and realized that the web of secrecy Mum spun around us had made me blind to so many good things in the world, things like truth and honesty and compassion.

As for Alicia, she became and still is a valued friend. Over the years she has taught me such a lot about unconditional love.

I participated in the course after that, as fully as I could. In addition to the group sessions you had to have an hour each week with one of the counsellors. I saw Glenda. We talked about the feelings the listening course was bringing up in us and mine were monumental. All the stuff I'd suppressed for so long came tumbling out. My sessions with Glenda released a torrent of emotion and with it came a flood of angry questions. Why did Mum maintain that unhappiness was just a normal part of married life? Why did she not protect her daughters? Why did she treat us like puppets rather than autonomous individuals? Couldn't she see we had a right to choice, to our own fulfilling lives?

Glenda suggested I go into counselling. She said I needed help. At first I was reluctant, but as my inner turmoil grew I agreed to it, breaking another childhood taboo. Sylvia agreed to be my counsellor. She saw me every week for about a year and she never charged me for it. She did that from the kindness of her heart. I didn't tell anybody about it, not even Raj; as far as he was concerned I was still doing a course. I told Sylvia everything. Week after week she sat there listening to me sobbing as I poured out the sorry details of my life. The knowledge that I could trust her with that was so important to me, but a question played in my mind and one day I asked her, 'Sylvia, how can you listen to all this? How can you take on all this sadness and still carry on with your life?'

She smiled and said, 'Don't you worry about that.'

She was the most giving person and she became someone I knew I could always turn to. She died of cancer five years ago and I miss her still.

CHAPTER 23

While I was doing the listening skills course I started talking to people about my idea for helping women with cultural and language barriers and the more I talked the more real it became to me. People gave me good advice, some offered to help. It was one of the women from the course who told me to get in touch with the Council for Voluntary Service and that's how I met Wendy Lloyd, who became my mentor. I went to her with a storm of ideas about how I wanted to help women and she gave me facts. She told me if I ever wanted to access any funding I'd need a constitution setting out my aims and objectives, and a management committee with at least four members. She was so supportive; she even helped me find the perfect name for my project: Karma Nirvana. From the whirlwind of ideas I threw out at her she had homed in on the important things: peace of mind and enlightenment.

We needed a proper base. 'Well, the Rape Crisis lot used to use the little room at the back. Maybe you could have that,' said Trish when I bumped into her at the women's centre.

'But I can't afford to pay rent, we haven't got any money,' I said.

She shrugged and smiled encouragingly. 'Ask if you can have it for free then. It's sitting there empty. Why not give the management a presentation then ask them. You've nothing to lose.'

I'd never heard the word 'presentation'; I had no idea what it was but Trish said all I had to do was talk about my plans with the same passion I'd shown her. She said it would be easy and once she'd persuaded me to do it, she put me on the agenda for the next management committee meeting. I was item number four.

The day came and I was so nervous. I paced up and down outside the meeting room waiting for my turn to come. Each minute seemed to last for ever and as time ticked by I could feel my confidence draining away. I hadn't got a presentation, I hadn't got any facts or figures, I hadn't even got any notes. All I had was my dream and how could I sell that?

Eventually I was called in. What actually happened in there is a bit of a blur. Somebody asked me to take a seat and I heard myself saying that if they didn't mind I'd rather stand. I felt hot and my mouth was very dry. I took a deep breath.

'I've got this idea, well, a vision really, of a project that would help women who are facing language and cultural barriers. I can't say exactly what that help would be because I haven't really started yet, but I know there are women out there who have got problems and who do need help. I first thought of it because of my mum, who died two years ago. She'd lived here almost all her life, but she never learnt English and when she was in hospital . . .'

Once I'd started the words seemed to fly out of me. I'd worried that I would be tongue-tied and forget what I wanted to say but once I got onto Mum it all came pouring out. I wanted them to see her as I did, a little old lady who'd worked hard all her life and paid her taxes and then, at the end, been let down by the people looking after her. I explained that she'd been hurt and humiliated because those paid to care for her didn't understand her needs.

My heart was racing, I felt like I was talking at a hundred miles an hour, and I could feel my hands dancing all over the place, but they seemed to be helping me to talk and so I didn't try to keep them still, I just went with it. I still do that today. If you made me keep my hands behind my back I'd be a mute.

When I'd explained about Mum, I told them about Robina, her awful suffering and how her agonizing death had happened because she didn't know where to turn for help. I shared with them the thought that was lodged like a thorn in my conscience: that a kind word or a sympathetic ear might have saved Robina's life. And then – I couldn't really believe I was doing this – I told them about me. I could never have done that before the listening skills course but the trust I'd found there gave me the confidence. Glenda, Sylvia, Alicia and the others had brought me to a place where I could look those women in the eye and tell them how I'd run away to escape a forced marriage and how I'd had to survive without my family ever since.

'I've had nowhere to turn for help, so you see, I know from personal experience that a project like mine is needed. I know there are other women like me and my mum and Robina. I see them every day in Derby, scuttling about like shadows, with their eyes on the ground. I know I could help those women, so I'm asking you now, please help me realize my dream.'

I stopped there, slightly breathless, and for a moment everyone in the room was quiet. The woman who broke the silence said: 'I think you're very brave,' and that really surprised me. Then several of them spoke at once and they were saying things like 'How can we help you?' and 'What do you see yourself doing?' and 'What will you need?'

'What I need is a room, a base for the project. Which is called Karma Nirvana, by the way, I think I forgot to tell you that. I wouldn't be able to pay for a room at the moment, but I'd pay when I could. This would be a good place for the project because so many women come here anyway. Some of those women must have issues I could help with, and you could tell them that I exist.'

'And what would you be offering them exactly?'

'To be honest with you, I can't say exactly

because I've got nothing to offer at the moment. I need to build up resources. But I envisage giving support, both emotional and practical, information and advice . . . I want to meet the needs that I'm presented with.'

The chairwoman rang next morning. They'd all been impressed by my passion, and I could move in as soon as they'd had the carpets cleaned. I was so pleased that I could hardly take it in. I had been so convinced that they were going to turn me down.

I collected the keys about a week later. It was a huge room, with a really big window that let in loads of light. It looked right onto the Rape Crisis Centre's office and that was an important link for me. There was nothing in it except the desk and the chair which were pushed into one corner, but I stood there in the middle of the empty space and thought, 'This is mine and it's going to be special. I'm going to shape this and put my mark on it and achieve something for every woman who walks through that door. That's my dream and I'm going to make it real.'

CHAPTER 24

I always knew that the best way to spread the word about Karma Nirvana would be through the exercise classes. Not the ones I did with Raj, in the leisure centre. Those were popular, but the ones that really mattered to me – and the ones I knew would be important to Karma Nirvana – were the ones I held in community centres in areas of social deprivation, areas like the one where I'd grown up.

It was mostly Asian women who came to those classes, and I knew for some it was the only proper outing they had in a week. Their husbands let them come because they knew they wouldn't meet any men there and because they could bring their kids. I didn't mind as long as the kids played quietly at the back of the hall; Maria was often there, sucking on her thumb as she slept in her car seat, and I sometimes brought Lisa. To make the women feel more comfortable I used to black out the windows with sheets of cardboard before every class. I renamed them the Karma Nirvana classes; I made sure everyone who came knew about the project and it wasn't

237

long before women started approaching me, wanting advice.

I had a few who wore flashy leotards, but most of them chose to exercise in their Indian suits, which was fine by me as long as they wore trainers. Some of them had husbands who insisted on it; others were just conditioned to it. There was one girl who stood out because she wore a shapeless old tracksuit which was so worn and hideous that I could only think she wanted to make herself look plain. Everything about her spoke of loneliness: she used to stick herself firmly in the back row and she never made eye contact. I wanted to talk to her about Karma Nirvana but before I got around to it, she approached me at the end of one class.

'Do you teach anywhere else?' she said, her eyes still glued to the floor.

'At the leisure centre on Mondays but I do Thursdays here as well.'

'I see. Thanks.' She started to turn away when I caught her arm and asked if she would like to get a coffee. 'I'm starting up a project that might interest you. I'd like to tell you about it, if you've time.'

Her name was Ayesha. We went to a café just down the road and stayed for about half an hour. I don't think she looked directly at me in all that time. I told her about Karma Nirvana and she seemed interested, but there was something absent about her, as though a big part of her was locked away. I got the impression she was weighed down by a secret she was keeping really close to her chest. I did learn that things hadn't worked out for her at home and she was living on her own. I resolved to look out for her, to persuade her to talk to me again.

'I really feel I'm getting somewhere now, like Karma Nirvana is actually coming together,' I said to Ayesha the third or fourth time we had coffee together after class. It had become a bit of a habit and she always hung back at the end of the hour, as if she was hoping I'd ask.

We always went to the same place, and we usually sat at the same Formica-topped table, right at the back where we could be peaceful. That was important because Ayesha spoke so quietly that I really had to strain to hear what she said. Not that she said much; mostly she just answered my questions as briefly as she could. When I told her about Karma Nirvana she murmured, 'That's good, you must be pleased.' I felt like I was trying to reach her through a pane of glass.

Suddenly I had a thought. I didn't question it, I just opened my mouth and said, 'Ayesha, did I tell you why I started Karma Nirvana?'

Eyes glued to the table, she shook her head. So I told her about Robina and me, and how even now my family wouldn't have anything to do with me. She didn't look at me while I was talking but she was so still and alert that I knew she was listening. 'That's why I'm doing it, Ayesha, because all these years I've felt so lonely and ashamed and I know, I just know, there must be so many other women like me.'

Ayesha had been fiddling with a paper serviette, folding and unfolding it, and when I said that last bit her movements became more frantic, she was almost shredding it. Her head was down and I saw a tear splash onto the table. She wiped her cheek with the back of her hand and I thought I heard a whisper. I craned right forward.

'When I was eight, my oldest brother raped me.' She quickly dragged her breath back in, to catch a sob. 'My uncle did it too. For years they went on doing it, sometimes every week. They did it to me over and . . .' She buried her face in her hands and turned towards the wall, her shoulders heaving with sobs.

What could I say to her? *Eight* . . . Younger than my precious Lisa, who was still quite unaware of the beauty of her firm, round, innocent body. If any man touched Lisa I knew I would kill him. But Ayesha's mother did nothing to protect her daughter; in fact I discovered later that she'd connived in the abuse.

Ayesha didn't tell me any more just then. I gave her Karma Nirvana's number and told her that if ever she rang it I'd get back to her as soon as I could. And she did ring, often. She kept coming to the classes, but I saw her at other times as well and I gradually learnt the full story of her suffering. She told me how as a child, sore and terrified, she'd plucked up the courage to say what her brother and her uncle had been doing. 'My mum slapped my face. She said, "Don't you dare disgrace this family. Cry at the bottom of the garden if you must, but don't bring your fuss in here." My brother must have known she said that, because he stopped being careful, he did it more and more.'

Aged sixteen, Ayesha was sent to Pakistan to get married. She was told she was going on a family holiday. I wasn't surprised to hear that, as a wife, she swapped one sort of abuse for another. Her husband wasn't much older than her, but he was hefty and bad-tempered. After one particularly violent assault she went sobbing to her mother who told her – again – to be mindful of the family name and stop complaining.

Those words struck me like a dart that went right through me and carried me back down the years to where I sat, watching my older sisters beg for my mother's sympathy. 'Not a word of this to anyone. It's a private matter for our family.' That's what Mum used to say as Dad drove us home after those terrible sessions. Now, for the first time ever, I realized that many, many of the Asian families we knew probably shared that same secret Mum was desperate to keep. It wasn't just us.

'I couldn't take it after that, Jas. I ran away,' Ayesha told me with the tears pouring down her face. We were sitting on the scratchy grey carpet tiles in my room, Karma Nirvana's office. I'd yet to get a second chair. 'I haven't seen them since, not Mum, Dad, not anyone. It's been eighteen months and they won't even speak to me on the phone.' I was holding her and she was spluttering through her sobs. We sat together in silence for a long time and when her thin shoulders had almost stopped heaving, she said really quietly, 'It's my little brother I miss most, Jas. And they've told him I'm dead.'

I know my listening to Ayesha helped her. She told me it did and, anyway, I could tell just by looking at her. As the weeks went by she stopped carrying herself like a whipped dog. She said that hearing my story, knowing she wasn't the only one, made her feel stronger. I knew she wasn't ready to make the mental break from her family that I'd made. She was a long way from that. But I tried to nudge her towards seeing things differently. 'You wouldn't treat your worst enemy like you've been treated, would you? You don't have to put up with it, you know, just because the person doing it's your mum.'

I helped Ayesha but also she helped me. I hadn't expected that, but it's true. Her story – which spoke so clearly of cruelty, denial and disownment – clarified my own experience and made me see with absolute certainty that I'd been the victim not the perpetrator of a crime.

That made me feel stronger and so did the knowledge that I was doing something good. What's more, being there for Ayesha helped me rise above my own problems. Raj's treatment of me was increasingly unpredictable. I'd chosen him, I knew I had to stay with him, but I felt I was walking on quicksand whenever I was near him.

Raj was constantly finding fault. It felt like I couldn't do anything right. When I angered him he'd bawl me out and then ignore me. He could keep it up for as long as a week and I used to think I'd go insane. I'd follow him about like a lost child, pleading with him to talk to me. I'd kneel down and pray that he would talk to me. I couldn't function unless things were right between us. Being strong for Ayesha was like a rock that I could cling to.

CHAPTER 25

In September 1994 I started at Derby University. I shouldered my bag with three new files and a block of A4 paper in it, and I felt this big grin spreading across my face as I walked across the grass towards the doors I'd fled through two years earlier. There were students everywhere, going about their business in every direction. Most of them walked in little groups, chatting and laughing, but they didn't faze me any more. I could hold my head up, I'd earned my place. At the age of twenty-nine I'd fulfilled my dream and I was going to college.

Raj started the same day as me, reading law, but he was in a different building. The first lecture I had was sociology and as I sat there waiting for it to begin I surveyed the other students. They all looked so young and carefree. Two girls just along from me were discussing all the things they were going to do in Freshers' Week. There was going to be a disco on the Friday and one of them, the plumper of the two, was fussing about what she should wear. It made me smile. Friday was going to be Maria's first day in the university crèche;

Raj's mum usually had her when I was out, but she was busy on Friday. I'd be racing to pick her up and then dashing across town in time to collect Lisa from school. I was longing to see Lisa but the weekends she spent with us were always tense.

It was my responsibilities more than my age that divided me from the other students. I was always leaving lectures in a hurry, rushing off the campus to take an exercise class, or to collect Maria or to do my jobs at Raj's mum's house. She didn't like me studying at all. She was proud of having a son at university but she made it clear she didn't know what I was doing there. If ever she saw me reading one of my textbooks or setting out my paper and pens ready to write an essay she'd stop me working. She was clever about it. She'd start talking to me, knowing I wouldn't dare ignore her conversation. Or she'd find extra little tasks for me to do. I was in her house, I couldn't stand up to her, but I didn't have to give in to her. I crept downstairs in the middle of the night to study at the kitchen table before sneaking back to bed at dawn.

I had to work hard to keep up with my studies, and there was Karma Nirvana too. With the help of Wendy Lloyd I was trying to access funding; at the very least I needed to maintain a telephone line and she was a genius at finding little pockets of money, grants I could apply for. As soon as the telephone was installed I made sure that I went to the office every day to check for any messages.

And I was trying to get the word out; when I could find the time I rang round hospitals, health centres, police stations and social services, making them aware of what we did and how to reach us. Some people could see the point straight away; the bored response of others made it clear they thought I was wasting their time.

I wasn't put off but I was more and more convinced that we needed some sort of focus, an event to launch the project. Early in 1995 I hit on the idea of a women's health day. 'Health's relevant to everyone,' I said to Wendy Lloyd. 'It's important to women of all ages, and to their families. And it's unthreatening so the Asian men won't mind their wives coming.' Wendy agreed and she encouraged me to do it. She was always encouraging and I'll be forever grateful to her.

The health day was a long time in the planning. I knew exactly what I wanted: lots of different speakers, stalls displaying information, interpreters so nobody should feel excluded, food, discussion groups . . . I wanted the whole place alive with activity and interest.

The first person I approached was an Asian nurse in the breast care unit of our local hospital. She was flattered and agreed. That was easy, but I had to do a lot of groundwork for the rest. Eventually I got speakers on mental health, depression, nutrition, cervical screening. I was really pleased about the screening because I knew it was something Mum had never done. She was far too embarrassed.

Several of the women I taught got involved. I found Punjabi and Urdu interpreters; one girl designed some flyers and we spent hours pounding the streets of Derby distributing those as widely as we could. Margaret Redfern, our local councillor, agreed to come and talk and, to my amazement, about a month before the scheduled day our local MP, Margaret Beckett, said she would come and open it. I was thrilled.

The night before it happened I was a bag of nerves. I went through my checklist again and again and went to bed exhausted at about midnight. The last thing I said to Raj was, 'What if it doesn't work out? What if no one turns up?' He groaned and rolled over. 'You've left flyers in almost every shop in Derby. Don't worry, it's going to be great.'

He'd agreed to come and help set up in the morning and then disappear before the event started. I'd let it be known that no men could attend the health day; I knew that would be impor-tant for some of the Asian women. I didn't want any of them being barred by their husbands from coming.

Next day I was at the hall by eight o'clock. It was the community hall in which I taught aero-bics but in the morning light it looked drab and dusty. The room felt stale and airless; in one corner there was a laden ashtray, forgotten at the tail end of some event the night before. I started wrestling with the sash windows, wondering how we were ever going to make this cavernous space look interesting and inviting.

My volunteers arrived in a flurry of noise and bright-coloured Indian suits and we worked hard erecting tables, arranging chairs, pinning up the posters I'd scrounged. Manjit and Nina filled the tea urns and set out all the cups and saucers and shortly after nine o'clock the food arrived: trays of sandwiches, sausage rolls, samosas, cakes and biscuits. Everything had been donated by a local supermarket. When the people manning the information stands arrived with all their bumph and booklets the picture I'd had in my mind began to take on proper shape.

We were ready just before our ten o'clock deadline. Jassey had dropped Lisa off and she was chasing a balloon round between the stalls. She was going to help in the crèche we'd promised to any mothers bringing children. They trickled in at first; by 10.30 there can't have been more than twelve people in the hall and I was starting to panic when there was a sudden influx. They came through the door in a steady stream: old women, young women, women pushing pushchairs and clutching small children. I stood by the door smiling and welcoming people as they flowed past me in a rainbow parade of saris, dresses, jeans, Indian suits and T-shirts. Shibana stood opposite me and we handed out evaluation forms, asking every woman who walked through the door to fill one in before she left the building. Wendy Lloyd

248

had said feedback like that would be invaluable in attracting funding.

Margaret Beckett arrived and complimented me on the turnout. Before I knew it I was standing beside her on the stage and she was doing the formal opening. She and Margaret Redfern both mentioned Karma Nirvana and the importance of filling in the evaluation forms, and I began to feel I was bobbing along on a wave of support and encouragement.

The day was even better than I'd hoped. The speakers gave clear, interesting talks and they all made themselves available for questions afterwards. The nurse who'd come to talk about cervical screening was surrounded by Asian women. Lots of the older ones were being helped by the interpreters. Submitting to that sort of screening is so alien to Asian culture – a threat to Asian women's modesty and a blow to their men's possessive pride – that I felt really proud to have created an environment in which they felt safe enough to talk about it.

At lunchtime I heard several women discussing what they'd learnt that morning. One said she was going to go home and fetch her mum. The whole place was buzzing – at one stage I'd say the hall was crammed with 250 or 300 people – and yet the atmosphere was so relaxed and easy.

We'd advertised the day from ten until four, and by four-thirty there were just me, Lisa and a handful of volunteers left. When the last chair had been pushed against the wall I was exhausted but I couldn't remember when I'd been so happy. It was all congratulations and hugging one another. Lisa counted the evaluation forms for me while we were packing up and she said there were 120. I had them clutched in my hand. I was guarding them with my life because I knew they were the key to Karma Nirvana's financial future.

CHAPTER 26

After the Women's Health Day Karma Nirvana's phone finally started ringing. I went to the office on the way from college and the light on the answering machine, which had been disappointingly dark all those months I'd been checking it, was blinking furiously. Some of the messages were blank and I worried that those were from women who had plucked up the courage to ring and then been scared off by the electronic voice of the answering machine. Lots of them were from social services departments wanting information about Karma Nirvana. A few were from people enquiring about the classes.

My original idea had been for a project that would help all women, but it soon became clear that it was Asian women who needed Karma Nirvana. Almost all the calls we took concerned Asian women; I was staggered by the number of them. It was as if a box of ugly secrets had been opened; some days it felt like nothing would stop them pouring out. Some of the first stories I heard still stick in my mind today.

There was the key worker from the YMCA who

251

rang to ask my advice about a seventeen-year-old girl in her hostel. 'She arrived here covered in cigarette burns which she says were inflicted by her brother, but she won't report him, even though he and the rest of the family held her prisoner for almost ten months. They locked her door and boarded up her windows because she wouldn't agree to the marriage they wanted. I can't reach her, Jasvinder. It's like she's dead inside, and now I think she's drifting into prostitution.'

There was a social worker who asked me to mediate between a client and her parents. 'I know her through the truant officer; her parents have been keeping her off school. She's fifteen and she's eight months pregnant, but they've not let her have any medical care at all. They're so ashamed of her condition they won't let her out of the house. I'm scared they're going to make her give birth at home, Jasvinder. She says she loves the father and he wants to support her – he's a Derby-born Asian like her – but I can't find him. He's disappeared and his family is saying nothing.'

And there was Maram. Maram was one of the first women to actually turn up at Karma Nirvana's office. She was visibly pregnant and very upset. 'My husband has disowned me. He has thrown me out and I have nowhere to go.' Through her sobs she spoke in Urdu. I later learnt she spoke no English. 'It is my fault, I know that, but I didn't know how to avoid what happened. I wasn't expecting it. I went to my ante-natal appointment and the doctor who saw me was a man. Always before it has been the midwife. He wanted to listen to my baby's heart. I knew my husband wouldn't like him touching me, but I didn't know the words to make him stop.'

I remember making Maram a cup of tea as I wondered what shocked me most, the way her husband had treated her or her belief that she had brought his cruelty on herself. It reminded me of the day I told Dad a man had flashed at me and Robina on the way home from school. My mild-mannered dad was furious and he raged at us: 'You must avoid these situations, do you want to bring dishonour on yourself?'

I rang the social services and asked for their help. The woman I spoke to agreed to find Maram emergency accommodation and came to collect her from the office. I gave Maram a hug before she left and made her promise to keep in touch.

She did. Three days later she rang me and said she was fine. 'I'm back with my husband, he forgave me.'

'Oh, good, that's good news, Maram.' It sounded suspicious to me. In my experience men – and women – motivated by honour don't have sudden changes of heart.

'He gathered the older members of the community in my mother-in-law's house, as many as could fit in and, in front of them, I begged his forgiveness. I went down on my knees and kissed his feet and begged and he forgave me. So you see, Jasvinder, now I am all right.'

Using the women's evaluation forms as back-up I applied for Lottery funding and, several months after the Women's Health Day, we were awarded £125,000 over three years; enough to establish a proper concern. Through the local paper I recruited three staff and a new management committee and as soon as my co-workers were in place I began to focus on forming links with anyone I thought was relevant: the police, GPs, voluntary agencies like Rape Crisis, primary care groups.

The better known Karma Nirvana became the more people dropped in, all wanting as much support, advocacy and advice as we could offer. My co-workers and I began to find it hard to get anything else done. The solution was to institute a weekly surgery when we were all available to talk. It was instantly popular.

I was learning more each day about the task ahead of me. A social worker with a desperate client told me that Asian women brought here as brides have no rights to benefits or legal aid until their status here is authorized. 'They're trapped with the families who brought them into the country,' she said. I realized that I might have to grow beyond Derby and start campaigning on a national level.

CHAPTER 27

Towards the end of my second year at university Raj and I were invited to a wedding in Leeds. It was Rachel, a woman I'd become very close to when I lived there. Raj had met her, but he said he didn't want to go. 'And if I don't go, you don't either.' For several days I wheedled and pleaded but he wouldn't shift. It mattered to me that I went and I finally decided to stand up to him. I told him I would go alone.

'Not unless I agree to it, you won't,' he said. It was all about control. He wanted me tiptoeing round him, begging him to let me go. I played along with it but I'd made my mind up, I was going to see Rachel married.

The day came and Lisa and I, dressed in our best, were heading for the front door when he shouted from the bedroom. 'You're to be back at six o'clock. Have you got that? Don't think you can come and go to suit yourself.'

'Okay, Raj. I'll be back by six,' I said, calm as I could. I was determined not to let him get to me.

'You better be, or you and your untouchable daughter can find yourselves somewhere else to live. I'm warning you, if you're not back by six o'clock, that's it.'

As we drove out of Nottingham Lisa was pale and silent and I knew she was worrying. 'Where will you go if he throws us out? I can go back to Daddy, but where will you go?'

'Don't worry, darling, he doesn't really mean it.' I didn't feel as brave about it as I sounded but I wanted to reassure her.

At the wedding we forgot our worries. It was a white wedding in a lovely little church. Rachel was marrying a rugby player and all his team mates were there forming a guard of honour. She looked so happy and the groom looked just like the cat that got the cream. They stood in the churchyard, posing for photographs, and even though they were laughing and excited they looked so grounded, standing there together hand in hand.

The reception was at the local football ground. There were old friends there, from the markets, and for the first time in months I relaxed. There were other kids for Lisa to play with and she was happy too. It was good to see her laughing; so much of the time she spent with me was shadowed by the bad feeling between her and Raj. I was so caught up with enjoying myself that I forgot the time and when I looked at my watch it was already five o'clock. I couldn't believe I'd been so careless. Nottingham was more than an hour's drive away.

I immediately rang Raj and asked if we could

stay a little longer; I wheedled and begged as he liked me to, but he was adamant. 'Be back here by six o'clock or else . . . Don't push me, Jas.'

My heart was really racing then. I pulled Lisa out of a group of girls who were all dancing together and told her we had to leave as fast as possible. She's always been biddable and, bless her, she didn't make a fuss. Having said my goodbyes I took off my high heels and hurried to the car as fast as I could. We were silent all the way, I was concentrating so hard on driving. My knuckles were white from gripping the wheel so tightly, straining to make my poor old car top its maximum speed of 60 miles an hour. The roads were full of Saturday evening traffic, cruising aimlessly, and it seemed to take for ever.

It was twenty past six as I pulled into the street where Raj's parents lived and I could see, almost at once, that I was too late. Raj's mum was standing by the front door, Maria on her hip, and Raj had just marched past her carrying a box of my books which he dumped on the pavement beside a couple of bulging bin bags, one of which had my favourite jumper spilling out of it.

'You stay in the car, darling,' I said to Lisa as I swung into the kerb and leapt out onto the pavement. 'Raj, I'm really sorry. I meant to be back by six, but I forgot the time and the traffic was terrible, I'm so sorry . . .' The words were rushing out of me and I really meant them, I was genuinely sorry and I thought Raj could have told that, but he just looked at me like I was dirt.

'I told you what would happen if you chose to ignore me . . .' He left the sentence hanging in the air as he turned and walked back into the house. I went to follow him but his mum was still standing in the doorway. She shifted a little to bar my way. She was looking so stern and cold.

I lost my nerve. I wanted to defend myself but there was nothing to say. I was helpless against both of them. 'Okay, Bibi-ji, I'll go,' I murmured to Raj's mum. I went to lift Maria out of her arms, but she wheeled away from me. 'The child is staying here. It's what her father wishes.'

I was so shocked I completely forgot about being respectful. I reached round and grabbed Maria under her arms, but Raj's mum held on tight. 'She is staying with her father,' she repeated.

'I'm not leaving without her,' I said, clutching Maria as firmly as I could.

'Rajvinder, come here quickly!' Raj's mum was pulling too.

Out of the corner of my eye I saw a neighbour's front door open. Raj's mum suddenly let go of Maria and I stumbled backwards. In the car Lisa's arms were open, ready for her little sister.

Raj and his mum stood there watching me as I struggled with the sacks of clothes. A couple of jumpers and a top dropped out as I was carrying them to the car. I told myself to walk tall and proud as I went back for them, but I knew I was scuttling like a thief. I rammed the box of books and files onto the back seat. I wanted to check that all my precious work was there, but I didn't dare.

I should have said something to Lisa as I got back in the car, but I didn't trust myself to speak. I was doing all I could to hold my tears back. As I pulled away from the kerb Raj and his mum were still in the doorway, their faces ugly with anger as they watched us drive away.

On the warmth of Lisa's lap Maria's wails juddered into whimpers and those soon stopped too. My daughters sat quiet as mice with frightened eyes and behind them the back seat was piled high with my possessions. My entire life was in that car and I didn't know where to go. My mind flashed back to the day that Jassey and I ran away to Newcastle and for one crazy moment I thought of going to his house. Even after all we'd been through I knew he'd have me back. I also knew that to take that step would be disastrous.

Habit turned me towards Derby and I drove down the A52 with tears pouring down my cheeks. When I'd been desperate to get back to Nottingham the road had seemed so long and slow, but now the miles flashed past. I was trying to think but my brain felt like cotton wool. I kept hearing Mum's warning that if I married Raj I'd end up getting divorced. I should have listened, but I was so used to her working for her own ends that I hadn't taken any notice. That felt like arrogance now.

Writing this more than ten years later, it strikes me that I was driving towards my home town, the place where I was born and brought up and where almost my entire family live, and yet I had nowhere to go. Of course, I could have turned to one of the women who had befriended me: Glenda, Sylvia or Alicia. They had taught me so much about support and sharing; they'd shown me that secrecy is a stifling bond rather than the protective cloak that Mum perceived it as. I should have trusted them, I know that now, but at the time I didn't. I panicked and in my panic I forgot all I'd learnt. I didn't want any one of those kind, wise women to know that once again I'd failed to sustain a relationship, I didn't want them to see me, with all my things in garbage bags, slinking shame-faced through the night.

And so I turned to Narinder, a friend of Raj's who had seen some of what went on between us. Narinder never intervened, never stopped Raj saying the things he did, but once when we were all three out together he waited until Raj left the table – to go to the toilet or to buy drinks at the bar – and then he let me know he sympathized. Narinder had seen me humiliated by my husband; he'd seen me shamed. With him I didn't have much face to save.

When his image popped into my mind, I thought of the tiny terraced house that Raj and I once picked him up from. I wondered if he'd fit us in. Stopped at a traffic light, I looked across at the girls: Maria had fallen asleep and the sight of Lisa's stoic little face made me realize I didn't have an alternative. I couldn't drive around all night.

I knew Narinder was in because I could see his telly flickering in the sitting-room. I knocked – a pathetic, apologetic knock – and then stood waiting. He opened the door and, as his mind registered what his eyes were seeing, I watched his expression change from annoyed to surprised to quizzical. Before he had time to ask me anything I said, 'Raj has thrown us out, me, Maria and Lisa. We've haven't got anywhere to go. Do you think we could stop here a bit?'

He was taken aback, I could see that, although he did his best to hide it. 'Of course you can, come in.' He stepped back to let me pass him in the narrow passage but then remembered. 'The kids, let's get the kids. And have you got bags?'

We hauled my stuff inside and I settled the girls in Narinder's back bedroom. I was glad to see the bed was big enough for three of us; I was so tired that the thought of sleeping on the floor made me ache all over. Narinder didn't ask me what had happened, he didn't make me talk much at all. He just made me a cup of tea and put me in an armchair and made it clear we could stay as long as necessary.

He said it again before he went out next morning and I thanked him. I didn't want to impose, but I still couldn't think straight. My mind was stuck on the fact that my marriage was over. I'd failed again. I couldn't look the world in the face. As if my shame was blazoned all over me I kept the curtains closed and lurked inside Narinder's house until Lisa and Maria became fretful and Lisa begged me to take them to the park.

Maybe that's when Raj saw me driving away from Narinder's house. Maybe it was just that after two days he'd exhausted all the other possibilities. Either way, at six-thirty on Monday evening he was there, hammering at Narinder's front door. The girls were scared, even Narinder looked alarmed. Raj was battering the door, rattling the letterbox and shouting through it, 'I know you're in there, Jas. You can't deceive me any more. Didn't I say you two were seeing each other?'

Narinder and I looked at each other. I told Lisa to take Maria upstairs to play in our room. Narinder opened the door and Raj burst through it shouting about how Narinder and I were having an affair.

'That's rubbish, Raj. You know it is,' I said.

'She needed somewhere to stay, Raj. You know that, mate. You threw her out,' said Narinder.

'So you sided with her! That's great. That's real loyalty from a friend.'

'I'm not siding with anybody, Raj. Don't be ridiculous. I took Jas in because she and the kids needed somewhere to sleep. End of story. What's going on between you and Jas is nothing to do with me.'

'Dead right, it's not. So kick her out.'

'I'm not going to do that, Raj. No decent person would.'

That riled Raj, I could see. He took a deep breath ready for another tirade but I cut in.

'Thanks, Narinder, but I'll go, we'll go. You've been very generous, but you don't have to put up with this and I can't see Raj giving up while I'm still here.'

'No! You won't go.' Narinder was a mild man but he sounded so determined that both Raj and I shut up and stared at him. He walked past us both and opened the front door. 'Look, mate,' he said to Raj. 'Why don't you go home and cool off a bit. There's nothing going on between me and Jas, I promise you that. But nothing's going to get settled while you're so angry. Come back and talk to Jas when you're feeling calmer. In the meantime she and your daughter are safe while they're here.'

That was brave of Narinder. Raj still had his fists clenched. He looked from Narinder to me and back again and I know he wanted to say something that would put him back in the ring but Narinder's calm reason had deflated him. He shrugged his shoulders and stamped out.

I didn't see him again for a couple of weeks but then, just as unexpectedly, he reappeared with a bunch of flowers and asked if he could talk to me. He took me to a restaurant and said he was so sorry, he loved me so much, he was so determined to change. He said that when he thought that he was going to lose me his life had looked so bleak. He did all he could to woo me and I fell for it. I lapped up his false flattery because I wanted it to be true, I wanted a good man who loved me. For years I'd been nobody's daughter and I needed to make up for that: I needed to be somebody's wife.

I made one condition though. I said we had to have our own place. I said I couldn't live with his parents any more, there was no way we could rebuild our relationship with them watching our every move. Raj agreed and that's how we came to Balfour Road.

His dad lent us the money for that house; it cost £13,000 in an area where anything halfway decent cost £23,000 and I wouldn't say we got a bargain. The house was as derelict as our marriage. It was two up, two down with a tiny unfinished bathroom and a little kitchen at the back. The floors were rough concrete except in the living-room where someone had got as far as laying one floorboard which you had to use like a tightrope when you crossed the room. The walls were bare and damp – so damp that mould grew on some of them that winter – and the window frames were the oldest in the world, they howled and shook in the wind. We used to hang blankets and towels over them to try and keep warm.

We first saw it just a few days after our reunion at Narinder's when we were still floating on a cloud of new hope and romance. I didn't see a wreck, I saw an opportunity and a project that would pull us together. I imagined it painted in pretty colours with fresh curtains at the windows and the dank yard outside transformed into a sunny patio. We'd barely moved in before those hopes were dashed.

When we were scrabbling round for furniture Narinder gave us an old sofa. It had a split in the seat with foam bulging out of it but it was usable. Within weeks of moving into Balfour Road I found myself sitting on that sofa night after night, with my course books open on my lap, wondering where Raj was. 'I've been giving classes, it's going really well for me at the moment' or 'I've been at the gym, if you're going to teach keep-fit you've got to look the part'. Those were the excuses he gave when he came home late and I wanted to believe him.

Often he came home at 2 or 3 a.m. About four hours after he'd crawled into our bed I'd climb out of it to get Maria ready before I began the round of dropping her at nursery, stopping to do my stint at Karma Nirvana and then going on to university. When I came back in the evenings Raj would be gone and the massive roll of lino that you had to dodge round to get up or down the stairs would still be there, untouched, with the box of tools lying unopened beside it. The home-making never happened.

CHAPTER 28

Balfour Road is in the heart of the Asian area and I knew I'd bump into my sisters sooner or later. Since Mum died we'd had no contact. I still saw a lot of Dad and Sunny. I was always being called round to talk to Sunny because he was in trouble at school; he was hard to handle and Dad needed my support. Sometimes when I was at Dale Road I'd hear news about my sisters. From what Dad said I knew that Gin and Yasmin were talking to Lucy again. They weren't talking to me. Yasmin hasn't talked to me since the day I ran away. And when Ginda went back to Shinda she withdrew again.

It was Gin I saw first. I was out shopping on a Saturday morning a couple of weeks after we'd moved into Balfour Road and she was walking down the street towards me. The pavement was crowded but we were only about thirty metres apart and I'm sure she saw me. I raised my hand in greeting and a jolt of recognition jarred her face, but only for an instant. Then, with her head turned away, she crossed the road and I was left with my fingers stopped mid-flutter feeling stupid.

I was gutted. It was fifteen years since I'd run away and still Gin could not forgive me.

I kept that sadness bottled up inside me. It was the start of my third year at university and I was trying to work out my schedule, making sure I gave enough time to Karma Nirvana and my studies. My main focus at college that year was a dissertation on Sikh women who had been disowned by their families. In the course of my reading I would discover that Guru Granth Sahib believed in equality between men and women and was against forced marriage as well as the caste system. Mum had always used his teachings as a weapon but I learnt they couldn't have been more different from what she taught me.

By the end of that term, I was pregnant again, fluttery with hope as I carried the life that was meant to put Raj and me back together again. We were so rarely together it's remarkable it happened, but I wasn't sorry. I thought it might help. How many women have made that mistake?

At three o'clock one February morning the phone rang. I was half awake anyway, my ears straining for the sound of Raj's key in the door. Maria was asleep beside me and Lisa was there, on a mattress on the floor; she was spending more and more time with me by then. I wanted to reach the phone before the ringing woke them up and I hurried downstairs, one hand instinctively covering my just swelling belly, goose-pimples rising in the pre-dawn chill.

'Hello?' As I grabbed the receiver I climbed onto the sofa, getting my feet off the cold, bare floor. 'Hello. Who's this?'

'I'm ringing to tell you that your husband is having an affair.'

It was a woman's voice, cool and silky and sounding rather pleased. I felt like I'd been punched in the stomach, '*What*?'

'Your husband is having an affair and I felt you ought to know.'

'I'm sorry, but who *are* you?'

'I thought you should know,' she said and then the line went dead.

I dropped the receiver and wrapped my arms around my belly. I remember rocking and howling like a madwoman as my fragile fantasy of happiness was shattered. Weeks of suspicion poured out of me as I gave myself over to sorrow.

I'd forgotten all about the kids until I heard a creak on the stairs. I looked up and saw Lisa, face frightened, shoulders hunched against the cold.

'What are you doing there? Get back to bed!' I bellowed at her, my poor vulnerable child. She fled and I went back to rocking, guilt now added to my misery. I was still huddled on the sofa, staring blankly at the grey dawn, when Raj came home at six o'clock.

He denied it. I probed and probed but he wouldn't admit to anything and in the end I gave up. I let life go on as it was because I couldn't see how to change it. I felt as powerless as I had in Nottingham.

A few weeks later the woman rang again; she told me her name was Jane and said she knew me from my classes. That detail seemed so cruel.

By the time I was four months pregnant, my belly visibly swollen, my back beginning to ache, I was struggling to maintain the pretence that Raj and I could go on together. We shared nothing except a cold, crumbling house, Maria and the creation of the life that was growing inside me, a life that I was determined would grow up in an atmosphere of love. And where was love in the sour misery I carried with me through each day? In the sharp craving for affection? In the sullen moments of despair?

It was seeing my baby on the scan – thumb in his mouth, ankles neatly crossed, heart pumping like a piston – that made my mind up.

The sonographer thought I was crying because she'd told me my baby was small for my dates and I didn't disillusion her. I accepted her comfort and kept my sorrow to myself. But as I lay there listening to her pointing out my baby's heart and lungs and liver ('all there, all healthy, your baby is going to be *fine*'), as I wiped the cold gel off my belly and struggled back into my clothes, as I made my next appointment and hurried back to the car, all that time something was hardening inside me. By the time I got home I'd made up my mind.

When Raj came in that afternoon I said, 'It's over, Raj, and I want you to go. Now. You know why. There's nothing to discuss. I'd like you to leave today.' Lisa was still at school and Maria at nursery; I'd planned it like that because I didn't want them to witness any ugly scene.

'Yeah, yeah.' He was standing there, nodding his head and grinning, like he'd heard it all before. I didn't argue or repeat myself. I picked up the phone and, with him there watching me, I phoned his dad.

'*Papa-ji*? I want you to know that it's over between me and Rajvinder because he's been having an affair. He's been seeing another woman for weeks and I can't pretend any more. I'm going to divorce him, *Papa-ji*, and I wanted you to know the reason why.'

I don't know if they believed me; I doubt Raj's mum did. But it mattered to me that I told them. I didn't want to take the blame. When I put the phone down Raj was still standing there, looking dumbfounded.

'I'm going now, to get the girls. I'll be out for a while. Please be gone when we get home.'

I never wavered. I'd thought I might go to pieces in the car, out of Raj's sight, but I didn't. I felt almost elated, stronger than I had in months. The next day I went out and bought a couple of tins of vivid pink paint and I covered the walls of the bedroom, working with a sort of manic energy. That was our main room, our only room really because it's where we kept our one electric heater. The girls played in there, I worked, we all slept

270

there; after Raj left it was often the three of us in the double bed huddled together for warmth. I wanted to make it look bright to cheer us all up, to convince myself that the future was going to be all right and that night, with the still damp paint casting a rosy glow on the faces of my daughters as I kissed them, I thought it might be.

My confidence lasted about as long as it took to wash the smell of Raj from my sheets. A sense of failure dogged me. A few days after Raj had left, Lucy cut me dead in the street and I was actually glad; I couldn't face her. I was determined that Dad shouldn't find out what had happened and I'm pleased to say he never did.

I'd wake in the small hours, my chest tight, my heart fluttering, cold sweat on my back. Unable to sleep, I'd take my mind through the day ahead: the girls, Karma Nirvana, my dissertation, the baby growing inside me . . . I felt like a midget at the foot of a mountain. My sense of loneliness was overwhelming and, as it got light, it took all the willpower I had to drag myself out of bed.

At about seven o'clock I'd wake the girls and they'd sit on the bed eating cornflakes while I got ready. Cornflakes were cheap and there were bad weeks when they had them for every meal. I often went without; eating was too much effort. Lisa had chosen to live with me by then, but there were times when I sent her back to her dad because I was just too tired to keep pretending I was fine. I could feel her constantly watching me and the anxious look on her face wrung my heart. Maria was too little to notice. She'd go off for the day with Raj and come back babbling about the fun she'd had with him and Jane. The pain that caused me was as sharp as any knife.

With Raj gone we had no car, so each day I picked up a heavy bag of books and heaved Maria into my arms then ran to catch the bus. She would scream at me 'Stop jiggling me, Mummy, it hurts' and my heart would pump so fast I thought it might burst. I had to take Lisa first and then catch a different bus back to Maria's nursery before going on to Karma Nirvana.

Those days without a car almost broke me and my distress must have shown because it was during that week that my tutor first suggested I defer finishing my degree until the following year.

'I mean, look at yourself, Jasvinder, you're exhausted, anyone can see that. You're having a baby, you've got your job . . . does your husband help at all?'

'We're separated actually,' I said, biting down hard on my bottom lip to stop myself crying. I was okay until someone was kind to me.

'Well, all the more reason. Why drive yourself so hard? Lots of people defer. There's no shame in it – especially with such good reason.'

I smiled briefly. 'I don't want to. Thanks for your concern but I'll be fine.' I wouldn't even consider his suggestion. I was stressed, yes. But work was my only sanity.

My dissertation required a lot of research so I often went into university in the evenings. I'd get Maria from nursery and – when she was with us – Lisa from her after-school club and we'd get there about six o'clock. First we'd go the refectory and get the girls some food. Things like beans and chips were cheap. Then I'd go to the library and look up the information I needed in journals and do some photocopying and collect any notes the tutors had left for me. At about eight I'd pick up the kids and take them home to bed.

I was in the habit of going in at weekends too by then. I'd take Lisa and Maria and ask the librarian if I could bring them in with me. I was completely honest with her, I just told her I really wanted to do this degree but I didn't have any childcare so I needed her help.

There was a corner of the library filled with children's books that were used by the students doing teacher training and she said Lisa and Maria could sit there as long as they were quiet. And they were quiet, bless them. Lisa was like a little mother to Maria, reading to her and playing with her for hours at a time. I never had to say a word. We'd have a break at lunchtime. I can remember sitting on the same bench in the freezing grey days of February and the hot sun of May. We'd eat the sandwiches I'd brought and then go for a little walk in the grounds before going back to the library. I did that every Saturday and Sunday for about two years.

My days were so full I had no time to think but come the evening, with the girls settled, my thoughts began to spiral. Loneliness grew inside me. I'd failed at every relationship I'd tried to make and I hated myself for it. By day I fought for the rights of Asian women and by night I craved acceptance from the very community I'd rejected. I sat huddled in a blanket with my sociology books open, staring at the same page for what felt like hours on end, willing the information to sink in. I longed for company. I'd set myself up as a pioneer but what I wanted to be was ordinary. I wanted a family.

It must have been spring when Raj and I finally separated but when I look back I remember all the days as dark and grey. I see myself as cold and hunched, pulled in, as if nursing a physical injury. I thought a lot about death. Oblivion seemed so alluring. I had all these suicide plans and I think if the baby hadn't started kicking I'd have done it. It was the baby that stopped me, the baby, Maria and Lisa.

CHAPTER 29

One day, when I was really low, I rang Karma Nirvana and asked for a few days off. The chairwoman told me to take as long as I needed. 'You should have some maternity leave anyway, Jas,' she said. And I was grateful. The state I was in I wasn't fit for support work; I barely had anything inside myself to give my kids, let alone anyone else.

I might have collapsed completely had it not been for Trish, who heard what had happened from my chairwoman. Our paths must have been criss-crossing since the day I made the presentation at the women's centre, but somehow we rarely met. She turned up on my doorstep one evening at about nine o'clock, after the girls were in bed.

'Hello, Jasvinder,' she said. 'Don't think me nosy, but I've come to see if you need help with anything. I heard your husband left you. Can I come in?'

She walked into my life and made it her business to look after me. In the bleak weeks that followed Trish became my saviour. She brought round nourishing food and forced me into eating properly, she listened to my woes and made me laugh. When I was at my lowest ebb she took me to live with her for a fortnight, even giving up her bed for me and Maria and sleeping on the sofa. She became my friend, the best friend I've ever had.

When necessary, Trish minded the girls for me as I attended what felt like endless hospital appointments. I'd had completely straightforward pregnancies with Lisa and – until my placenta abrupted – with Maria too, but this one was full of problems. The baby was small and I was so strung up that I kept fainting and having palpitations. I was closely monitored.

By May the baby was kicking hard; heels, knees and elbows jabbed my belly. As he became more and more real to me I dreaded bringing him back to the drab dereliction of Balfour Road where, by that stage, you could almost taste the sadness in the air. I made enquiries and found that with my Karma Nirvana salary I could get a tiny mortgage. I told Trish and she encouraged me. A desire to move was added to my stress.

At my six-month appointment my blood pressure was so high the doctor wanted to admit me to hospital for monitoring.

'But I can't come in. I'm a single mother, I've got kids to look after. And I'm taking my finals in a month, I've got a dissertation to finish. I've got so much work to do, honestly I can't come into hospital.'

The doctor said I had to, for the sake of the baby. He sent me up to the ward straight away and Trish, bless her, sorted everything out. The girls went to their dads' and after work that day Trish brought me in washing things and something to sleep in and a pile of books. Those were the only things I really wanted. I lay in bed, wired up to a monitor, working through my files. Trish had told my tutor and he was really supportive; he even arranged to have some lecture notes sent in to me.

I did rest though. Once I was lying down tiredness hit me like a truck. For the first time in months I slept through the night and two or three times a day I'd find myself nodding off, book in hand. I'd been there about four days when I woke from a nap to see Jassey sitting beside me. I was astonished. After he'd got residence rights for Lisa and I'd married Raj there had been nothing but bitterness between us. I hadn't seen him for about four years. I remember thinking that he looked older, that he'd put on weight.

'Is Lisa okay?' I asked, instantly anxious.

'Yeah, yeah, she's fine. It's not her I've come about.' He paused, looking uncomfortable, but then carried right on.

'Look, Jas, I wanted to say I'm sorry it didn't work out for you and Raj. I've heard it's been really hard for you. Lisa's told me a bit, and other people, you know what the grapevine is like.' He gave a wry smile. 'I wanted to say I'm sorry, and also that I'd like you to come back to me, Jas, I

277

mean it. I'd accept your children as my own, Maria and this one.' He made a little bow towards the bump beneath the sheet. 'I'd marry you again and we'd be a family, I'd look after you . . .' He paused, his cheeks flushed, and fixed me with the open, completely honest gaze I remembered so clearly. 'I mean it, Jas, what do you think?'

For an instant a picture of his house – our house – flashed through my mind: the pink-painted living-room, the flower-filled garden, tomatoes in my greenhouse. I thought about sharing responsibilities and not worrying about money every second of every day. I looked into Jassey's kind, hopeful eyes and thought about companionship. It could all be so easy.

'No, Jassey,' I said. 'I'm grateful for the offer, really. But it wouldn't work, you know that. You don't deserve to be hurt all over again.'

CHAPTER 30

The day my finals started was very hot. By 10 a.m. my clothes were sticking to me. I was seven months pregnant and my bump ached. I remember the sense of tension as we all stood outside the exam room fanning ourselves with our hands. When the doors of the examination hall were opened all you could see was an army of desks set out with rigid precision. Even the exam papers seemed to have been laid down perfectly straight. We'd all been given desk numbers; I found mine and sat down, glad to do so because my head was swimming. The windows, high up in the walls, were open but the room was close.

The first hour passed quickly. The air was thick and still with concentration. I felt lucky with the questions and had no trouble recalling the facts I needed, my pen seemed to skim across the page. But halfway through the second essay my energy began to flag. Pinpricks of light danced before my eyes. I felt light-headed and wished I'd had some breakfast. As I put up my hand to ask for a glass of water the dancing pinpricks became a wall of white light that blinded me.

My desk seemed to tilt and the floor was rising up . . .

I dimly remember hands lifting me, my feet clumsy on the floor, a cool room with a fan, a slim hand holding out a glass of water. I heard a voice telling me to relax, there was no more to worry about. 'But I didn't finish the paper. I've got to go back. The exam isn't over.' I tried to get up but the nurse put a restraining hand on my shoulder.

'It's over for you, dear. You can't go back in once you've left the exam hall.'

'But I have to. I've *got* to finish.' Suddenly I recognized the woman standing behind the nurse as one of the invigilators; it was Professor Sharma, who I knew and liked. 'Did you bring me here?' She nodded. 'Well, then you know exactly what happened. You know I haven't cheated. You have to let me go back in. Please, this means so much to me. And I feel fine now, honestly.'

The nurse and the invigilator exchanged glances. I could see them weighing rules against reason and whether or not I was fit enough to finish the paper. Ungainly and feeling heavy as a heifer I swung my legs off the couch and stood up, determined to convince them I was fine.

'All right then, you win. But let's be quick.' The invigilator led the way back to the exam hall and as we reached its doors, looked at her watch. 'It's twelve-fifteen. You came out at five to twelve. I'll arrange for you to have an extra twenty minutes at the end, so don't put your pen down when the others do.'

I got through the exams. I finally handed in my dissertation. Three years of study ended but I didn't feel jubilant. At the end of my last exam I left the hall caught up in a stream of excited students. I pushed my way to the side and stood back against the wall to let them pass, feeling old and tired as I watched them laughing, high five-ing one another, screwing up their notes as they danced their way across the campus to celebrate in the pub. I wouldn't have joined them, even if they'd asked me to. Completing the degree meant nothing to me; I'd always known I had the willpower to complete it. What mattered to me was passing it and I wasn't going to celebrate until I knew I'd done that. I hurried to the car park, keen to be on time to pick up Maria and Lisa.

The baby was due in August and with every week that passed I became more determined to move out of Balfour Road: the thought of four of us living in its one habitable room was terrible. But I wasn't prepared to walk away with nothing as I had done when I left Jassey. As I saw it, Raj was the guilty party and if he wanted me out of the house, he'd have to buy me out of it.

I wanted to move out of the Asian area. It made me feel claustrophobic, just as I'd felt in White's View. I'd grown used to my sisters snubbing me but I resented the way disapproval spread through the community. Try as I might I couldn't ignore the curious stares, the reproving glances, the way women drew aside in huddles keeping their children close when I went in and out of shops around Balfour Road. I knew I was gossip-fodder and I hated it.

I'd found a house about four miles away in Oakwood. It was tiny, but it was detached and it had three bedrooms. I went to see it with Trish and the girls one July afternoon and all the rooms were really sunny. I remember Maria lying on the carpet in a beam of light and saying, 'Look, Mummy, I'm sunbathing indoors.' All the rooms had carpet; we kicked off our sandals and walked about barefoot just for the pleasure of the soft, clean feel of it. Everything was so finished compared with Balfour Road; to Lisa's delight there was even a Jacuzzi in the bathtub. And it had a garden, just a scrubby little lawn with a couple of neglected flower beds, but I could imagine the baby there, sleeping in the sunshine in his pram.

I made an offer straight away and stayed up late that night, juggling figures, working out how I could possibly afford it. I was getting cleverer with money by then. In my three-year struggle through university I'd got used to searching for loans, grants, hardship funds – anything that would allow me to complete my studies. I'd learnt by then that there was help available, but only if you asked for it.

I went into labour on 12 August 1997. I was woken by the first, unmistakeable cramps, and I remember thinking 'I'm so tired, I don't know if I can do this'. I got myself to the hospital and Trish joined me there. Raj had asked her to, because he was working. Trish was wonderful; she stayed with me as I laboured, rubbing my back, smoothing my hair off my face, holding my hand when the midwife examined me. With every contraction I felt like I was being flattened.

Raj arrived just as I was being prepared for a Caesarean, all ready to prove himself the attentive, anxious father. I'd wanted a normal delivery, but the midwives had convinced me that wasn't going to happen. I was really scared and I wanted Trish right beside me, but when Raj arrived it was all 'Ah, here's the father', and calling him in and squeezing Trish out and I was so out of it I couldn't do anything. But when the midwives said, 'It's a boy, Jasvinder', when they gave him to me, wrapped in a little blue blanket, Trish's squeals of joy were the loudest. I'll never forget those cries of jubliation. I looked down at him, fanned out his tiny fist, checked he was perfect and then, as they finished stitching me, I thought, 'It's over, please someone take this baby and let me get some sleep'.

The children and I moved in to Calver Close, Oakwood when Joshua was two weeks old. It wasn't much of a move; just clothes and books and the tatty old mattress from Balfour Road. I didn't want to take anything from there, but Raj said I should take it and we didn't have any other sort of bed so I swallowed my pride in order to be practical.

I remember our first night in that house. We all slept in one room, me, Lisa and Maria on the mattress and Joshua on the floor beside us in his little Moses basket. There were no curtains and moonlight streamed through the window and lit up the faces of my sleeping children. Lisa with her long black hair strewn across the pillow and her brow slightly furrowed, anxious even in her sleep; Maria, thumb in her mouth, pressed tight in beside me and Joshua, flat on his back with his arms thrown back beside his head, his tiny chest rising and falling beneath his pale blue sleepsuit. His mouth was making little sucking movements and I knew he'd wake soon for a feed because my breasts felt hot and swollen.

I propped myself up on my elbows and lay there waiting for his cry, ready to scoop him up and hold him close before his hungry wails woke Maria and Lisa. I was tired but that night I also felt exhilarated. I took a deep, satisfied breath and caught the scent from Trish's roses. She'd brought them round earlier, all ready in a vase, and they were sitting on the windowsill, a bright splash of promise. I was proud of myself and I don't know that I'd ever before felt that. I'd bought a house, a house that was mine alone, and I was going to make it a home for my children. I might be exiled from my family and its history, but I suddenly felt confident that we could make it on our own.

Next morning, while I was feeding Joshua, Lisa rummaged in my old box of books and found herself a pen and paper and we started making a list of goals: things that we were going to save for.

'I'm going to have a bed for myself,' she said.

'I'm going to have a bed for myself and a television,' I countered.

'I'm going to have a bed for myself, and a television and something to put my clothes in.'

'I'm going to have a bed for myself and a television and a car that I can rely on to get us down the motorway . . .'

That was nine years ago and it was the start of a game that's never ended. 'Speak what you want, Lisa, even if it seems a million miles away,' that's what I told her. 'Speak what you want because once you've sown that seed you can work towards it.'

My results from Derby University arrived a few days after we'd moved in. I picked the envelope off the mat and stood there staring at it. Inside was the piece of paper that would realize or dissolve the dream I'd worked so hard for. It was five minutes before I could bring myself to open it. Then, as I pulled the flimsy paper out of the envelope and unfolded it my hands were shaking so much that I could hardly focus on the word First.

'First! Lisa, Maria, Lisa, I got a First. Quick, come and look. I got a First.' The girls came running and we were shouting, laughing, dancing up and down the tiny passage until Joshua took fright at all the noise and started howling. I took him from his basket, kissed him, soothed him, sat down on the mattress to feed him. The girls flopped down beside me and Maria, leaning against me, said, 'Mummy, what's a First?'

I freeze-framed those minutes with the four of us sitting on the mattress. I did it deliberately and even today I can play them through my mind like a video: five minutes of hard-earned, perfect happiness.

When my tutor, Graham Fowler, rang a few weeks later I thought he was going to congratulate me, and he did. But then he asked if I would give the vote of thanks on behalf of the students on graduation day. I was overwhelmed by the honour, it was the last thing I'd expected. With 3,000 students in the university, why pick me? He said it was because I'd worked so hard and overcome so much to finish my degree, which surprised me because I'd tried to hide my situation from my tutors. I hadn't wanted them feeling sorry for me; my training in secrecy was dying hard.

When the day came I felt sick with excitement and nerves. I'd hired a mortar board and gown and I wore them over a dark suit and a scarlet shirt; I wanted to look smart. The main hall was

286

packed with chairs. We graduates were all sitting in the front rows and our guests were behind us. I remember craning round, scanning each row of people. I spotted Raj. Jane had walked out on him by then and he was single again. I'd said he could come because I needed someone to hold Joshua. He was sitting between Maria and Lisa with Joshua on his lap and I found myself looking at him quite dispassionately. I knew I'd shut that door for ever and I was never going back. It was my dad I was really looking for. I'd invited him but he'd been noncommittal. I so wanted him there.

I hadn't found him by the time the Chancellor of the University started speaking. He introduced the guests – Dame Helena Kennedy was there to collect an honorary degree, she's the only one I remember – before addressing us all. Then in a long slow crocodile every single graduate filed up onto the stage to be presented with their certificate. The Chancellor shook each hand and had a quick word with everyone; it seemed to take for ever. And then it was me.

My legs felt like jelly and my hands were clammy as I stood behind the lectern. I was still looking for Dad as the Chancellor introduced me. I'd have given anything to have seen him sitting there, staring up at me. I wanted to see his face, pleased and proud as he watched his only graduate daughter in her mortar board and gown. The applause following the Chancellor's words was brief, and then there was this enormous silence, which I had to fill.

Graham had said to speak for fifteen minutes and in the end I think I managed ten. I was shaking when I started. I hadn't made any notes but somehow I knew what I was going to say. It wasn't anything grand.

I started by telling them about the day I first set foot on the campus, more than five years previously, when I was looking for a place to do my A levels. I told them how *mortified* I was to find out it was a university because that seemed so high above my station. I told them how I ran off with my tail between my legs, and that made them laugh.

The laughter relaxed me. I found myself saying what it was like doing A levels at the age of twenty-seven, having scarcely opened a book since I'd left school. I explained that my reasons for doing those exams were practical – I wanted to be able to support myself – but that once I'd started, the books had brought me so much unexpected pleasure. Reading had opened up a whole new world for me.

I said I'd been teased for being a mature student, and I explained what it had felt like being a single mother, pregnant and doing a degree. I said how very, very hard it had been and how my tutors had done everything they could to help me, right down to suggesting that I defer my degree. 'I could never have done that,' I said. 'I wanted this degree so badly, it meant so much to me, that from somewhere – and even today I don't know where – I got the determination to keep going, to see it right through to the final exam. And I'm so glad I did because when I opened that envelope saying I'd passed, that I'd got a higher grade than I ever expected, I nearly burst with pride at my achievement. Seeing that word First was one of the best moments of my life. But that is just the start for me, I'm sure of that.'

I had to pause for breath then and there was a spatter of applause across the audience, but I suddenly realized that I hadn't finished, that I had something else to say, so I raised my hand up off the lectern to make them stop.

'My mum and dad came here in the 1950s to look for work,' I said, and I could feel the audience settle down as they sensed something different coming. 'They came here from the Punjab, to a country they didn't know, with a language they didn't speak, far, far from everything familiar to them, so that they could give me, my brother and my sisters, a better chance in life. It's taken me a long time to realize how much they gave up for us, how much they sacrificed to make sure that we had the opportunities they never had. I may not always have seen eye to eye with my parents, I may not have shared their values, but I'm grateful, so grateful to them for that.'

There was another bit of clapping but I didn't stop for it, I went right on. 'I'm pleased to say I seized those opportunities, I can look back now and say I grabbed them and made the most of them and that's why I'm standing here today. If someone like me, who left school with no qualifications, who came to university a single mum with two kids, and had another on the way, if someone like me can get qualifications, anyone can. And I look forward to seeing my kids following in my footsteps. I want to see you on this stage one day, Lisa, and you, Maria, and Joshua.'

I stopped then and the whole place exploded with clapping. Everyone stood up. Dame Helena Kennedy came over and kissed me, and she had tears pouring down her face. It was extraordinary. The applause seemed to go on and on, and while I was stood there, waiting for it finish, I was still looking for my dad. Finally, just before I left the stage, I faced the fact he wasn't there. I didn't blame him. Some of my family wouldn't have liked him coming. I understood that, but it didn't make the hurt I felt any easier to bear.

I went round to see him a few days later. I took him a framed copy of my graduation photograph and told him that the speech went well. He didn't say much but he did look pleased and to me that meant a lot.

CHAPTER 31

With my degree over and Joshua settled into a routine, I went back to Karma Nirvana with a burst of new energy. Towards the end of my first week back a ward sister at the local hospital rang to see if we could send someone to talk to a young Asian girl brought in by a stranger who had found her collapsed in the street. Her name was Zainab.

I took the call and felt concerned immediately. Sister said the doctors thought she'd swallowed something highly toxic; judging by the marks and the smell on her clothes it was probably bleach. Although she had been admitted almost a week before no one had been in to visit her, no one had even rung to enquire. The stranger who picked her up couldn't tell them anything except the area of Derby in which he found her and she didn't seem to have been carrying a bag or anything else that might tell them who she was.

'All we've got out of her is her name. But it's clear she doesn't speak English. Would anyone from your team have time . . . ?'

'Of course, I'll come myself, I'll come tomorrow,'

I said, running my next day's appointments through my mind as I spoke. I knew it would be a squeeze, but support work is the basis of everything Karma Nirvana does and to this day I make it a priority. I went in first thing next morning and a nurse directed me towards a bed occupied by someone so tiny that she hardly made a bump beneath the sheets. All I could see was a mess of dark hair on the pillow and a tangle of tubes leading up to various drips. I walked across and stood beside the bed.

She turned her head towards me; her face was yellowish grey. For a second I thought I saw a spark of curiosity in her huge, dark eyes, but then she sighed, as if the whole thing was too much effort, and looked away.

'I've come to see you, to help you if I can.' I drew a chair up to the bed. I didn't say anything else. Fear pulsated off her almost palpably and instinct told me to go very slowly. I put my hand over hers where it was lying limply on the bedspread and sat quietly for about half an hour. Then I got up. 'I've got to go now, but I'll come back tomorrow.'

She turned her head again and this time held my gaze.

Over the next few days I visited that girl as often as I could. She was one of those people – there have been a few since Karma Nirvana started – who got under my skin. Supporting them has become an important part of my life. When we first met there was something about her complete desolation that I recognized from my own dark days in Newcastle.

Sitting beside her, I told her about that time in my life, I told her the whole story right down to my still being estranged from my family. It had helped me get through to Ayesha and I hoped it might have the same effect now. She listened to me silent and wide-eyed and when I got to the bit about having to finally accept that my mum cared more about the community than she did about me, tears began to pour down her face. I stopped talking and she cried for about five minutes before she dried her eyes and said, in Punjabi, 'I know how that feels.'

It had taken until she was strong enough to sit in the chair beside her bed for a couple of hours each day for me to be able to coax a few words out of her, and the sister had been right, she spoke no English. The way her eyes would go glassy with fear and confusion as they fixed on the face of the person speaking reminded me so much of Mum. The doctors wanted to know exactly what she'd swallowed and although she didn't want to talk about it – I think she was ashamed of what she'd done – she eventually admitted it was household bleach. Half a bottle of it. 'You can tell her she's lucky she's not dead,' said the doctor who'd asked me to find out. 'She may well find that her digestion has been permanently damaged.'

She crept down the road to recovery. One mild

October day I asked the ward sister if I could take her for a walk in the hospital grounds. We went very slowly; it took quite a time to work our way through the maze of corridors and Zainab was already tired by the time we made it outside into the fresh air. There was a bench a few hundred yards from the exit doors and we decided to stroll over and rest on that. Zainab sat there with her eyes closed and her face tilted up towards the sky taking in great gulps of air. She looked like someone really thirsty who'd been given a drink.

The ward sister had told me as I left the day before that I was still Zainab's only visitor. 'She's got her social worker now, and she's trying to decide what's to be done with her when she's ready to leave. We still don't know anything about her. Will you find out what you can?' I said I would. I felt Zainab trusted me by then.

I began very gently; I asked her if, when she left hospital, she'd be going back to her family. Her eyes widened in alarm and she shook her head vigorously.

'Where is your family, Zainab? Sister says she hasn't heard from them since you came into hospital. Do they know you're here?'

She shrugged and a shadow of the desolation I first knew in her flashed across her face. 'My mother and father are in Pakistan. I don't know if they know I'm here. My husband – he's my father's cousin – is here in Derby. He's probably told them that I've run away.' She dropped her head and the bitterness in her voice was blunted by tears. 'My father will be so angry with me; I've shamed him, but I couldn't stay there any longer, they were so cruel,' she sobbed.

I held her hand as she told me how her husband had raped her the week she arrived in England. 'I didn't know him. We didn't meet until the wedding; I was sixteen and I was shy. For three days he was patient but then he forced me . . .' Her cheeks flushed with shame, but having started her story, the indignities she had suffered poured out. 'He hurt me so badly I didn't want to do it again, so he kept on raping me. He hurt me so much, but I had no time to rest. Every morning I had to get up at six and do housework, make the meals, wash the clothes, clean the rooms. They treated me like a servant. Sometimes I did not sit down until ten at night, and if I was slow or missed something, my mother-in-law would beat me. When I wasn't working, she would lock me in my room. For two years I didn't walk outside in the streets, Jasvinder.' Her voice was flat and sad.

'Why didn't you tell someone? You should have told the police,' I said. I had my arm tight round Zainab's shoulders now. It was as if I was trying to press feeling into her, all the love and care she'd been starved of for years. For all the trust between us, she still felt tense and rigid in my grip.

'How could I? I don't . . .'

'. . . speak English.' I finished the sentence for her. 'Of course, how stupid of me.'

'And it's not just that. I was never alone; even

at the doctor's my husband or my mother-in-law would come in to the appointment with me. And anyway, my mother-in-law said if the police or anybody else in authority knew I was here I'd be arrested and put in prison for being here illegally. That's what she said. Is it true, Jasvinder?'

I reassured her that it wasn't and led her gently back inside again. She was obviously exhausted. I was tired too, but once I'd said goodbye to her I went to the Karma Nirvana offices and rang the number Sister had given me for Zainab's social worker. I told her all I'd learnt and she promised to try to find safe accommodation for Zainab when she was ready to leave hospital. 'I think she'll need someone to keep an eye on her,' I said. I wasn't sure Zainab shared her doctor's opinion that she was lucky to be alive.

When I'd put the phone down I sat there for a few minutes, preoccupied, haunted by the last thing Zainab had said to me, her eyes dark with pain. 'The social worker wants to contact my parents; she doesn't understand how angry they would be. I am their daughter, but if they knew what I'd done they would disown me. My parents care more about honour than they do about me.'

I know what that feels like. I've been there. I understood her anguished disbelief. How could anyone turn their back on their own child for the sake of a concept? How could that be considered honourable? To me it seemed a cause of shame.

*   *   *

Zainab was released from hospital into a Derby refuge and I went to see her there a couple of days after she'd arrived. It was a nice enough place, shabby but well looked after. The staff were friendly and keen to help, but there were no Punjabi speakers among them so Zainab was reliant on an interpreter who only came sporadically.

I'd found her sitting on her bed which, according to the refuge staff, was where she spent all her time. She looked totally dejected and withdrawn. The room was small: just big enough for a single bed, a narrow hanging cupboard and a small chest of drawers. In an effort to brighten the place up someone had stuck a travel poster to the wall, advertising holidays in France. Save for her actual presence there was nothing to show it was Zainab's room. She'd left her in-laws' house with nothing; she had nothing.

It suddenly occurred to me that, although she must have been in Britain for two years, incarceration in her in-laws' house meant Zainab knew almost nothing of this country or its people. Her suicide attempt had caused her to be picked up and dumped, unprepared and empty-handed, into a western way of life. She had nothing familiar to cling to.

'How do you get on with the other people here?' I asked her. She shrugged. 'They only speak English. They can't talk to me, so they ignore me, and they go like this –' she wrinkled her nose in a show of disgust and waved her hand in front of her face – 'when I make Indian tea . . . It is better that I stay here by myself.'

I'd heard similar comments made by some of the women who visited our surgeries. 'In the end I couldn't stand the loneliness so I went back home.' 'They kept suggesting I call my mother and tell her where I was.' 'The other women kept their kids away from mine . . .' But it was the first time I'd seen it for myself. It dawned on me that there might be a case for specialist provision for Asian women and as I sat beside Zainab on her bed that afternoon I made two resolutions. The first was to get Zainab to sign herself up for English lessons. The second was to find myself some shift work in the local refuges; I needed to know more.

CHAPTER 32

In August 1999 a man called Mohinder rang me out of the blue. I'd known him when I was a child because he spent a lot of time with Prakash. She helped his family settle in Britain and I'd been brought up to call him *Py-ji* which means brother. I knew he'd got married, had two kids and moved to Derby but I hadn't seen him for years.

'I need to talk to you, Jas. Can you come round to my place?'

I was suspicious. 'What is it? Can't we just talk on the phone?'

'No, no, we need to see each other face to face. But you won't regret it, believe me. Why not come round tomorrow afternoon. Say five o'clock?'

I agreed. I was still uneasy but I was curious. Next day I knocked on his door at precisely five o'clock. It was a big house, right in the Asian area; he'd obviously done well for himself.

'Ah, Jas, come in, come in. How about some tea?' he said, leading me through to the kitchen. He was making out that he was all hospitable but I could tell he was nervous: his face was covered with a light film of sweat.

'No thanks, *Py-ji*. Why don't you just tell me what you want to talk about?'

'Ah yes. Well, the thing is this, Jasvinder, I have managed to find you a suitable match.'

'You've done *what*?'

'I've found a husband for you. Be realistic, Jas. Who is going to want you now? Three children and two divorces to your name – who will look at you? Your family was good to me and now, in return, I have made it my business to help you. He is a good man, believe me. He is an accountant, good job. And he is currently in Leeds. I will arrange everything, don't worry. Just say the word and I will get the papers so you can sponsor him into the country . . .'

I was dumbfounded, so surprised – and angry – that I couldn't say anything. I just stood there looking at him. He would have run on and on if my mobile phone hadn't interrupted him.

It was Sunny and his husky fifteen-year-old's mumble had been replaced by a clear voice, tight with panic.

'*Massi-ji*? You've got to come quick. It's Dad. I think he's dead.'

I didn't need telling twice. It was the way Sunny said 'think' that made me shut off all emotion and move as quickly as I could. If I got there fast it might not be too late. I was half way to the front door when I shouted over my shoulder, 'I'm going to my dad's. Call an ambulance. Sunny thinks he's dead.'

It took me less than ten minutes to get to Dale Road. The front door was on the latch and I ran right through it to where Dad was lying on the living-room floor. His mouth was open and his skin was grey. Sunny was crouched down beside him, tears streaming down his face.

I was down on my knees and trying to remember years back when St John's Ambulance came to Littleover School and showed us mouth-to-mouth resuscitation. I pinched Dad's nose and, covering his mouth with mine, tried to breathe life back into him. His skin was cold but not icy and I thought that must be good. I breathed into him once, twice, three times and each time I turned my head to fill my own lungs I saw his chest rise and fall. I breathed into him a fourth time and as his chest fell with the exhalation it gave a sort of rattle. I thought he coughed.

'I think he's coming back, Sunny,' I said, and redoubled my efforts. I was pressing on his chest now too, taking it in turns to breathe and press, breathe and press. I was frantic, trying to pump life back into him. I was still doing it when the ambulance men came and told me, very gently, that he was dead.

They took him to the hospital and I followed in my car with Sunny and Mohinder, who'd followed me to the house. My sisters were there, screaming and crying.

Sunny was beside himself that evening as we waited in the hospital. He'd been playing football with his mates when Dad had his heart attack and he kept saying if only he'd been home he might have saved him. I tried to console him and the others did too. Concern for him was the only thing that linked us; other than that there was nothing between us but awkward space.

Later, when the doctor said we could go, I went back to lock Dad's house up. I'd thought I'd spend some time there but I couldn't, I couldn't even bring myself to go upstairs. The house was already full of ghosts. In the living-room I looked down at the spot where I'd tried to bring Dad back and thought about my mouth against his and how I'd tried to force life back into him. For most of my life Dad had kept me at arm's length and then, at the point of his death, I'd been so close to him it was obscene.

Back in Oakwood I hugged my kids a little tighter, held them a little longer than I normally would. Joshua was only two but he sat on my knee and wiped the tears off my cheeks with his sticky little hands: 'I love your dad, Mummy,' he said. Lisa was really cut up. She'd become quite close to Dad.

They moved him from the hospital morgue to the chapel of rest and I went to see him there. I'd been told I could spend as long as I liked with him and I stayed quite a while. I wanted him to have company; I hated the fact that he'd died all alone. On the living-room floor he'd been dishevelled, with his wispy hair spread out everywhere, but now someone had made him look all neat and tidy. He seemed at peace and talking to him seemed so natural. I had all the time I needed because, after all those years, he didn't have to worry about other people knowing I was with him.

I talked to him about the time we used to spend together on the allotments and how much that had meant to me. I reminded him of the old car he used to drive us to school in; how its wipers didn't work and how he used to make me lean out of the window and wipe the snow off as he drove along. I told him how much I loved him and how I wished things had been different between us. I said I knew how hard his life had been here in England and how brave I thought he and Mum had been to leave India, to make that sacrifice for us. I wondered – I still do – what my life would have been like if he had stayed on his farm in the Punjab. The last thing I said was that I would look after Sunny for him, always.

I was very grateful to be able to stand by my dad's body and say all that. I felt I said things I'd been keeping bottled up for years. I couldn't do it when Mum died because my sisters wouldn't let me near her; they washed the body and did all those things for her. I asked if I could help but they wouldn't let me: 'If the hands of an outcast touch her she'll be contaminated,' that's what they said.

This time I'd hardly got home from the chapel

of rest when Gin rang. 'We've got to get this funeral organized,' she said, as if we went through a 'to do list' together every day. 'You have to get him a suit; you'll have to put a suit on him.'

After the mouth-to-mouth, that was the second most personal thing I ever did for my dad. I didn't know what size he was so I drove round to his house and measured his best suit, his only suit, the one that smelt like him, hair oil and cigarettes. Then I went into town and went round the shops trying to find the suit he'd want to wear for all eternity. He'd turned away from me in life but I was looking after him in death. I was talking to him in my head, telling him how strange that felt.

Sunny wanted to buy him some dark socks with cartoon characters on them so I got those and then, from the house, we fetched a couple of things to put in the coffin. The only one I remember is a picture of Mum. We dressed him up in the suit and the socks and the new brown tie I'd bought him and he looked so smart. I think Mum would have been proud.

After the funeral, when I was ready, I went back to Dale Road to start packing up Dad's things. I was the one my family had never wanted in the house, the one who was always having to scuttle off and make herself scarce, but now Mum and Dad were gone there I was, all by myself, clearing up. I just got on with it.

In the fridge I found the last lot of fruit I'd brought him. It was hard to make him eat properly after

Mum died. I tried buying vitamins, but he said he couldn't remember to take them. He was tired and diminished. Even though Sunny was living there with him he seemed so alone.

I was upstairs, doing his bedroom, when I saw my graduation picture on the wall. I hadn't seen it since the day I gave it to him and I thought he'd put it away and forgotten about it, but there it was. It was in the corner, not in a prominent place, but it was on the wall all right. Dad couldn't say how proud he was of me in life, but I suddenly felt he was saying it in death. I took the photograph down and I'm looking at it now.

We had to go to the solicitors to have the will read. I'd driven Dad there to have it drawn up but I had no idea what it contained because I'd sat outside until he was ready for me to drive him home again. The first thing the solicitor said was that Dad had made me and Ginda executors of his will. To me that spoke volumes. I had never expected to be the one holding the keys to his property and dealing with his matters. I always thought it would be Balbir because he was the only son and sons are so precious in Asian families. Besides, I was the one who dishonoured the family.

That's what they all said for years, but in the end it turned out differently. Dad spoke to me in death. At the end, it was me he trusted to do the right thing. I still miss him. I still wish I'd told him I loved him before it was too late, told him and my mum. But I'm glad of the things he said to me when he died and I've tried my best to carry out his wishes, even though it's sometimes been hard.

Dad left everything to Sunny. Ginda walked out of the solicitor's office in disgust when she heard that. To me it seemed fair: Sunny had no one else in the world and anyway, who were we to question what Dad wanted?

CHAPTER 33

The summer after Dad died, Lucy arrived on my doorstep unannounced. I was her last resort. Lucy had wanted to stay with Gin, but Gin's husband hadn't forgiven her. The truce between them was always uneasy. She had abandoned her arranged marriage with his nephew – to him that was hugely shameful.

Of course I said she could stay. I still had dreams of us being a proper family then. That summer Lucy seemed sad. One night she and I started to talk about our upbringing and why our mother was the way she was. I told Lucy:

'I think she and Dad both thought they were doing the best for us.' I was telling her what I'd so often told myself. I'd worked hard to accept that as the truth. I wanted to put my childhood to rest and leave my bitterness behind.

'But she never showed love for us, she never hugged us or kissed us . . .' Lucy was beside herself, but what could I say?

The love Mum showed was conditional. It was dependent on us being what she hoped for and expected: diligent daughters, obedient wives, dutiful

307

daughters-in-law, model Asian citizens. I believe now that those were the things she thought would make us happy, keep us safe.

When I was young I thought my mum was motivated by arrogance. Her obsession with the hierarchy of caste, with the family's reputation, with our honour, I thought all those things were signs of her pride. Now I wonder if she was driven by fear. In some ways she and Dad were just like I was when I ran away: displaced persons, severed from their roots and families. In England their precious community was the only framework they could cling to, the only familiar thing they had.

I've come to terms with my childhood. I feel close to Mum and Dad, even though they are dead. As for my siblings, they're not family in any real sense. We don't talk to each other now.

Most of the news about my family I get second-hand. I read in the local paper that Balbir set fire to a carpet in his house. It was attempted suicide but, because of the risk to his neighbours, he was done for arson and ended up in prison. Sunny told me Balbir was beaten up while he was there for being the brother of 'that bitch who helps girls run away from home'.

Sunny was my link with the family but in the past few months that's changed. Inasmuch as I could I treated him as my own. The year after Dad died I sold my house in Oakwood and moved back into the Asian area. I bought a place on Warwick Avenue, just as I said I would when we were on the school run, all those years ago. I did it for Sunny so that he could come and live with us without moving away from everything he knew.

In 2002, when Sunny was eighteen, I kept my promise to Robina and took him to Canada to meet his dad, Navtej. On that first visit we were welcomed and fêted and treated like kings. Navtej had remarried but he never had another child. He said he'd like Sunny to come and live with him and, a year later, Sunny went.

I can't say I was sorry. Since he'd reached his teens Sunny had been questioning my values: 'Why do you do the work you do?' 'Why can't you be like Ginda-*masi*?' 'How can you let Lisa have a boyfriend?'

Sunny went to live in Canada but he wasn't happy.

He rang night after night after night, until I agreed to fly over and sort things out. This time there was no welcome. A family meeting to discuss Sunny's future became a furious row. All the old insults were hurled at me: 'You married a *chamar*, you disgraced your family, you're no better than a prostitute . . .' We packed our bags and left and there's been no contact since.

My story became Sunny's story. His family was no more able to accept Sunny's individuality than my parents could accept mine. In the Asian community the will of the family still comes first.

I tried to help him with his life. I always knew he was ashamed of what I do, but when I heard he was saying to people, 'When I marry I won't let my wife talk to my *masi*', I challenged him. We're not talking any more, which makes me very sad.

I've moved away from him, I've moved away from all of them. I got used to living in the Asian area because I'm strong enough now not to care what people think. But the day Gin and Yasmin ignored Lisa and Maria out in the street – deliberately cut them dead – I decided I was moving. I'm not exposing my kids to the hurt I've known; I'm not handing down that legacy of rejection.

Three years ago I bought a house in a little place just outside Derby. I joke that I'm the only Asian in the village but the fact is, I love that. I'm away from my work, away from the community into which I've never fitted comfortably. I can come home and shut the door and nobody bothers me; I am at peace.

Lisa has left home now. Last year, aged twenty-one, she graduated in law from Leeds University and I nearly burst with pride as, sitting next to Jassey, I watched her in her gown and mortar board, collecting her degree. The odds were against her, and look what she has achieved. After a spell living with her father, Maria has come home and at the weekends she, Joshua and I can escape into the country for a walk or a bike ride. I am giving them the childhood full of unconditional love that I wanted for myself. I've built us a safe little world, a sanctuary where I can retreat to recharge my batteries, ready for the work ahead.

CHAPTER 34

Not long after I met Zainab I started doing shift work in the local refuges and what I saw there convinced me of the need for specialist provision. Women who end up in refuges have had their lives pulled up by the roots. If they are to survive, an anonymous hostel won't do; they need something familiar, something as close as possible to what they've known and lost. I'm thinking of women like Shazia, a young Muslim girl, brought up in Birmingham, who was taken to Pakistan 'for a holiday' aged fifteen and married to a cousin whom she didn't even meet until the ceremony. After the wedding her family flew home and although Shazia begged and pleaded to be allowed to return with them, they left her in Pakistan for several months. They wanted to be sure she 'formed a relationship' with her husband. She had no choice: he forced himself on her the day her family left. Shazia told him how unhappy she was but he didn't care; he made no bones about the fact that all he wanted was a passport into England. She was allowed home only when she had promised to go through the procedures necessary to bring him over here.

Back in Birmingham Shazia wrote to the British Embassy explaining her plight and begging for their help. She explained that she'd been forced to marry her husband and forced to fill in the forms sponsoring him to come to England. She sent the letter via a friend so her parents wouldn't know about it, but she never got a reply. In desperation, three weeks after the man she had grown to hate arrived in this country, Shazia rang the police and asked to be given safe escort from her parents' house. She packed some bags and hid them in readiness but when the police arrived, when her mother started screaming and wailing and begging her to stay, she didn't have the strength to go and get them. She left empty-handed.

When I first saw her – a couple of weeks after that happened – she was sitting on her bed with that blank, shocked look you see in newspaper photographs of refugees. She had turned her back on everything she had ever known or loved. She was many miles from home with nothing at all familiar in her surroundings. The first thing she said to me was, 'Do you know where I could pray?' She was trying to cling to the shreds of her identity and there was nothing in that refuge to give her any help.

Shazia reminded me of my sixteen-year-old self. She'd had that same traditional upbringing that leaves you so vulnerable and unprepared for real life; if you can't conform you can't cope. She had to feed herself in the refuge, but she wasn't sure how to do it. 'How many loaves of bread will I need, Jas?' she said. Like me before I ran away, she'd never gone to the shops without having been told what to get. Her uncertainty ran much deeper than what she should eat. 'I don't know who I am any more, Jas,' she said as we sat talking. She was looking straight at me and the fear and confusion I could see in her eyes took me right back down the years. 'I ran away because I couldn't be the person Mum wanted, but I don't know how to be anybody else.'

To my mind you didn't have to look further than Shazia to see the need for specialist Asian women's refuges. She was going to need so much support before she could rebuild her life. And I wanted her to be able to rebuild it as an Asian woman. Running away mustn't mean you have to shrug off your whole identity. Pull-back to the culture you grew up with is very strong. I'd learnt by then that turning your back on bits of it doesn't mean that you reject it altogether. I'm proud to be an Asian woman and I wanted Shazia to be able to come through her trauma and feel the same.

When my shift was over I went back to the Karma Nirvana offices and started making a list of people to talk to, people from the police, health and social services. I knew they wouldn't all be sympathetic, I knew the people already running refuges might see it as muscling in on their patch; after all, there's only so much funding to be had. But the thought of Shazia kept me going. Do you know what she said to me just before I left? I was walking out the door when she caught my arm.

'I ran away to be free, but now I feel I've swapped one prison for another.'

I approached the national charity Refuge and asked if they would be prepared to form a partnership with Karma Nirvana to set up an Asian women's refuge and they agreed. I envisaged one house large enough for eight women, but by early 2001 – when we were racing to submit a funding application before the April deadline – I resigned myself to the fact that I wouldn't find that in Derby. I re-worked the plans for our pilot project using four two-bedroom properties instead.

We had the support of the local housing association but some of the properties they offered us defied belief. More than once I walked through the front door and gagged because of the smell. I got used to walking round them with a scarf or a handkerchief pressed over my nose and mouth. I saw kitchens thick with grease, carpets infested with fleas, houses in which the window frames had rotted and fallen out, or the ceilings had collapsed because of damp. We saw houses where I couldn't imagine keeping a dead dog, let alone a woman in need of solace. But the deadline meant we had to decide and eventually I took a leap of faith and picked four.

The funding application was successful and as soon as the money came through the renovations started. It was all done properly; the houses were stripped out and made good top to toe and within sixteen months all four of them were looking fantastic. I know many of the women who contact Karma Nirvana fear that running away will mean living in a hovel – just like Jassey and I did – but these houses prove them so wrong. They've got gardens, blinds at every window, washing machines, furniture – all of it brand new. We even managed to scrounge some prints to brighten them up a bit and a few books and toys for the kids.

But to my mind the important things in those houses are the big cooking pots, the *chapatti* pans, the racks of Indian spices and, in the living-room, the area set aside for prayer mats. When I got into the kitchen of one of those refuges nowadays I'm enveloped by the smell of Asian cooking; it's a warm familiar smell that wraps itself around me like a quilt. That's what I envisaged when I began my fight for specialist provision.

We opened those four refuges in 2002. Each one was designed to house two women and their children and in that first year Karma Nirvana provided emergency accommodation for fifty-two women and their children and had to turn more than one hundred and twenty-five others away. To me that was more than proof of need and I immediately started advocating specialist provision as a national project. It has been a slow process, but there is now an Asian women's refuge in Stoke-on-Trent and talk of one in Burton.

That was the start of moving my work beyond Derby and now, increasingly, I am campaigning across the country, talking to police officers, social workers and teachers about the issues facing Asian women in Britain. Almost everywhere I go I find such thirst for knowledge, and such need. Often I talk in schools and when I do, among the kids who approach me to ask questions at the end, there are invariably one or two hollow-eyed Asian girls who murmur, 'What you talked about . . . it's happening to me.'

The stories I've heard from the women who seek help from Karma Nirvana are echoed wherever I go. So many Asian women suffer at the hands of their families who hurt them in ways that a stranger never would. Their torment is invisible because honour-based violence happens behind closed doors, but it is there, creeping like a cancer through our society.

Not everyone is willing to accept this. Not long ago, in Derby, I was addressing an annual meeting of magistrates on the subject of murder in the name of honour. When I'd finished talking three men stood up, wanting to speak. Two were supportive but the third, a Muslim Pakistani, a respected leader within his community, said: 'I've lived in

Derby all my life and I have never heard of anything like the issues you discuss. Who are you anyway? I've never seen you before. I think you are an impostor.'

He denied any knowledge of honour-based violence despite the much-publicized case of Rukhsana Naz who – just like him – lived in Derby all her life. She went to my old school, Littleover. Rukhsana was nineteen years old and six months pregnant when her mother sat on her legs while her brother strangled her to death. They did it because she refused to abort the baby she was carrying, and they suspected it was not fathered by the man she had been forced to marry when she was just fifteen.

Hers was just one of the 5,000 honour killings that take place, worldwide, each year.

Luckily the British authorities, who in the past have been caught up in a fog of ignorance and misplaced cultural and religious sensitivity, have started to acknowledge the problems that Asian women face here. Honour killings are now recognized as such. Two terrible cases were reported while I was writing this book. The brother and cousin of twenty-five-year-old Samaira Nazir stabbed her eighteen times before cutting her throat, because she wanted to marry for love. They made her little sisters watch them do it, and the two girls ended up spattered with Samaira's blood. Nineteen-year-old Arash Ghorbani-Zarin was stabbed forty-six times by the brothers of the girl who was carrying his baby, the girl with whom he planned to spend his life.

Of the four men directly involved with these murders three were under twenty. Older men often use young relatives to do their dirty work, but what frightens me is that the younger generation seem to feel even more strongly than their elders do about the subjugation of women. I heard that despite our dreadful legacy, one member of our family has often said, 'If I had a daughter who went out with a Muslim I'd chop him into little pieces and gladly do time for it.'

As director of Karma Nirvana I am pleased and proud to be able to play my part in addressing these threats to Asian women. I have been asked on several occasions to advise on issues facing the Metropolitan Police body currently reviewing 120 murder cases to see if they should be reinvestigated as honour killings. So far it has been deemed that at least twelve of them should. I have developed close links with the Forced Marriage Unit which was set up by the Home Office and the Foreign and Commonwealth Office and now deals with more than 250 cases each year, some of them involving girls as young as ten years old. I am also asked with increasing frequency to offer advice on cases of honour-based violence that are brought to court. On a continuing basis, I feel privileged that so many women trust me with their stories of pain, and the fact that I can be a tool in their healing process is something I never take for granted.

Although many British Asians condemn honour-based violence and are delighted at the way its prevalence is now being exposed, not all of them share this view. The work I do makes me an object of hatred to some people. Last year, on a Saturday night, I was curled up on the sofa watching television with Maria and Joshua when my mobile phone rang. 'Where's Nadia? We know she's with you; we found your number in her bedroom.'

I knew exactly who the woman was, and her icy rage turned my stomach cold. About ten hours previously her daughter Nadia had called me from their home in a prosperous town just south of London, her voice shaking with fear.

She had been kept prisoner in the house for the previous two years while her family arranged her marriage to one of her first cousins. She didn't go to school, she didn't see friends; she was sixteen and she never went anywhere alone. Her step-father had stuck nails and barbed wire along the top of the fence surrounding their property just in case she tried to run away.

She told me most of that later. At the time all she said was that she'd found my number in a magazine article, and she needed my help. With hundreds of miles between us all I could do was outline her options, but it must have given her some courage because two hours later she rang again.

'I've done it. I got out of the house. I've escaped and I'm in the high street, please help me.'

I did what I could. I persuaded her to ring the

local police and I rang a friend of mine in the Metropolitan Police. He dropped what he was doing and drove out to find her. By the time he got there she was in the local police station, getting more and more hysterical as an officer tried to persuade her that the best thing would be to let him take her home. I thought, once again, how lucky I was with the police officer who first found me and Jassey. Once Nadia had convinced my friend of the danger she would now be in at home, he took her back to London and arranged refuge accommodation.

When Nadia's mother rang that night I denied all knowledge of her daughter and hung up, but I knew I wouldn't be able to deflect her that easily. An hour or so later my mobile rang again. It was a male voice, ugly and menacing. 'We know you live in Derby, we know people who could find your house quite easily. Tell us where Nadia is or you might find yourself chopped into little pieces.'

I was scared, and impressed as ever by the efficiency of the Asian network. Two calls later – in which my children and their schools were mentioned – I rang the police. By the end of that weekend a panic button had been installed in my house and an officer had left me with a list of precautions to try and ensure my safety, things like varying my route home and never getting out of the car without checking first.

Taking those precautions made me stop and think, but only briefly. There is so much to do that

I know I will continue this work until my dying day. I am currently researching a Ph.D on honour-based violence and I am also working to establish a National Friendship Network.

The women brave enough to stand up for themselves and escape from families who bully, abuse and imprison them face disownment, immense sadness and loss. In fleeing their families, they are forced to leave behind the communities they grew up in, the faces and places they have known all their lives. These women need friends who will understand them and support them, who will be the background to their lives as they struggle to rebuild their identities. A pilot project for the National Friendship Network is now under way, shaped by the views of people who have contacted Karma Nirvana in the past. I persuaded the Forced Marriage Unit to fund the training in skills such as listening and confidence-building of nineteen people who will be the first friends/mentors in this network, and I am now back on familiar territory: chasing further funds to make my vision real.

Last week a woman called Usha came to Karma Nirvana. She was seventeen. Having been tricked into a marriage abroad when she was just fifteen she was then kept prisoner in her home in Stoke for more than a year while she saved to 'bring her husband over'. When the school's welfare officer came looking for her, Usha's mum would push her into the cellar and lock the door. She was

322

always very polite to the welfare officer, offering her a cup of tea, grateful for her concern; inviting her to call again if she wanted to. 'It's just that Usha is not well today, she's sleeping,' she'd say. Or, 'Usha has had to go round to her auntie's to look after the children while Auntie takes Uncle to hospital.'

She was charming enough to convince the welfare officer that all was well and after a while she stopped calling. At first Usha tried to get help. She dialled 999 a couple of times, but when the police arrived at the door her mum would just say, polite as ever, 'Sorry, you must have got the wrong address. There's no one of that name here.' Then she'd beat Usha for making the call.

Eventually, like so many of us, Usha seized her chance and ran away. For the previous year she had been moving between bed and breakfasts, always on the run. By the time I met her she was in turmoil. She wanted to go home, but she was afraid of what would happen if she did. She had started self-harming, cutting herself. She showed me her thin forearm, criss-crossed with scars, some of them faded to faint silver lines but others still a vivid red. 'I don't want to do it; I feel really bad about it . . .' she said, struggling to look me in the eye. 'But it's the only way I can cope . . .'

In the months since she'd fled, wherever she sought refuge, her family had bombarded her with mobile phone calls. They used every trick they could think of to get her to come back.

'Your mum's got cancer . . .'

'Your uncle's died . . .'

'Your grandma's dying and she's asking for you . . .'

Every last iota of emotional blackmail was brought to bear and I knew that, despite all she'd been through, Usha longed to give in to it.

'I can't help it,' she whispered. 'I really miss my mum.' It's for women like Usha that I am determined to make this network happen. Friendship can never truly replace family but it helps, I know that. I was once where Usha is.

CHAPTER 35

One cold grey morning towards the end of 2005 I found myself on a train trundling north towards Dundee University. I was going to address the law faculty on the subject of forced marriage and honour-based violence. I'd been invited to do so by Jim Haslam, professor in the university's school of accountancy, business and finance. He had read about Karma Nirvana in one of the papers and it touched a chord. He wanted to help me spread the word.

· The lecture theatre was packed that morning. There was the expected crop of fresh-faced students, eager with their A4 note-pads. But Jim had opened the invitation out beyond the university and there were a score or more of adults; social workers and health professionals, a couple of men from the police.

I could give this talk in my sleep if I wanted to, the material is so much part of me. But it never fails to move me because the facts are so appalling. Did you know that the suicide rate among young Asian women in Britain is three times the national average? I believe that many of them, like Robina, are driven to kill themselves; it's just a cleaner, more convenient form of murder. I will never take for granted the suffering that so many of them have to bear.

I fill my talks with stories of women like Shazia. She has moved on from refuge provision now; she's got a boyfriend and a job. Hers is a success story, although she still grieves for her family with whom she's had no contact since the day she left home. I often talk about Chandi, an eighteen-year-old girl I met when the Forced Marriage Unit brought her back to Britain. When Chandi's family said she and her sixteen-year-old sister were going on holiday to Pakistan, Chandi took the precaution of telling a friend. 'Here's where I'm going. If I'm not back in a month tell the police,' is what she said.

With that quick conversation, Chandi saved herself. She had been in Pakistan ten weeks when representatives of the British Embassy in Islamabad arrived in the village to which Chandi had been taken and – amidst scenes of hysterical anger – removed her from her new in-laws' house. In all the chaos, her younger sister, already traumatized by her sudden move from a north London suburb to a remote rural village and the unwanted attentions of the man she had been forced to marry, panicked and refused to leave, much to Chandi's distress. 'Mira got seven As in her GCSEs, Jas, but she doesn't know that,' Chandi told me. 'She's stuck there sweeping the cement floor of her mother-in-law's house.'

When I finished talking that morning at Dundee University you could have heard a pin drop. Looking up and down the rows of faces they looked genuinely shocked. Then hands started going up and the questions started. 'Why isn't forced marriage a criminal offence?' 'What happens to the women when they get brought back?' 'What can we do to help?' I got the impression that a lot of them, particularly the adults who'd come in from outside, were appalled by the fact they'd been in ignorance about these things happening in Britain. Jim had set aside half an hour for questions but it wasn't nearly enough; they were so thirsty for information that I could have talked all afternoon.

Eventually, when I stepped onto the train that was going to take me back to Derby, it was packed, standing room only. Wedged up against one another in the aisle, it was easier to talk than not, and I found myself telling the man I stood next to what I'd been doing in Dundee. He had never heard of forced marriage or honour killings and, as I was explaining, I watched the colour drain from the face of the elderly man standing next to him; he went deathly white.

I apologized. 'I'm sorry if I've upset or offended you. I know it sounds shocking but, believe me, it does happen.'

'I know,' he said. He was looking at me so intently I was almost scared. 'One of my chemistry students, a brilliant Asian girl . . . She came from Bradford but she was studying where I used to teach, at Glasgow University . . . It was years ago. She was doing a Ph.D. I did a lot of work with her and, as the months went by, she started to confide in me.'

He was craning towards me, oblivious to the press of people round us. 'She told me that her parents had arranged a marriage for her, but she didn't want to see it through. She told me they had a lot of arguments but I thought, "So what?" Most students argue with their parents. Even when she said her family was going to kill her because she wouldn't marry the man they'd chosen I didn't take it seriously. I couldn't believe that would happen. All I said was, "If you're really worried you should go to the police."'

Guilt stained his face, but he looked me straight in the eye as he said, 'I did nothing to help her and a week later she was dead.'

He read about it in the newspapers, a far-fetched story even by Asian standards. One night at 3 a.m. the girl went downstairs to the family garage to change the tyre on her car. Apparently she did not use the jack correctly and it collapsed, causing the car to fall and crush her head.

It was reported as a tragedy, an accidental death.

UNWELCOME SETTLERS

Robert J. Horton

CHIVERS

> British Library Cataloguing in Publication Data available

This Large Print edition published by BBC Audiobooks Ltd, Bath, 2009.
Published by arrangement with Golden West Literary Agency.

U.K. Hardcover ISBN 978 1 408 43260 0
U.K. Softcover ISBN 978 1 408 43261 7

Printed and bound in Great Britain by CPI Antony Rowe, Chippenham
and Eastbourne

CONTENTS

CHAPTER I

INTO THE SUNSET

The new-born town of Angel glowed like a splash of gold upon the gray surface of the plain, as its clusters of rough, unpainted buildings and drab-colored tents caught the reflection of the sunset in the high skies above the mountains toward the west.

A streamer of smoke trailed against the southern skyline as a train raced northward across the prairies. It pulled up at the bright new station, with its cinder-bedded platform, and disgorged its passengers with a semblance of the haste and excitement which marked all the activities of the homestead rush.

'New West Hotel?' bawled an angular individual from Missouri, who had been one of the first to answer to the call of 'free land.'

'New West Hotel! Free rig.'

Neil Sterret and his wife, Dora, after gazing about at the crudely animated scene for a few seconds, allowed themselves to be escorted to the conveyance which the hotel runner indicated. Other new arrivals crowded in with them, an overflow of baggage was pushed in between their feet, the runner swung up onto the rear step, and they went rattling away over the uneven dirt roads which formed the streets of the town.

1

At the hotel, which was a two-story wooden building, unpainted and uncarpeted, Neil wrote his name and his wife's on two lines of the bulky register.

'Two rooms,' he said to the man behind the desk, 'for my sister and me.'

The hotel runner, now officiating in the capacity of a bellboy, helped them upstairs with their hand luggage. When he had left the suitcases and grips in their rooms and departed, the girl turned to the man and spoke.

'Why did you say "sister," Neil? Now that we are here they are certain to learn sooner or later that we are married.'

Neil Sterret dropped into a chair and made a gesture that expressed his disgust. 'Hasn't it occurred to you that these people out here in this primitive country would think it strange that a man and his wife should require two rooms? It's the first place we've been where we had to register our names since we left Illinois. The brother-and-sister stuff went without question on the train.' He snorted. 'Dora, when is this foolishness going to end?'

'Now, Neil, don't let's start that argument all over again,' replied the girl, her face flushed.

'Well, it is foolishness, now that we're here,' retorted the man heatedly. 'What did you marry me for if—'

'For the last time, Neil, I'm going to tell you

2

that I married you because I promised your mother I would, two years ago. You were different then.'

'You never loved me, to begin with,' complained the husband bitterly.

'Yes, I did,' declared Dora, 'and I would love you just as much now if you were the same, but in the two years since your mother died you've changed. You know it. Oh, Neil,' she continued, with a sob in her voice, 'if you will only make a man of yourself out here I will love you just as much again. When you insisted that I marry you and come out here to the West to your uncle's ranch, where you could make a new start and become a real man, I consented because I wanted you to make good because I wanted you for my husband if you did make good. Doesn't that show that I cared, and that I'm ready to care again?'

'Don't cry,' said Sterret petulantly. 'This is a man's country out here, and I'll fit in.'

'I hope so,' said the girl softly.

The rays of the setting sun, filtering in through the window, gave her hair a rich, golden hue as she removed her hat.

Neil Sterret could not repress an exclamation of admiration as he noted the trim figure of the girl, her flushed cheeks, the glow in her gray eyes under long lashes, the rounded contour of her arms as she raised her hands to put in place stray wisps of hair.

His dark, handsome face, marked with early

signs of dissipation, flushed. 'But a year, Dora, is a long time,' he pleaded.

'It won't seem long when we have a goal to strive for,' she replied cheerfully, 'and if you make good your promise in a year, we can be really and truly married for a long time.'

'What'll Uncle Brodick think?' he countered, frowning.

'Just what we tell him, Neil, and we'll tell him all that he doesn't know now. We'll tell him how your mother looked after me when my parents died, how we fell in love with each other, how your mother wanted us to marry, and how I promised her I would marry you; how you—you—made a few mistakes back in Illinois; how I agreed to your plan to wed and come out West with you, with the understanding that ours was to be a—a formal marriage for a year while you made yourself over out here in this new and splendid environment. Oh, he'll help us, Neil; he'll help you to make good!'

'Well, I'll leave you to do the telling of it, since you made the bargain,' said Neil.

'Look!' exclaimed the girl, pointing to the red banners in the sky above the far-flung range of mountains. 'It's just as if we'd come right into a sunset, Neil. Isn't it beautiful? No, not beautiful—magnificent, majestic! Neil, back there where we came from we never dreamed there was a country like this. I can feel the change in my very blood; it's tingling

4

already. Don't you sense something like an inspiration?'

'I suppose so,' he said, himself impressed with the mighty grandeur of the scene. 'Well, let's go down to supper.'

Seated at a long table with many others, they ate heartily. There were three long tables in the room, and from one of these tables a large, red-faced man watched them closely during the meal. He followed them out and indicated them with a motion of his thumb to the clerk as they passed into the narrow hallway leading to the stairs. The clerk nodded, and the large man turned on his heel and walked away.

Neil Sterret saw his wife to her room. 'I'm going out to look the town over and try to find out if uncle's man is here for us,' he said casually.

'You won't get into trouble, Neil? You know, things must be very different out here, and—'

'I can take care of myself,' he answered crisply. 'Go to bed when you're ready. I'll tap on your door to let you know I'm back when I go to my room.'

He stood in her doorway for a time surveying her as she lit the lamp upon the table. He seemed for a moment on the point of advancing across the threshold; then he turned suddenly and stamped down the stairs.

5

CHAPTER II

A NEW CODE

Angel's main street was but dimly lighted, and such illumination as it had came from the stars which dotted the high arch of the heavens overhead. But from the buildings on either side, most of them one-story, hastily-put-together affairs with false fronts, came a faded radiance from kerosene lamps and the sounds of revelry.

Scores of horses stood at the hitching rails. Some were tied and others stood with drooping heads, the bridle reins dangling free at their feet. The pound of hoofs echoed among sounds of screeching phonographs, tinkling glasses, laughter, shouts, jingling spurs, and the occasional bark of a dog.

Something in the very air dry, exhilarating, carrying the tang of earth and grass sensed a new country in the making.

Neil Sterret felt its spell, and his wild blood thrilled to a new sensation. He noted the attire of the men. Most of them wore khaki trousers and shirts. Others appeared in chaps and spurs, with bandanna handkerchiefs about their necks, knotted behind and hanging low in front under the opened bosoms of their shirts. These, too, were armed. Butts of big, black guns protruded from holsters slung low on thighs.

It was with great interest that Neil saw that these men were given plenty of room as they swaggered about with their queer, swaying gait; they seemed to spurn men of less picturesque garb. But the thing that interested him most, perhaps, were the hats these men wore—broad of brim, with a high crown almost invariably dented or pinched in. These big hats seemed a symbol of something which Neil wanted to become—a real Westerner.

He stepped into a store and bought himself such a hat. He was surprised that the huge, gray headgear should feel so easy and light on his head.

'Throw that other thing away,' he instructed the storekeeper with a swagger, pointing to the small, neat, brown fedora which he had worn lately.

Once again he went out into the cool, scented spring night. He walked, this time, to the edge of the town, where he could see the gray reaches of prairie stretching out under a high-hung canopy of stars, to where the black shadow of Angel Butte and the serrated outlines of the higher mountains traced a jagged pattern against the night sky.

He breathed deeply. 'Lord, it is a man's country!' he said aloud.

When he returned to the center of town he entered a building whence issued a strange medley of distorted sound. He paused, breathless at the scene.

It was a long, narrow room. Swinging lamps hung from the rough-board ceiling, and other lamps flared from in front of reflectors attached to the walls. On the right side of the room ranged a bar, with glasses and mirrors behind, and, tilted above, so that it was almost over the heads of those who stood drinking their soda pop and 'one-half,' was a highly colored lithograph of Custer's last fight.

On the left side were arranged a number of tables, about which scores of men were grouped. In the rear was a lunch counter. The air was hazy with tobacco smoke, and the place echoed to the tinkle of glassware, the rattle of money and chips, the squeaking of an ancient music box, and the hoarse laughter and talk and curses of many men.

Neil hesitated a second, walked to the bar, and took a drink. Next he turned his attention to the tables. His blood leaped when he saw that men were buying chips and gambling them in a strange game. It was the famous 'black jack,' or 'twenty-one,' of the West.

Neil saw the dealer shuffle the cards, deal one around the table to each man, one to himself, and repeat the performance. The dealer then looked at his own two cards.

'I'm hittin', boys,' he said.

Immediately the various players began to call for cards.

'Hit it!' cried one. 'Too many.'

The dealer took this man's cards, placed them face up under the balance of the pack he held in his left hand, and raked in the chips the man had wagered.

The next man scraped the table with his two cards, which evidently was a signal that he wished to draw, for the dealer instantly dealt him a card.

'That's good,' said the player, and placed his chips upon his cards.

So it continued around the table, some players drawing cards and 'staying,' others drawing cards and 'breaking' and losing their bets, some drawing no cards at all but standing pat on the original two.

Then the dealer began looking at the various hands, taking up all the cards, paying some bets, taking in others, and announcing a stand-off in some cases, in which event he did not take the bet or pay it.

Last of all he exposed his own hand two face cards.

'Twenty,' he announced, and began a new deal.

Neil saw men expose hands consisting of an ace and a face card or a ten. 'Twenty-one,' the dealer would announce. 'That's the name of the game.' And men exposing such a hand would assume the deal, placing their chips in the center of the table to be sized up by the man running the game; for the 'house' was in

9

on every deal on a fifty-fifty basis.

Gradually Neil comprehended that the object of the game was to get twenty-one or as near to it as possible without getting more than that exact count. He learned that the aces counted eleven, the face cards and ten-spots ten each, and the other cards according to their figures. A face card and seven counted as seventeen. He noticed that the players seldom drew to this count or above it, for they seemed to feel that the chances of getting a four-spot or less were greatly against them. He noticed, too, that when the dealer turned up a twenty-one count on the first two cards he took all bets without permitting any one to draw except, of course, another twenty-one, which would be a stand-off. But, most important of all, he noted that the best chances for winning lay with the dealer.

As he became more familiar with the play, he felt the fever for gambling burning in his veins. Gambling had been one of his faults in the two tragic years which lay behind him. He had promised Dora never to gamble again; it had virtually been one of the principal provisions of their pact. He wiped huge drops of perspiration from his brow and went to the bar frequently for another drink forgetting his promise not to touch liquor, too.

When he returned from one of these trips for refreshment he found vacant a seat behind which he had been standing. After hesitating a brief interval he dropped into it, opened his wallet, and flung a twenty-dollar note to the dealer. 'All blues,' he ordered.

The man in the slot pushed over eight blue chips Neil started. He hadn't watched the buying in of chips closely and had assumed the blue ones were worth a dollar each. He felt he couldn't very well explain, and so he wagered a blue chip as nonchalantly as possible under the circumstances. If he lost them all he could quit. He had had exactly one hundred and ten dollars in his wallet after paying the expenses of the trip and buying the hat.

He lost the first blue chip and then another. He doubled and lost again. He bet the remaining four chips to get even, and the dealer raked in all bets on a black jack-twenty-one.

'How many?' asked the man in the slot cheerfully. The dealer was holding up the deal waiting upon him.

'Twenty again,' said Neil, striving to smile as if losing money were nothing to him.

On the last blue chip of the second stack he won the deal with a natural twenty-one hand. But he couldn't take the deal and be prepared to offstand the bets with five dollars in chips which he now had on the table. Nor would the five which the house man would put in with him be enough. Yet the deal offered what was apparently an excellent chance to win.

Neil drew out his wallet and tossed the

remainder of his capital to the center of the table. 'You handle the cards,' he said to the man in the slot, who had done so several times for players.

The deal broke even on the first round of the cards. Neil saw with elation—although not without a subtle sense of misgiving—that the players were making sizable bets. Some wagered the limit of twenty dollars in checks on the second deal. The eighteen count which turned up for the bank on this deal was not sufficient to win all the bets.

'Are you going all the way?' the man in the slot asked Neil.

'Sure,' replied Neil, thinking the man meant to ask if he would go for all he had put in the center.

On the third deal a player who had wagered twenty dollars turned a black jack and won immediately on his count of twenty-one. Only two players drew cards, and these announced that they were good. The man dealing turned up a thirteen count. 'Come on, eight-spot,' he said in coaxing tones, as he turned a card from the top of the pack. A face card fell.

'That breaks us,' said the dealer. 'Hard luck, but it goes that way sometimes; that's what makes the game. Let's see—we haven't enough chips.'

He sized up to all bets around the table. 'You owe forty dollars for your half of the overs,' he announced to Neil.

12

Neil paled. 'But—but all the money I had on me was in the center,' he explained lamely.

'What's that?' snappily asked the man in the slot. His dark face clouded and his eyes burned. 'Didn't you say you'd go all the way? There wasn't enough checks in the center to meet all these bets—you saw that, didn't you?'

'I—I didn't understand what you meant,' faltered Neil, the perspiration breaking out upon his forehead anew. 'I thought you meant would I—I go for what I had in the center.'

'Now, don't come any of that on me,' continued the dealer. 'Cough up!'

'Just got in with an Eastern bank roll an' wants to make us believe he's broke,' jeered a man of tanned visage who wore a rattlesnake-skin band about his wide-brimmed hat and leather cuffs adorned with silver ornaments. 'Well, we got a different code out here, stranger. Pay up like a man!'

'But I tell you I haven't any more money,' blurted Neil, his face red.

'I'll frisk you,' shouted the dealer, starting around the table as the other players leaped back out of the way, 'an' if you're broke I'll take it out of your tenderfoot hide, you cheap homesteader.'

'Ratty, you shut up an' sit down!' The words came in cool, even tones from behind Neil's chair.

Neil looked up to see a large, red-faced man standing behind him, looking grimly at the dealer, who had halted suddenly.

'You ain't meanin' to say you'd let him get away with a thing like that, are you, Lentu?' demanded the dealer of the red-faced man.

'Didn't he just tell you he didn't understand what you meant?' demanded Lentu coolly. 'Don't you suppose there's any one comes into this country who don't understand blackjack? You sit down, Ratty, and do just what you would have done if he had said he wasn't going all the way. Pay the overs out of the bank.'

Ratty slunk back to his place in the slot, trembling with rage.

Neil rose, but his movement was arrested by the sound of another voice, cool and drawling.

'Now, Lent, just because Ratty is goin' to let this cheap skate get away with his four-flush play is not sayin' I'm agreeable.' It was the man with the ornamented cuffs—plainly a man of the ranges, for his black, hairy chaps showed as he knocked back his chair and gained his feet.

Neil glimpsed a lightning movement of Lentu's arm at his side; then he gasped. In the flash of an eye his champion had drawn a gun. Held at the hip, its long, black-blue barrel was aimed directly at the heart of the man who had espoused the dealer's cause.

'Out, Ben, out!' said Lentu meaningly, meeting the other's hard gaze unflinchingly. 'You're not in the know in this play.'

For some moments the two eyed each other

14

steadily. Then the cow-puncher sat down. 'All right, Lentu, if that's the way it is,' he said simply, and turned his attention again to the table as the other players resumed their chairs.

Lentu put up his gun. 'Come along,' he said to Neil, and the two left the place.

In the clear, fresh air Neil breathed deeply. This, then, was the West. All the experiences he had had in the past—thrilling as some of them had seemed—were as nothing compared to what he had just gone through. Gun play! Such speed!

From within he heard the sneering, high-pitched voice of Ratty shouting: 'A man's hat don't make a man out of a boob.'

In that instant there was born in Neil's heart an innate, consuming hatred of the dealer.

CHAPTER III

SEEDS OF TRAGEDY

The man, Lentu, led Neil to a back room in the rear of the New West Hotel bar.

'Bring up a bottle,' he instructed the bartender, with a wink, as they passed through to the rear room.

While they were waiting for the order to be executed Lentu regarded Neil thoughtfully. When they had been served and were again alone Lentu spoke:

'Name's Sterret, ain't it?'

Neil nodded wonderingly.

'Old Amos Brodick's nephew from Illinois?'

'Yes,' replied Neil readily. 'Are you the man sent by my uncle to take us out to the ranch in the morning?' He had forgotten to make inquiries concerning their escort.

'No; my name's Lentu,' explained the other. 'But I heard in a sort of roundabout way that you was coming out, heard your name, saw you come in, checked up on the register, and just happened into the Prairie Flower saloon when your trouble started. I'm ready to believe what you said about not understanding what the dealer meant an' all that. Those fellers are layin' for the homesteaders; but you're not a homesteader, of course.'

'No, I'm not,' affirmed Neil.

'There're a whole lot of things you've got to learn about this country,' said Lentu, pouring two more drinks from the bottle and then setting it well aside.

'Yes, yes,' agreed Neil eagerly. 'I don't know why you have befriended me, but but I wish I could ask you to teach me to handle a gun like yourself.'

Lentu smiled. It was not his part at that time to tell the young man before him that skill of the kind he had exhibited is not easily taught or acquired, that gunmen were more often born than made, and that the practice which

16

perfected them was the natural outgrowth of an early inclination and aptitude.

'I'll do what I can,' said Lentil seriously. 'But I want to tell you something of conditions hereabouts. Maybe it will all be for your own good. I hope you think I'm in earnest when I say I'm interested in you.'

'I can see that by the way you acted tonight,' said Neil quickly.

Again Lentu smiled; but Neil was toying with his glass and thinking of Ratty, the dealer, and did not see the grim, baffling, designing quality of that smile.

'Sterret,' said Lentu earnestly, 'this has always been a cattle country. Of late we've had some sheep, but they came in because the homesteaders began to crowd the range. Sheep can graze on less land than cattle—of course, you know that.'

Neil did not know it, or had not known it until then, but he inclined his head as if the knowledge had always been his.

'Well, now,' continued Lentu, choosing his words carefully and striving to impress his listener as much as possible by the earnestness of his tone, 'we could stand a few homesteaders. They gathered in little groups for their own protection'—he paused long enough to wink significantly—'and as long as that was the case we could take care of them easily. But now the government has set up a yell about free land, and the poor fools think

17

all they've got to do is come out here and file, and a farm will sprout.

'Sterret, listen to me.' He was in deadly earnest now, and his eyes narrowed as he leaned on the table toward the younger man. 'This isn't a farming country. Here and there in the river bottoms we've raised some oats; but on this open range, out on the flat lands away from water, on the benches? Never!' He struck the table with his fist, and Neil reached forward to steady the lamp.

'These homesteaders,' Lentu went on, 'inexperienced, land crazy, deluded, are flocking in here to do something that never has been done before—to take away the range that's rightfully ours, to starve our stock and make paupers of us. Do you think that's right, Sterret?'

Neil looked into the grim face before him, into the cool, gray eyes that bored into his own. 'I—I don't know much about it,' he confessed.

'If a man walked in here, poked a gun in your face, took your watch, and made away with it, would you think it was right?' demanded Lentu.

'Of course not,' said Neil hotly. 'That would be stealing.'

Lentu leaned back. He drew tobacco and papers from his shirt pocket and proceeded to roll a cigarette. 'That's what they're doing to us,' he said quietly. 'They're stealing our range, using the land act as a gun, an' taking the grass away from our cattle. The country has to have cattle, Sterret.'

Neil nodded. That fact was indisputable.

'And there are plenty of farming countries where it rains once in a while,' Lentu pointed out. 'You come from one.'

Again Neil nodded. There was logic in what this man said.

Lentu put a light to his cigarette. 'Then why,' he continued, 'should these harebrained homesteaders come out here to steal our range and scatter or kill our herds when there is plenty of farming land elsewhere, and this is a natural stock country?'

Neil could only ponder the question; he could think of no answer. 'I don't know,' he said finally.

'And nobody else does,' declared Lentu. 'Listen, Sterret. Your uncle, Amos Brodick, is a cattleman. He always has been a cattleman. The time has come for the cattlemen in the Angel Butte district to stick together. Don't you think he should stick?'

'Why certainly,' replied Neil instantly. 'He'll stick. Who said he wouldn't stick?'

Lentu merely waved a hand deprecatingly and rose. 'I was just acquainting you with the way things stand out here. Thought I'd tell you right off how we are fixed. You're going up to the Brodick ranch and—you'll be a cattleman yourself. We have to understand each other.'

Neil felt flattered as he followed Lentu out.

'You better go to your room,' advised Lentu. 'It's late, anyway, and you ain't very well acquainted out here yet. I'll see you again. Good night.'

It was not until Neil had reached the top of the stairs that he recollected he had forgotten to ask Lentu where his ranch was or whom he represented.

He knocked lightly on the door of Dora's room. 'You awake?'

'Yes, I was worried about you,' replied the girl. 'Where have you been?'

'Just looking the town over,' he answered.

'Is your uncle or his man here to take us to the ranch in the morning?'

'No. I looked everywhere but couldn't find any one; but some one will be here in the morning,' he said.

'Neil, are you sure?'

'Yes, there was a man who knows, who said they would. Don't worry.'

'Good night, Neil.'

For a minute he was silent, and then: 'Good night, Dora.'

He went to his room, closed and locked the door, and lit the lamp. He laid the new hat on the table, and for a long time sat looking at it, a queer, bright look in his eyes.

'I guess this is the country I've been looking for,' he muttered finally.

And long into the night, to the early hours

of the morning, he tossed and turned in his bed and stared for extended intervals out of the window at the stars and the velvet black shadows of Angel Butte and the mountains beyond.

In the hotel bar below, Lentu and the cow-puncher Ben were talking.

'So that was who he was,' Ben was saying. 'An' did you talk some sense into him or did he have some to start with?'

'Well, he's got the makings now, anyway,' Lentu said, grinning. 'Come on, I've got to go down and square myself with Ratty, or he'll think I'm sidin' with the land grubbers.'

'Ratty was plumb puzzled,' declared Ben as the two started for the Prairie Flower saloon. 'An' you had me goin' for a spell. Amos Brodick's nephew. Lent, you've got more sense than the hull outfit put together!'

'It ain't sense,' said Lentu grimly. 'It's precaution.'

CHAPTER IV

SECTION TWENTY-TWO

Neil and Dora had just finished breakfast in the morning when they were approached by a tall, blond young fellow who swung his dusty, wide-brimmed hat behind him as he inquired:

'Is this Mr. Sterret?'

'That's me,' said Neil.

'Yore uncle sent me to get you and take you out to the ranch,' said the man. 'I'm Walt Frost, one of yore uncle's hands.'

'This is my wife,' said Neil, introducing Dora.

Walt Frost bowed. 'Glad to meet you, ma'am. Are you ready to go? I've got the buckboard, an' the horses is rested up; I've been in since five o'clock.'

'How is Uncle Brodick?' asked Dora.

'Oh, I plumb went an' forgot to tell you that yore uncle said he was sorry he couldn't get down to meet you, but, you see, we're puttin' the cattle out on the forest range, an' he reckons to keep an' eye on the proceedings. Yore uncle is well, ma'am.'

'I guess we're ready to start,' said Neil. 'You might help me down with the grips.'

'Shore I will. You bet,' agreed Walt, and he followed Neil upstairs.

When they had carried the baggage to the narrow platform in front of the hotel Walt announced that he would go for the team and asked them to wait a short time.

'Isn't he a nice fellow?' said Dora as they stood on the platform beside their baggage. 'Did you notice his laughing blue eyes and how brown his face and hands were—the color of bronze from the sun? Neil, isn't the sun bright out here?'

Neil was about to reply when the hotel clerk touched him lightly on the arm. 'About your bill, Mr. Sterret. I thought perhaps you had forgotten,' he said politely. 'Or perhaps you wish it charged to your uncle's account? All his men stop here when in town.'

Neil had grown cold when he heard the first words and remembered that his funds had been exhausted the night before, but he brightened when he heard the clerk's final statement.

'Just put it on uncle's account,' he said lightly.

'That's all right, Mr. Sterret. I shouldn't have asked. Was everything satisfactory?'

'No complaint to make,' said Neil.

As the clerk stepped back into the hotel Dora spoke. 'Oh, Neil, why don't you just pay the bill and not bother uncle about it? I'm sure he'd be better pleased if he knew we hadn't asked any—any favors in getting to the ranch.'

'Never mind,' said Neil. 'We haven't any too much money, and I'm going to work for uncle, am I not?'

'Yes—only I thought—'

'He'll never see it on the bill, anyway,' Neil broke in. 'They don't look at bills out here; they just pay 'em.' He remembered what the cow-puncher in the blackjack game of the night before had said. 'Uncle would want us to charge it, anyway.'

Dora was silent, thinking.

23

In another minute Walt Frost drove up in the buckboard, and the hotel runner came hurrying out to help them load their baggage and wish them 'good luck' as they sped away behind two splendid bays.

Across the railroad track, past the livery stable and feed corrals and numbers of small shacks and tents, they made their way and eventually emerged upon the prairie which sloped gradually upward in a long acclivity to the shoulders of Angel Butte.

Dora could not repress an exclamation of ecstasy, and Neil, sitting beside her on the rear seat of the buckboard, felt an indescribable thrill as the panorama of a far-flung, wild, lonely, colorful expanse of plain and rolling hills and mountains was unfolded before their eyes.

The vast reaches of level ground, golden under the sun, were splashed with the blooms of prairie cactus; eastward and northward the great, undulating stretches of virgin prairie reached to the blue rim of the horizon; in the northwest the dim, serrated outlines of the mountains hung against the sky and ranged in a hundred-mile semicircle around to the southeast, surmounted at intervals by white peaks, and in the western foreground, toward which they were heading, the pine-clothed sides of Angel Butte sloped down to the grassy flatlands.

'Neil, Neil, did you ever think the world

24

could look so big?' exclaimed Dora, somewhat overawed by the magnificence of the scene.

'It ain't so big but what it's beginning to be crowded, ma'am,' said Walt over his shoulder.

Neil remembered the talk of Lentu the night before. 'There are strange things happening here, Dora,' he said seriously.

'Strange? What do you mean, Neil?'

'I hardly know myself,' answered Neil truthfully.

He ignored her further questions as they drove over the smooth prairie road, and soon she forgot to be inquisitive as the grandeur of the view again awoke within her something akin to inspiration and awe.

As the sun ascended in the illimitable blue arch of the heavens they rounded the north shoulder of Angel Butte and began a long ascent.

Suddenly, from around a bend above, two horsemen came into view, riding furiously. Walt gave vent to a startled exclamation and pointed excitedly. Almost immediately another rider could be seen, urging his mount at breakneck speed in pursuit of the pair ahead. White puffs of smoke broke from in front of the third horseman.

Walt pulled up the team just as the flying pair reached the buckboard. Before there was time for explanations or questioning the third rider reached them.

Neil recognized Lentu. He waved to him,

but Lentu paid no attention to them. Instead he addressed himself to the two who had halted when they had come up to the team. 'What were you doing up on the north half of twenty-two?' he demanded crisply.

'The north half of that section isn't filed on, is it?' asked one of the men.

'If you mean that it's still open on the maps I reckon you're right,' replied Lentu, holding his gun in view.

'Well—we—we supposed if it was still open on the maps, it was opened to filing,' explained the first man, visibly nervous.

Lentu urged his horse close beside the speaker's. He looked the man square in the eye; fixed him with a narrowed, dangerous gaze. 'It's open on the maps and open to filin', but it's across the line,' he said steadily.

'Line? What line?'

'Suppose you ask 'em down at Angel,' replied Lentu. 'An' when you find out what I mean maybe you'll be more careful in the matter of judgment.' He tapped the horn of his saddle with the barrel of his gun. 'Understand,' he continued in the same cool, ominous voice, 'it's open on the maps, an' it's open to filing, only—it's across the line. So long.'

The two men, evidently from some other part of the country, swung their horses about, after a few seconds of indecision, and rode away.

26

Lentu turned to the occupants of the buckboard.

'Howdy, Walt! Hello there, Sterret!' he greeted. Walter merely nodded curtly. Sterret returned the greeting verbally and, after Lentu had replied with a formal remark about the weather, introduced Dora.

'A pleasure, Mrs. Sterret,' said Lentu, swinging low his hat. 'An' now, if you folks don't mind my breaking trail for you, I'll be back on my way.'

He whirled his horse and was gone in a cloud of dust.

'You know him?' asked Walt of Neil before he started the horses.

'Met him last night,' answered Neil. 'Say, Walt, who is he?'

'That's Lentu,' said Walt quietly.

'I know his name; but what about him?'

'He's foreman for the Double S.'

Dora, who had crouched against Neil at sight of the gun, now recovered herself. 'But why was he chasing those men and—and firing at them?' she asked. 'And what did he mean by the north half of twenty-two?'

'We'll be at the ranch in an hour,' was Walt's cryptic reply.

CHAPTER V

AMOS BRODICK

Shortly after noon they crossed the west shoulder of Angel Butte, where it was joined by a spur from the mountains, and looked down into a beautiful valley between pine-clothed hills, through which wound a stream of clear water called Wild Horse Creek.

Walt pointed with his whip to the lower end of the valley, south of the butte, where a set of substantial ranch buildings showed the center of tilled fields looking like green squares of velvet with silver bands, where the irrigation ditches gleamed in the bright sun-light of midday.

'The ranch,' he said proudly; 'the 3-X-Z.'

On the lower slopes of the hills cattle were feeding, and a band of horses was grazing along the creek bottom upstream from the ranch. South and west the green ranges rose in long steps, studded with virgin stands of pine and fir, to the white peaks which reared against the sky.

Again Dora and Neil stared in wonder, silenced by the glory and stupendous beauty of the scene. It was as if they had stepped from the plain into the mountains. And then the panorama was shut off as they drove down into

28

a wide cañon, its sides covered with firs, and began the descent to Wild Horse Creek.

Dora gasped and squealed with fright as the buck-board rattled along the narrow road with less than a foot to spare between the edge of the road and the precipitous side of the cañon.

Soon, however, they came out upon a better road in Wild Horse Valley and drove swiftly down along the stream. Walt stopped the team, got out with a large drinking cup, and handed them each a drink of the clear, cold water.

'It's the best water I ever drank!' said Dora, asking for more.

'Yes, it's tolerably fair water, ma'am,' agreed Walt. 'This creek is fed by mountain springs. But wait until you drink some of the spring water at the ranch. Yore uncle had it piped from some springs about a mile up the creek on the south side, an' it's supposed to be the best water hereabouts.'

Half a mile farther they reached the upper end of the ranch and then rode between green fields and pastures. At last they turned in between two high gateposts, while a boy held the gate open lest it swing back, and drove up to the vine-covered side porch of the ranch house.

A woman, Amos Brodick's capable housekeeper, welcomed them.

'Mr. and Mrs. Sterret!' she exclaimed, visibly excited and delighted. 'So you're here 'way back from Illinoy. I declare you must be tired. I'm Mrs. French, your uncle's housekeeper. Come right in. Louis, Louis! Come here and help with their things. That's my boy,' she explained as a freckled, brown-haired lad came bashfully forward.

'He's a little backward with strangers,' went on Mrs. French while she led them into the first room off the porch, which proved to be the dining room. 'Expect you'll want to tidy up a bit. Right this way, Mrs. Sterret, dear. Louis, you show Mr. Sterret where to wash. I declare you must be starved. Now just fix yourself up a bit, Mrs. Sterret, and I'll have your dinner ready in a jiffy.'

Ten minutes later they sat down to a dinner of roast beef, mashed potatoes, thick gravy, pickles, creamed corn, jellies, cold tomato sauce, biscuits, honey, raisin pie and jelly tarts—all served with pitchers of rich milk and cups of steaming coffee.

'Your uncle is up the creek putting the beef herd on the forest reserve range,' said Mrs. French, hovering about them as they ate. 'He'll be back for supper, an' he'll sure be glad to see you all. Now don't be back-ward 'bout helping yourselves; we eat all we want out here and ain't ashamed of it. Dear me, I declare I'm glad to have a woman to talk to on this ranch, Mrs. Sterret.'

'Won't you just call me Dora?' asked the girl, who already had taken a great liking to the housekeeper.

'Well, just listen to that!' blustered Mrs. French, very much delighted. 'Of course I will, dear—Dora it is. I declare I'm glad you are regular folks. I was afraid you might be a little high-toned, coming from the East that a way.'

'Neil, perhaps Mrs. French can tell us why the men were shooting over there when we came up,' said Dora, again remembering the shots and the strange actions of the men they had met.

'Oh, it must be Martin's doings,' said Mrs. French quickly. 'They are trying to stop the homesteaders from locating around the butte. Was it anything to frighten you, dear? I'm so sorry.'

'But is it right for them to shoot at men, Mrs. French?'

'No, deary, it isn't.' Mrs. French looked worried for a second. 'But your uncle will tell you about it, or I will later. And it's nothing for us to worry over.'

'When will Uncle Amos be back?' asked Neil.

'Late this afternoon. He has to help the men. We are short-handed now because it's hard to get men for a cattle ranch.'

'I should think the homesteaders would be looking for jobs,' said Neil.

'Some of them will work, Mr. Sterret, but they're inexperienced. We've only got about twelve men now, not counting the cook.'

'Can't uncle get all the men he wants?' persisted Neil.

Mrs. French made a gesture of helplessness. 'It doesn't seem that way,' she confessed. 'Things are none too good lately.'

'None too good? What do you mean by that?'

'Well, Mr. Sterret, you better wait and talk with your uncle. He can tell you more than I can,' said Mrs. French as she began to clear the table.

Dora offered to help, and Neil went out to look over the ranch. Louis accompanied him and showed him the bunk house where the men slept and kept their belongings, the cook house and men's dining room, adjoining the bunk house; then they went to view the barns and corrals, and Louis took him to the stream behind the hay barn, where they caught a mess of trout.

Just before sundown Amos Brodick and several other men came riding furiously down the valley and swung in to the barns amid a cloud of dust.

Ten minutes later Amos Brodick was greeting his nephew.

'Mighty glad you took it into your head to come out to this country,' he boomed cheerfully in a hearty greeting as he gripped Neil's hand. 'An' now, Neil, where's your wife?'

Dora came out upon the porch when Neil called and offered her hand a bit timidly to the big man who was to play such an important part in their destinies.

'Waal, now, Neil, you sure picked a good looker,' declared Amos. 'That ain't flattery, young lady; we tell people what we think of 'em out here as often as not. Now let's all go in an' get supper. I'm hungry enough to eat ground hog tonight if we didn't have anything else.'

After supper Neil and his uncle sat on the porch, where they could see the high light in the western skies and the white gleam of the limestone cliffs against the dark green of the pine growth on the hills.

Dora, who had been talking with them, had gone into the house and again was busy helping Mrs. French.

'That's a queer story Dora and you have told me,' said Amos Brodick. 'But I guess the little girl has the right ideer. You know, Neil, a man's got to have a woman's respect to be the right sort of husband, an' this is a country which makes men—or starts 'em on the road to making themselves.'

Neil avoided further talk about his and Dora's affairs. 'What's this I hear from Lentu about the trouble the homesteaders are making out here?' he asked.

Amos Brodick frowned. 'It wouldn't be my ideer, exactly, to have you worrying your head about our troubles the first day you get here,' he said. 'But one reason I was glad when you decided to come was because I kinda need the help of some one of my own blood. I'm all alone here, and I ain't always sure who to trust.'

'I understand you are finding it hard to get men,' prompted Neil.

'Yes, and that's a bit strange, too,' said Amos. 'Of course there ain't as many men in this country now who know this business, the cattle business. But the dry-landers, as we call 'em, who are filin' on the land, seem scared to come out Angel Butte way to work. I think Lentu an' his crowd have got 'em buffaloed.'

'What's Lentu got to do with it?'

'Lentu is foreman for Martin, who owns the Double S. Martin and McCabe, of the T-C, and Pierson, of the old Angel Butte Cattle Company's ranch, the A B C, have gotten together with the ideer of fightin' the homesteaders. The Double S, T-C, A B C, and myself own quite a piece of land in here; enough so we can run quite a bunch of cattle, although not as many as up to a year ago.

'This combine, as I call the Angel Butte crowd, aims to keep ranging cattle north and east of the butte by intimidating the men who've filed on land there—by gun play, if necessary. They've made the north half of section twenty-two an outlaw piece by scarin' off people who've come up there to file on it; say that's as far south as locatin' can be done. An' it's wrong, to my notion.'

34

'Aren't you with the combine, Uncle Amos?' asked Neil.

'Not in that way,' replied the older man quickly. 'I ain't aiming to try to fight the government, for that's what it amounts to. We had the free use of this land for grazing, but it never belonged to us. We've grabbed off a chunk as it is. Now, if the government wants to come in and say we're goin' to give away that land, why, it's the government's right. I can make out pretty well by breeding better stock—goin' in for quality more'n quantity—an' the combine can do the same.'

'But won't the combine look at it as if you wasn't sticking by the stock interests?' demanded Neil.

Amos Brodick turned and regarded his nephew in the half light. 'I can see you've been thinking a lot about what Lentu has been telling you,' he said earnestly. 'Now don't go too much by what he says. Your interests are here with me, for now that you're out here I don't mind telling you that I figure on teaching you how to run this ranch and on leaving it to you when I die. Don't think too one-sided, one way or the other; but think fair.'

Two horsemen came riding down the valley road, and one of them turned in at the gate and spurred his horse up the road to the porch.

'Hello there, Swain,' called Amos. 'Get down here a minute; I want you to meet my nephew, Neil Sterret, son of my sister's. He just got in from the East. Neil, this is Swain, my foreman.'

When the two men had shaken hands Amos and Swain spoke about range matters for a few minutes. 'We've been putting the beef herd on forest-reserve range today,' explained Amos to Neil as the foreman vaulted into the saddle to take his horse to the barn.

'By the way,' said Swain after he had mounted. 'I met a hombre riding slow this way leading a pack horse. Stranger hereabouts, I guess. Asked him if he wanted a job, an' he said he couldn't make up his mind.'

'What kind of a lookin' feller?' asked Amos.

'Tall, dark, clean-shaven,' replied Swain. 'Sat his horse like he was used to saddle leather an' had a gun slung handy. Seemed a cheerful sort of cuss with a don't-give-a-darn air about him as if he was plumb sure he could take care of himself. I don't know—there was something in the way he sat, or held his arm, or—Oh, I don't know what, but he looked to me—'

'Swain, what're you gettin' at?' demanded Amos impatiently.

'Well, he impressed me the first crack out of the box as being a gunman, maybe,' explained Swain as he rode away. 'He might likely be down this way,' the foreman called back over his shoulder.

'I'd like to have a look at him,' mused Amos

Brodick as they turned into the house. 'I wonder if it could be anybody I know.'

CHAPTER VI

THE STRANGER

When Neil came down from his room at dawn the following morning he was surprised to find that the others, including Dora, were all up and about. After breakfast Amos Brodick took him out to the barn, where he showed him a rangy sorrel in a box stall.

'That's your horse, Neil,' said Amos, 'an' I guess about the first thing you better do is to get used to a saddle. Walt'll show you some saddles, an' you can pick out the one that suits you best.'

Neil explained that he had done quite a bit of riding on the farm in the East, and his uncle nodded approvingly. 'You'll have to be on a horse a good bit of the time out here,' he told Neil, 'an' the main thing is to get over the soreness soon's you can.'

Dora, too, was given a mount, and that afternoon, when Neil and Walt had ridden up the valley to look after some stock grazing in the bottoms above the ranch, she rode along the trail which led north up a long draw toward the east shoulder of Angel Butte.

Lured on by the beauty which revealed itself in the vistas of pine-rimmed stream and picturesque cliffs, she rode farther than she had intended, and suddenly she realized that she was tired and stiff in the saddle.

She dismounted to rest in a little mountain park near the head of the draw, where the sides of the hills on either hand crowded in against the narrow trickle of stream and trail. She tied her horse to an aspen and reclined against the soft bed of grass and moss. The sides of the draw were thick with chokecherry bushes, while in the open spaces among the timbers higher up grew the low, gray vines of the cedar, or juniper, berries. Wild roses and other mountain flowers were scattered about in profusion, and the breeze was sweet with the scent of blossoms and the resinous tang of the timber.

The peaceful beauty of the scene and the stillness of this region so new and strange to her impressed her with a sense of quiet and repose. With eyes half closed she began to dream of a new life in which Neil would find himself, and happiness would come to them both.

Soon she was dozing, and then she slept, falling a victim to the seductive powers of sun and breeze and the altitude of the hills which so often affect people unaccustomed to them in this combination.

She was awakened by the pound of hoofs

and opened her eyes with a startled cry to see Neil dismounting before her.

'They told me you'd come up this way, and I followed you, thinking you might get lost,' he explained as he threw the reins over his horse's head with a motion he already had learned.

'I rode farther than I intended and got off to rest,' said Dora sheepishly, as she fixed her hair and rose to her feet.

Neil stepped toward her. 'Dora, you look positively adorable,' he said in unsullied admiration. 'You look sweet enough to kiss.'

She drew back from him. 'Now you're forgetting your promise,' she reminded him.

'But, Dora, can't a man praise his wife?' he demanded.

'I suppose so,' she said doubtfully, her face flushed. 'But is that all you mean, Neil—just praise?'

'No, it isn't,' he replied earnestly and truthfully. 'Dora, we can't go on this way for a whole year. I realized it today. I need you to help me make good. And, as it is now, people will wonder; they will laugh at us behind our backs. Didn't you see the queer look on Uncle Amos' face last night when we were talking about how how it was we came out here? Dora, I never could stand being ridiculed.'

'Neil, no one who knows will ridicule us, and they will have all the more friendly interest in you. Why, Mrs. French said it would prove the best thing in the world for you—'

'Oh, hang Mrs. French!' shouted Neil. 'So you've been telling her everything, and soon the whole ranch will know.'

'But I had to tell Mrs. French, Neil. And suppose the whole ranch does know—'

'I tell you I can't stand it,' he interrupted. 'It's all foolishness. And you know it's all different in this country; a man's wife is his wife out here!'

'Let's go back,' said Dora hurriedly, starting for her horse.

'Not until I've kissed you and had a better understanding about things,' he exclaimed, leaping to her side.

'Neil!' She screamed as he seized her in his arms.

When he kissed her she screamed again and struggled to release herself.

From the slope behind them came the rattle of falling rocks and gravel; then a cool, ominous, drawling voice:

'Turn that girl loose!'

Neil released his hold and whirled to confront a tall, dark man who wore a gun low on his right thigh.

Dora, flushed and panting, with eyes flashing fire, could not resist a grateful glance toward the newcomer.

'What business is it of yours?' demanded Neil angrily.

'Just this much,' retorted the man, striding toward him, 'your presence and actions don't appear pleasing to the young lady, an' that's enough to excuse my butting in.'

'I want you to know that this girl is my—'

'Never mind what you want me to know,' interrupted the stranger coolly. 'I already know what I've seen with my own eyes. Suppose you beat it out of here—pronto .'

'You've got a lot of nerve,' blurted Neil, with baffled rage blazing from his eyes.

In a flash the stranger's gun leaped into his hand. 'You goin' to obey orders an' lope?' he demanded ominously.

'I'm not going to go without—'

'Wait,' cried Dora. 'I'll go first.' She untied her horse and, leading him to a rock, used the boulder as an aid in mounting. 'You can follow me, Neil,' she called back.

Neil climbed into his saddle. 'I haven't got any gun,' he said with a sneer as he gave the sorrel the rein.

'Maybe it's a good thing you haven't,' said the stranger, putting away his own weapon.

When Neil had gone the man climbed quickly to a point where a horse stood on a thin ribbon of trail. 'Lucky for the girl I happened to be scouting down this way,' he muttered to himself. Then he laughed. 'No gun!'

He turned his horse up the mountain toward the summit of Angel Butte. But as he rode he twisted frequently in the saddle to survey the country.

41

CHAPTER VII

GOSPEL OF THE RANGE

Early next morning the newcomer in the Angel Butte section rode slowly down the north slope of the butte and from a point of vantage scanned the open country to the north and east. He sat his horse quietly, rolled and lit innumerable cigarettes, tipped his hat to shade his eyes from the bright sun, and evidently enjoyed the lonesome panorama of wild, open distances spread out before him.

Despite his apparent calmness there was about him a subtle attitude of impatience; his eyes, alert and keen, roved constantly over the scene and frequently searched the timbered areas behind him. Occasionally he twisted and turned in his saddle and spoke vaguely to his horse—a perfect specimen of the enduring Western cow pony.

His attention became focused upon two riders who were making their way slowly up the long, grassy acclivity toward the western shoulder of the butte.

And suddenly he started and uttered an exclamation of surprise as he noted spurts of dust in the road just ahead of the riders, who now halted instantly.

'Bullets!' he cried in amazement.

He whirled his horse about and spurred along a cross-cut toward the two men sitting their mounts in indecision.

Rounding a rise of ground he whistled as he descried two other mounted men speeding from the west side of the butte toward the motionless riders.

'Now what kind of a game is this?' he asked aloud as he urged his horse at a tangent toward the place where the men were likely to meet.

When he reached the spot the four were engaged in what appeared to be a one-sided conversation. The quartet regarded him questioningly as he rode up and reined in his horse.

'Well?' snapped one of the men who wore chaps and spurs and was armed with a six-gun and had a carbine slung in its sheath from his saddle horn.

'Nice day,' said the stranger casually.

'Just right for ridin'; don't let us delay you none,' said another of the men, dressed and armed like the first speaker.

The other two men were attired more after the manner of the towns and were not armed. They plainly were flustered.

'I was wondering what it was all about,' said the stranger pointedly.

'It don't concern you onless yore a dirty, lowdown homesteader,' said the first man, whirling his horse to confront the stranger.

The stranger smiled. 'An' if I am a homesteader?' he suggested.

'Then yo're on dangerous ground,' snappily replied the other. 'This pair has just found out where they stand,' he continued, indicating the two men who were not armed.

'We're homesteaders,' confessed one of the men, 'and we understood the north half of section twenty-two was open to entry, also some land south of it, and we came up to see it.'

'An' you can go back an' tell the locator that told you about it that the next time a party comes up here we're goin' to shoot to hit something beside the grass roots,' shouted the spokesman for the armed pair.

'That's mighty rough language, friend,' observed the stranger.

'We don't aim to decorate the truth up in no parlor style,' retorted the other.

The stranger's right hand hovered stiffly above the black butt of the gun at his right side, and he regarded the speaker with an unwavering gaze as he spoke to the homesteaders.

'You seen this land you're talking about?' he asked quietly.

The homesteaders at first did not realize he was speaking to them. Finally one of them answered: 'If you mean us—yes, we've seen it.'

'And you're sure it's open to entry?' continued the stranger.

44

'Yes, it's open and a good piece, too.'

'Then why don't you go ahead and file!' said the stranger crisply as the gun leaped to his hand ahead of the concerted attempt of the two armed men to draw.

'You fellows don't hardly figure you're bigger than Uncle Sam, do you?' he demanded of the pair who had gone motionless when his gun had appeared.

'Yo're a stranger in these parts, ain't you?' sneeringly asked one of the men.

'Sure,' replied the stranger. 'But I get at home quick when there's gun play goin' on.'

The homesteaders, visibly relieved and with revived confidence, turned their horses and rode away in the direction of the town, miles eastward.

And the two men confronting the stranger also turned their mounts westward. 'I've got you spotted,' said the spokesman in a tone which meant much. 'Yo're Brodick's gunman!'

But the stranger merely laughed—a merry, tantalizing laugh—as the pair dashed away. Then he rode slowly back toward the east side of the butte, whistling as though his mood had changed; as though something he had craved had taken place to disrupt the monotony of the peaceful scene before him. And in his gray eyes was a leaping fire of excitement, evidently relished.

The two men who had intimidated the homesteaders rode at a furious pace up the road and turned in at a stone ranch house near the pass over the west shoulder of the butte.

Dashing up to the house they dismounted, flung the reins over their horses' heads, went to the door, and knocked. Almost instantly the door was opened, and the men walked into what was plainly an office room.

Lentu, who had opened the door, greeted them gruffly. A large, gray-haired man with a florid face and bushy eyebrows sat at a desk.

'What's up?' he demanded. 'I thought you were guarding twenty-two.'

'So we was,' explained one of the men. 'But a new hand's been taken in the game.'

'New hand?' queried the man at the desk. 'Come, talk up.'

'Well, I guess as owner of the Double S you'll be surprised to learn that the homesteaders has got a new ally,' said the man, reveling in the element of suspense he was creating.

'Out with it,' snapped Lentu, glancing significantly at his employer.

The man then told of the meeting with the homesteaders and the stranger.

'It must be the man we saw riding down the Timber Creek trail night afore last when we was keeping an eye on old man Brodick's movements,' concluded Will Martin, owner of the Double S.

'Describe him again, an' don't overlook anything,' said Lentu eagerly, his eyes glowing.

46

Once again the men described the man who had interrupted their play with the two homesteaders.

Lentu swore. 'I wonder who it could be. It's a gospel of the range that a gun-fightin' ex-cowman won't even associate with a dry-lander.'

'I'll tell you what I think,' said the spokesman for the two men who had brought the news. 'He came from around the east side of the butte; you people saw him ridin' down Timber Creek the day old Brodick put his beef herd on the forest range; I'll bet he's Brodick's gunman!'

'I've always figured he'd try a trick like that,' cried Martin, striking the desk with his fist. 'Lentu, this thing is coming to a show-down!'

Lentu sat upon a chair near the desk. He motioned to the two men standing. 'Go back and keep an eye out. Send some one to the top of the butte with a glass an' tell him to watch the east side. Florry's around with nothing to do—send him.'

When the men had departed he turned to Martin. 'You're dead right,' he said earnestly. 'I'd liked to had a chance to put another bee or two in that fool Sterret's ear, but it looks as if we'd have to go ahead.'

Martin shifted uneasily. 'I ain't positive, Lentu, that we're on the right track in this business with old Brodick '

'You ain't goin' to let him cut loose an' fight

47

us in the bargain, are you?' interrupted Lentu.

'No, no,' said Martin, avoiding the other's gaze. Then his eyes blazed. 'It's up to him to stick!' he exclaimed.

'Sure—sure it is,' agreed Lentu in a purring voice, 'and as long as we're going through with this thing we might as well go all the way. If Brodick has hired a gunman—' He tapped the butt of his six-shooter significantly.

'I know,' said Martin, upon whom the movement was not lost. 'You're fast, Lentu; you're powerful fast. That's one reason I've hung on to you through thick an' thin. You'd been strung up once if I hadn't come to the front for you.'

'An' now you're drawing down the interest in full,' said Lentu. 'I'll send the word to the T-C and the A B C.'

Again Martin shifted as though he were ill at ease. 'You think it's your idea then so soon?' he faltered.

'Tonight!' said Lentu, rising.

A few minutes afterward riders were pounding toward the T-C ranch in the west and the A B C in the southwest ten miles.

At sunset a number of mounted men were at the Double S. Their horses fed in the corrals while they ate and talked in the ranch house. It was dark when the cavalcade filed into the road that led over the west shoulder of the butte and down the cañons to Timber Creek and the Brodick ranch.

And while they walked their horses under the pale glow of the stars a man cut down through the timber on the south side of the butte and waited in the shadows near the Timber Creek trail.

CHAPTER VIII

AN ULTIMATUM

Dora sat at her window. The ranch house was still, and the only sound to be heard was the occasional stamping of the horses in the pasture inclosure across the road. The fields and the timbered sides of the hills were bathed in silvery moonlight, and the limestone rimrock, which traced a series of broad steps up the slope of Angel Butte in the north, was ghostly white.

More and more Dora was impressed by the silence and majesty and overwhelming bigness of this new country. But there were tears in her eyes. Would Neil respond to the wholesome influence of this great outdoors? Had she made a mistake? Was the man she would make over past the point where environment would affect him?

His increasing disposition toward an intolerance of their relations worried her. His outburst of two days before remained fresh in her mind; as did the picture of the tall, dark man with the gray eyes who had come so unexpectedly to her rescue.

And Neil's declaration: 'A man's wife is his wife out here!' Was she being selfish?

Deep down in her heart she knew she loved this prodigal. She had loved him when she had promised his mother to marry him. And she suddenly realized that if he failed to make himself the man she wanted for her true husband it would break her heart.

As she gave free rein to these troublesome thoughts and pondered her problem she became conscious of a new sound a muffled, baffling, indefinable sound. It seemed to come from the west, from the direction of the trail up Timber Creek.

She leaned out of the window, tipping back the screen to do so, and soon caught sight of a number of dark shadows in the road which wound down along the creek. Nearly breathless with interest she watched until the shadows solidified into horses and men. They rode to the gate and there dismounted while one of their number proceeded to the house and knocked upon the door.

In a few seconds she heard some one stirring downstairs. A shaft of yellow light slanted across the grass beneath, as the door swung back and she heard Amos Brodick's voice.

'Howdy, Martin. You're visitin' kinda late,

ain't you? Come in.'

'No, I don't think I'll come in, Amos, thanks,' replied Martin. 'Some of the boys are here with me.'

'I was wonderin' who was out there by the gate,' said Amos, advancing upon the porch with the lamp. 'What's the cause for the crowd, Martin?'

'No harm in a crowd, Amos, when you don't know what to expect,' was Martin's rejoinder.

'An' what're you meanin' by that?' Amos demanded, surprised.

'We want to talk to you privatelike,' explained Martin steadily. 'McCabe an' Pierson are out there, an' some of the men off my place an' the T-C and the A B C ranches. We want to have a conference with you.

'Well, what's the matter with my house?' asked Amos sternly.

'There's no use waking everybody up, Amos; suppose we go out by the corrals.'

'This looks to me like a danged dark way of doing business, Martin. I want to ask you again what the idea was in bringing so many men if you just wanted to talk with me, an' why you didn't come in the daytime since you all claim to be honest men.'

'We came in a hurry,' Martin retorted sharply. 'Only McCabe, Pierson, Lentu, an' myself want to talk to you. I'll call 'em in if you aim you've got to have it that way, but there ain't no sense in wakin' the house up an'

51

having 'em all wonderin' an' askin' questions.'

'Maybe you're right, but it looks queer to me,' Amos said, after deliberating. 'But wait till I put this lamp in, an' I'll go out an' hear what you've got to say.'

Dora heard Amos Brodick go back into the house. The shaft of yellow light was blotted out. In another minute Amos had joined the man Martin before the house, and the two of them were walking toward the corrals. She saw the man with her uncle raise a hand and saw three others from the horsemen by the gate join them. They disappeared around the corner of the horse barn, and again the night was still.

Though she could not, in her excitement and bewilderment, form a dependable idea of the nature of the mission of Martin and the others of the mounted men, she surmised that in some way an attempt was being made to intimidate Amos Brodick. And while she could not know it, her surmise was not far from the truth.

'Look here, Brodick, this thing has come to a show-down,' exclaimed McCabe, owner of the T-C, when the five men had reached the west side of the barn, which was farthest from the bunk house.

'That suits me,' replied Amos Brodick instantly. 'Lay your cards down.'

'Are you in with us to keep this end of the range tight?' demanded McCabe.

'What do you mean by "keeping it tight"?'

'Keeping the rats out of it!' said Lentu, speaking as if he snarled the words.

McCabe silenced the Double S foreman. 'Let me talk,' he snapped; then, turning to Amos Brodick: 'We mean to keep it tight by keeping these land-grabbing fool homesteaders an' all others with bunch grass for brains off it,' he said evenly. 'Listen, Brodick, the time's come to throw a good live scare into that bunch an' make 'em lay off the Angel Butte country forever!'

'If that's the play, men, I don't want a hand,' said Amos Brodick. 'I've got enough to 'tend to without going in for a range war. I've been in one o' them, ain't I, Martin?'

'Don't throw *that* up at me,' said Martin with a side glance at Lentu.

'I'm not throwing up anything against you, Martin,' said Amos sharply. 'Bygones is bygones with me—so far's that's concerned. But I'm not going into a losing game when I can see the handwritin' against it on every plot the land offices are handin' out.'

'Amos, if you ever mention the Sand Creek hangin' business again, I swear I'll kill you,' said Martin. 'I'll—'

'Shut up!' said Lentu.

'I wasn't intendin' to mention the Sand Creek hanging,' said Amos dryly; 'but now that you've brought it up I can point to it as one reason why you an' me couldn't go into the

53

same deal on any proposition.'

'Wait a minute,' ordered McCabe. 'Here, Brodick, this isn't a personal quarrel. Bad blood between you an' Martin has got nothing to do with this business we're talking about— making the Angel Butte range tight. Now, Brodick, you're a cattleman. We're cattlemen. We own quite a bit of land hereabouts, an' we own lots of stock. We've got to put a stop to this homestead business or we won't have the range for our stock. The forest reserve is a joke, an' you know it. We've got to stick together. Either you're for us or you're against us!'

'Now that ain't exactly fair, McCabe, an' well you know it,' replied Amos.

'We're gettin' right down to cases on this proposition,' said McCabe. 'Martin an' Pierson an' I are in to stick. We've run our stock together for more'n twenty years, an' you've done the same. It's your place to stick with us. That's it—you're either for us or you're against us.'

'It looks to me, boys, like there was more behind this thing than just keepin' the homesteaders off like you say,' drawled Amos.

For a moment there was silence.

'What's your answer?' demanded McCabe.

'You boys knew before you came down here that I wouldn't agree to no war against the homesteaders,' continued Amos in his drawl, which was a danger sign.

'What do you say?' roared Martin.

'It looks pretty much to me like there was something sort of personal in all this business,' said Amos.

McCabe motioned to Martin to be silent as the other started to reply. 'You can look at it any way you choose,' he said to Amos, 'but we're askin' you for the last time if you're goin' to stick with us. We'll never ask you again.'

'That's a threat!' cried Amos. 'An' no man livin' can threaten me into anything. Get out of here!'

'We'll take that for your answer,' said Pierson quickly, speaking for the first time.

'An' don't forget who said it,' warned Amos Brodick as the four men turned to go.

Dora, still watching from her window, saw the men reappear. Her uncle walked alone toward the house, but directly in front of the porch steps he stopped and, standing in the full light of the moon, watched the men as they mounted their horses at the gate and rode rapidly away up the valley.

Amos Brodick walked slowly down the walk toward the gate, looking after the disappearing horsemen, apparently thinking. As he reached the gate a figure darted from the screen of a clump of pines in the pasture across the road, vaulted the fence, and hurried to the gate.

The girl caught a dull gleam of metal in her uncle's hand as he challenged the newcomer, but the gleam vanished when the lone visitor laughed and said in a rich, musical voice: 'Just dropped in to get acquainted, Brodick. I see you been receiving callers.'

'An' who are you?' demanded Amos.

The other removed his hat and spoke a few words in an undertone, leaning close to Amos Brodick's ear. Dora started in surprise as she recognized her champion of the incident with Neil in the cañon on the east slopes of Angel Butte.

'Come in,' she heard Amos Brodick saying.

The two men entered the house, and Dora crept wonderingly to bed.

CHAPTER IX

THE UNFINISHED SENTENCE

In the first flush of dawn the stranger rode up the cañon trail to the west shoulder of Angel Butte. He saw three men before the main gate to the Double S ranch; two of the men were sitting their horses in the road, and the third was standing by the gate with his shoulders against the crossbars.

As the stranger approached, lounging in the saddle, he drew the attention of all three. Noting this fact, he began to whistle a vagrant tune of the ranges; also he pulled the broad brim of his black, high-crowned hat well forward to shade his eyes from the bright rays of the early morning sun.

'Howdy,' greeted Martin of the Double S, scowling as he stepped a bit forward from his position by the gate when the lone rider came up.

'Howdy,' returned the stranger without checking his horse.

McCabe, master of the T-C, pushed his horse casually into the path of the newcomer. 'Ain't you goin' to stop a minute?' he asked.

The stranger pulled up his horse and favored the speaker with a searching glance. 'I've got plenty of time,' he drawled. 'Was you wanting to ask me, maybe, about something?'

A ranch hand came running from the direction of the house. He made a sign to Martin, who then waved him back.

'I reckon you're out takin' the mornin' air,' observed Martin, a gleam of anger in his eyes.

The stranger whirled his horse in Martin's direction so suddenly that the rancher leaped back against the gate. And now the stranger's eyes gleamed with a grim ferocity as he leaned over the saddle horn toward Martin.

'What's the use beatin' around the bush?' he demanded.

McCabe and the other rider closed in a bit, scenting an emergency; their hands dropped toward their pistol butts.

Martin, momentarily taken aback, rallied with flashing eyes at this show of support from

McCabe and the ranch hand with him. Though Martin was unarmed he did not fail to discern the angle at which the stranger hooked his right arm above the gun at his side.

'You're a good guesser,' said Martin. 'Maybe you was just wantin' to know about the road to Angel. The road you're on will take you to town if—'

The stranger laughed harshly. 'Martin, I can find my way to a town by instinct. I'm that smart, understand.'

'Maybe your friends that was figurin' on filin' on twenty-two is in there waitin' for you!' roared Martin in quick anger.

'Oh! That's it,' said the stranger in a soft, musical voice. 'You heard about that, eh? Well, now, that land's open to entry, ain't it—or, isn't it? You know I ain't right smart in everything, Martin; maybe that land's yours, now.'

Martin, who had been startled to hear the man call him by name, motioned to McCabe to be silent. To all outward appearances the baron of the Double S now was cool. 'You're a cow-puncher?' he asked in more agreeable tones.

'I have punched cows.'

'Are you lookin' for a job?' asked Martin pleasantly.

'That would depend on who was offering it to me,' replied the other coolly.

'I might be able to use a man on the Double

58

S,' said Martin.

'Why, you sure ain't gettin' short of guards for that twenty-two tract already!' exclaimed the stranger in mock surprise.

'No, we're not gettin' short,' cried Martin, once more burning with anger.

'Wait a minute, Bill,' McCabe put in. 'Let me ask this feller a few questions—'

'No, let me answer 'em before you ask 'em,' the stranger cut in evenly, shifting his keen gaze back and forth between the two ranch owners. 'I ain't lookin' for a job, an' I ain't telling you who I am or what I am—I'm that independent,' he went on. 'It's none o' your business. Maybe I'm just passing through, an' maybe I'll elect to stay aroun' here a while. Maybe I like to fish, an' the fishing's good in the creeks hereabouts. Maybe I'm goin' in for homesteadin', an' maybe I was just attracted to that little fracas over on twenty-two because I like to see fair play. That's some more of my business. I've got all kinds of business; you wouldn't think I had so much business; I'm just chock-full of it. An' it's none o' yours. That's the main point—it's none o' yours. You're wantin' to warn me to get away from Angel Butte. This is a free country, an' I'm over twenty-one. I've camped on the east side of the butte, an' that's on forest reserve. I don't like people aroun' close, maybe; it's just possible I don't like to be crowded. It's likely I don't reckon on being bothered. You was goin' to

59

warn me, and I'll beat you to it—don't you bother me!'

A glance, rich with significance, flashed between McCabe and Martin. 'Nice morning,' said McCabe with a sneer.

'An' so far it's been a healthy one,' rejoined the stranger as he turned his horse back into the road.

'Was there anything you overlooked saying?' asked McCabe with mock politeness.

'I think I was intending to include the intelligence that you men could go to blazes so far's I was concerned if you behaved proper,' drawled the stranger, grinning. 'But we'll let it go since I forgot it.'

Gently he put the spurs to his horse, but as he moved off his eyes sought Martin's and narrowed. 'How do you stack up as a guesser?' was his parting shot.

He rode leaning far to the left in his saddle and glancing back over his right shoulder.

'Told us more'n he thought,' was McCabe's comment.

Martin nodded silently. 'Brodick's hired a gunman,' he said.

Shortly after the stranger had passed from sight around the north side of the butte, McCabe and his man took their departure.

*   *   *

The last two weeks in June passed with quiet

marking all activities in the country adjacent to Angel Butte. None appeared to inspect section twenty-two and thus possibly draw the fire of the guards who had been stationed by the combine to protect their dead line. The stranger, camped on the east side of the butte, was seldom seen except by the lookout stationed on the crest of the butte by Martin and the ranchers associated with him.

Amos Brodick now had all his cattle on the summer range within the forest reserve. His men were repairing the irrigation ditches and attending to the distribution of the waters which assured bountiful crops of hay and oats and alfalfa and sedan grass, and nourished a large and varied garden close to the house.

In the vicinity of the little town of Angel, homestead shacks began to appear. The small, unpainted, board structures looked in the sun like splashes of gold against the broad, brown vastness of the prairie country which stretched eastward to the blue rim of the far horizon. Gradually these splashes of gold crept westward toward the rolling flanks of Angel Butte, from the pine-rimmed crest of which the combine's watchers stood vigil.

Neil Sterret apparently was absorbed in the routine activities of the ranch. He spent much time on his horse and made several trips to the Double S, where Lentu treated him with a great show of friendliness and gave him pointers in the use of the weapon which he had obtained from his Uncle Amos, and with which he yearned to become as proficient as the other men of that country. He failed to tell his uncle of these trips or of the glamorous pictures which Lentu painted in Western phraseology of the day when the 'good old order of things' would again come into its own.

Dora, visibly pleased with what she considered a good indication of the beginning of Neil's redemption, nevertheless was worried by an intangible feeling of uncertainty and foreboding which appeared to hang in the very air.

Amos Brodick was often preoccupied at meals. She noticed that he never went abroad without his gun, and that the other men of the ranch were constantly armed. The unusual sight of pistol butts banging so close to swinging arms and looking so formidably businesslike carried to her mind a suggestion of impending tragedy—of strife and bloodshed.

She had never mentioned to her uncle the fact that she had witnessed from her window the visit of the mounted men in the night; that the appearance and departure of the unknown man from the east side of the butte was known to her. But she knew these events were much in the mind of her uncle, for since that night he had displayed a stern side to his character and had been much concerned over the slightest of departures from ranch routine; he had held his men under closer rein. His attitude since that night had been one of increasing alertness about the affairs of his domain.

Whether any others on the ranch knew of the night visits she could not be sure, although she suspected that some of the men might be aware of the incident, or Amos Brodick might have told them what he wouldn't think of confiding to his women folks, with whom he ever assumed a cheerful demeanor.

And then one day near the end of June, Neil astonished her by asking his uncle point-blank at the dinner table if he knew the 'nester' on the east side of the butte—darting a swift glance of warning at her as he put the question.

'Why do you call this man whoever he is—a nester?' his uncle countered with a steady questioning gaze.

'That's what people are who—who haven't any business around, isn't it?' demanded Neil, although his face reddened under its fresh tan.

'Nester is a bad word, Neil, my boy,' said Amos Brodick kindly. 'It's a word that's sort of goin' out of use nowadays. It used to mean a man who came in and squatted on unsurveyed government land; but now there is no cause to call any person by such a name.'

'Well, he acts suspicious, doesn't he, Uncle Amos?'

'It isn't anything unusual for a man to come

along and camp in this country where there's good fishing and hunting, Neil.'

'But it doesn't look right when there's so much work an' everybody's short of hands,' Neil protested. 'They say this fellow won't work because he doesn't have to work like other folks. They say he's a gunman and a killer and a bandit and too dangerous—'

'Who says that, Neil?' asked Amos Brodick sternly.

Neil's face paled as he saw he had talked himself into a trap. He could not tell his uncle he had heard those sentiments just expressed from Lentu. 'Oh—some—of the boys,' he replied lamely and covered his confusion by attacking his dinner. 'That fire guard who went up on Telltale Peak tother day said something about it. Guess everybody round here thinks he acts suspicious.'

'You must discount anything ill you hear a man in this country saying about another,' said Amos Brodick. 'Men do not usually say another is a suspicious person without some basis of fact. Mere talk directed at another is liable to be for personal reasons. Just now, with the homestead rush beginning, you're liable to hear most anything from the combine.' He looked at Neil sharply, but the youth did not betray any incriminating interest.

'Has the—the combine got it in for that fellow?' he asked, feigning surprise.

'That I do not know,' said Amos Brodick with a frown. 'The combine's notions don't interest me, unless—'

Those about the table waited expectantly for him to complete the sentence, but instead he finished his dinner in silence and went out.

CHAPTER X

WARNING THE STRANGER

Although Dora sensed that Neil's statement regarding the stranger on the butte was made partly for her benefit, she could not, for some reason unfathomable to herself, believe that the man with the calm, steady gray eyes and upright bearing, who had championed her cause when Neil had been indiscreet, was in reality a killer—a murderer. Something about him as she remembered him on the occasion of their chance meeting—seemed to dispute Neil's subtle intimation.

But of these things she had little opportunity to think during the days when preparations were under way for harvesting the crops, when both she and Mrs. French were kept busy in many ways attending to household affairs.

Neil, she felt, was improving. His making over was to be a slow process, but it had unmistakably begun, she reasoned. Thus her days, although constantly overshadowed by vague worries, were not entirely unhappy.

Then came the announcement that the family and most of the hands would go to Angel for the annual Fourth of July barbecue and ball. It had been the custom for years to attend this affair, and the men had asked for the privilege again, Amos Brodick explained. He laughed and joked in a hearty manner in anticipation of the celebration, but Dora saw that under it all he was inclined to be apprehensive.

The men drew straws, and in this way two were selected to remain at home and keep an eye on the ranch and attend to the distribution of the water. It was very warm, and the crops required constant irrigation.

'It'll be some celebration,' Neil said to Dora. 'An' if that gunman up on the butte takes it into his head to go down to town he's liable to get his head shot off!'

'Neil! Why would any one have cause to do such a thing?'

'I don't like to tell you these things, Dora, but this is a wild country out here, and everybody ain't always what they seem. There's some who think he's a bad man, and that it ain't safe to have him around.'

'Have you been talking to some of the men from the other ranches, Neil? I haven't heard any one here say anything about this man, except you.'

'You don't see much of the men here, do you?' he countered. 'And they wouldn't be telling you things to disturb you. I don't want you to be repeating what I say, but there's liable to be some entertainment that ain't on the program down in Angel on the Fourth.'

'Neil, I believe you would like to see something happen!'

'There's got to be things happening in a country like this, and if I don't see some of them I won't know how to act when I get into a mix-up,' he explained. 'You've got to be ready for anything out here. That's why I wear this gun, and why I'm learning how to use it. It's part of a man's rig out here.'

'But, Neil, guns and strange happenings like you—like you hinted might take place in Angel, don't seem to fit in with this peaceful scene around us. The fields and the cattle grazing look a lot like our old home.'

'Huh!' he snorted. 'You've got more' n one silly notion.'

His words kept repeating themselves over and over in her mind and increased her worries that afternoon, so that she decided to ride out into the cool, pine-scented cañon on the eastern side of Angel Butte.

Once more she rode far up the narrow, winding cañon with its pines and firs, its golden slopes whereon grew the berry bushes, ripening now, and with its outcroppings of limestone, resembling carvings high above, or thrusting pinnacles upward until they bore the appearance of spires of celestial cathedrals.

She came upon the stranger suddenly as she turned a bend of the trail about a huge boulder almost covered with vines, with its base in a bed of green kinnikinnick. He was sitting on a ledge of rock idly gazing at the steep slope opposite. His horse grazed near some young alders behind him.

He turned quickly as he heard her horse, and his eyes glowed with surprised recognition, but he spoke no word of greeting.

Dora checked her horse in momentary indecision, while Neil's imputation that it might be dangerous for this man to go to the celebration in Angel flashed through her mind. She was surprised to find herself thinking that she should warn him.

'Nice day,' he said finally, removing his hat as she continued to stare.

She started in confusion, and then, speedily making up her mind, she urged her horse toward him.

'There is something which I—I feel I should tell you,' she began, conscious of her awkward position. 'Something perhaps you should know, although you may think it's silly.' She looked at him doubtfully. He was not one who looked as though he would submit to being shot down without capably resisting.

She was reassured by his laugh, which

disclosed a row of white, even teeth; they set off the deep tan of his face to excellent advantage. 'What is it you want to tell me?' He smiled up at her as she sat her horse.

But now she found it hard to put into words the warning which she felt it her duty as one human being to another to give him. 'Are you are you planning to—to go down to Angel for the—the celebration?' she faltered.

'Hadn't thought much about it,' he confessed.

'You'd better not go!'

'Not go?' He looked much surprised. 'An' why not, ma'am?'

'Because you're—you're liable to be killed.'

Again she heard his merry, musical laugh. 'I told you you might think it silly,' she reproved him a bit haughtily.

Instantly he became serious. 'Why do you think I might be killed, ma'am?'

'I cannot tell you why, nor do I know there is any such possibility. I heard something to the effect that there might be trouble in store for you in Angel on the Fourth, and I decided it would be only common decency to—to put you on your guard. Personally I have little interest in the matter.'

He rose. There now was no mistaking his seriousness. 'I understand, ma'am,' he said in a respectful voice, 'an' I sure appreciate your kindness. I'll keep my eyes open.'

'Then are you going?'

'I just couldn't very well stay away—now.' He smiled.

'But it might be very dangerous. I don't know that it would, but—'

'I am not unaccustomed to danger, ma'am,' he interrupted. 'To get right down to cases I don't mind it a bit. I rather like it!'

'Oh!' The girl's thoughts raced back to Neil's hint that this man was a gunman—a killer. She studied the frank and open features of the man before her. He didn't look bad, she had to confess to herself. She wished she had the courage to question him about himself. 'Can you tell me what a gunman is?' she asked suddenly.

The man started. He stared at her searchingly. 'I reckon a man that can get his shootin' iron into action tolerably fast would be a gunman,' he replied, continuing to look at her curiously.

'Would he necessarily have had to kill anybody?' she queried timidly.

'Not necessarily, but quite probably,' he drawled with a whimsical smile.

For some reason his answer, or the way he said it, seemed sinister—repelling. She could not resist a glance at the worn butt of the pistol which protruded from the holster at his right thigh. Nor was this glance lost upon him. He stepped back a pace, again smiling.

Thoughts of Neil, of his practice with his weapon, came to her. 'I wonder if you could tell me: Does the West make bad men?' she asked, spurred on by an earnest impulse for Neil's welfare. 'One new to the West,' she added quickly, 'would it be likely to prove unfortunate for him?'

She thought she caught a gleam of understanding in his eyes as he replied. 'Ma'am, the West either makes a man or breaks him thorough. If he has the right stuff in him it makes him every time. Sometimes it makes a bad man over, an' if he can't be made over in the West he can't be made over anywhere, I reckon. The West gets credit, I expect, for a lot of bad men who were bad when they came here an' got worse. As for the women' he bowed gracefully and gallantly 'ninety-nine times out of a hundred a woman finds herself out here!'

The girl felt her color rising, but again her thoughts reverted to Neil. 'But the spirit of the West makes for good, doesn't it?' she asked anxiously.

'The spirit of the West, ma'am, is in her skies, her air, and her land,' he said with a sweeping gesture. 'You can judge for yourself. It depends on what a person has inside of him.'

As he concluded she saw that his face was grim, and that there was a cold, almost harsh look in his eyes.

'Thank you,' she said as she wheeled her horse. On the way back down the cañon she felt a thrill as she recalled his last words and the unfathomable air about him as he had said them.

Was this man, then, really dangerous? Was it true that he was a killer? Time and again she pictured with fascinated imagination that worn, black gun leaping into a thin, browned hand and blazing flame and smoke under the shock of crashing bullets. For the first time she thought of him and of the guns with an indubitable feeling of fear. She put spurs to her horse. And as she rode swiftly toward the ranch house she found herself looking forward to the celebration in Angel with undeniable dread.

CHAPTER XI

ANGEL MAKES HOLIDAY

Early on the morning of the Fourth the ranch was astir with preparation for the journey to town. The day's initial chores were accomplished long before breakfast, which was served fully half an hour earlier than usual both in the men's and the ranch-house dining rooms.

Soon after breakfast several of the men departed, riding horses which had been curried and combed with unusual care and adorned with martingales as a special piece of equipment in keeping with the holiday attire of the men; with their high-crowned hats of plush with colored bands, neckerchiefs of brilliant hues, and shirts of purple and yellow and pink. The holsters, belts, and leather cuffs of the men all were highly polished and ornamented with silver. They made a gay display as they rode away in the golden hour after full dawn.

Dora and Mrs. French, Uncle Brodick's housekeeper, were dressed in holiday garments also, and when Walt Frost drove the buckboard up to the front gate, they donned dusters as a protection against the grime of the road.

Amos Brodick called them and led them to the waiting buckboard, for he had announced that he would himself drive them in. The two women were seated in the second seat, and Amos and Mrs. French's boy, Louis, sat in front.

Neil, resplendent in full Western regalia, with white angora chaps, Stetson, belt, and gun as leading features, came out to see them off, and the balance of the men mounted with Neil and trailed after the buckboard as Amos gave the rein to the horses.

The road up the creek was hard and fine, and they made good time. In less than an hour they were climbing the long acclivity to the west shoulder of the butte. When they reached the summit of the pass, Amos checked the horses and pointed to two buttes far in the northwest.

'Square Butte an' Crown Butte,' he said, 'and way beyond 'em in the shadow of the big mountains is the Teton country.'

Dora thought Mrs. French shuddered as she listened; he looked askance at the elderly housekeeper.

'We used to live there,' said Mrs. French.

Amos Brodick turned in his seat to glance at her. 'An' well out of it,' he said, apparently for her ears alone. 'Way in the north you can just see a peak of the Sweetgrass Hills.' He pointed with the whip. 'Guess they must be most two hundred miles away. An' that streamer of smoke way straight ahead in the prairie is the smoke from the smelter in Great Falls.'

Dora breathed deeply at the vast panorama and slowly turned her gaze toward the east, where the town of Angel could be dimly seen. Again she felt a tremor of misgiving. And yet—could this glorious scene of far-flung skies and towering mountains and unending vista of rolling plain, all gold and blue under the bright sun, be merely a setting for tragic deeds, for passions raging unbridled in the minds of men who knew and loved this environment?

Her reverie was interrupted by the resumption of motion. They rode swiftly by the gate of the Double S ranch. No one was in sight. Dora felt better when they had passed and were well on the road which followed the

74

gently undulating slopes down to Angel.

The town was dressed in holiday array after the Western fashion. Scores of small fir and balsam trees had been cut on the timbered slopes of the foothills and were fastened about the fronts of the buildings, tied to posts, and lavished about the interiors of restaurants, saloons, and stores. Bunting hung everywhere with loose ends waving in the gentle breeze, and flags, although in the minority, were given conspicuous places.

A large dancing platform had been erected about two feet from the ground, with a canvas roof, and sides formed by interlacing branches of many fir and balsam trees placed close together and held by scantlings and ropes.

Horsemen rode into town from all directions, and the dust flew in clouds. A band played. Cow-punchers, gay in chaps and bright in colored neckerchiefs and shirts, rode along the main street and thronged the bars. Homesteaders in khaki were in the majority, perhaps, but they gave the men from the ranges a wide berth. Phonographs screeched, glasses tinkled, shouts sounded, spurs jingled, and now and then the general noise was punctuated by the sharp bark of a six-shooter unlimbered in high hilarity.

And over all was the sun and the drifting veils of dust and the blue of clear, high skies, blending with the purple tints of distance, and the vague, indefinable atmospheric exhilaration which is of the West and the West alone. Elbow room and freedom!

Amos Brodick drove to the evergreen-draped entrance of the New West Hotel. 'Get a room for the ladies, where they can primp up a bit before dinner,' he told the lanky hotel runner who was on duty wearing a large badge that announced the legend, 'Commitee.'

While Amos went to put up the team, taking the boy, Louis, with him, Dora and Mrs. French were shown to a room which would serve as a headquarters for their stay in town. As the room was at the head of the stairs leading up from the narrow hallway between the bar and the small lobby, they were able to hear with great distinctness the loud talk, laughter, and shouts of the throng below.

Suddenly above the many voices mingled in jest, greeting, and conversation, the two women heard another voice on the stairway which they recognized with a start of interest.

'You don't know what you're saying, Will,' said Amos Brodick.

'The devil I don't!' Dora recognized the voice of the man who led the night riders weeks before the man Amos Brodick had addressed as Martin.

She looked at Mrs. French and saw that the housekeeper also knew the voice and was standing with a hand to her throat and with unmistakable terror in her eyes.

'The devil I don't know what I'm talking

about,' roared Martin. 'You've been my enemy ever since that Sand Creek business, Amos Brodick—tryin' to make out you're betten'n I am. You're startin' a feud, Amos, that's what you're doin'—startin' a feud you won't be able to finish.'

'Don't talk like that, Martin,' pleaded Amos. 'I have nothing particular against you—'

'Then why don't you come to the front with McCabe, Pierson, and me? You think you can slip one over on us, an', darn your soul, you can't get over the hill with it!'

'Martin, you're drunk,' said Amos Brodick sternly.

'Oh, I'm drunk, am I? I'm drunk because it's the Fourth of July, an' I've got forty men in Angel at my back. I'm drunk because you think you're betten'n I am. But I'm a-talkin' cold turkey, Amos, an' you've got to be white or yaller; an' if you're yaller—'

'Now hold on,' Amos broke in in a thick voice that quivered with anger. 'Don't call me yellow—don't make it more'n I can stand.'

'You ain't yaller? You ain't? Then what have you got that gunman staked out up on the butte for? We ain't blind. We can see. What was he down there on twenty-two butting into the play an' takin' sides with the land rats for? What was he doin' up by my place the mornin' after we went down to your ranch to try an' reason with you? Baitin' us—tryin' to start something so he could pull his gun an' do your

77

dirty work—'

'Martin, stop!' cried Amos in a voice trembling with strong emotion. 'You don't know what you're saying, an' you'll be sorry for this when you think it over.

'Ain't he your gunman?' demanded Martin thickly. 'Ain't he?'

'No—no—*no*!' thundered Amos.

'Well, who is he?' asked Martin.

'I can't tell you who he is '

'But I can tell you who he is,' cried Martin. 'He's the Left Hand, that's who he is—which is as much as anybody knows about his name. He's got as many killings behind him as he's got ca'tridges in his belt, an' he's wanted in half a dozen counties, an' you know it. The Left Hand! Wearin' his gun on the right side to pull wool over our eyes. An' you bringin' him over from Meagher County. Thought none of us would spot him. Ratty, the dealer, knew him the second he put eyes on him this mornin', so you—'

'Martin, for the last time, will you stop!'

Mrs. French ran to the door, opened it, and stepped into the narrow upper hall, with Dora close behind her. On the top step stood the boy, Louis.

The housekeeper leaned over the railing. 'Amos!' she called.

'Go back,' called Amos Brodick.

'Oh, that's all,' sneeringly said Martin, who was standing two steps below Amos, halfway

78

down the stairs. 'I just wanted you to know, Amos Brodick, that we're on to your play, an' we'll have your gunman before this night's over, an' you'll have to do your dirty work yourself if you're able—'

In one leap, as both Dora and Mrs. French screamed, Amos hurled himself upon Martin. The pair, locked in a seeming death struggle, landed at the bottom of the stairs, and almost simultaneously with the crash of their bodies came the report of a gun.

Dora, white as death, caught the housekeeper as she swooned. Louis ran down the stairs despite her warning to him to come back. Then there was a hurried tramping of many feet, and the cries of men. The girl forced herself to look over the railing.

Amos Brodick, with a crimson stream flowing down his face, was standing back against the wall on one side. Swain, the ranch foreman, was at his side, grim-faced, with eyes narrowed and gleaming. Martin was in the hands of two other men, neither of whom Dora knew. Behind, in the space between the bar and the lobby at the end of the little hallway, many men were jammed. On the floor between Amos Brodick and the man, Martin, was a pistol.

Swiftly Amos reached inside his coat under his left shoulder. He tossed his weapon to the floor beside the one which already lay there.

'Now say the word, Martin, an' we'll go after

them—an' the best man wins!' said Amos in cold, earnest tones.

The men jammed in the hallway backed away. Martin crouched forward, and just as his body became tense for a leap toward the weapons, Lentu pushed his way through the crowd.

One flashing glance at the postures of Brodick and Martin, and he had stepped between them and picked up the guns. He handed Amos his weapon and, keeping Martin's pistol in his own hand, led him quickly away.

Swain and Amos Brodick climbed the stairs. Mrs. French had recovered and was weeping, with her arms about her boy. 'Amos,' she said as they entered the room, 'maybe we better go home.'

Without answering her, Amos turned to Swain. 'Tell the boys to bunch up and quit drinking. And you better—' He whispered something in Swain's ear in an undertone.

'Do you know where he is?' asked Swain.

'No find him,' replied Amos.

'Don't you think we'd better leave?' Mrs. French asked in a pleading voice.

'Leave? Now? Not if it's my last day on earth!' said Amos Brodick.

CHAPTER XII

THE CHALLENGE

After Amos Brodick had cleansed his face, and Mrs. French had cleaned and bandaged the slight wound on his left temple made by Martin's bullet, they went down to dinner.

They ate at one of three long tables piled high with food in the hotel dining room, which was lavishly decorated with evergreens and bunting. Dora noticed that throughout the meal, Swain, the foreman, lingered near the door, and once or twice she saw men from the ranch approach him, speak a few words, and go. She was struck, too, by the fact that Amos had kept them waiting a few minutes until places were available at the lower end of the room, from where he could see all the others in the room.

Mrs. French could not disguise the fact that she was in a veritable torment of worry, and, even after they had left the dining room and were seated with scores of others in a grand stand where they could watch the bucking-broncho contests and other sports, she kept glancing about anxiously and paid scant attention to the feats of Western skill exhibited before them.

After this show came the greased-pig and

greased-pole contests, staged in the main street in the open block between the hotel and the depot, and these the party watched from the upper porch of the hotel. There were horse races and roping contests up and down the street, and a parade of all the cow-punchers present, mounted, and riding four abreast.

They saw Lentu in this parade, and Dora heard Amos Brodick mutter: 'Paradin' his crowd for my benefit.'

'Did you say something, Amos?' Mrs. French asked quickly.

'Nothing,' replied the cattleman shortly, although his eyes glinted and he kept looking after Lentu and those riding with him.

When the 3-X-Z men Brodick's own passed, with Swain riding at the head, Dora saw Neil with them and clapped her hands. He looked up and waved his hat, his face flushed through the tan, a broad grin on his lips.

Dora was instantly concerned with a peculiarity of his manner—a symptom she had seen before in the Eastern State which they had left. She turned to Amos Brodick.

'Uncle Amos do you suppose Neil—has—had something to drink?' she faltered.

'Oh, he might have one or two under his belt,' Amos said, laughing. 'Most of the boys put a few fire-crackers inside of 'em on a day like this to get ready to ride herd on the celebration. But I've shut 'em all off,' he added

82

with a frown.

'But Neil promised me he wouldn't drink any more when we came out here,' said the girl.

Amos looked at her kindly. 'Maybe the boys just naturally talked him into it. They're a hard bunch. Or maybe he's just excited because it's all so new to him. That's probably it.'

'I hope so,' said Dora, not without a feeling of doubt.

For two hours they watched the various activities in the street while the band played on the porch below them. It was a thrilling, novel sight, this scene of bronzed, active men at play. Nor was Dora the only one who viewed the rodeo with interest. The sides of the street were jammed with homesteaders who watched with amazement as the chapped and spurred wizards of rope and gun and horseflesh cavorted before them.

The soft glow of the sunset was mellowing the skies and sending waves of crimson-tinted color athwart the land when Lentu rode down the street on a beautiful pinto which tripped daintily as if dancing while the band caught the spirit of the exhibition and played, 'Put on your old gray bonnet;' and when Lentu made the pinto kneel in the dust of the street so he could lean over its head and brush the ground with his hat the crowd responded with a thundering burst of applause.

This was thought to be the end of the street

carnival, but as the throngs began to move they were suddenly arrested by the sight of a tall man arrayed entirely in black from the glistening ebony polish of his riding boots to the crown of his sable hat, riding down the street astride a magnificent black horse.

Horse and rider seemed to blend, except for the silver trimmings and trappings of the saddle and bridle and the man's modest adornments; and both the animal and its master were the very living embodiment of grace.

The crowd again broke into applause, for in the West a perfect example of spirited horseflesh and a capable, confident master in the saddle are quick to excite admiration and appreciation.

Both Dora and Amos Brodick started in surprise when they recognized the rider.

'Good Lord!' said Amos softly.

But Mrs. French heard him. 'Is that the man, Amos?' she asked quickly.

Dora sensed that the housekeeper associated his exclamation with Martin's accusations concerning the stranger on the butte.

Amos Brodick nodded in silence while his gaze roved among the throngs below. Dora leaned close to him, almost breathless with interest and apprehension.

'Will they—kill him?' she heard herself whispering.

'They wouldn't be likely to try it in front of all these people,' replied Amos. But Dora noticed that his right hand was inside his coat as he leaned over the porch railing.

The man rode straight down the street until he arrived at the place where Lentu had compelled his pinto to kneel. At this point the rider tossed a silver dollar into the road, to the very spot Lentu had touched with his hat.

He petted the horse gently on the neck while he spoke to him softly and urged him a bit with the spurs. Quickly the animal's four feet came together over the spot where the silver dollar had fallen, and he slowly pivoted—a beautiful sight, and one suggestive of diligent training and perfect understanding between horse and master.

While the band played softly and all eyes admired the feat, Dora found herself instinctively searching for a sight of the big, black pistol butt at his right side. She thrilled with new interest when she saw that it was missing. Then she noticed the rider was holding the rein in his right hand. As the horse swung slowly around, with forelegs crossed, and the left side of the driver was exposed, she suddenly gasped. The gun was there on *the left side!*

Left Hand! That was what Martin had called him—a gunman with as many killings behind him as he had cartridges in his belt. Could it be possible that this calm, almost boyish-looking man was indeed a ruthless, cold-blooded killer?

Her fascinated gaze lingered on the dull gleams of red which shot from the cartridge-heads in his belt. And instantly she became aware of the fact that this was not a casual exhibition but a challenge from Left Hand to the men who threatened him. The whole performance took on a new and powerful significance.

And now, at a word of command, the horse leaped aside as the rider swung low from the saddle and retrieved the silver dollar from the dust. With the outburst of applause, horse and rider glided up the street and were lost in a cloud of dust shot with the rainbow colors of the sunset.

'Come, folks, we'll go down to supper,' said Amos Brodick.

CHAPTER XIII

THE ANSWER

When the soft, hazy twilight had deepened into night, and when the great arch of the heavens was spotted with stars, the merrymakers repaired to the dancing pavilion for the climax and end of the celebration, which would last until the first gray banners in the east announced the dawn.

Neil came for Dora to take her to the dance. His face still was flushed, and Dora was soon cognizant of the fact that, whether or not the others from the ranch had ceased their calls at the bars, Neil was patronizing them in defiance of his uncle and with flagrant disregard for his promise to her.

With the knowledge, the old fear came back. Would Neil respond to his new environment, and, more troublesome still, was the environment just what she—they—had expected? The events of the day, coming so swiftly, seemed to presage some far more disquieting happening before the night was over. She observed that several of the men from the ranch appeared to be constantly near Amos Brodick. There was mystery, foreboding in the attitude of her uncle and these men; something sinister in the coincidence of Lentu and Left Hand, as Amos Brodick now unhesitatingly referred to him, taking for a brief moment the center of the stage at the day's celebration. Contemplation of these things temporarily drove from her mind all thoughts of Neil, except such as concerned his safety.

Regardless of what might take place during the night, she would contrive to keep Neil in the dancing pavilion.

Mrs. French accompanied them to the pavilion, stating that Amos Brodick would come along later. Louis was with some young friends. They found the benches along the sides of the place thronged, and dancing was going on as it had been all day.

'I suppose you've heard who your friend is,' said Neil when they went upon the floor. 'I mean your friend from the butte.'

It was the first time he had referred to the incident in the cañon. It had seemed to her in the weeks which followed that he had decided not to mention their unusual situation—to go quietly about the business of redeeming himself and then hold her to her promise, which she felt was fair and creditable in him. Now she chose to disregard his veiled feelings in the matter.

'Neil, I heard the talk that passed between Uncle Amos and that man, Martin,' she said quietly; 'so I know what they are saying about the stranger.'

'Well, he'll get his,' said Neil, as they swung into the dance. 'Lentu will attend to him before the night's over!'

'Neil! Do you know what they—Lentu and the others, I mean—plan to do?' she asked quickly.

'Oh, I've heard a few hints dropped,' he said significantly.

'Have you told Uncle Amos?'

'Told Uncle Amos?' He appeared surprised. 'Why, of course not. It's none of our affair.'

'But perhaps he would like to know what

you may have heard. And, if the man is in danger—'

'Why are you so interested in him?' demanded Neil.

'I am not interested in him, Neil, only as—well, I don't hardly believe he is what they say he is, and I don't believe Uncle Amos thinks he is, either. And, anyway, appearances up to now would seem to indicate that he is more on Uncle Amos' side than he is on the other—'

'It isn't a question of sides,' Neil interrupted impatiently. 'That fellow is known as Left Hand; he's a gunman who's come here to stir up trouble.'

'But you don't know that for certain, do you, Neil?'

'Maybe not, but it looks like it; and whatever becomes of him will be all right with me.'

Dora was quick to realize that Neil harbored a deep resentment, possibly hatred, against the man for having interfered that day in the cañon. She was dismayed at the thought that she, perhaps, was partly responsible for the animosity shown toward him. She didn't know the facts about his actions against the guards on twenty-two, except as Martin had mentioned them. Was Neil, then, somewhat responsible for the demonstration against the stranger? And the midnight visit after Martin and the others had gone!

'Neil, I am convinced you should tell Uncle

Amos all you know.'

'I don't know anything,' said Neil. 'If the fellow was all right why didn't he take a job on one of the ranches? Why is he meddling with the affairs of the combine? Tell me—'

'Why, Neil, the very fact that he is against the combine puts him on the side of Uncle Amos,' the girl protested.

'Maybe he's got his reasons,' said Neil, almost savagely.

'Neil, don't you see that the combine with Lentu and the others in it are the enemies of Uncle Amos?'

'Maybe they are and maybe not,' was his reply. 'Uncle Amos might be mistaken. Maybe they're not as bad as he thinks.'

Dora stopped the dance and led the way to a vacant place on the bench at the lower end of the floor.

'How can you be so foolish?' she asked him, her eyes flashing. 'Neil, have you no inkling as to what is happening about us? Can't you see that the combine is threatening your uncle? Can't you see he is worried and perhaps in danger? Do you know what happened this morning?'

'Swain told me about it,' he answered.

'And then you know that Uncle Amos might have been killed by that man, Martin.'

'Martin was drunk,' said Neil shortly. 'If Martin hadn't been drunk nothing would have happened. Anyway, there may be a quarrel between Uncle Amos and Martin that we don't know about. Such things are always happening out here.'

'Oh, Neil, I'm afraid you are playing the fool. Such things are not always happening out here. Mrs. French has lived here in this country all her life, and she is worried and apprehensive. There is something beneath it all; maybe it is a quarrel, and we know nothing about it. But whatever it is, Neil, it is serious, and Uncle Amos and perhaps ourselves, are threatened.'

'I'll tell you what is behind it,' said Neil with an exaggerated gesture and a superior lifting of his brows. 'The combine wants Uncle Amos to stick with them against these homesteaders, and this Left Hand has come along and butted into the game.'

'But you know why Uncle Amos won't stick with the combine, as you call it, Neil; it is because Uncle Amos does not think they are right. He says they are pushing against a stone wall. We must be loyal to him. We have only been here a short time, and we cannot know exactly what conditions are; we do not yet understand these men and their motives. And if Left Hand is taking part it may be that he is doing so to help Uncle Amos in some way.'

'Then why isn't he working on the ranch?' Neil demanded. 'Why doesn't he come out in the open?'

'I cannot answer that, Neil, and neither can

you; but I feel that you are incensed against
this man because he—he—objected when
you—'

'And I've a right to be,' said Neil bitterly.
'But there's no need to tell everybody this.
Here comes Mrs. French.'

When the housekeeper joined them Neil
excused himself. 'I'll be back in a minute,' he
said. And Dora, at a loss for a reasonable
excuse to detain him, watched him go.

Neil entered the nearest saloon, a small
place lighted by a single swinging lamp above
the bar, which ranged along one side of the
short length of the room. Throughout the day
he had avoided the Prairie Flower saloon, the
first place he had visited after his arrival in
Angel. He had not forgotten the incident of
the black-jack game when Lentu had come to
his rescue in the altercation with Ratty, the
ferret-faced dealer. And the dealer's parting
fling, 'A man's hat don't make a man out of a
boob,' had burned in his memory. He hated
Ratty, for he felt that Ratty had made a fool of
him. Even now, as he ordered a drink at the
crowded bar, he fingered the butt of the gun in
the holster at his right thigh.

This day, attired in cowboy fashion, and
mingling with the men from his uncle's ranch
and at sly moments with men from the Double
S and other ranches of the combine, he had
noticed a measure of respectful deference paid
him by the men in khaki or overalls from the

homesteads. They, like he, were fascinated by the new environment in which they were thrust; but he had the advantage of a make-up—although he discounted this fact if he was aware of it.

While the men from his uncle's ranch tolerated him in friendly fashion, those from the ranches of the combine apparently accepted him as an equal—or treated him as such. They made much of him; invited him to drink with them, listened when he talked, and now and then confided something to him. It was all very flattering. And they told him Left Hand would get his!

As Neil finished his drink he felt a touch on his arm and turned to find Swain behind him. The ranch foreman nodded toward the head of the bar, where there was a little open space between the men drinking at the counter and the front wall of the building near the door. Neil followed Swain to this comparatively quiet location and found two other 3-X-Z men there.

'Bad business to be licking up that stuff, son,' said Swain kindly.

Neil resented the fatherly way in which the foreman had always treated him; resented his calling him 'son,' which seemed to him to be a patronizing term. At times he suspected Swain of humoring him, which was more maddening than all the rest.

'Oh, I guess I can take care of myself,' he

replied, scowling.

'Against orders today,' Swain pointed out. 'I suppose your uncle meant to include you with the rest of us.'

'Why certainly. I'm one of the outfit, ain't I?' asked Neil, smarting under the imputation that he might not be in the same classification as the others.

'That's why I mentioned it,' returned Swain with a smile.

Neil, mollified by this reply, suddenly turned to Swain with an inspiration. 'What do you think of this fellow Left Hand?' he asked, striving to veil his intense interest in the subject.

'Don't know much about him,' was Swain's cryptic answer.

'Well, what do you think of the grand-stand play he staged this afternoon on the horse up there in the street?'

'Was it a grand-stand play?' countered Swain.

'What else could it be?' sputtered Neil.

'He might have been drawing his enemies out into the open or something like that,' Swain intimated, after some hesitation.

'Drawing his enemies out in the open! Rats! He hasn't come out in the open himself, has he?'

'That's according to how you look at it,' replied Swain, although he did not offer to explain what he meant by his answer.

'They'll probably send Lentu after him,' observed Neil, watching the foreman closely to ascertain the effect of this. But Swain remained silent.

'Has anybody seen Left Hand since his stunt in the street?' Neil asked.

'I suppose so,' Swain answered evasively.

'Maybe he's lit out of town to avoid trouble.'

'Think so?'

'I heard—happened to overhear—a couple of combine men saying that Lentu would drift into every saloon in town tonight looking for him,' Neil asked.

'Well, he may have a chance to see him right here,' was Swain's astonishing reply.

'Is is Left Hand coming in here?' gasped Neil.

'No, he ain't coming—he's here,' said Swain, pointing cautiously toward the distant end of the bar.

Neil looked in the direction indicated and saw the man called Left Hand standing close to the end of the bar. He had his particular nook pretty much to himself, and he was standing with his back to the bar. Neil saw there was an open door in the rear of the place, apparently leading into a back yard. Left Hand kept his gaze darting at frequent intervals from the back door to the front of the room, yet his attitude was that of one merely lounging in lazy fashion after a drink or two.

Although Neil thoroughly hated this man

95

for his interference between him and Dora in the cañon on the east side of the butte, he nevertheless respected the reputation that the combine's men had given him. He was thrilled by sight of the weapon strapped securely to the man's left thigh; thrilled more at the prospect of a meeting between this man and Lentu, another reputed gunman of lightning ability and accuracy. Would there be trouble? Neil fervently hoped so.

As if in answer to his unvoiced wish there was a commotion in the front doorway. Martin, of the Double S, entered, with an authoritative-looking man at his side, and followed by several of the combine's employees.

'There he is,' shouted Martin, pointing out the man at the lower end of the bar. 'Know him?'

The crowd broke away from the bar, leaving an open space in which Martin and the men with him confronted the stranger.

'Can't say that I know him,' said the authoritative-looking man coldly.

'No?' roared Martin. 'Well, that's Left Hand, wanted in half a dozen counties. Now, Mr. Deputy Sheriff, what you going to do about it?'

The officer stepped forward a pace. Instantly the smiling face of the man with his back to the bar froze in grim lines, and his eyes narrowed.

'What's your name?' demanded the deputy.

'Smith!' The word seemed to crackle, it came so short.

'Smith!' echoed Martin in a jeering voice. 'Do you see where he wears that gun, sheriff on his left side? Do you—'

'There's more'n one left-handed man in these parts, Martin,' interrupted the deputy. It was plain he was not unmindful of the menace which shone from the eyes of the man accused. 'And I'm not goin' to accept an identification if it's no betten'n on the word of Ratty, that crooked little dealer.'

'That's up to you,' retorted Martin as the deputy swung on his heel and departed. 'Scared stiff,' he added savagely.

'How about yourself?' Left Hand asked with an amused smile.

'I'm an old man,' Martin began, but ceased speaking as another pushed in front of him.

Neil held his breath as a hushed silence fell over the whole room. The faint strains of music from the dancing pavilion and occasional noises from the street outside were all that disturbed the stillness as Lentu confronted his man.

It was the first time these two men had met face to face. Lentu was scowling ominously, his chin outthrust, while the other appeared to smile grimly, yet with something hinting of keen satisfaction, though his eyes glowed with a sinister light.

Lentu leaned a bit forward, his scowl wearing away as he stared intently at the other. 'Left Hand?' he murmured, half to himself, yet loud enough for all in the house to hear.

'The same,' was the unexpected, startling answer, given with another smile, in cool, clear tones.

The two men remained motionless, standing in a half crouch, arms and hands tensed for lightning strokes at the slightest indication of action on the part of one or the other.

Men who were minded to move away remained rooted to the spot in fascination. Five seconds, that seemed an eternity, slipped by, and suddenly from the front of the room came three shots. The room was plunged into darkness as the glass from the shattered swinging lamp fell to the floor. And with the sound of the falling glass came darting streaks of fire and the sharp thunder of exploding cartridges; then followed stillness and the pungent odor of pistol smoke and a slow, gasping sound as men recovered their breath.

'Strike a light!' It was Lentu's voice.

There was a shuffle of feet behind the bar, and an extra lamp was lit.

Its pale gleam disclosed Lentu standing in the open space with a gun in his right hand. Left Hand was nowhere to be seen. Lentu shoved the weapon into its sheath and pushed his way out of the crowd.

Neil surged through the front doorway with

the throng which was leaving. In the open air he stood looking about him with a vague stare, thoroughly sobered by what he had seen, and with the new and amazing burden of knowledge which was his.

What did it mean? Why—why—why? He kept asking himself this as he slowly made his way toward the dancing pavilion. Gradually, as his senses became normal, he remembered; and with remembrances he felt the sharp prod of a painful curiosity.

The three shots which had shattered the lamp had come from almost over his right shoulder. He had stepped forward half a pace when Lentu had entered. And Swain had been standing at his right side!

CHAPTER XIV

THE SAND CREEK HANGING

Shortly after midnight Mrs. French, Amos Brodick's housekeeper, prevailed upon Dora to return to their room in the hotel to get some rest. She explained that such affairs as the celebration dance always increased in good-natured violence toward morning—a violence to which Dora was unaccustomed and by nature antagonistic—and that Amos would be around to call them for breakfast before daylight in order to get an early start for the ranch.

She might have spared herself the long explanation, for Dora was quite ready to retire to their room. The excitement of the day had so troubled her thoughts that her brain seemed numbed to further mental effort. She had heard about the meeting between Lentu and Left Hand, and Amos Brodick had advanced the confidential information that Left Hand was unhurt and had left town. She refused to concern herself any further about the matter.

Neil had appeared thoughtful and absent-minded—something she attributed to the after-effect of what he had consumed in some under-cover, law-defying place, and the thought caused her disgust. He told her Swain had said that Martin and most of his men had ridden away. He had seemed repentant of his former aggressive belittling of her theories and arguments, but this had given her no satisfaction, and she said good night to him with relief.

When the women reached their room they found Mrs. French's boy, Louis, already asleep in a cot at the foot of their bed. Dora undressed wearily, but after they had gone to bed she tossed and turned in restless contemplation of the many disturbing angles to the series of events which had transpired since she and Neil had arrived at the Brodick ranch.

'You must try to get some sleep, deary,' said Mrs. French. 'Close your eyes and forget everything.'

But the woman's tone told Dora that she, too, was worried and thinking. She felt a bond of sympathy between herself and the elderly housekeeper who had always been so kind to her.

'I can't sleep, Mrs. French; I just can't. If I knew what it was all about I would feel easier. And, Mrs. French, what could that man Martin have meant this morning when he said Uncle Amos had been his enemy ever since that Sand Creek business, and that Uncle Amos thought he was better than Martin was himself?'

'Hush, deary; you must never mention that 'less you whisper.'

'But what is it, Mrs. French?' Dora persisted. 'Can't you tell me? You can trust me if it shouldn't be repeated.'

'Oh, there's plenty who know about it,' said the housekeeper. 'But it isn't talked about very much. There'd be no harm in telling you, but I'm afraid it would upset you, dear.'

'Mrs. French, I would like to hear about it. If it is in some way responsible for the actions of those men toward Uncle Amos I would like to know about it. I am sure I wouldn't worry so much if I knew everything; and if I can't know everything, I do want to know as much as I can. Of course I cannot insist that you tell me unless you feel free to do so.'

Dora sensed that Mrs. French was really aching to unburden herself of the story and was content to wait until she should begin. Presently the woman rose to make sure that the boy, Louis, was asleep.

'Do you remember yesterday morning'—it was now long after midnight—'when we reached the top of the pass over Angel Butte, dear?' asked Mrs. French.

'When Uncle Amos was pointing out the landmarks in the distance? Yes, I remember; and didn't you say you used to live somewhere up north—'

'In the Teton country,' supplied Mrs. French. 'Your uncle, you'll remember, said we were well out of it. He was right. I always shudder when I think of what happened up there. Yet it was the finest country I was ever in—or it seemed that way to me; long stretches of nearly level range with the mountains close behind. My Louis was born up there. His father worked for your uncle. After he was kicked so badly by a wild horse and died from it I became your uncle's housekeeper, and he has always been good and kind to Louis and me. Amos Brodick is a fine example of a real Western gentleman, dear.

'One night when we were living up there some men came to the ranch and asked for your uncle. They talked to him in the little front room off the parlor that he used for an

102

office. It seemed that two men had stolen some mules at least the men who came to see Amos claimed the mules had been stolen. They said the suspects claimed to have brought the mules down from Canada, but that it was a lie, for the men had abandoned them and started north when they found they were exciting suspicion.

'Your uncle went with the men to a conference at a near-by ranch where it was decided to follow the two men accused of stealing the mules. I have heard two sides to the story which was told by the suspects. One was that they had brought the mules down from Canada, as I told you; and the other was that they had taken the mules from a man who owed them a big sum in wages which he refused to pay. I don't know which is the true story—if either of them is true.

'But Amos thought there was something else behind the business. He said it looked to him as though some of the men were enemies of the two accused of stealing the mules. Anyway, he proposed that they notify the proper authorities and send them after the two men and bring them to trial. His suggestion was sneered down, and when he saw the bitterness shown he refused to join in the chase and came back to the ranch. Two of the men rode part way back to the ranch with him, entreating him to join them, and even threatening him, but he would have nothing to do with the matter.

'Well, the others went after the two suspects. They finally cornered them in a cabin near Sand Creek, which used to be in the reservation. The men in the cabin stood the posse off with their guns, and finally one of the posse advanced to talk with them under a flag of truce, which was a white handkerchief or something tied to a stick.

'This man told the pair in the cabin that they were cornered and outnumbered and didn't have a chance to get away. But he said the posse had decided to give them a chance to defend themselves in the courts, and that if they would give themselves up the members of the posse would see that they were safely transported to Fort Benton, where they would be given a fair trial on the charge of having stolen the mules, and would be released if they were innocent.

'The men said a fair trial was what they wanted and denied they had stolen the mules and said they had fled because of the hostile way the posse had acted. So the man with the flag of truce repeated the promise that they would be taken safely to Fort Benton to be given a fair trial and released if found not guilty. Then the two suspects, assuming that the word of the posse was good, just as the word of most men in the West is good, gave themselves up.'

Again Mrs. French rose and bent over the

cot where Louis was lying, to make sure he was asleep. 'When the men surrendered, the members of the posse were surprised to find that they had a boy with them,' the housekeeper continued in a very low voice. 'They didn't know the name of the boy or the names of the men, either. They took the weapons which the two suspects had and put a guard in front of the cabin in which were the suspects and the boy. He was only a young boy about nine or ten years old. Just about Louis' age.

'That night the other members of the posse made the guard stand with his face to the cabin wall, and then they went up behind him and blindfolded him. They told the men in the cabin to come out and quickly tied their hands behind their backs. Then they took them to a cottonwood tree and, without giving them a chance, hanged them!'

Dora cried out in horror. 'Hanged them after they had promised— Oh, Mrs. French, that was terrible!'

'Hanged them until they were dead, after they had got them to surrender with a flag-of-truce promise to see that they got a fair trial,' said the housekeeper. 'And they drove the little boy out upon the prairie in the dead of night alone and without food. He was never seen or heard of again! In after months bones were found in the vicinity, which showed that the boy had died on the prairie or had been killed by wolves and his flesh eaten by the wild animals.'

'Oh, that was horrible, Mrs. French. What did they do to the men who were in the posse?'

'The law was not very strict,' replied the housekeeper. 'It was hushed up. I think they did have some kind of hearing about it, but there was not enough evidence. The story leaked out bit by bit, but it could never be proved just who were responsible.'

'But Uncle Amos knew who they were, didn't he?'

'He knew some of them yes,' whispered Mrs. French. 'But even if he had decided to testify he would never have lived to reach the witness stand. The affair turned public sentiment against the unknown members of the posse, and they would have killed your uncle rather than let him live to testify against them. And not only would your uncle's life have been at stake if he had been minded to tell what he knew, but his cattle would have been run off or killed, and he had to protect his bankers, to whom he owed a large sum at that time. Pressure was brought to bear on him through these bankers, for the members of the posse had influence behind them, and many were said to be prominent.'

'And how does that business affect Martin and uncle's relations?' asked Dora, although she suspected the truth.

'Don't ever tell a soul that I told you this,'

cautioned Mrs. French in a faint whisper. 'Martin was one of the posse, and his man, Lentu, who was young then, was the leader!'

'Oh,' said Dora softly, 'I begin to see.'

'Two years after the hanging we moved away from up there, and your uncle bought the place south of Angel Butte. Later, when the homesteaders began to appear in the country north, and there was talk of irrigation, Martin and McCabe moved down this way, too. Martin and Lentu know your uncle knows much about the affair they were mixed up in, and although it happened many years ago, and is very seldom talked about now, Martin has always thought your uncle would tell what he knew before he died. Your uncle hasn't had much use for Martin or Lentu since that business up north.'

'Were any of the others of the combine in that affair?' Dora asked.

'I don't know, deary, although I suspect McCabe. I wouldn't be surprised if they were, though. And I've believed lately that they want to get Amos involved in this homestead war so that he will be equally guilty with them if anything should happen, and so seal his lips about the other. But I think your uncle believes in letting bygones be bygones, as he told Martin, and has never thought of telling what he knows.'

'Mrs. French, do you believe Uncle Amos has hired this gunman, Left Hand, to protect him, or for any other purpose?'

'No,' replied the housekeeper quickly. 'I know Amos Brodick, and I know he wouldn't hire any one else to fight his battles. Now, deary, we must try to get some sleep, for we'll have to start for the ranch in three or four hours. Do try to sleep.'

But Dora found herself at dawn still pondering the riddle of the man in black with the gun strapped to his left thigh.

CHAPTER XV

THE COMBINE PREPARES

When Swain told Neil that Martin and most of his men had ridden out of town he was mistaken. Several of the Double S and other combine men did ride away, but Martin and Lentu met within an hour after the affair with Left Hand in a small room over the Prairie Flower saloon.

'A fine mess you made of things,' Martin accused when they had lighted the little lamp in the place and stood facing each other.

'Now don't start that line of talk,' said Lentu savagely.

'Why, not? You didn't go through! '

'That lamp being busted was enough to throw anybody off his guard,' growled Lentu, settling his big frame in a chair, and staring at the lamp on the small table with its greasy oilcloth cover.

'Sure it was; but it gave you a chance to get him. You shot six times—I counted the shots; and you missed him every time!'

'Because it was dark an' he ducked,' Lentu said, snarling.

'Of course he ducked. Got plumb away in clean fashion. But you didn't duck, Lentu. He could have potted you by the flashes of your gun as easy as not easier, maybe.'

'But he didn't,' observed Lentu, not without a show of genuine surprise at the fact of his life being spared at the very moment he was trying to kill another—and by his intended victim.

'He could have dropped you where you stood,' said Martin.

'That's twice you've said that,' said Lentu angrily.

'Well, what do you make of it?' Martin inquired, sitting down in a chair across the table from his right-hand man.

'Brodick's scheme. Probably decided it would look too raw—if Left Hand could have got away with it.'

Martin laughed sneeringly. 'He couldn't have helped getting away with it if he'd wanted to plug you. And all my work bringing that deputy around so he could see this Left Hand was a gunman and give you some excuse for putting him out—forced to draw—for nothing.

Lentu, it looked to me as if you was sort of rattled and maybe—maybe—'

'Don't say it,' warned Lentu with a dangerous gleam in his eyes.

'Well, I won't,' decided Martin. 'Only— Well, I've never seen you hesitate before, and—'

'Maybe I saw more'n you did,' growled Lentu, again becoming thoughtful. 'But we'll let that go. I wonder who shot the light out.'

'Why, I thought one of the boys shot it out when he saw the play was hanging fire, to give you a better chance,' said Martin. 'One of our boys, I mean.'

'Like fun one of our boys did!' shouted Lentu. 'Martin, you're gettin' raw. None of our boys shot that light out. I took pains afterward to ask 'em. They was all right behind me and you, an' the shots came from behind them.'

Martin frankly was puzzled. He stared at Lentu in astonishment. 'Well, who could have shot it out, then?' he asked in bewilderment.

'Some of Brodick's crowd, likely,' replied Lentu.

'But what good did it do 'em? Left Hand didn't try to take advantage of it, unless it was to get away.'

'That's just it,' said Lentu earnestly. 'He took advantage of it to duck an' get away. Didn't want to shoot it out with me, probably.' But Lentu's last words did not carry any great conviction, and Martin noticed this.

'That feller's got a reputation of bein' able to shoot just as fast as he can think,' said Martin dryly.

'Then why didn't he start to draw in the first place?' Lentu insisted. 'I was ready for him. I expected it. I was just going for my own gun when the light popped out.'

'If that light was shot out by one of Brodick's men it was because they didn't want a killin' between you two fellers just now,' said Martin in a convincing tone. 'Whichever of you fellers is the fastest with your shootin' iron, an' I strongly hope you are, they didn't want any fatality at present. Now that's the upshot of the whole business if one of Brodick's men shot the light out.'

But Lentu was hardly listening to him. He was musing. 'I believe—there—was—another reason,' he said slowly and softly. 'But I'm not going to be fool enough to tell anybody no, not even you. Say, Martin, this game is going faster and further than we thought—ain't it?'

'You just finding that out?' Martin asked, sneering. 'You're not gettin' cold feet, are you?'

'Stop that kind of talk, Martin,' said Lentu sharply. 'None of us can get cold feet now. If anybody shows any signs of laying down, I'll—'

He ceased talking and rose to his feet as a peculiar knock sounded on the door. Then he opened the door to admit McCabe.

'He's cleared out,' said McCabe as soon as

the door was closed. 'Lit out on that black horse of his goin' north, an' none of the men could keep him in sight. That's some piece of horseflesh. Wonder where he had him cached?'

'Oh, that's nothing,' said Martin. 'That's just one of the things to wonder about that feller. Looks to me like he's got us all buffaloed,' he added with a grin at Lentu.

'Yes? Maybe he has.' McCabe spoke angrily. 'Well, you sure made a smart play this mornin', Martin; goin' after Brodick that a way an' talkin' your fool head off.'

'Never mind that,' said Lentu sharply. 'I've explained all that to him. He says he's willin' to take a little valuable advice from now on.'

'Good thing,' observed McCabe. 'Maybe we all need some of that. Learn anything more about who shot the light out, Lentu?'

Lentu shook his head. 'But I ain't quit tryin' to find out,' he remarked. 'Things have got to move sprightly from here on. Listen—'

For half an hour the three men spoke in whispers, seated about the table with their heads close together. Finally Lentu rose to his feet, started toward the door, and then suddenly swung to confront the others. 'An' if any of the bunch starts to feeling bashful about the game,' he began, 'he'll '

He nodded silently and went out.

*   *   *

An hour or more after midnight, Neil, feeling the reaction from the excitement and indulgences of the day, slipped quietly out of the dancing pavilion and made his way to the little barroom where had occurred the meeting between Lentu and Left Hand.

The place held a peculiar fascination for him. The sight of the two men facing each other, of their tenseness and the breathless air of expectancy, the sudden shots from over his shoulder, the darkness and the sharp cracks of Lentu's gun—all burned in his memory.

He knew, deep down in his heart, that he had wanted to see gun play; that he would have given speed to Lentu's draw if he could have done so by thinking. He hated Left Hand. He had begun to believe that the man was a hero in Dora's eyes.

There were not many in the place, and none of the 3-X-Z men—Brodick's outfit—was there. Neil gave his order, and he had not consumed it before he was joined by Lentu.

'Believe I'll have one myself, old-timer, if you don't mind drinking with me,' said the Double S foreman genially.

Neil felt flattered, for all eyes were upon his companion. When Lentu looked slowly about, however, the others in the place turned again about their business.

'Tough luck you ran up against tonight,' Neil volunteered.

'That was a bit tough,' agreed Lentu after they had finished. 'Have another, Sterrett— I'm feeling sort of reckless myself, an' you seem to be the only one in Brodick's crowd who ain't afraid to celebrate like a man.'

Inwardly and outwardly Neil glowed. A man's praise, this was!

'There's only one thing botherin' me,' said Lentu in an undertone as they again had recourse to the refreshment the bartender surreptitiously slid toward them. 'I can't figure out who fired the shots that smashed the lamp.'

'Spoiled your chance to get your man, didn't it?' Neil suggested as they drank.

'It sure did—an' it would have been good riddance to have dropped that hombre,' said Lentu.

Neil's hatred against Left Hand again flared red.

'The shots came from around me somewhere,' he said softly.

'Yes, guess they did,' drawled Lentu without looking at Neil. 'Must have been some friend of his back there.'

'Would you go after the man who smashed the lamp if you knew who he was?' asked Neil with real concern.

'Oh, I wouldn't say that,' said Lentu. 'Only I'd know what to look out for the next time. Can't say I care so much who used the lamp for a target; just curious to know if it was one of our gang.'

'I don't believe it was,' said Neil craftily, pouring himself another drink. The next time! Did Dora think Left Hand was a hero? Was she glad for more than one reason that the man had interfered between them?

'No, I don't hardly think either that it was one of our crowd,' Lentu was saying. 'Still, you never can tell.'

'I'm quite sure it wasn't,' said Neil. The next time! He looked at Lentu with fresh interest. This man had been his friend, hadn't he? The other had been—

'Lentu, those shots came from over my shoulder,' said Neil in a low voice, vibrant with suppressed excitement.

'That so?' said Lentu, affecting but a mild interest.

'Yes. They came from over my right shoulder. I was standing beside a man just before you came in and when you came I stepped a bit ahead of him.'

'Oh, that doesn't mean whoever you was standing near fired 'em,' said Lentu. His tone might have indicated to Neil that he was but little concerned; but the youth could not see the glitter in his eyes, for they were centered upon the glass he held in steady fingers. 'I don't suppose you remember who that man was, anyway.'

'Yes, I do. It was Swain,' said Neil quickly.

'Oh, well, it doesn't make much difference,'

drawled Lentu.

Two minutes afterward they parted, Neil going back to the dancing pavilion, and Lentu crossing the street.

Lentu went directly to the Prairie Flower. He found Martin and McCabe at the bar. 'Swain fired the shots at the lamp,' he told them crisply. 'I got the truth out of young Sterret.'

A short interval of silence greeted this announcement.

'That don't leave any doubts as to who Left Hand's working for,' said McCabe.

'And don't leave us any too much time,' put in Lentu. 'I'll get the bunch together, an' we'll slope.'

In the hour before dawn the stillness of the west end of the main street was broken by the pound of hoofs. Dora, lying sleepless, rose upon her pillow and looked out of the window. She saw a number of riders racing in the moonlight; watched them until they merged with the shadows which slanted across the first easy slopes at the foot of Angel Butte.

CHAPTER XVI

THE FIRST STROKE

It was Walt Frost who drove Dora, Mrs. French, and the boy, Louis, to the ranch early in the morning. Amos Brodick saw them off and explained that he could not go back to the ranch that day, as he had some business to attend to in The Falls, which would necessitate his going to the smelter city. He said he would return the next day and instructed Walt to leave his horse in Angel for him to use when he came back.

Swain, Neil, and the others of the men started for the ranch at daybreak and reached home before nine o'clock. After a second breakfast in the bunk-house dining room, Swain announced that he would ride up Wild Horse Valley to look after the upper herd which was grazing near the head of the creek and would likely have to be moved in a few days to fresh range.

Neil had the length of the irrigation ditch up the valley—some six miles—to ride, as the daily inspection of the ditch was one of his regular duties. Swain, riding fast so that he could complete his inspection and return to the ranch that night, left him at the end of the upper pastures and pushed on. Neil rode leisurely along, keeping a casual eye upon the amount of water in the ditch, and pausing momentarily at the flumes which occasionally wound around some point of rock or bridged a low place. He found everything in good order and the leakage remarkably small, considering the hot, dry weather which had been the rule during June, instead of the rainfall which he had been told was usual during that month each year.

As he made his way up the creek on the fine, hard trail, with the greens of pine and fir on the slopes of the mountains which hemmed in the little valley, shining in welcome contrast to the sear browns and yellows of the grass and gravel in the open spaces near the creek, he noted the general dryness of the forests and remembered the warning of the fire guard who had been sent up to Telltale Peak to be careful about matches and burning cigarettes.

He dismounted frequently for long, cooling drafts of the clear water in the creek the nectar of mountain springs. He liked to mount and dismount, to hitch up his chaps and gun belt, to take off his wide-brimmed, high-crowned hat for a glance of satisfied admiration while he mopped his brow with the huge bandanna he carried in a hip pocket.

Neil liked to ride, too, for he was becoming adept in the saddle, and, in addition to its being a novelty to him, it gave him a chance to give free rein to his imagination. Today, with

118

the memory of the events of the day before fresh in his mind, he could see himself as the aggressor against such men as Left Hand and Ratty, perhaps—a pair whom he hated thoroughly.

Eventually he came to the end of the irrigation ditch, where the water was taken from Wild Horse Creek. Everything was all right, and here he dismounted, threw the reins over his horse's head so the animal could drink and graze, loosened the saddle cinch, and then, taking the bit of lunch he had brought along tied on the cantle of the saddle with the ever-present and most-times superfluous slicker, he sat down in a little clump of aspens and firs for a bite and an hour of lazy leisure.

As he ate and then leaned against a tree, Neil considered the problem of his situation with his wife Dora. If she was infatuated with Left Hand, as he had begun in a narrow, jealous way to suspect, it was probable that such an obstacle between them would be removed sooner or later by Lentu; for Lentu had sworn to get the newcomer and had impressed Neil with his vaunted ability to do so. Indeed Neil was prepared to assist him, if opportunity should offer.

He had purposely refrained from thrusting his attention upon Dora, believing that in time she would 'come round' to his way of thinking. It was a silly business and would have to end some time. She would be sensible enough to see that before the year was up. And doubtless as he grew more familiar with the ways of the West, and became more like the men of the country, she would come to look upon him differently—with more respect.

It would all adjust itself in time, he reasoned. And when the time was ripe he would convince her that her attitude in the matter was foolish and futile and unfair, and she would give in. That would end it. He wanted Dora, of course; he had no semblance of doubt in his mind on that score.

As the afternoon wore on, Neil prepared to go back down the creek to the ranch. However, it was always with regret that he left the upper parts of the valley, for he loved the sight of the pine-clothed mountains crowding in and the silence and open vistas between the trees up the creek. In this instance he remembered that his uncle was not at the ranch, and it would not matter in any event if he was a little late in returning. Two miles above was a point where the walls of the valley narrowed, nearly cutting it in halves, save for a gap between the cliffs.

Why shouldn't he go on up the creek into the upper half of the valley and meet Swain and ride back to the ranch with him?

He debated the matter for a minute and decided that was what he would do. It was a glorious day, cool in the upper reaches of the valley, and the ride back to the ranch in the twilight would be delightful.

So he tightened his saddle cinch, mounted, and turned his horse up the trail which led through the gap toward the head of the creek. Neil had been to the head of the creek once before and knew approximately where the upper herd of cattle was grazing. He half expected to meet Swain coming back, but about two hours afterward he found himself at the place where the trail to the bench on which the cattle were grazing led off from the creek, and he had not seen anything of Swain.

He turned to his right and followed the broad trail to the top of the ridge on that side where a broad benchland reached northward for several miles—a plateau covered with excellent grass. The beef cattle were supposed to be using this range. But Neil sat his horse and stared in amazement across the tableland. He looked east and west and north scanned every foot of ground with his startled gaze and muttered to himself in astonishment.

There was not a single head of cattle in sight! The plateau was bare of stock, without a living thing to greet the eye on any portion of it.

'Where—have—they—gone?' Neil said aloud to himself.

Had Swain decided this range was so well eaten off that it was no longer suitable for the upper herd? The range didn't look so bad, Neil reflected. And had Swain moved, or attempted to move, the cattle alone? Impossible! The upper herd included more than three hundred head. Neil turned his horse and looked across the little valley to summits of the mountains opposite. He started in surprise as he looked, and his gaze froze.

Almost directly across from where he sat his horse was the pass which led over the divide toward the Smith River country. And on the slope of a mountain behind the lap of the pass he saw numbers of slowly moving objects— cattle!

And, as he watched the movement of the cattle in puzzled surprise, he saw a number of white puffs of smoke appear and drift in veils until they were dissolved by the breeze. He heard several dull, reverberating echoes. The movement of the cattle apparently increased in speed. Pistol shots and running cattle!

Instantly there flashed across Neil's thoughts a word with which he had conjured— rustlers!

His uncle's cattle had disappeared; there were now cattle in the mountains south of Wild Horse Creek where there had been none before; those cattle were moving toward Smith River, and pistol shots were urging them on.

He drove his spurs into his horse and plunged down the trail to the creek. And now he noticed something which had escaped his attention on the way up. The tracks on the trail had the appearance of having been freshly made within a few hours that day! He had seen no cattle on the way up the creek, although he had heard his uncle declare that the beef herd when it moved would move down the creek into the pastures before shipping. No, there was little doubt in Neil's mind but that the band of stock south of Wild Horse was Amos Brodick's beef herd. And, as he reached the narrow floor of the valley, splashed through the creek, and speedily began the long climb on the other side, a new and more wildly startling theory formed in his excited mind.

Might it not be that Swain himself, taking advantage of Amos Brodick's absence from the ranch, was trying to make away with the cattle?

So excited was Neil that he did not notice the dying sun in the western skies as he urged his horse up the trail. And when he reached the pass he was more or less astonished to find that the twilight was beginning to fall—the long, hazy twilight of the high hills, when the colors of the sunset lay upon the trees and ground with the thickness of a shroud or a carpet.

He galloped through the pass and came in sight of the herd. It was milling on the lower slope of a mountain above the wide trail which led down the south-west side of the divide. Neil's view of the trail below was shut off by an outcropping of limestone on the left and a thick growth of timber on the right.

As he checked his horse in sudden indecision the sharp staccato of a volley of shots sounded below and ahead of him. He rode to the farther side of the limestone, where he could see the trail for a short distance. Here he halted again, uncertain as to how to proceed in a situation with which he was unfamiliar, and under circumstances in which he had had no experience.

Just as he had made up his mind to ride slowly ahead until he could see what was going on, he heard another volley of shots. A moment afterward a rider came into view, thundering up the trail, twisted in his saddle and firing at some invisible target behind him. Almost with the echoes from his shots the rider dropped his weapon, sagged in his saddle, toppled to one side, and fell in a crumpled heap upon the dust of the trail almost at Neil's horse's feet as his mount thundered madly on, riderless and thoroughly frightened.

Struck motionless and dumb with his first sight of tragedy, Neil stared down at the white features and wide-open, unseeing eyes of the man lying twisted in the trail. Terror was mirrored in his fixed gaze as he recognized the dead man.

It was Swain, the foreman.

Before Neil could fully comprehend the significance of this knowledge he again heard the rapid pound of hoofs and raised his head

124

in time to see three other riders come into view the leader with a gun in his right hand held up level with his head and tipped back over his right shoulder.

Quickly the gun snapped forward, but in the very act of firing, the man tipped its muzzle so that the bullet went wild. His eyes started with surprise as he brought his horse to a rearing halt, and from his throat issued a gurgle of inarticulate oaths.

The two men behind him drew up close to their leader, who continued to stare first at the body of Swain upon the ground and then at Neil, looking at him in horrified fascination.

'You happened along just in time,' said the leader, sheathing his gun. 'Right on the spot.'

'Lentu!' cried Neil, for the leader was indeed the Double S foreman. 'Lentu—you've killed Swain!'

CHAPTER XVII

SHADOWS OF DOUBT

Lentu and Neil stood by their horses at the head of the valley wherein flowed Wild Horse Creek. The soft mantle of night had fallen over the mountains, but its canopy, which arched above the serrated outlines of the towering ridges, was aglow with stars, and the

125

floor of the valley was bathed in a pale light.

Lentu had taken his cue from Neil's question as to what Swain, the foreman, had been up to.

'Of course he was tryin' to steal the herd,' Lentu was saying. 'We was crossin' the divide to see about some cattle that's for sale over on Smith River an' caught Swain driving the bunch through the pass. When we asked him where he was taken' 'em he started shootin'. Then we knew something was wrong an' took after him. You saw what happened. We didn't intend to drop him; we was only tryin' to stop him.'

Neil shook his head in perplexity. The sight of violent death up there in the hills the death of a man whom he had known intimately shocked him and left him nearly speechless.

'Now look here, Sterret,' Lentu continued, 'you know this fellow Left Hand ducked out of Angel mighty quick last night, ridin' north. He an' Swain probably had it made up to get away with Brodick's cattle. Like as not he cut around over the hills an' made it to the other side of the divide an' is coming back up the trail to meet Swain, he thinks, an' help him. That's probably why Swain was so anxious to see him get away down in Angel that he shot the lamp to pieces to stop me killin' him. It looks mighty like a frame-up, doesn't it? Of course it does! Now I'll take my two men an' drill on down the trail on the other side, an' maybe we'll hit up with this Left Hand. If we do we'll fetch him in, some way. If we don't we'll lay for him an' some time find out what he had to do with this business.'

'But, what'll I do?' asked Neil in apprehension.

'Go right back to the ranch,' said Lentu. 'Tell 'em you saw the cattle bein' moved in the pass an' took up there an' saw Swain chasin' 'em an' firin' his gun, an' then he came ridin' up to you firin' an' fell off his horse beside you dead.'

'And what'll I say to them about you and—'

'Don't say anything about us,' said Lentu harshly. 'Just forget you saw us at all. That's the only way we can corner the other man. You better tell 'em when you get to the pass you found Swain layin' there dead.'

'But maybe they'll think I—that I—I killed him,' Neil stuttered. 'It looks bad for me!'

'Not unless you go tryin' to blame it on somebody else,' replied Lentu quickly. 'If you was to tell 'em you saw us, for instance, we'd just prove an alibi—which we can do, for nobody saw us come up here—an' that would make it look bad for you. But they'll know you didn't do it; don't worry. An' even if some fool person was to think you did it he couldn't prove anything. You're safe so long as you stick to the story I told you—comin' up here an' seein' Swain chasin' the cattle an' then findin' him dead.'

'They may think it's funny I didn't try to bring the body back to the ranch,' said Neil doubtfully.

'No, they won't think that, either,' Lentu contradicted. 'Swain's horse bolted. You couldn't get his body on your horse an' take it down there alone, with your horse cuttin' up as he would be certain to do. Besides you was too shocked—see? All you thought of was getting back to the ranch an' tellin' what had happened. An' Swain's horse is probably almost there by now, so you'd better ride fast. You'll likely meet 'em comin' up to see what's happened.'

'All right, I'll start back,' said Neil, preparing to mount. 'Won't the 3-X-Z bunch be liable to take after you fellows?'

'They'll never get a sight of us,' Lentu promised earnestly. 'Don't wol ry about that. We'll be gone, an' goin' fast; an' if we have any luck we'll have Left Hand in a tight place within forty-eight hours. Leave it to us. An', say, Sterret—'

Lentu stepped close to Neil. His eyes had narrowed and were unmistakingly cold and menacing.

'As I say, it would look bad for you if you was to mention us in this thing. Besides that, there's another reason why you better forget all about us when you begin to talk.' Lentu's hand dropped like a flash of lightning to the butt of his gun. 'It might not be healthy for

128

you, understand? I'm your friend an' all that, but—*be careful!*'

The insinuation and the man's attitude were not lost upon Neil. He shuddered involuntarily as he nodded.

Lentu smiled grimly and stepped back as Neil mounted. 'So long,' he called softly.

As Neil urged his horse through the creek and went thundering down the trail, Lentu half drew his gun with a muttered oath. Then he vaulted into his saddle, motioned to his two companions who were waiting near by, and the three rode directly up the creek to a rocky and little-known trail that led into the higher mountains and far to the north around the plateau range to the ridge which joined the west shoulder of Angel Butte.

Neil, riding like mad down the Wild Horse trail, found his thoughts racing in keeping with the speed of his mount. Swain dead! Killed by Lentu! Had he really been trying to steal the cattle? Had it actually been a plan of Swain's and Left Hand's to rob his uncle? Had they known in advance that Amos Brodick was going to The Falls? Or was Lentu lying?

Again and again that question entered his mind. Was Lentu lying? Or— He actually checked his horse as a new theory presented itself. Had Lentu and his men been trying to run the herd off, and had Swain caught them in the act and been killed as a result? It seemed reasonably doubtful that Swain, a man who had worked for Amos Brodick for years, would deliberately plan to do such a thing at this time when, more than likely, he had had better opportunities in the past.

Neil's heart rose in his throat as he remembered the feud between the combine and his uncle. On the face of it what he had seen was in Swain's favor. He had been firing back over his shoulder; riding away from the cattle, not with them or ahead of them, as would have been the case if he had been driving them and had been taken unawares from behind. He had been fleeing back toward the ranch!

Lentu's first indecision now was explained. He had not expected to find Neil there, of course; had been nettled, in a quandary as to what to do. And then Neil's own question as to what Swain had been doing, and possibly some other silly questions he had asked in his excitement and speedily forgotten, had shown Lentu what course to take.

But there was the matter of Left Hand. Swain had shot the light out to help him. That was queer. And Left Hand had not ridden back to Angel Butte. Neil had heard some of the men from his uncle's ranch say that Left Hand had gone north. But even then—

No! Neil believed in his heart that Lentu was guilty.

Did he dare go back on his promise and tell all he knew? Lentu's parting words had

130

virtually been a threat of death if he told all.

Neil felt that his hands were tied. He knew he could not bring himself to tell everything, for even as he thought of it he saw the cold, menacing, deadly gleam in Lentu's eyes as his hand had darted to the butt of his gun and he had made his threat.

It was with genuine terror that Neil rode around a bend in the trail above the head of the irrigation ditch and saw two men riding furiously toward him. His heart was in his mouth until he recognized Walt Frost and another man from the ranch. Swain's horse had carried the mute message of trouble to the 3-X-Z.

'Swain's been killed!' cried Neil as the two rode up.

'What's that you're sayin'?' asked Walt in astonishment. 'Cool down a big, Sterret. What is it?'

And then Neil, terrified because of his situation, and a captive to his fears, told the story in breathless snatches just as Lentu had advised him. He had ridden up the valley to meet Swain, had gone on up to the plateau, had seen the cattle in the pass, had found Swain lying in the trail dead when he arrived there to learn what was the matter, and he had seen no one!

'Go back to the ranch,' said Walt. 'Tell Williams, he's acting foreman now. He sent us up to find out what had become of Swain. An' watch out for yourself on the way back.'

In another moment Walt and the other were out of sight, riding madly up the creek trail.

Neil wiped the sweat from his face and hands. As Lentu had predicted, there had been no questioning of his story. And what, indeed, would his object have been in doing harm to Swain? It did seem ridiculous that any suspicion should be attached to him. More than likely there would be none. He was safe, unless—

Again came the vision of Lentu's sinister attitude at parting.

He was safe, and he would remain safe!

'Watch out for yourself on the way back,' Walt Frost had said.

There was no need of that, Neil told himself bitterly. He rode on toward the ranch with his secret burning in his soul.

CHAPTER XVIII

THE UNEXPECTED MEETING

At the ranch, Neil told the news, in a calm voice, although his face was pale under its tan and his features were drawn and strained. Dora, catching the look of numbed horror in his eyes as he described the finding of Swain's body, felt sorry for him and was drawn strangely toward him.

Mrs. French had made a light in the dining room, and it was there that Neil told his story to Williams, who, as assistant foreman, automatically stepped into the shoes of the dead man.

Williams listened intently, and by no word or action did he display any doubt of what Neil said. Even as he noted this fact, with secret relief and satisfaction, the youth also felt the queer pang within his breast. Did Williams suspect Swain's actions? Was that queer emotion which he felt within him a sense of loyalty to Swain? Whatever it was, Neil was glad when the ordeal was over and his account of the affair had been accepted at its word value.

'I will ride up to join Walt and Dan,' said Williams after a thoughtful pause. 'The cattle will be safe in the pass until tomorrow with two men watching them. They can rest a day before we put 'em back on the range. I'll have the cook put up some grub for Walt an' Dan an' leave 'em up there or, no, I'll stay up there myself an' send Dan down with the body. Neil, when you've had something to eat an' some sleep you ride down to Angel to meet your uncle when he comes in on the noon train from The Falls. Tell him what has happened. He will know what to do.'

When Williams had left the room Dora went up to Neil. 'Go and lie down, Neil,' she said softly, 'and when it is daylight I will call you, and we'll have a good breakfast ready for you to eat before you start for Angel.'

As Neil looked at her he felt again that indefinable emotion within him. Was he— could it be that he was ashamed? There was plenty of time yet to tell the whole story, he reasoned to himself. But he shuddered as he remembered Lentu and his threat: 'It might not be healthy for you, understand?'

Neil understood.

Dora, mistaking the look in his eyes for one of compassion for the dead man or realistic awakening of his soul, put her hand gently upon his arm. 'Go lie down, Neil,' she urged. 'You have a hard ride before you. Don't worry. Uncle will know what to do.'

But Neil was worried. What would his uncle say? What would he do? What could he say or do? Neil, much fatigued and feeling the reaction from the excitement, dropped asleep, fully dressed, debating this in his mind.

When Dora woke him the dawn had come over the land. He ate his breakfast in silence and went out to find a fresh mount saddled and waiting for him at the gate. Sleep had done him a world of good, and now, as he rode over Angel Butte, his spirits revived in the fresh morning air, and he sighed with relief as he felt the strong, certain muscles of the horse beneath him.

He saw no sign of life, as with considerable

apprehension, he passed the Double S ranch house. He did not know, naturally, that Lentu and Martin watched him from an upper window.

'He's goin' down to meet Amos,' said Martin. 'Now, Lentu, do you suppose do you suppose—'

'Not a chance in the world,' said Lentu, sneering. 'He's kept his mouth shut. He's lucky, after dropping in the way he did. I didn't figure Swain would be up there, let alone that young brat!'

As Neil reached the last of the rolling slopes of the butte and swung into the nearly level stretch of prairie leading to Angel he saw the smoke-streamer left by a train drift along the horizon to the north. He spurred his mount to a last long spurt and arrived at the little railway station almost as the train was pulling in.

Covered with dust and breathing heavily, he confronted his uncle with his news as soon as Amos Brodick stepped from the train.

Contrary to Neil's expectations, Brodick did not indulge in any exclamations, but stood looking dreamily out over the wide prairie to the west. Neil thought he saw something like a film shading his uncle's eyes; but the face of the old cattleman was grim and forbidding.

'I didn't reckon it would come so soon, Neil,' said Amos finally. 'Come I must get back to the ranch.' He saw Neil's horse standing covered with sweat. 'Put him up in the New West barn,' he instructed. 'I'll go over an' get the horse Walt left here—he's fresh.'

Amos Brodick swung up into the hotel stage as he finished speaking. Neil mounted and rode slowly to the barn. He told the man in charge to saddle the other horse and then met his uncle as he was coming out of the barn.

'Listen to me, Neil,' said Amos Brodick. 'There's a deputy sheriff in this town named Mills. I've asked for him, an' he's out in the country a ways, they tell me; but he's expected back soon. You stay here until he gets back and tell him about Swain. Tell him I asked for him to come out to the ranch, but not to make any fuss about it. He'll know what to do. Then you come home. An' don't do any talking.'

Neil promised to carry out the orders. His uncle got his horse and started for the ranch.

Late that afternoon the deputy sheriff returned to Angel, and Neil met him on the porch of the hotel. The officer received the news much the same as Amos Brodick heard it —without visible emotion or more than ordinary interest. This coincidence impressed Neil. Was life, then, held so cheaply in this new country?

'I shall have to do some work before I leave here, tell your uncle,' said Mills. 'I'll try to get up there tonight.'

That was all the deputy said as he moved quickly away. Somehow Neil had felt that

136

when the news was conveyed to the proper authorities it would be the signal for immediate action—the sending out of a posse, perhaps. But, apparently, Swain's death was causing not even a ripple in the official life of the county. It met with seemingly stoic indifference. It was almost as if it had been expected!

Yet all this gave Neil an increased feeling of security. His story so far had been accepted without question. Very likely he would not even be asked to repeat it. There was little danger of his having to incur the vengeful enmity of Lentu in an effort to ward suspicion from himself. His secret and his life were safe!

And yet, with this satisfying knowledge came a new sense of responsibility which was puzzling to Neil. He considered this as he rode out of Angel in the hour preceding the sunset. For the first time he felt himself a factor in the strange tangle of events which had transpired since he and Dora had come to the ranch.

He awoke suddenly to the realization that the feud between the combine and his uncle was a matter of life and blood. Lentu had said they were fighting for the open range, standing at the frontier to prevent its corruption by fool-headed farmers or would-be farmers who knew nothing of the country or its customs. He had painted a vivid picture of stirring scenes and wild range life that would come back into its own if the combine won—pictures that appealed to Neil's imagination, that thrilled and enthralled him. He had insisted that Neil's uncle would in time 'wake up' and come to see things the combine's way, and that Neil would have an honored place in the activities of the victors when all the things he promised should come to pass. And he had taken sides against Left Hand, whom Neil hated, and against whom he felt utterly at a disadvantage. It was as if Neil had the deadly speed and accuracy of Lentu's gun between him and Left Hand in what he construed as his fight to keep Dora. Yes, it was better to have Lentu's gun for him than against him.

Nevertheless, the killing of Swain had served to impress Neil with the seriousness of the situation. His uncle against the combine! Again he felt that peculiar inner emotion which he did not understand. It seemed as if a new and strange trend of ideas were endeavoring to break through the barrier of argument built by Lentu—a barrier the Double S foreman was prepared to maintain by force.

When Neil's horse topped the last but one of the long, rolling slopes on the northern side of Angel Butte, the sunset was dying in the skies over the high mountains westward, and long banners of crimson and gold, slowly fading into the hazy purple of the twilight, hung athwart the heavens. Neil halted to view the scene, fascinated by its beauty and its hint of infinite spaces.

Gradually his gaze became fixed on a swiftly moving, golden cloud of dust that whirled toward him along the grassy slope, and he soon made out a rider following a dry cattle trail which once had marked the thundering progress of the buffalo herds but now resounded to the dull, methodical pound of a horse's hoofs.

Closer and closer came the rider ahead of this swirling dust cloud, and Neil, thinking to avoid him as a sensible precaution, drove the spurs into his own mount. But the rider cut across, up the slope, and gained the trail a bit ahead, where he waited until Neil arrived.

Neil started in surprise not unmixed with apprehension when he recognized the rider silently sitting his sweating, steaming horse in the trail, covered with dust which showed plainly in matted layers against his black chaps and shirt and high-crowned hat. His left side was toward Neil, and the youth saw the big, black butt of the gun which snuggled tight against the man's side, and caught the gleam of the sunset's fading fires on the cartridges in his belt.

It was Left Hand, arriving back at Angel Butte after a long, hard ride.

In a flash Neil remembered Lentu's hint that this man might have been involved with Swain in an attempt to steal his uncle's cattle. Had Lentu and his companions found the man at an appointed rendezvous waiting for Swain, and chased him?

'Just getting back from the celebration?' greeted Left Hand amiably as Neil's horse stopped.

'An' what if I am?' demanded Neil, emboldened by the other's apparent lack of hostility.

Left Hand's smile departed instantly. 'Has your uncle got back to the ranch?' he asked coldly.

'My uncle's at the ranch, of course,' replied Neil.

'Anything happened up your way?' asked Left Hand sharply.

Neil couldn't resist the impulse to answer: 'Maybe you know as much about it as I do! '

'What is it?' snapped Left Hand.

'I don't know why I should be answering—'

'What has happened?' Left Hand interrupted. 'Come, speak up—quick!' The man's left hand darted downward to his pistol, and his eyes flashed dangerously. 'Speak up!'

'Swain's been killed,' answered Neil, his face paling.

'Swain!' said Left Hand softly. For a moment he appeared deep in reflection. Then he looked at Neil somewhat curiously. 'Let me give you a tip, young fellow,' he said coldly. 'Stay away from Lentu and his crowd. Show some sense. An' if I was you, I'd leave that gun at home.' He drove in his spurs and rode swiftly down the trail, leaving Neil mad with futile anger.

As Neil started on up the trail he thought he heard an oath and a laugh borne back upon the breeze from the disappearing horseman. Once more his hatred of Left Hand aroused his suspicions as he hastened over the shoulder of the butte and turned down toward the ranch.

CHAPTER XIX

A GRAVE CONJECTURE

When Neil arrived at the ranch he found that Swain's body had been brought down from the pass in the mountains, and that plans had been made to bury it next day. The men had made a coffin from available lumber stored in the hayloft of the horse barn, and in short shifts they watched over the body.

Deputy Mills arrived at the ranch that night, and to him Neil repeated his story in the presence of his uncle and Williams, the new foreman, and Walt Frost. Williams and Frost testified that an examination had revealed the fact that Swain had been shot twice *in the back.*

The officer put a few perfunctory questions to Neil, but neither he nor Amos Brodick nor any of the others seemed openly to doubt for a minute that Neil had told the truth and the whole truth.

Whatever surmises Amos Brodick might have indulged in, he did not put into words. He was strangely silent and grim. The officer stayed at the ranch that night and remained alone with Amos Brodick in the dining room until a late hour. He departed early in the morning.

Swain was buried the next day. The men stood around the coffin and the open grave while Amos Brodick read a burial service. Mrs. French and Dora, silent and fearful and with tears in their eyes, were present. When Amos had finished with the service the coffin was lowered into the grave, which had been dug in the lower slope of the butte above the pasture north of the house, and inclosed in a special fence. It was in a spot where the sun would almost always shine, except in bad weather, and where, according to the men, 'Swain would have liked to lie if he could have chosen the place himself.'

After the burial the various activities of the ranch became normal again. July slipped away without disturbance of any kind. The beef herd had been put back on the plateau at the head of Wild Horse Creek, but two men now were constantly on guard. It was planned to move these cattle down the creek in the early part of August and to graze them on the way, for Amos Brodick had the prior right, from the forest service, to most of the grazing land along the creek.

The north shoulder of Telltale Peak, which joined with the ridge that flattened out into the plateau where the beef herd was grazing, could be seen from the ranch. It had been arranged that in event of trouble on the plateau the men stationed there were to make a smoke signal on the north shoulder of Telltale Peak, and assistance from the ranch would be dispatched immediately.

All the men—and the women, too—had been carefully instructed by Amos Brodick to be alert for the sign of this smoke signal, and to report it to him at once if it should be seen. A fire in the same spot was to be the signal at night.

Now there was a lookout constantly on watch during the night. The men arranged these lookouts among themselves, and the duty never was neglected.

Aside from these precautions, the regular work of the ranch was carried on in the regular way. Neil had his duties and performed them willingly. In fact he had a genuine desire to learn as much as possible about ranch life and work. And his uncle, evidently desirous that he should learn the business from the ground up, as the saying has it, accorded him the same tasks—in so far as his experience would permit—and subjected him to the same discipline as the other men. He received his orders from Williams, and the new foreman could find no fault with the way in which he obeyed them. The men were quick to enlighten him when the occasion demanded and, for the most part, treated him as one of them, despite the fact that he slept in the house and ate his meals at the ranch-house dining table. He looked better than when he had arrived, too, and he had gained strength with his coating of healthy tan.

Neil studiously avoided thrusting his attention on Dora, and he saw that this attitude on his part, and his steady application to his work, were effectively pleading his cause with her. Her pleasure frequently showed in her eyes when he would come in to supper tired and hungry and smile wistfully at her. But he was too shrewd to attempt to go further than the smile as yet.

Amos Brodick, busy with the many affairs of the ranch, found but little time in which to pay any attention to the peculiar situation which existed between his nephew and Dora. Indeed the rancher seemed at times to be enjoying the little drama being played before his eyes and under his patronage.

'He's coming along all right,' he said to Dora one evening when she had pressed him very subtly for an opinion as to Neil. 'I think maybe along about Christmas time you two—' And then he broke out into a hearty laugh as Dora, blushing, left him alone on the porch.

But Neil, although he never voiced his

thoughts, rather resented the fact that his uncle did not see fit to confide in him concerning his affairs. Amos Brodick, busy from early dawn until late at night, was accustomed to sit alone in his little office in the front of the house after he had finished for the day. Sometimes Neil detected a worried look in his uncle's eyes, and often he caught him standing musing with that expression which signified that his thoughts were many miles away.

Only once during these weeks of the glorious summer of the foothills, with their blending of the heat of the prairie lands and the cool, pine-scented breezes of the higher ridges, did he make so bold as to interrupt his uncle's thoughts at night with a reference to the feud, as it now was generally called.

'Lentu and some of those others claim they can keep the homesteaders out up here just like they say they've kept the sheep out,' Neil had said, supplementing his remark.

His uncle's eyes had flashed. 'They can't seem to see that what they're tryin' to do is just the same as tryin' to stop the tide from coming up with a shingle. They can't stop it. An' sooner or later they're goin' to have it hammered into them—or shot into them— that folks are thinkin' different about the matter of the law now than they did—well, some years ago.'

This was as much as Neil had been able to

145

get out of his uncle with regard to the combine. And Neil couldn't help but contemplate in sheer astonishment the quiet manner in which the death of Swain had been received. There had been no attempt so far as he knew at investigation. The incident appeared closed with the lowering of the dead foreman's body into the grave and the taking of precautions to prevent another such tragedy.

It was then that a strange, awesome thought came to Neil, but he refused to give it credence. Still it recurred to him many times during the weeks after Swain's death, and it caused him to see his uncle in a new light—an uncomfortable light. He strove earnestly to put the thought aside. It was merely conjecture, surely.

But from Dora, during their occasional talks, he learned more than from his uncle. It was from her he heard what Martin had said on the morning of the celebration in Angel. He decried the possibility of Left Hand being a gunman hired by his uncle, and agreed with Dora that this could not be true. Yet it set him thinking and again brought up the disagreeable conjecture.

From Dora, too, he heard the story of the Sand Creek hanging, which but served to add a new, sinister aspect to Lentu's unsavory reputation and attest to his viciousness.

Dora sought to convince him of the

146

ruthlessness of this enemy of Amos Brodick. 'Just think of such a man!' she cried. 'A man who would deliberately murder two men under a flag of truce and drive a young boy out upon the prairie alone to die!'

This but served to convince Neil the more that his course in following Lentu's instructions regarding the story of Swain's death had been logical.

'And so you see,' Dora had continued, 'whatever can be said, it does look as though Left Hand was on our side since he is against Lentu and Martin and the others.'

There it was again. Neil ground his teeth in ill-concealed rage. Why did Dora persist in sticking up for Left Hand? She had not forgotten the man, then. In Neil's mind Lentu's hatred for Left Hand compromised his undeniably bad qualities.

Left Hand a hired gunman of his uncle? Neil did not believe it. If such were indeed the case, why wasn't he on the ranch and close at hand? And if it were true, was it also true that Neil's conjecture was correct?

For the first time he deliberately asked himself the question: Was his uncle afraid?

Could this be the reason why little or nothing had been done about Swain's death?

Neil, mentally debating the matter from all angles, was compelled to conclude that everything pointed to his conjecture being the truth.

And then, one day late in July, Walt Frost returned from Angel with a load of supplies and some astonishing news.

'Left Hand has filed on the north of twenty-two and is building a shack there!' was his startling announcement.

The gunman had thrown the combine's defy of a deadline for homesteaders into its teeth and was boldly and openly taking possession of the forbidden ground!

CHAPTER XX

THE MIDNIGHT VIGIL

The news of Left Hand's surprising move was the subject of exhaustive speculation among the men on the ranch, with the exception of Amos Brodick, who showed neither great surprise nor visible interest. His only cognizance of the new and amazing turn in affairs was to repeat his admonition to the men to be constantly alert in the event of a signal from Telltale Peak, which would announce a second attempt to rustle his cattle.

Neil, convinced that it was some kind of trick on the part of Left Hand, succeeded in sowing seeds of suspicion against him in an insidious way. He told of his meeting the man as he returned to the vicinity of the butte from a long, hard ride; intimated in a subtle way that Left Hand might know something of Swain's death, because Neil was not convinced for a certainty that the theft of the cattle was not a plan of Swain's and the gunman's.

Neil now saw his uncle in a new and depreciative light. He actually believed that Amos Brodick stood in deadly fear of Martin, Lentu, and the others of the combine!

'But, Neil, there is as much reason why Left Hand should file on a piece of land as anybody else,' Dora had argued, when Neil had hinted at the way he felt about the whole matter.

'He could have filed when he first came here,' Neil had retorted. 'And if he's wanted by the authorities as they say, he had to file under some name besides his own—whatever it is— and he couldn't very well except to keep and prove up a homestead under an assumed name.'

Meanwhile the whole ranch watched for the fulfilling of the combine's threat against any one who should dare to file inside of the dead line laid down in the spring.

The combine's guards had been withdrawn, it was learned. Possibly they didn't want to clash with Left Hand. But it was generally believed that the combine had assumed that its threat had made good and had not expected a filing on twenty-two.

During July the newly erected shacks of the homesteaders had crept steadily westward from the town of Angel; now they had reached the eastern flanks of the butte, although they had not encroached upon the north side, where there was a vast expanse of range still used by the combine as grazing land for its cattle.

There was one shack in this territory now, however. It was the shack which Left Hand had built in a day after he had had the rough lumber hauled out from Angel, and had sat beside the driver, gun in hand and with a rifle behind him, to answer any leaden messengers of protest which the combine might speed in his direction.

But there had been no show of hostility while the shack was being built. Peace and quiet reigned upon the butte, which reared its majestic bulk against a clear blue field of sky, brilliant with sunshine, glowing in gold and green, topped with spires of limestone that gleamed with the whiteness of marble.

Dora had found a trail which wound around the east side of the butte to its crest, and on several afternoons when she had been riding she had followed this trail to the summit, to gaze out upon the far-flung scene of prairie grandeur with its background of purple mountains—the Rockies, the Big and Little Belts, and, in the southeast, the Highwoods.

On the afternoon following the announcement that Left Hand had filed on twenty-two and was building a shack there, she rode again up the winding trail to the top of the butte. On her first trip, weeks before, she had seen a glimmer of Left Hand's camp through the pine growth midway of the descent of the east side of the butte. But the camp had disappeared. Left Hand had moved to some other section of that side of the butte, possibly down by the deep sluice boxes cut in the limestone near the foot of the butte, where the waters of Band Creek, augmented by those of Wild Horse Creek, surged on their way to join the mighty Missouri.

This afternoon the girl viewed with a thrill the little structure of rough boards which stood alone far down the north slope, a tangible, visible, saucy-appearing defy to the combine. Forlorn, insignificant as it would have looked to a stranger in the locality, Dora knew, nevertheless, that it portended something mighty in the lives of those who lived around the butte. The very stillness of the air and peaceful beauty of the scene held a note of sinister foreboding—as of a wild animal asleep before the hunt.

Sitting on a boulder in the shade of some gnarled and wind-twisted pines, Dora lost track of the passage of time and was suddenly brought to her senses by the soft shading of the light and the delicate rose tints of the skies, which proclaimed the sunset.

Hurriedly she rose and went for her horse, grazing in a meadow a short way down the slope. As she prepared to mount she heard the rattle of stones upon the rocky trail. In another moment, while she hesitated in wonder and with a vague feeling of alarm, Left Hand came into view riding up the trail, and pulled in his horse close to her.

He shook his head slowly and scowled.

Although Dora had heard many stories which tended to stamp this man as a dangerous, ruthless character, she found that she was not afraid of him—had never been afraid of him. Neither did she find herself considering him in the same light as she considered Lentu, another gunman and reputed killer. Although she could not reason exactly what it was which convinced her, she felt that there was a difference between the two men, even though they might each be deserving of the reputations bestowed upon them.

Left Hand continued to shake his head as he looked at her. The scowl quickly faded, however. 'You shouldn't be doing this,' he said finally in a tone of reproval. 'It isn't exactly safe.'

'What have you reference to, Mr. Left Hand?' asked Dora with a tilt of her head.

'You shouldn't come up on this butte not these days,' replied the man.

'If that is what you think, you will be kind enough to tell me why,' she retorted.

'Because there are dangerous men around

here, and while maybe you don't understand, it isn't altogether safe for you to go so far away from the ranch, ma'am—up here especially.'

'If I am to believe all I hear you are one of the dangerous men, Left Hand,' she said, gazing at him keenly. She noted that his eyes looked troubled, and his face was grim; he had forgotten to remove his hat.

'Perhaps,' he replied quickly and, she thought, whimsically. 'But you have nothing to fear from me, ma'am.'

'Of course not!' she exclaimed, but found herself at a loss for further words.

'It might not be the same with all the men up here,' he went on. 'An', besides, now that I've put that button on the landscape down there'—he pointed toward the lone shack in the north—'I'd like to have this place up here clear so I can keep an eye on it, an' there's others that might not like the idea of my being up here, an'—well, this ain't liable to be the healthiest spot around here, ma'am, if you know what I mean.'

Dora knew what he was endeavoring to convey. She mounted to obtain time in which to think, and decided upon a bold question.

'Left Hand, do you know what they—what some people are saying about you?' she asked.

This brought a short laugh. 'I could manage a guess.'

'I don't mean about your—your business,' she said.

153

'My business?' he asked sharply. 'What do they say is my business?'

Dora could not find the courage to tell him in so many words, but she nodded toward the gun strapped to his left thigh.

'Oh, that!' He smiled, and she thought he looked relieved.

'And they say you are in the employ of my uncle,' she continued. 'His—his gunman.'

Again the short laugh. 'And you want to know if that's true, eh, ma'am?'

'If I have the right to ask,' she faltered. 'I am not altogether familiar with customs out here, but—'

'Don't worry,' he interrupted cheerfully. 'You needn't have any fears 'bout me being in your uncle's pay. And in return for that information I wish you'd promise not to come up on the butte again for a while, anyway.'

She was about to reply to this when they were both startled by the approach of another rider. Left Hand whirled his horse and called to her over his shoulder to move away from behind him. His hand closed over the butt of his pistol as Neil came into view riding a sweating, nearly winded horse. Neil halted and stared at them with eyes which nearly popped from his head, and which flashed with anger.

'So this is the way it is!' he ejaculated with a sneer.

Dora urged her horse forward. 'Neil, I came up here for the ride and the view, as I've often

154

come, and Left Hand happened to find me here and—'

'Happened!' Neil cried.

Dora flushed at his tone and what it implied.

'That's what she said,' put in Left Hand. 'I happened upon her here an' told her it wasn't safe for her to be coming, if you want to know.'

'Just giving her a little advice, I suppose,' said Neil, sneering again.

'You got any objections?' queried Left Hand coolly. 'I suppose you're just hanging around here to give folks advice—women especially,' said Neil, now white-faced with anger.

'You could take a little advice yourself without its hurting you none,' Left Hand observed. 'An' what I was telling the lady was on the square—about her coming up here.'

'I want you to understand,' Neil flared, 'that the lady you're talking about is my wife!'

'Neil, you don't understand,' Dora implored.

'I understand that this fellow is meddling with somebody else's wife,' said Neil viciously.

'My advice to you,' drawled Left Hand, 'is to try an' be worthy of your wife an' not be a—coyote!'

With a veritable scream of rage Neil's hand dropped to the butt of his gun, but the calm, forbidding look in the other man's eyes arrested his movement. Instinctively he knew that he had not one chance in a thousand of

155

drawing his weapon before the other could get his gun into action.

'Don't do it, my boy, don't try it,' cautioned Left Hand. 'And don't get any fool ideas into your head about this chance meeting of mine with your wife. She's telling you the truth. This is not a safe place for her at present, an' I came up here to tell her so. Take her back, for it'll be dark before long. An' remember what I said about the—coyote.'

Dora guided her horse ahead of Neil's and began the descent. 'Thank you,' she called back to Left Hand.

'Don't mention it, ma'am,' returned the gunman.

Neil, tortured by futile rage, turned his horse. 'The odds are on your side,' he called back to Left Hand. 'They're on your side this time.'

'I aim to have 'em that way most of the time,' said Left Hand coldly, as he watched the riders disappear.

'I guess it's a good thing I happened to see you striking up this trail,' Neil called to Dora after a time.

'Don't talk to me, Neil,' Dora cried with tears welling in her eyes. 'Don't speak to me—now.'

Back on the summit of the butte Left Hand tied his horse in a thick clump of trees under the lee of a huge outcropping of limestone. He went to the north end of the rocky ridge on the crest of the butte and, after a long, searching gaze at the wide panorama below him, rolled and lit a cigarette and began to pace slowly back and forth along the rim, where he was in the shadow of the twisted pines, but had an unrestricted view.

Slowly the crimson banners of sunset shaded to gold and blue in the west, and the soft, hazy, purple veil of the twilight drew across the land and gradually deepened into night—the clear, cool night of the foothills, with the darkened vault of the heavens alive with stars.

At the coming of the dusk a faint light showed in the single window of the little shack—the window on the south side toward the butte. As night descended the light shone brighter and brighter until it, too, appeared like a star—a star fallen to rest against the velvet-black background of prairie.

Left Hand watched it with eyes agleam as he paced the rim of the summit. His features were tense; his attitude that of impatience, but not indecision. He was biding his time.

'If that lamp'll just hold out long enough,' he muttered to himself, 'maybe it'll attract attention.'

He kept his gaze roving toward the dark slope in the direction of the Double S. Now and then he would walk nearly around the crest of the butte to west and south, where he would pause and stare whimsically in the direction of the Brodick ranch, and then quickly retrace his steps to the north rim of the summit.

'His wife,' he said softly to himself. 'An' she asking me one day what the West did to a man. An' him, blind as a bat, actin' like a danged coyote!'

The moon, which had appeared with the coming of night, sank closer and closer to the mountain tops. There it seemed to hang just above the peaks and then slip quickly behind them. The darkness deepened. Still the light shone in the window of the little shack below—a blazing symbol of defiance.

Left Hand's watch showed the hour of midnight as he scanned its face in the flickering light of a match behind the shelter of the rocks where his horse was tethered.

Now he kept his gaze fixed on the long, black slope which led to the west shoulder of the butte and the Double S. An hour passed. He looked down toward the light. It had dimmed as if it were going out, or as if it had been turned low.

'Just as I figured,' he said to himself, then suddenly straightened and strained his eyes toward the Double S. At the upper end of the slope he saw a shadow—a blotch of ill-defined darkness against the background of the slope barely discernible in the pale glow of the stars. Again he saw it, and then it blended with the blackness farther down the slope.

Left Hand hurried to his horse, untied him, and led him down the trail and around through the pine growth to the north side of the butte. Mounting, he descended swiftly in the cover of the sparse timber until he reached its lower fringe. Here he tied his horse again and then began to creep silently and stealthily down the slope.

There were now two blotches of darkness, two vague forms stealing down the slope toward the dim light in the shack window.

CHAPTER XXI

A SINISTER PROPHECY

The night wind breathed in the prairie wastes as the two shadows glided toward the shack. One moved quickly down from the southwest slope; the other cut across from the fringe of timber, moving slowly and pausing at regular intervals, keeping close to the ground in order to blend with the blackness of the plain.

When the first shadow reached the shack it crept slowly to the window, and gradually the outlines of a man's head and shoulders stood out against the faint glow of the dimming lamp within. The second shadow moved rapidly but silently now. And when the man before the window, having satisfied himself that there was no one inside, turned quickly to look about him, he found himself staring into the bore of a six-shooter held in a steady hand. Slowly his stare traveled from the gun to the face above it; became fixed upon the eyes which transfixed his. His hands went high above his head.

Without speaking Left Hand stepped forward and possessed himself of Lentu's gun. He motioned with his pistol toward the front of the shack, and Lentu moved around to the door, still keeping his hands elevated. Left Hand opened the door and followed Lentu inside. He lit another lamp upon the table and put out the one which was smoking and empty.

'I sort of expected you'd call,' said Left Hand. 'I fixed that light on purpose so you'd think it was an invitation. Sit down, but put your hands on the table!'

Lentu obeyed the commands. 'I didn't know but what that light was a blind,' he said surlily. 'I don't care if it was. I came down here to see you.'

Left Hand dropped into the other chair by the table, a corner of which separated him from Lentu. He stared at Lentu with a directness which momentarily nonplused the other. There was an undefinable but easily distinguishable gleam of hatred and gloating in that stare an undubitable menace, absolutely sincere.

'I say I came down here on purpose to see you,' Lentu repeated.

'Yes?' Left Hand seemed to lisp the word so that it carried something of a hiss as it left his lips.

'Oh, I intended to get the drop on you if I could,' Lentu said with a smirk, and the grimace he intended for a grin seemed strangely out of place. 'But that's as far as I had intended to go tonight.'

Left Hand laughed. Lentu thought he detected a note in the laugh which made it seem more sinister than the other's continued, disconcerting stare.

'What did you want to talk to me about?' asked Left Hand coolly. 'I mean, what did you think you wanted to talk to me about? Or, did you have to have the drop on me to talk?'

Lentu wet his lips. His eyes had narrowed. He was not a coward. But there was something in the cold, almost fiendish gleam of the eyes which looked into his own that gave him a new sensation. He did not try to grin again.

'I'm asking you what you wanted to talk to me about,' Left Hand reminded him sharply.

'Why, it's just this—it's—well, Left Hand, I don't know what your game is, but, whatever it is, why couldn't it be played better on our side?'

In the silence which ensued, the gentle drone of the prairie wind could be heard. This sound was quickly drowned in a harsh, mirthless laugh from Left Hand a laugh that sent a chill into the very marrow of Lentu's bones. It was almost like the laugh of a

161

madman. Indeed, it seemed to suggest downright savage joy.

'Lentu, you're a fool,' said Left Hand grimly.

'You might get more from us than from old Brodick,' said Lentu.

'I'll get all I want from you!' cried Left Hand.

Again Lentu felt the strange sensation, the chill. He avoided that stare. Could it be that the unknown thing he felt was fear? Was he to be shot down in cold blood?

'So you came here with a proposition?' Left Hand said suavely. 'Because I've crossed your dead line an' planted a shack on twenty-two? Because you think I'm working for Brodick?'

'Because we could use you,' retorted Lentu, and he probably spoke the truth.

Left Hand leaned on the table. His eyes were glowing with a strange, fierce gleam. 'How do you know I ain't working for myself?' he asked.

'A gunman like you don't deliberately butt into anybody's play unless there's something in it for him, does he?' countered Lentu. 'I know your reputation—'

'But do you know me?' demanded the other sharply.

Looking straight into the burning eyes before him, Lentu felt the same thrill which had crept over him when he had confronted the man in the saloon at Angel the night of the celebration. The sweat stood out upon his forehead in glistening beads while his mind tugged vainly at the strings of memory. And, as he met the other's stare, he knew the look would mean but one thing—death. Left Hand intended to kill him! He glanced swiftly about him, and as he glanced Left Hand smiled; his face seemed to light with joy and satisfaction with triumph.

'No chance,' he said softly; 'not a chance. Lentu, you—haven't—got—a—chance! Don't you see I'm sitting here gloating over you? That's what I'm doing—gloating! And yet you're sure goin' out of this shack alive! I'm goin' to let you go just like a cat lets a mouse go an' then catches it again an' kills it! If you could only think maybe you wouldn't get out of here so easy. But you can't think yet. You're right. I'm workin' for somebody. That's why I've got to let you go. Now, ain't that strange?'

Left Hand laughed, but the other didn't join him in his mirthless hilarity.

'You say you know my reputation, Lentu? Well, I want you to be sure—*sure,* understand? Do you remember the night we met in Angel? I always wondered why you didn't draw that night, Lentu. You didn't make a move until you thought you had the advantage. An' now we're here alone in this shack, an' you're wishing you had your gun that I threw in the corner. Lentu, do you see that knot in that middle board of the door?'

Left Hand's voice seemed to purr as he pointed to the knot midway the height of the door.

'Now that ain't such a big knot, Lentu; it's a lot smaller than a man's heart—a right small mark, to get down to cases. Now you watch!'

Left Hand slipped his gun into the sheath of his left side, and rose to a half crouch. 'Now, Lentu, hold up your right forefinger. Don't worry, I'm not goin' to shoot it off, nor shoot you. You don't know why, but you're as safe here with me tonight as if you was tucked in your own bed. All I want you to do is crook that finger now that you've got it up there.'

Lentu hesitated. But, looking into the man's eyes in the glow of the light from the lamp, he realized that Left Hand meant just what he said. Lentu's eyes glittered. The fool was actually going to give an exhibition of his speed with his gun. Deliberately going to give him a chance to view him in action; to compare his speed with his own—Lentu's. It was like exposing one's hand at poker and then going on with the game. It might give Lentu an advantage in a future meeting. Was the man a supreme egotist? Was he overplaying his hand? For the first time Lentu smiled naturally as he crooked the finger.

But the smile died cold on his lips. It seemed to him as if he had hardly moved his finger—just decided to move it when the left hand of the man before him moved faster than the eye could follow, and the sharp thunder of the gun shattered the death-like stillness.

Lentu's eyes popped in amazement at the magical, lightning swiftness of the draw he had witnessed. Slowly his fascinated gaze shifted from the weapon at Left Hand's hip to the knot in the door. It was punctured almost directly in the center!

'You see!' cried Left Hand gayly. 'Did you see?'

Lentu remained silent. He had seen fast work with a gun; had had to beat some fast men. But never had he witnessed such speed as Left Hand had exhibited. What was the object? Coolly he appraised the other as he sat down and again leaned upon the table. And then the question formed in Lentu's mind shone in his eyes. Could he, Lentu, draw and shoot as fast as that?

It was as if Left Hand could read his very thought. His eyes burned into Lentu's with deadly seriousness, and his lips tightened as he slowly shook his head with an earnest conviction.

'You ain't got a chance, Lentu; that's what I want you to remember. That's the way I want it when the time comes. That little show I staged wasn't a bluff.' Left Hand pointed to the bullet hole in the knot in the board of the door. 'I wanted you to see; I wanted you to know. You won't have a chance!'

Lentu's face turned a purplish red with

anger. Was the man trying to scare him—to frighten him out of an encounter which he predicted?

'I ain't got a chance now,' he said, openly sneering.

'An' you didn't have one down in Angel, though you didn't know it. An' you won't have one the next time. A man always gets what's coming to him, Lentu.'

'So you're a preacher as well as a gun fighter,' said Lentu as he sneered again.

'Not a preacher, Lentu! I'm a prophet!'

Left Hand walked to the corner where he had thrown the other's weapon. He picked it up, broke it, spilled the shells on the floor, handed it to Lentu, and motioned toward the door. As Lentu went out Left Hand extinguished the light and followed him up the long slope, but when Lentu reached the top and turned around, he was alone.

CHAPTER XXII

A TRIANGLE

The following day Neil, outwardly cool and composed and reserved in his attitude toward Dora, inwardly raged in bitterness toward Left Hand. The fact that he believed Dora's statement that she had merely ridden to the

166

top of the butte for the exercise and the view did not alter his conviction that the man had followed her there that he was deliberately soliciting her favor; and her look of reproval at breakfast merely caused the tumult in his thoughts to flare the more ominously.

After breakfast Amos Brodick instructed Neil to ride to Angel with some letters for the post. These had to do, he said, with the prospective sale of the beef cattle, which were to be brought down from the plateau range within a week—as soon as the alfalfa hay had been put up.

On the ride to Angel, Neil kept a sharp lookout for sight of Left Hand, but his vigil was unrewarded. He saw no one in the vicinity of the Double S, either. He stared darkly at the shack on the north half of section twenty-two, erected, as he knew, by Left Hand, but to all outward appearances deserted.

'Builds a shack and then hides in the timber,' growled Neil savagely as he drove in his spurs and hastened toward the prairie town of Angel far below.

It was still some time until noon when Neil rode into the town and went directly to the general store, which contained the post office. After posting his uncle's letters he took the horse to the hotel barn to be rested, watered, and fed against his return. Then he sauntered around to the front of the hotel and the main street. He was in an ugly mood, and this mood

167

was not improved by his reflection that he could think of no way in which to get even—as he thought the case required—with Left Hand.

In this frame of mind he entered the Prairie Flower saloon. It was the first time he had been in the place since the memorable night when he had participated in the blackjack game and incurred the displeasure of the dealer, Ratty.

Almost as soon as he walked in through the door he caught sight of the dealer. He walked to the bar and called for a drink—such as was sold openly. The strenuous nature of Neil's thoughts gave him a courage and aggressive appearance which was far different from the impression he had made on that night some two months before. In addition, he felt a dawning confidence in himself.

Watching in the mirror behind the bar he saw the dealer looking at him curiously and apparently disdainfully. This nettled him and aggravated his temper, which already was raw. Only a few were gathered around the table where the game was in progress, as it nearly always was in progress both day or night.

As Neil finished his drink—the only one he intended to take that day, he told himself—he was surprised to see Lentu enter hurriedly by the back door, which was open, and signal to two men in cow-puncher garb who were standing near the table watching the game. Lentu spoke to the men a moment, and then

168

the two went out of the rear door. Neil assumed that they were employees of the combine.

Lentu seemed surprised to see him there when he came to the bar. He insisted that Neil drink with him, and Neil, finding that the liquor—a special brand which a wink from Lentu brought forth—fanned the flame of his angry passion and, becoming more vengeful in his thoughts, told the Double S foreman of the encounter with Left Hand the evening before, and of his suspicions. Lentu's eyes glistened as he paid marked attention to Neil's words and then deftly ascertained that Neil had concealed the most important phase of the incident of Swain's death in the story he had told his uncle and the others. He appeared satisfied. He said nothing to Neil of his extraordinary session of the night before with Left Hand in the shack on the north slope of Angel Butte.

A bell sounded from a restaurant next to the saloon, and most of the men around the gaming table left to get dinner. Ratty closed the game temporarily, and when his boosters went out to eat he crossed over to the bar.

He stood at the lower end between Neil and the door, at Neil's left. Lentu stood at Neil's right and nudged Neil's arm as Ratty came up to the bar. 'He's got more respect for you than he used to have,' said Lentu in an undertone.

The remark pleased Neil, who leaned

against the bar with a swaggering, confident air.

But Ratty's forthcoming remark did not seem to indicate any great degree of newly acquired respect. 'I see you've added chaps an' spurs to the hat,' he said with the suggestion of a sneer.

Neil's eyes glittered and narrowed in surprise and anger, Lentu glanced significantly at the bartender.

'Did you ever stop to think that you've got as much as you can tend to if you look after your own business?' retorted Neil.

'I'm capable of doin' that, young feller,' said Ratty.

'He's bluffing,' Lentu whispered to Neil with hardly a movement of his lips. 'He's scared of you, an' is tryin' to cover it up. I know him like a book—the coyote.'

At the word coyote Neil bristled. Left Hand had used that word in connection with himself the evening before. At the very thought of it Neil's anger rose again. Here was another enemy who had humiliated him, present in the flesh to receive the brunt of his rage. Ratty did not look very dangerous, and Neil had the spur of his wrathful thoughts to drive him on.

'An' what's that hanging on his side?' Ratty snickered as he put down his glass. 'Why, darn my stars if he ain't gone to packing a gun!'

Neil's eyes blazed with fury.

'What you totin' that aroun' for, son?' Ratty

170

taunted with a wink at Lentu. 'Do you see how quick they get to be bad men when they come out here from the East?' he asked the bartender.

'Pull your gun an' send a couple of shots over his head,' whispered Lentu excitedly. 'He'll run like a scared rabbit. He ain't armed, anyway. Hurry up. Throw a scare into him!'

And Neil, approving the idea in a flash, and in the same instant recollecting that he had Lentu behind him, in any event, pulled his gun and fired twice over Ratty's head. The bartender dodged down behind the bar at the first move. It seemed to Neil that the second shot sounded considerably louder than the first. And then he looked at Ratty in unfeigned amazement as the dealer's body swayed back from the bar and toppled to the floor.

'Good Lord!' cried Lentu loudly, running to bend over the fallen man. 'Great guns, Sterret,' he gasped, 'you've killed him!'

An icy chill of horror and fear struck at Neil's heart as he stood and stared down at the body of the dead dealer and then looked open-mouthed at his gun.

'Put that gun up, quick,' snapped Lentu, as he turned the body over and withdrew a snub-nosed revolver from one of the dead man's hip pockets. 'Ratty just couldn't draw fast enough for the kid,' he explained to the bartender as the man came slowly from his hiding place. Lentu dropped Ratty's gun close to the stiffening fingers of the hand which stuck out from under the body.

'Sterret, get out that back door,' commanded Lentu. 'Get your horse an' get out of town as fast as you can ride an' keep your mouth shut!'

Still Neil remained rooted to the spot with horror, unable to comprehend the tragedy which had befallen him in such an incredibly short space of time. The sweat burst out upon his face and forehead and hands as he returned his weapon to its sheath. There must be some mistake, he thought wildly—some kind of accident. He had shot high; he had not intended to—

'Hurry an' make your get-away, you fool,' roared Lentu. 'A posse might not stop to ask questions except with a rope. I'll head 'em off if I can. Are you going, or—'

Neil didn't wait to hear the rest of it but ran for the back door. As he leaped outside he turned for a fleeting glimpse over his shoulder and caught swift sight of Left Hand standing in the front doorway. For an instant he wavered, wondering; then he dashed for the hotel barn, got his horse, and rode like mad out of town in the direction of the butte.

Driving home his spurs with a cruel viciousness that made his horse snort with pain and extend itself to the utmost, Neil dashed across the open country to the bottom of the first of the series of long, easy slopes which led up and around the north side of the butte to its western shoulder and the cañon trail down to Wild Horse Creek.

Here Neil slacked his pace somewhat. What if he were followed? Wouldn't his pursuers go straight for the ranch and find him there? Then what? His distorted brain pictured a noose swinging from the limb of a tree and himself standing under it striving to explain what had happened to a posse of grim-faced men. What would he say? What could he say? He needed time to think, and above everything else he wanted to know if he was followed.

He looked quickly about him, and his gaze, as he checked his horse, centered upon the tumbled country to the south, below the eastern side of the butte, where Brand Creek wound through the sluice boxes cut in the soft limestone. There he could hide and watch!

Without further thought about the matter he turned his horse from the trail and rode rapidly south until he had gained the shelter of the bad lands, with their growth of cottonwoods and willows near the sluice boxes. He mounted to the top of a rise of ground and, after securing his horse among the trees on the west side, crawled to the edge of a limestone ledge on the east and fixed his gaze upon the open trail in the northeast, over which he had ridden from Angel.

He hardly had time to settle himself for his vigil before he saw a cloud of dust racing on the wind from the direction of the town. His heart swelled in his throat. A posse? Men, maddened and eager for vengeance, already upon his trail? With the thought Neil became strangely quiet and composed—clearheaded and able to think.

Speedily he realized that it was too small a dust cloud to be made by a body of horsemen, and this surmise soon proved to be correct; for he made out a single rider coming rapidly on the main trail to the butte. A few minutes later he recognized the form in the saddle as Lentu.

Neil was at first prompted to mount and ride out to the trail to meet the oncoming horseman. But before he could yield to this impulse he was stayed by another. He felt a wave of hot anger toward the Double S foreman. Lentu had told him to shoot. It was not Lentu's fault, perhaps, that he had followed the suggestion; but Lentu had been responsible for it, just the same.

Again Neil was struck with wonder at the result of his shots. He would have sworn at the last bar of judgment that he had aimed high, much higher than Ratty's head. He remembered that second shot; it had sounded louder than the first. Could it be that the cartridge was overloaded, and that the bullet had split, and part of it had gone low and killed Ratty? But he caught himself smiling; little as he knew about weapons and ammunition such a thing did not seem probable or possible. He decided that he would not ride out to meet Lentu; he watched as the Double S foreman disappeared around a bend on the first slope.

Thinking clearly now, Neil realized that the affair looked mighty bad for him. He had had trouble with Ratty. Doubtless every man who frequented the Prairie Flower saloon knew about the altercation which had taken place on the occasion of Neil's first visit there. He had not been in the place since—until this day. And on this second visit Ratty had been shot and killed by—but Neil could not bring himself to say, even in a whisper or in his thoughts, that he had committed the crime.

All the enmity he had felt toward Ratty had been blotted out by the feel and sound of the shots and the gruesome sight of the crumpled body on the floor. Neil hated heartily the very recollection of the bravado he had felt earlier in the day. He was not a killer, and he knew now what he had not known before—that he had no desire to be a killer, to take life.

Without looking at it, Neil drew out his gun, broke it, removed the empty shells, and flung them away from him in hearty disgust. He loathed the very feel of the pistol as he hurriedly slipped in two new shells and returned it to its sheath. He thought it would be best not to have two empty shells in the chamber.

He forgot it on the instant as he sighted

another small dust cloud whirling above the trail out from town. An officer? He watched breathlessly as the rider approached and then uttered a startled cry of amazement and consternation.

The rider had left the main trail to Angel Butte and had cut off to the south. He rode for some distance directly south and then swung toward the west. Neil leaped to his feet and then crouched motionless on the very edge of the limestone in an agony of indecision.

The rider was coming in his direction! He was coming fast. And, though Neil's every instinct urged him to flee, he remained as though rooted to the spot.

CHAPTER XXIII

THE SIGNAL

High above the glistening rock dome of Telltale Peak at the head of the narrow valley wherein Wild Horse Creek nursed its waters, hung a mass of feathery clouds. They had been there the day before—a thin wisp of shadowy veil that had gathered form during the night. The cloud mass attested to the warrant for the tradition of the peak, which was that the appearance of this vapor banner high over its summit foretold a change in weather—a storm. Already the wind had gathered volume and was whistling across the ridges and down between the timbered slopes of the valley and over the prairie lands, from the west.

Lentu, arriving at the Double S on his lathered horse, found a number of men there waiting for him, including those he had sent out from Angel. He quickly changed his saddle to a fresh steed in the big corral and ordered the men to mount. Time and again, as he went about the business of changing horses, his gaze sought the sky above the ridges west of the ranch in the direction of Telltale Peak, which he could not see because of the nearness of an intervening rib of range which joined the west shoulder of Angel Butte.

'Did that young cub from Brodick's place ride past here?' he demanded of one of the men.

'If he did he must have changed himself into a breath of wind,' was the answer. 'We ain't seen hide or hair of any rider but yourself an' the boys that came from town.'

Lentu frowned but vouchsafed no comment. Vaulting into the saddle he led the men out upon the long, undulating north slope of the butte. Here he paused to make sure of the direction of the wind. The sear, dry, brown-gold grass of the prairie rippled in waves as the wind caressed it, shaping it momentarily into miniature windrows, smoothing it again, bending it, wrinkling it, flattening it, tossing it

177

until the whole vast reach of the plain appeared to be trembling violently; and the motion always was toward the east, toward the single shack in the foreground on the north half of twenty-two, toward the other shacks which dotted the flatlands east of the slopes of the butte, toward the town of Angel with its rough-board structures and its board-floored tents, dry as tinder, highly inflammable, needing but a spark in the gathering force of the wind to become a caldron of flame and a fiery heap of smoldering embers.

Lentu spread his men in the shape of a fan, the farthest being two miles out across the slope, and he himself took up a position at a point near the trail on the west shoulder of the butte, where he awaited a favorable moment to give a prearranged signal. The men all had dismounted. Lentu slowly raised his hands, and for a moment they all bent low, then leaped back into their saddles and raced madly for the trail behind the Double S ranch house, which wound along the north slope of the western ridge toward the plateau near Telltale Peak, though there were a number of trails which surmounted the ridge and threaded thin paths through the timber to the valley of Wild Horse Creek.

*   *   *

It was Williams, the new foreman, who called

Amos Brodick from his little front office in the 3-X-Z ranch house in the early afternoon.

'There's smoke on Telltale Peak, sir!'

Amos Brodick rose quickly from his desk and ran out upon the porch. Far at the head of the valley, its gleaming dome and the darker shadow of its right spur outlined against the skies, was Telltale; and curling from the right spur was a spiraling feather of smoke.

'Saddle my horse!' shouted Amos. 'You and Walt Frost and one of the other men come with me. That's a signal from the men with the cattle.'

The ranch was in a hubbub of excitement. Men were running from the fields and the garden toward the house. Williams waved them back, with the exception of one who was to accompany Frost, himself, and Amos Brodick.

'If you hear firing, or if we have not sent word or returned before morning, send the other men,' Amos Brodick told Mrs. French. 'Let's see. There'll be five left, an' when Neil gets back he'll make six. Keep Neil an' the cook an' another here, whatever happens. This may be Martin's work. It may just be trouble with the cattle. But we can't leave the ranch an' you women unprotected. I think maybe there'll be other help coming if it's serious.'

The women watched white-faced as the four men galloped up the creek trail.

Amos Brodick's face was grim, and his eyes

were burning with the fire of combat as he led the way up the valley, riding hard and keeping his gaze on the trail ahead and the smoke signal, which loomed above the right spur of Telltale. As they slowly neared the head of the valley, where the trail to the plateau cut through the timber and up the ridge to the right, the cattleman checked his horse with a startled exclamation, and pointed high to the left and straight ahead.

The men swore softly as they looked. In the timber under the lee of Telltale and farther down into the valley flickering tongues of red were licking at the dry underbrush and trees, and leaping high with showers of sparks where the wind caught them and fanned them as with some gigantic bellows.

'The forest is afire!' cried Amos as he spurred his mount. 'That's what's the matter. The boys are having trouble gettin' the cattle out!'

Pushing their horses to their utmost speed the four men rode for the head of the valley and the trail to the plateau. Already the fires were climbing the slope toward the tableland, where were the cattle. If it reached the plateau it would sweep across it on the wind in an incredibly short time. The only trail from the flatland where the cattle were grazing, over which the stock could be driven safely out, was that which led down into Wild Horse Valley. If the fire should reach this trail before the cattle could be removed it would mean their extermination and would involve Amos Brodick in a loss from which he could recover only with extreme difficulty if at all. Payments and interest were due upon his place, and he was depending upon the beef herd to tide him over the lean years which had followed his removal from the Teton country after the affair of the Sand Creek hanging.

As the horses plunged across the narrow strip of valley and began the climb to the plateau, one of the men who had been left in charge of the big herd appeared suddenly in the trail sitting his horse and holding up a hand, palm outward, as a signal for them to stop.

'What's the matter?' demanded Amos angrily. 'Why ain't you tryin' to get the cattle out?'

'Because the minute a man's head shows on that plateau it's the target for shots from the timber,' was the answer.

'Shots? Whose?' demanded Amos.

'That I don't know,' the man replied. 'It began about noon, when we first saw the smoke from the fires in Wild Horse Valley. When we started to round up the cattle an' drive 'em to the trail the bullets began to whistle through our hats. My other horse was shot dead under me. Several of the steers was hit by hot lead an' keeled over. Then we built the signal fire. The cattle has got a whiff of the

181

smoke, an' they're bunching up.'

Without further questioning, or seeing fit to answer, Amos spurred his horse on up the trail. The man's story had established the fact that the forest fires had been set. The combine had boldly started to wipe out his cattle!

In the shelter of a fringe of timber to the left of the head of the trail Amos Brodick halted and considered the situation from every angle. The cattle were indeed bunching almost in the center of the big expanse of table-land. Around this plateau there was a sparse growth of timber leading to the ridges in the west and south and sloping down in the north and east. Already the smoke from the fire was beginning to drift across the plateau—and this drifting smoke gave Amos an idea.

'Where did the shots come from?' he asked the punchers, who had been in charge of the cattle. 'Which direction, I mean?'

'Seemed to me like they come mostly from the north side, an' maybe a few from the east,' replied one of the men, pointing across the plateau.

'Martin an' his gang are hidin' in the timber,' said Amos. 'I'm goin' to drive 'em out along with the cattle! Here, string out, you fellows—in the timber down the west side there. Shoot on sight if you meet anybody. When you get below the line from west to east where the cattle are bunching up, put a match to the timber. It'll burn fasten'n lightnin' in

182

this wind, an' it'll shoot a powerful lot of smoke across that north end of the plateau. When the smoke starts we'll ride out an' get the cattle started this way.'

'But the grass on the plateau?' exclaimed Williams.

'It's pretty well eaten down,' said Amos; 'it won't burn any too fast. It's the smoke from the timber I want. Hurry up, men—get goin'!'

When the smoke from the newly set fires began to roll out across the table-land, augmented by more smoke from the fires in the valley below the south ridge, Amos and the other dashed out upon the plateau and, firing their guns in the air, began to drive the cattle at a furious pace toward the south trail. Choking and gasping in the smoke they virtually stampeded the herd in the direction of the trail.

A scattering volley of shots came from the north side of the plateau, which now was submerged in a pall of smoke, riding eastward on the wind. The shots soon ceased, and Amos and Williams galloped ahead to guide the cattle into the head of the trail. The first flaming forerunners of the forest fire below were licking at the fringe of timber just to the west of the head of the trail when the cattle passed thundering down toward the valley.

Amos Brodick plunged on, ahead of the herd. Smoke and sparks filled the air as the fire raced eastward down the slopes of the valley. The rapidity with which the fire gained ferocious headway was astounding but not unnatural, for the timber, underbrush, and grass had known no rain in weeks of drought, and the forest and floor of the valley were sear and dry. Fanned by the wind, which increased in velocity as the clouds above Telltale Peak thickened in certain harbinger of a storm, the flames literally tore on their way, leaping from treetop to treetop, enveloping the trunks of trees in a fiery sheet, racing through the underbrush and along the ground.

On both sides of the valley the fire was raging and eating down toward the creek-bed and toward the trail, over which hung a thick curtain of smoke pierced by sparks and flying embers a hot, suffocating blanket that shut out the rays of the sun and bathed the floor of the narrow valley in a weird, unnatural, saffron-colored light, which distorted the perspective and even hid the flames so dangerously near.

When the cattle reached the bottom of the trail they were between two walls of fire with the smoke-pall closing down upon them. There was fire behind them also, for the flames had swept from side to side in the head of the valley. In a rift of the dense, suffocating curtain above and ahead, Amos caught a glimpse of men topping a ridge far down the creek. Then the wind closed the gap and shut off his view.

'Stampede 'em down the trail,' he shouted

above the sullen roar of the burning forest. 'Martin an' his men are goin' to try to head us off down the creek!'

The men galloped back and forth behind the plunging herd, firing their guns and shouting madly, while Amos Brodick rode far ahead of the cattle, his eyes fixed in a stare as he strove to pierce the curtain of smoke.

Some miles below, the valley would widen out; cliffs of limestone and ledges and rim-rock strewn with boulders and shale would impede the progress of the fire. If the cattle could be driven below this point, where the sides of the valley would close in for a short distance, they would be safe from the flames. The men, too, would have to pass this point to reach safety.

If the place was blocked by enemies it might mean death for both cattle and men. Amos Brodick's gun was in his hand as he galloped down the trail. Surely the men left at the ranch would be riding up the valley, for the smoke of the fire must long since have been seen by them.

Now a new factor added to the uncertainty. It became noticeably darker under the pall of smoke. The storm was gathering in the west, drawing a thick veil of clouds over the sunset. Night would come speedily. To get the cattle through in the darkness would be a herculean task.

A gust of wind broke the smoke curtain

ahead, and, as Amos Brodick took advantage of the fleeting view, his pulses throbbed with uncertainty and apprehension. There were mounted men in the bottleneck of the valley ahead.

CHAPTER XXIV

INFORMATION

Standing motionless on the edge of the limestone which capped a rise of ground below the east slope of Angel Butte, Neil watched the lone rider coming toward him at a furious pace on a big, powerfully built black horse. He recognized the magnificent steed which the man rode before he could make out with certainty the identity of the rider in the saddle. When he saw that the man approaching him was Left Hand he became aware of the fact that he too had been recognized.

Left Hand was gesturing toward him with his hat.

Neil quickly repressed an instinctive desire for flight when he recollected that his own mount could not be expected to outrun Left Hand's horse, and that, since the man was an outlaw himself according to reports, he had nothing to fear from him. He remembered, too, that he had caught sight of Left Hand standing in the front doorway of the Prairie Flower when he made his hurried exit by the rear.

He climbed down from the top of the rise, mounted, and rode boldly out into the open as Left Hand came pounding up with a serious expression on his face.

'You didn't go on over the butte, then!' exclaimed the gunman. 'Lentu would have stopped you if you had, I guess. What're you doing—hidin' out down here?'

'I was waiting to see what would happen,' confessed Neil.

'You needn't worry,' said Left Hand curtly. 'I told 'em I cracked Ratty from the doorway. Lentu beat it fast; but I guess the bartender sort of believed me. He knew Ratty had identified me an' probably thought I had it in for him for that reason. Anyway, it'll bother 'em if they figure on startin' anything.'

'You you mean you—took—the—blame!' stammered Neil.

'Oh, I didn't do what I did because of any sympathy for you, nor for friendship's sake, either,' said Left Hand. 'I had my reasons, an' I haven't got the time to explain 'em now. You goin' to the ranch?'

'Do you think it's—er—safe?' asked Neil anxiously.

Left Hand's contempt shone in his eyes. 'You're a sorry sight. Look here, Sterret, it's time you woke up to a few things. You've been actin' like a fool. The West isn't a case of chaps an' handkerchiefs aroun' the neck an' guns that go off permiscuously. It's a case of men playin' the part of men whether for good or bad—you've got to go all the way one way or the other. Don't you see your uncle's got a whole lot of trouble on his hands? It's life or death with him. There's a bunch of mean-thinking, hard-shooting hombres in the game against him. Just for my own information I'd like to know what side you're on! '

'Uncle Amos never told me he was in such a peck of trouble,' said Neil surlily, his anger again swiftly rising against this man.

'It isn't one of those things you can talk much aboutto a kid that's got a lot of fool notions in his head,' retorted Left Hand. 'You've got a pair of eyes an' some ears, haven't you? You can see an' hear, can't you? Don't you know Lentu's been fillin' you with a lot of soft stuff catering to you with good reason? Why? Because Lentu and that outfit is figurin' to get your uncle an' get him cold. They know you're due to inherit the ranch, an' then they think they'll twist you round their little finger an' make you dance to their tune— an' maybe make you the goat in the end for the whole business. Oh, you're smart, all right. Why, for all I know you may be in on the deal; maybe you want the ranch so bad—'

'That's a lie!' cried Neil hotly. 'That's a lie, Left Hand, an' you know it!'

'I hope so,' said the other with a sparkle in his eyes. 'But it looks a little that way. Maybe you've just been slow to see how things stood. Maybe they've had you buffaloed.'

'Wait a minute, Left Hand!' cried Neil. 'While you're doing so much talking maybe you'll tell me who you are.'

'I'm Left-hand Smith,' was the smiling reply.

'That gives a lot of information,' Neil said with a sneer. 'Where did you come from when you got back to the butte that night after Swain was killed? Tell me that! '

Left Hand eyed him curiously. 'I came from the Smith River country.'

'Sure; and it was over that way that Swain was killed.'

'Do you know who killed Swain?' Left Hand asked quickly.

Neil avoided the eyes which stared at him. 'Maybe that's why I was asking where you had been on that ride,' he said boldly.

'No, it wasn't. But I'll tell you what I was over there for. I went over to see the forest ranger. Now come on, we'll hit for the ranch by a trail I know on the east side of the butte. I overheard 'em planning something up at the Double S last night, an' maybe there's trouble in the air. You can come along or stay—it's up to you.'

Neil watched the man swing his horse up toward the slope. After a moment of indecision he followed. Up and up they rode on a dim trail, which led through the sparse timber growth, until they reached the top of the last slope under the crest of the butte. Here Left Hand paused and pointed toward the north. Neil looked and cried aloud in his amazement. The entire north slope was wreathed in smoke, and a line of fire was racing eastward toward the homestead shacks on the plain and the town of Angel. Already the north of twenty-two, where Left Hand's shack had stood, was a blackened vista instead of waving tufts of grass. The fire was sweeping eastward on the high wind at a fearful rate.

'That's some of your friend Lentu's work,' Left Hand called back. 'Done to keep the folks down to Angel busy while they do their dirty work up here, an' to discourage the homesteaders.'

He swung his horse into the trail which wound around the east side of the summit of the butte and down toward the ranch. When they came out of the timber on the south side Left Hand pointed again, up the valley this time, as he urged his horse to as great a speed as the trail would allow.

As Neil looked up the Wild Horse Valley he saw the smoke signal rising from the right spur of Telltale Peak. More than that, he saw other veils of smoke, lower down, drifting up from the timbered slopes at the head of the valley.

They arrived at the ranch within a few minutes. The men were throwing saddles on their horses in the corral. Mrs. French and Dora were out in the yard looking up the valley.

'Where is Uncle Amos?' Neil shouted to Dora as he drew rein with Left Hand at the main gate.

Dora came running toward him with an anxious face. 'He's up the valley,' she answered. 'Oh, Neil, he saw the signal and went up there with Williams and some of the other men. He said there must be trouble with the cattle on the plateau range. And now, Neil, the men say there's a forest fire up there.'

Left Hand had ridden through the gate directly to the corral. Neil saw him talking to the men; it looked as if he was giving orders. Mrs. French came running toward Neil.

'Your uncle said you and two of the men were to stay at the ranch if the others went up the valley,' she said.

'Have some one else stay in my place,' Neil shouted as he turned his horse. 'I'm goin' up there.' He drove in the spurs and galloped up the road, passed the upper fields and pastures, and entered the broad trail which led straight up the creek.

Far ahead he could see a pall of smoke hanging over the upper valley. Even as he looked the outlines of Telltale Peak were lost in the haze and then blotted out by the dense, rolling banners of smoke. The clouds had gathered high in the west, and dusk was beginning to fall. The wind was stronger. Thunder muttered in the distant skies, and then Neil wondered if what he had heard might not be the echoes of shots reverberating among the hills.

He was conscious of a new feeling, a new sensation; something within him seemed to have changed. He was sober, serious, and yet he sensed an unusual exhilaration as if he were freed from something which had been gnawing at his spirit. He thought of Swain, shot from behind, and a new kind of anger thrilled him; he thought of the burning prairie, of the raging fire ahead, of his uncle charging into the very teeth of it all, and he was strangely glad— relieved.

Close behind him he heard the hammer of hoofs and turned to look as a horseman shot past him. It was Left Hand galloping like mad up the trail on his splendid black steed.

CHAPTER XXV

BEFORE THE FLAMES

Amos Brodick did not check the speed of his galloping horse when he glimpsed the unknown riders in the neck of the valley through which he and his men and his cattle must pass to safety. He plunged ahead under the deepening smoke curtain with one thought outstanding in his mind; cattle and men simply must get through the neck, and before dark.

He now was far ahead of the herd, although he could hear the thunder of the flying hoofs above the roar of the wind and fire and the increasing muttering of the approaching storm. There was but scant possibility that the storm would break in time to stop the ravage of the flames and leave the upper part of the valley safe. The cattleman realized, too, that there would be no stopping of that wild, stampeding, frightened herd of cattle until the terrorized animals had passed the neck between the upper and lower valleys and had spread out in the wide space below and recovered, undriven and unharassed, from the nameless fear which possessed them.

Now a second rift in the drifting smoke veil ahead gave Amos another glimpse of the men in the neck of the valley. There were several of them, one or two on each side and three in the center of the gap. They had dismounted and apparently were working at something, holding their nervous horses by the rein and bending and twisting at their mysterious task. One man was mounted and evidently directing the activity of the others.

As the smoke closed downward again, shutting off his view, Amos quickly surmised the thing which the men ahead were doing. At this strategic point a barbed-wire fence had been stretched across the valley from the rockbound sides late the previous summer. This fence had been put there to prevent the cattle grazing in the lower valley from drifting to the upper section. It had been a necessary precaution. In the spring, when the beef cattle were driven up the valley to the early-summer range, the wire had been pushed back to the rock walls to leave the trail open. It would have been strung across the neck again when the herd was on the late-summer range down the valley.

The combine forces now were stretching the wire across the gap, tightening it and making it fast to a few scattered trees near the center of the pass. When the terrorized forerunners of the stampeding herd hit this wire it would tumble them over. The cattle, pushing on from behind, would pile up, and soon the entire herd would be a struggling mass, choking the gap, trampling, stamping, pounding, smothering, dying in the racing flames and stifling smoke of the fire, cutting off the escape of the men behind, and leaving no evidence against the men who had brought about the catastrophe.

It was a fiendish plan, and in his brief interval of mental reflection, Amos Brodick saw that this had been the program of his enemies from the start. The fires had purposely been set at the head of the valley; the two men in charge of the herd had been prevented from starting the cattle down, to give the flames ample opportunity to gain sufficient headway; little resistance had been offered when Amos and the others had arrived on the plateau.

Martin and his aids had deliberately and successfully driven them into a trap!

Amos had a sickening, maddening sense of running into the teeth of insurmountable odds as he spurred his horse unhesitatingly toward the gap, and toward the barrier which he knew his enemies were prepared to enforce with bullets. Having gone this far, it was a fight to the death. There was no doubt in Amos Brodick's mind as to who had been responsible for Swain's death. He had known the moment he heard it that it was the work of the combine—a warning to him. Neither was there any skeptical view to be taken of Martin's confessed animosity toward him. There had been truth in what Martin had said that morning of the celebration in Angel; Amos had avoided the other rancher since the Sand Creek affair; and though Martin had no reason to fear that Amos' lips would not remain sealed about the whole cowardly business, neither Martin nor Lentu had been sure of it; hence the effort to involve him in the range war against the encroaching homesteaders, and this new plan to ruin him and probably kill him and let the forest fire wipe out the evidences of the crime.

195

The smoke curtain thickened, and the hazy atmosphere below it became shot with sparks. A forked tongue of lightning blazed above, followed by the first deafening crash of thunder. Amos saw the horse, ridden by the one man ahead who remained in the saddle, veer suddenly and leap in his direction. The rider, who had been leaning far to one side directing the men working with the wire, was thrown out of the saddle and dragged by one stirrup as the frightened animal dashed up the valley in long bounds.

Amos' face turned nearly purple with rage when he recognized the features of Martin bobbing as his shoulders were rapped upon the ground. Then Martin's gun spoke, and the horse stumbled to its knees. Martin dropped his gun in his haste to clear himself of the horse. Amos, white-faced now with burning fury, leaped from his own mount to confront his archenemy. He had lost all consciousness of the situation in which he was placed; he thought only of confronting Martin and punishing him for his perfidy. Shoving his own weapon into its sheath, he flew at Martin in a grim frenzy of rage, to deal out with his hands the retribution which he knew was due the man. His fingers closed on Martin's throat as the other recognized him with bulging eyes, terror-stricken.

Back and forth in the trail and on the gravel and grass of the creek bank Amos and Martin fought. Although evenly matched in the matter of weight and strength and age, Amos had the advantage of a righteous cause and the added incentive of a fury which made him a veritable demon of vengeance. Martin would prove no match for him in that terrible struggle. He realized this and, clutching at Amos Brodick's flying fists with one hand, drew a knife from his belt with the other.

A scream of unnatural laughter issued from Amos' lips as he knocked the knife aside as if it were a plaything and planted his left fist again in Martin's face. There was unspeakable fear in Martin's face now, for in the steady gleam of Amos Brodick's eyes he saw death for himself mirrored. Why didn't McCabe and the others come to his rescue? Even as he asked himself this despairing question he heard pistol shots from the gap and knew that help from that quarter now was improbable. There was fighting ahead in the pass.

Clouds of smoke rolled over and upon the struggling men. Glowing sparks and fiery embers showered down on them unnoticed. The hot breath of the burning timber was in the air about them. Their eyes smarted and watered. And above every other sound the hiss and crackle of the fire, the thunder crashing in the skies, the wind howling through the gap— was the increasing roar of the stampeding herd plunging down the trail, coming closer and closer on its race for the pass, with men behind driving it remorselessly, while they choked and gasped in the smoke and flying, flaming debris of the fire.

Toward all this rode Left Hand and Neil and the others.

When Neil had nearly reached the gap between the upper and lower valleys he took a short cut which led up a ridge, around which the creek and the trail circled to some distance southward. As he reached the top of the ridge a startling sight unfolded before him.

The head of the valley was entirely shrouded in a dense blanket of smoke in which tongues of fire leaped and played. Through the gap he could see now and then the forms of two men locked in what appeared to be a death struggle. In the neck of the pass Left Hand was charging into the smoke toward a group of riders near the center. Neil could see the red flashes from Left Hand's gun as he galloped into the gap. From the ridge to the right a second body of men was riding down. Neil soon recognized Lentu in the lead.

Behind all this were the billows of smoke, the darkened skies, flashes of fire and lightning, the crashing detonations of thunder, and a sullen roar coming nearer and nearer— cattle running wildly for the outlet to the lower valley!

Now Left Hand's horse darted off to one side, rearing and plunging as his rider reloaded his weapon. Puffs of smoke began to spring into the wind from Lentu and the other riders charging down from the north. In the brilliant light from a flash of the impending storm Neil saw clearly the unmistakable form of his uncle in the smoke and sparks that filled the upper valley just beyond the gap. Another figure was reeling back from a rain of blows. Martin! And Neil had once thought his uncle was afraid!

The youth's face and neck flushed with shame as he drew his gun and galloped madly down the ridge straight for the gap and the converging lines of horsemen. Bullets whistled past him, and he heard the welcome sound of the other men from the ranch pushing their horses at breakneck speed down the ridge behind him. A fusillade of shots greeted Lentu and the others as they reached the floor of the valley.

Then riderless horses dashed down the trail, and Neil and the men behind him rode straight for the gap through which Left Hand had passed.

As they neared the gap they could see Amos Brodick staggering toward them, dragging a dead weight. The sharp staccato of pistol shots came from within the gap. Two riderless horses dashed out. Then they discerned in a rift of the swirling smoke that Amos was striving to pull his senseless enemy to safety; for behind him appeared a bobbing line of black, coming on and on, kicking up clouds of dust that mingled with the heavy-hanging, rolling smoke; snorting, bellowing, staring with reddened eyes and mad with terror—the stampeding herd.

Neil and the others shouted shrilly in their efforts to warn Amos of his danger of being trampled to death—an end which seemed certain with the rapid onrush of the cattle. The cattleman, having vanquished his enemy, now was showing the stuff which made the spirit of the West a synonym for courage and fairness, by trying to save him.

Tears of pride and admiration and terror welled in Neil's eyes, and his heart throbbed in his throat, leaving him gasping and speechless as he saw that it would be impossible to reach his uncle before the plunging, thundering herd. His hands dropped at his sides as his horse reared and half turned in the hot breath of the fire and smoke. He would have covered his eyes, but he hadn't the power to move a muscle. An inarticulate wail of anguish died on his tongue as he saw Left Hand riding like the wind toward Amos Brodick.

Half a minute—perhaps less—and the cattle would be upon the man afoot and his burden. Over Left Hand's head and left side a rope was whirling in a wide noose. Suddenly it shot through the smoke and spark-filled air. True as a bullet whistling toward its mark it flashed, dropped over Amos Brodick's shoulders, and tightened instantly as Left Hand eased it to its hold on the horn of his saddle. Then the magnificent black responded to its master's command and leaped. Amos Brodick was jerked from the ground, his hold upon Martin's collar was pulled free, and in another few seconds he was dragged to the shelter of a mass of rock close to the right wall within the gap.

Out of the pass several men rode, holding their hands high above their heads, their horses plunging and snorting. Neil and the others with him covered them with their weapons and drove them back against the south wall on the outside of the gap. From the black and smoke-streaked sky overhead came a series of vivid flashes of lightning, and Neil, whirling his horse to look within the gap, saw the figure of Martin lying motionless in the path of the cattle, almost under the flying hoofs.

The heavens shook with the crashing, ear-splitting artillery of the storm, and then opened to let down the rain in blinding torrents upon the burning forest. The men huddled at the sides of the gap as the thundering herd swept through the pass, shaking the earth and walls of rock until the very air seemed to tremble with the smashing, grinding, pounding impact of hoofs.

With the rain the heavens grew lighter, and, when the cattle had passed, Neil looked wonderingly about him. Williams and the men who had been driving the cattle before the fire had halted before the little group of horsemen and were staring darkly at the prisoners. There was no sign of Lentu, but three forms could be distinguished upon the north slope; one of them was crawling down, while two were motionless, huddled in grotesque postures against the brown earth and rock down which coursed rivulets of water.

Neil turned his horse into the gap. He saw Left Hand's black horse standing in the lee of the rocks where he had dragged Amos Brodick out of the path of the herd. Left Hand was upon the ground, bending over a motionless form. But was it motionless? Neil saw his uncle raise an arm. He was alive. Left Hand had taken the one possible, desperate chance to save Amos Brodick's life and it had succeeded.

With a cry of joy Neil spurred his horse toward the figures in the shadow of the rocks.

CHAPTER XXVI

A NUMBER OF ARRESTS

Amos Brodick's face lit with a rare smile as Neil knelt beside him and gripped both his hands in a warm, tight clasp. Unable to speak because of his joy that his uncle was alive, his feeling of shame that he could have suspected that his uncle had been cowed by the combine,

Neil remained silent, retaining his grip of Amos Brodick's hands and smiling bravely into his eyes. Left Hand remained aloof, himself smiling whimsically and regarding the youth with new interest.

'There, there, Neil, don't try to squeeze my fingers off,' said Amos with an attempt at gruffness. 'We've had a little trouble, but it looks like it was over. You better put your slicker on, for it's rainin' like speckled wild cats.'

'Are you all right, uncle; are you sure you're all right?' asked Neil brokenly and anxiously.

'I'm fine and fit,' averred Amos stoutly, although he groaned as he slowly sat up under the leaning rock. 'Just a bump or two that I was fool enough not to miss on the way over here. By Jiminy, Smith, you just naturally roped an' threw an' dragged me like I was a bull calf on the way to a brandin'!'

Left Hand laughed softly. 'It was rough work, all right, Brodick—doggoned rough work, I'll allow. But it was the only way I could see to get you out from in front of that herd in time. If you stayed there a few seconds longer you'd been trampled to death certain for sure, an' I took a chance on jerkin' you over here, thinkin' a broken arm or leg or sprained back wouldn't be as bad as gettin' run over by a bunch of stampedin' steers, an' that if it broke your neck, well—that would have been quicker an' easier than the other, maybe.'

203

'Man, man, I ain't blamin' you none,' said Amos with a good-natured scowl. 'You saved my life, Smith. I hear they call you Left Hand on account you can draw an' shoot so swift on that side, but I say you can throw a mighty slick rope with that left of yours into the bargain. An' how about what became of—'

'Martin?' asked Left Hand in a low voice that seemed cheerful. There was a satisfied gleam in his eyes as he shot a glance out into the downpour toward a dark spot which showed against the pools of water in the tracks left by the cattle.

'Yes. What of him?' Amos Brodick seemed to anticipate the answer.

Left Hand slowly shook his head. 'He didn't get away.'

'The cattle went over him?' said Amos with a shudder.

'The whole herd,' replied Left Hand. 'All they left was a shadow. And just what he deserved!' he added grimly.

Williams, the acting foreman of the 3 -X-Z, Brodick's outfit, came riding up to them. 'We took the guns away from that bunch out there,' he told Amos. 'Got 'em herded under guard. McCabe an' Pierson are in the bunch.'

Left Hand tossed his head angrily. 'Lentu?' he asked sharply.

'Made his get-away when he saw how things was lookin' in the gap, the boys who came up with Neil say. Left two of his men dead an' one badly hit—Ben, the Double S cow-puncher. He's cussin' Lentu right an' left for bein' a quitter an' a dirty double-crosser an' gettin' him plugged.'

It was now nearly dark with the rain continuing to fall in a steady deluge. Although the air was still thick with smoke and steam, it was cooler.

'I'll want to talk to Ben,' said Left Hand, while Williams stared with a puzzled expression first at Amos Brodick and then at Left Hand.

Amos nodded toward the gunman. 'Smith's in charge, now, Williams.'

'We'll have to get you out of here first,' said Left Hand, looking at Amos. 'I expect you're too sore to ride to—'

'There's a cabin and some corrals 'bout a quarter of a mile below here on the south side of the creek,' Amos interrupted. 'I can make it that far with a couple of men to steady me, an' after a rest I'll be all right.'

Left Hand gave his orders quickly. 'Send a man back here, Williams, to help Neil get his uncle down to that cabin. Somebody will have to lead their horses. Brodick's horse has bolted. But don't pay any attention now to the horses that are gone, or the cattle. They can be rounded up an' seen to in the morning. I'll take a look out here where Martin was run over, an' then we'll take the prisoners down to the cabin, too—keep 'em there tonight.

There's plenty to do tomorrow. That's right,' he concluded as he saw Neil take the slicker from his saddle and offer it to his uncle.

'Put it on, Brodick; don't be squeamish. And, Williams, send a man who's got a fast horse down to the ranch for some bandages an' coffee an' sandwiches, an' some whisky—if they've got it—an' tell him to ride like blazes!'

As Williams left to carry out the orders Left Hand mounted the black and rode quickly out into the upper valley. He returned as Neil and Walt Frost were helping Amos Brodick out of the gap.

Amos looked at him inquiringly.

'Martin an' two others were killed by the cattle,' said Left Hand briskly. 'The other two might have been shot before,' he added cheerfully, 'but the cattle finished the job.'

He saw that Amos was progressing all right, aided by Neil and Frost, and then went to join the men with the prisoners.

Night had descended as the injured men and the cavalcade of riders reached the cabin and corrals. There were two rooms in the cabin, and in one of these McCabe, Pierson, and the other men captured, were quartered with two armed guards sitting in the doorway watching them. The cabin had been used by men looking after the cattle in the valley; it contained a stove, some rude furniture, a cupboard filled with dishes, and some foodstuffs, a lamp, and a lantern. The lantern

206

was swung from the roof of the room containing the prisoners, and the lamp placed on a table in the other room which contained also four bunks, two superposed on each side of the room, and a stove at one end.

The wounded cow-puncher was placed upon one of the lower bunks, and Amos Brodick rested in the other. Williams built a fire in the stove after ordering the horses unsaddled and put into the corral. The saddles were piled in a corner of the room occupied by the 3-X-Z men, Left Hand, and the wounded Ben.

Left Hand examined the Double S puncher and found him mortally wounded in the left side. The man was delirious by spells, and groaned and swore fearfully in his lucid intervals, asking for water, which Left Hand gave him.

'You're going out, man,' said Left Hand in a kind voice. 'I'm afraid you haven't a chance with that hole in your side. Where did you fellers come from, Ben?'

'It's Lentu's work,' cried Ben in a mixture of rage and pain. 'He's a dirty quitter. Said they wouldn't have a chance to hang anything on us; wouldn't be anything left to tell who done it when the fire an' cattle got through wiping out the traces. An' he turned an' run at the first sign that things was goin' wrong; first—breeze of—bullets drove—him—off.'

'That's Lentu's style every time,' said Left

Hand, laving the dying man's brow with cool water. 'He's never been known to give a thought for anybody but himself. He doesn't care how many are killed in his schemes if he makes his get-away with a whole hide. You oughta have known him, Ben. Tell me, who set the fires, Ben?'

As the puncher tried to rise to a sitting posture, Left Hand addressed Amos Brodick, Neil, and the others aside. 'Listen to this if he talks,' he warned them. 'Who set the fires, Ben? You don't owe this crowd you've been running with anything.'

'Martin an' McCabe's men set 'em in the head of the valley,' said Ben with an effort. 'Lentu had us set the prairie blazing on the north slope o' the butte. Said it would teach the homesteaders a lesson an' keep 'em busy down at Angel while we fixed things—up—here. Lentu's scheme, an'—Martin's—an' McCabe's—'

'Shut up, you yellow rat!' roared a voice from the other room where the prisoners were. 'What good is it going to do you to talk? You're the quitter, you yellow rat!'

In a bound Left Hand reached the doorway into the other room, and, hitting out between the guards who had been too startled to move, he knocked McCabe to the floor with a crashing blow to the jaw.

'I suppose you'll talk, eh?' said Left Hand in a voice trembling with anger. 'You'll talk all right; but it'll be in a courtroom with a government charge over your head. Here, some of you gag him,' he called to the 3-X-Z men.

In a few minutes McCabe was bound and gagged on the floor against the far end of the second room. 'If these fellows start anything shoot right into the bunch of them,' Left Hand instructed the guards. 'Let 'em have it for keeps. You've got the authority!'

He returned to his place beside the bunk whereon Ben was tossing weakly again in the throes of delirium. When the dying man next had a lucid interval he appeared too weak to speak. He swallowed a mouthful of the water Left Hand held to his lips and then swiftly sank into a stupor.

'I don't think there's a chance to hear anything more from him,' said Left Hand turning to Amos Brodick. 'He's lost too much blood to last much longer, an' he may never come out of it again unless that feller gets here from the ranch with a bit of liquor in time. It might rouse him for a spell.'

They sat quietly and watched the rapid breathing of the stricken man. There was no sound save the occasional crackling of the fire and the rain beating upon the roof of the cabin. Neil sat near his uncle and glanced continually at the stern face of the gunman who had dashed fearlessly into the gap toward the men of the combine and had so daringly saved his uncle from death under the hoofs of the stampeding cattle.

Suddenly Amos Brodick spoke. 'They were stringing the wire when you came, eh, Smith? Was that what they was doing?'

Left Hand nodded. 'The black went through it like it was a piece of binding twine,' he said with a faint smile. 'They'd have had the other strands up in a minute, though, an' piled up the cattle. I should have got up here this mornin', for I sneaked up to the Double S ranch house last night an' heard 'em planning this thing. But I follered Lentu down to Angel to see what he was up to down there.' He looked quickly at Neil, and the young man remembered with a painful start the killing of Ratty.

But Left Hand shook his head warningly when Neil would have spoken.

A cry from the bunk where Ben was lying attracted their attention. The cow-puncher was staring with eyes of reason and vainly endeavoring to raise his head. Left Hand aided him and again offered him water. 'What is it, Ben? Try to say it.'

'They—wanted—to—get Brodick,' whispered Ben as a veil seemed to drop over his eyes and a red froth bubbled on his lips.

'Yes yes?' cried Left Hand, while the others strained to catch any sound from the man's lips.

In another moment, however, Left Hand

laid the head back upon the coat pillow he had arranged at the head of the bunk. 'He's gone,' he said softly. 'Another mark checked up against Lentu. Lord! I can't think of that cur without—'

Neil drew back from the man in wonder as he saw his whole body become tense with the rage and hatred which burned in his flashing eyes. The gunman clenched his hands and compressed his lips into a thin white line as he stared, unseeing, over the heads of the others in the room. Only Amos Brodick, watching him in fascination, seemed unsurprised by the fearful intensity of the man's passion.

When the mood had passed Left Hand covered the face of the dead man. Hardly had he done this when the messenger who had been sent to the ranch returned, bringing coffee, whisky, sandwiches, cloth for bandages, and liniment.

Neil and Left Hand rubbed the liniment on Amos Brodick's bruises, while Williams made hot coffee.

'The cook sent word he'd bring the buckboard up at daylight for Amos,' said the messenger.

'I think I'll be able to ride in the morning,' returned Amos. 'I'm good for a few years in the saddle yet, thanks to Smith, here. By golly, man, you sure didn't lose any time in thinking.'

Left Hand merely smiled in answer, and then, as Williams was getting out the cups for the coffee, he stepped to the doorway into the other room and called to Pierson. The cattleman came to the doorway with a surly, questioning expression on his face.

'Come in an' have some coffee,' Left Hand invited. 'I'd like to have a little talk with you.'

Pierson entered the room and sat down on a bench near the bunk where Amos Brodick was lying. 'I'm not going to talk,' he said. 'You can save yourself the trouble, whoever you are, of asking me any questions.' He looked at Left Hand, who laughed.

'Don't be a plumb fool, Pierson,' said Left Hand. 'We've got enough information from Ben besides what *I* know to put you fellers in the penitentiary, an' that's where you're all goin' fast as you can be taken to The Falls an' given a fair trial. There's only one thing, Pierson, an' that's this: Some of you may not have to serve as much time as some of the others—say, McCabe, for instance. Have some sense.'

Left Hand leaned toward the man and opened his shirt. All who were in the room started in surprise as they caught the gleam of a badge pinned to Left Hand's undergarment. He was standing, however, so that the prisoners in the other room could not see it through the doorway.

'I see,' said Pierson, sneering in plain contempt. 'I suppose they've promised you immunity from some of your own stunts to be an assistant ranger or a deputy of some kind. You're a rotter.'

'That's a government badge, Pierson,' said Left Hand softly. 'McCabe an' you an' Lentu are up against the Federal game this time. There ain't goin' to be much leniency shown this trip.'

Neil and the others had now recovered from their astonishment. Only Amos Brodick had the air of having known it all along. In an instant Neil realized why Left Hand had not drawn against Lentu the night of the celebration in Angel. He had wanted Lentu and the others to go ahead with their schemes and thus run into a government trap. He realized that the combine's move against the homesteaders and his uncle constituted a grave offense; but something in Left Hand's manner also convinced him that it was more than any promise such as Pierson had intimated, which had prompted the gunman's decision to accept the mission from the Federal authorities.

'Pierson, I have nothing against you,' Left Hand was saying. 'I took this job as a special inspector of the land office for different reasons than you think. You'll learn all this in time. I don't expect you to talk now. I'm just giving you a little friendly advice, for I believe you're the best of the crowd you've been herdin' with. I want you to think over what I'm telling you. Your crowd is going over for a good stiff term in the pen. Some of them may hang. McCabe an' Martin an' Lentu had their reasons for wanting to get Brodick mixed up in a deal where they'd have a club over his head. They used you for one of their tools, just like they used all the men with 'em on their ranches—just like they used that poor dead Ben, there. Now some of these men are goin' to talk before they get through with it. They're goin' to spill the whole thing from beginnin' to end—all they know. It'll make the court feel a little inclined in their favor, maybe. You don't owe as much as you think to McCabe an' the others. Just ponder this over between here an' the jail in The Falls, an' see if it wouldn't be showin' good sense on your part to get yourself off with a light sentence. This is just friendly advice from me an' I ain't goin' to say no more about it.'

Left Hand rose and, after drinking a cup of coffee, got his saddle from the pile in the corner.

'It's gettin' on toward morning,' he said to Amos, 'an' I've got to hit Lentu's trail. Take McCabe, Pierson, an' their crowd down to the ranch in the mornin' an' send word to the deputy in Angel. He'll come after 'em to take 'em to The Falls. Likely the forest ranger an' his guard from Telltale will be along asking about the fire, an' they'll help with the prisoners. You an' your men are special deputies now, an' that bunch in there an'

Pierson here are under arrest. I'll likely be back this afternoon.'

Neil followed him out of the door. The storm showed signs of beginning to let up. Rain still was falling, but in lessened volume, and the wind had abated.

'I suppose the deputy'll be wanting to take me along,' he said to Left Hand.

'Never mind about that till the time comes,' said Left Hand as he strode away in the darkness toward the corral to get his horse.

CHAPTER XXVII

ON ANGEL BUTTE

Neil could not avoid thinking about his predicament as the morning approached. It was plain that Left Hand had assumed the responsibility for the killing of Ratty to shift the blame from Neil temporarily. What his object was in so doing Neil could not fathom. Neither could he tell his uncle about the matter in the presence of the others and after Left Hand had admonished him to be silent. Although the mystery of Left Hand's identity and his purpose in that section of the country had apparently been explained, there were still several angles to the business which were as puzzling as ever.

215

At dawn the cook arrived from the ranch with the buckboard, and preparations were speedily made for the departure from the cabin. Amos Brodick rode in the buckboard in advance of the cavalcade of horsemen, McCabe, Pierson, and the others riding closely guarded by the 3-X-Z men. As Left Hand had predicted, the forest ranger and the guard from Telltale Peak arrived early on the scene and, after hearing an account of what had happened from Amos Brodick, joined the men escorting the prisoners.

There seemed scant possibility of Lentu and any he might have with him attempting to attack the men guarding the prisoners and release them on the way to the ranch. Nevertheless the party kept a sharp lookout going down the valley and was prepared to frustrate any such design. It had stopped raining, and the sun had come out bright and clear.

McCabe rode sullen and frowning, keeping his eyes upon the horn of his saddle, his hands tied behind his back, as were those of Pierson and the others. The men were mostly silent, but an occasional grumble led Neil to believe that Left Hand's prophecy that the men would be willing to talk would be fulfilled.

The cattle were discovered grazing far down the valley, apparently none the worse for their experience of the day before.

Neil heard the forest runner telling Williams

that Left Hand had visited him at his headquarters on Smith River, and that he had expected trouble. He said it was his belief that in securing the services of Left Hand as a special officer the government had carried out a plan to fight fire with fire in the matter of dealing with the combine.

'The government sent a man just as speedy with his gun as any they had on their side,' said the ranger. 'I had instructions to give him any assistance he might ask for, and that I could give, but he told me he could handle the situation alone. Well, I guess the 3-X-Z outfit helped, all right.'

'But he ain't got Lentu yet,' said Williams in a worried voice. 'I'll bet Lentu's well on his way out of the country.'

'Don't believe it,' replied the ranger. 'He'll try to get this Left Hand, mark my words.'

When the guards and prisoners finally rounded the last bend in the wide trail above the upper pasture and came in sight of the ranch house they saw the buckboard standing at the main gate, while Amos Brodick was listening to Dora and Mrs. French. They appeared to be in great excitement, talking rapidly and gesturing up the creek and toward Angel Butte.

Neil and the forest ranger spurred their mounts ahead of the rest and soon arrived at the ranch house. They saw Amos disappearing within the house, followed by Mrs. French, who was still talking.

Dora came running toward Neil, her face showing pleasure and relief at finding him unhurt; it showed also that she was greatly excited and the bearer of news.

'Oh, Neil, I am glad you are safe,' She exclaimed as he checked his horse and looked down upon her seriously.

'What are you and Mrs. French so excited about?' he asked. 'Uncle is safe and the cattle got out. Why, Dora, are you crying?'

There were tears in the girl's eyes. 'I'm so glad,' she said again. 'But, Neil, there have been more than a hundred men at the ranch this morning from Angel—the big posse, and every man is armed and Lentu is leading them!'

'Lentu!' cried Neil. 'A posse? What—what are they after? Who—'

'They're after Left Hand, Neil. Lentu told them in Angel that Left Hand had set fire to the prairie over there to stop them from following him after he had shot somebody in town. And, Neil, the whole town came near being burned and would likely have burned if it hadn't been for the rain coming just when it did.'

'But Lentu—why, we saw Lentu late yesterday afternoon up the valley, and when we started shooting he fled for his life,' said Neil in wonder. 'He—he must have gone straight to Angel!'

218

He could not help but marvel at the man's courage and persistence. Then he remembered that Lentu was not aware that Left Hand was a Federal officer. He probably thought he could capture him and get the posse excited enough to hang him before they could learn the truth. He did not listen to Dora's explanation that one of the posse had said Lentu met them as they were leaving Angel at dawn. What if Lentu should succeed? Would it not absolve Neil of all connection with the murder of Ratty? Would they not accept his statement that he had fired high to scare Ratty, and wouldn't Lentu himself tell them that? Evidently they did not now believe that Neil had killed the dealer, for if they thought that, they would not be looking for Left Hand alone.

'They have got the butte surrounded,' he heard Dora saying. 'Did—did Left Hand kill somebody down there, Neil? You came back with him, didn't you, yesterday? And uncle says he saved his life.'

Neil started guiltily. He looked at Dora. 'No he didn't kill anybody,' he heard himself saying suddenly. 'Listen! What was that?'

From the direction of the summit of the butte came the sharp echoes of a volley of shots.

'They've cornered him up there!' cried Neil. 'Did you women tell Lentu and the posse we were coming down this morning?'

219

Dora nodded.

'And Lentu thought Left Hand would cut off up the butte to look for him, and he led the posse up there!' Neil decided.

Amos Brodick came limping out of the house just as the men with the prisoners arrived. 'Let me take your horse,' he called to Williams, and when he had mounted he motioned to the forest ranger. 'We've got to go up there,' he called, pointing toward the butte.

Neil wheeled his horse and joined them as they rode out of the gate, through the north pasture, and up the trail leading to the summit of the butte. His face was grim, and a determined light shone in his eyes. He pushed his horse into the lead and held him to as stiff a pace as the steepness of the trail would permit.

They heard more shots as they climbed the butte, scattering shots, and as they neared the summit they heard shrill shouts and the sound of many horses. As Neil urged his mount up the last steep pitch in the trail to the summit he felt a wild exultation in his blood as his body thrilled to a strong emotion. What was more, he knew the source of that thrill; knew it came from a new and satisfying sense of loyalty toward his uncle.

Deep down in his heart Neil realized that he had been a fool; he acknowledged that he had been mistaken in his conception of the West, had been foolish in his desire to pose as a member of the rough, wild school of men who had taken the law into their own hands and attempted to rule by the speed of their gun play and the intimidation of others less skilled with their weapons. He took pride in the courage of his uncle, in Amos Brodick's inherent respect for a square deal. He was wrathful now when he thought of the manner of Swain's death, and there no longer was any suspicion in his mind but that it had been Lentu and the men with him who had been attempting to run off the cattle that day and thus cause trouble and loss for Amos Brodick.

At the top of the final pitch in the trail Neil found himself in a jam of other mounted men. Some were leaping out of their saddles and running afoot toward the north side of the crest of the butte. Neil got off his own horse and followed them.

On the north side of the summit a strange sight con-fronted his eyes. Left Hand, unarmed, was standing white-faced before a group of shouting, maddened men. But Neil could tell by the flashing of Left Hand's eyes that he was not white-faced with fear but with almost uncontrollable rage and fury.

'That's the man you want,' he heard Lentu crying. 'He shot Ratty when Brodick's kid nephew an' I was having a little fun with him, shooting over his head. He set the prairie fire to help make his get-away. I saw him! He's a gunman with a record as long as from here to

Angel, an' Ratty was just another notch on his gun handle, an' if the whole town had burned up he'd have laughed.'

Neil tore his way through the crowd. 'That's a lie!' he shouted to the men behind Lentu as he crowded between Lentu and Left Hand. 'If anybody shot Ratty I shot him myself, although I was trying to fire over his head to scare him. That's the truth. And it was Lentu himself who set the prairie fires to cover up an attempt to kill my uncle and steal his cattle and to scare the homesteaders. One of the men with him confessed to that before he died yesterday.'

With a roar of rage Lentu swung on Neil, but the youth dodged the blow, and the men behind Lentu held him back. Neil saw his uncle and the forest ranger pushing their way to his side. He saw, too, with a start of astonishment, that Dora had followed them and was on the summit of the butte.

'And that isn't all,' Neil shouted to the mob of men crowding before him. 'That man Lentu shot and killed my uncle's foreman, Swain, and I saw him do it. He told me to keep still and threatened to kill me if I told the truth!' Neil was looking at his uncle now.

'He lies!' screamed Lentu in a fury. The silence which had fallen over the men was shattered by a shot. Neil felt a blow high on his right side and was swung partly around with it.

He saw Lentu struggling with some men.

Neil drew his gun and handed it to Left Hand behind him. 'He'll try to get you,' he said as he sagged to his knees.

Neil knew he had been shot. His uncle and Dora were soon supporting him. He saw Lentu break loose from the men and run to the edge of the rock on a corner of the summit and leap off.

The forest ranger held up his hands and began to speak. 'This man is a government agent,' he explained, 'sent here to prevent Lentu and Martin and McCabe and the others with them from intimidating the homesteaders. Martin was killed with some others yesterday when they fired the forest up Wild Horse Creek and tried to kill Brodick's cattle and himself. One of the men who died confessed that the prairie fire was started by Lentu. As for this shooting you are talking about, I know nothing concerning it.'

Left Hand spoke now for the first time.

'You can blame Lentu for that into the bargain. I saw that play in Angel. If you had listened to me instead of to Lentu you would have learned something. Lentu got Sterret here to fire a couple of shots over Ratty's head to scare him, for Ratty was talkin' kind of mean about Sterret. The shots Sterret fired went over Ratty's head, an' you'll find 'em high in the wall. But with Sterret's second shot Lentu fired himself an' killed Ratty, likely so he could scare Sterret an' get him in his power

223

in the deal against his uncle. Lentu had good reason, an' he has no more respect for a man's life than I have for a pack rat.'

'We'll hang him!' shouted several of the men in the posse.

'No!' thundered Left Hand. 'Absolutely not! I'll look after him.' He opened his shirt to reveal the badge pinned beneath. 'I want him on several counts—myself, understand. You are not to touch him.'

He repeated this when the men continued to grumble, and finally they agreed to allow him to settle with Lentu. One of the men returned the gun which Left Hand had dropped when he had fallen in climbing to the summit of the butte. Lentu would doubtless have killed him when he was thus unarmed except for the presence of the posse.

Neil could see Left Hand striding across the summit of the butte and heard him as if from far away ask about his horse. Then Left Hand disappeared, and the others who were grouped around seemed to assume hazy shapes hard to distinguish. There was a low hum of voices in his ears. Hands were feeling at his side; tender hands which he knew were Dora's. He thought he heard his uncle swearing, but he wasn't sure. He felt as if he wanted to doze and closed his eyes. A numbness stole over him, and then everything was blotted out in black oblivion.

CHAPTER XXVIII

OUT OF THE TWILIGHT

Gradually there came to Neil's ears a sound as of waves washing against a rocky shore. It grew fainter, then clearer, with a sort of musical rhythm that swelled until it resembled the clinking of cymbals at a distance, and when Neil opened his eyes at last he recognized it for the clattering of harnesses and the crunch of wheels against a road.

He saw the blue, sun-filled sky overhead and then became aware of Dora's face looking down upon him. He was aware, too, that she was holding his hands. A dull, aching pain throbbed in his side, as if in accompaniment to the click of shod hoofs and iron tires. He knew he was being transported in a spring wagon, but a question must have shown in his eyes, for Dora spoke to him quickly.

'We are taking you to Angel where the doctor can look after you,' she said in a sweet voice. 'You mustn't try to talk or move, Neil; just keep quiet, and you will be all right.'

He wondered vaguely at the sob in her voice. He remembered he had been shot. There was the pain in his side to remind him of that. But just how he came to be shot was a confused blur in his mind, the same as the

225

sight of Dora's face now was blurred, and the sky seemed farther and farther away and becoming darker. He tried to grasp one of the girl's hands, but again the oblivion of senseless blackness intervened as he lost consciousness for the second time.

Then it seemed to Neil that there were innumerable intervals when he saw light and felt the throbbing pain in his side—a pain which also seemed to be in his head, his arms, and his neck all through his body. He sometimes felt the burning sensation of a high fever, and he dreamed strange dreams and awakened suddenly many times to find himself talking. Water water! Could he ever get enough water!

There was singing sometimes now, too; singing and shouts and shots. Then the hot breath of a forest fire would play upon his face; thousands upon thousands of steers would thunder by with a horrible racket, and he would just have time to leap clear of the flying hoofs and would awaken to find himself panting for breath.

In brief, lucid intervals he recognized Dora, dressed in white, sitting near him. He was in bed, now; it was a white bed, and there were white window curtains fluttering on one side of the room. And he was thirsty—oh, so thirsty!

Once he recognized his uncle at his bedside, and with him was another man with a beard and spectacles, who held his wrist and watched him, his gaze burning into his own. The pain was not so bad now, but there was the sensation of the fever and the delirium which accompanied it, Neil tossed and turned in an agony of unrest, while his tortured mind made him the helpless prey of a thousand hallucinations and dreams in which there almost always figured two men—a burly, red-faced, evil-looking man, and another who was slender and dark and who smiled a cold, deadly smile.

At times when he dimly made out the figure of Dora beside him he imagined he saw tears in her eyes. Twice he tried to talk to her, but the words would not come. He had grasped her hand in a weak clasp once and felt the touch of her lips on his brow, but then had come again the delirium and the fever and the horrible, unquenchable thirst and aching of his hot fever-racked body.

Thus for three weeks Neil hovered between life and death, and just when it seemed that he must have entered the twilight preceding the long, long night of the grave, when the doctor whom Amos Brodick had brought from The Falls stayed two days and two nights at his bedside, he fell into a natural sleep which lasted most of the day and all of a night, and then he woke, with a moist brow and clear of eye, free of the fever and the delirium and the thirst.

He saw Dora and his uncle and the man

whom he took to be the doctor. The latter smiled at him cheerfully, but immediately put his fingers across his lips to signify that he shouldn't try to talk.

'Young fellow, you can thank your stars for a good constitution,' he said in an agreeable, gruff voice. 'Now you must be still and quiet, and we'll give you a little nourishment; then you must sleep some more, and soon you'll be well.'

Neil could see the bright sun shining outside the window, through which came a vagrant, sweet-scented breeze. Dora was busying herself arranging the pillows about him and smoothing the bed coverings. She smiled at him, and his uncle, too, appeared greatly pleased.

'They run in the family, doctor those constitutions like Neil's,' he said in a hearty voice. 'He'll be all right now when he gets a few good feeds of beef an' mutton an' the like.'

Neil smiled wanly, realizing that this pleasantry on his uncle's part was due to the elder man's joy in his recovery. It was good to know that people were glad one was going to get well. Neil sipped the orange juice and white of an egg Dora brought him, keeping his eyes on her face the while. When he once made as if to speak she placed a cool finger on his lips and shook her head.

'You must sleep again, Neil,' she said sweetly.

And for another week that was what Neil did most of the time—sleep. His wound was dressed every day by the Angel doctor, and Neil was told it was healing rapidly.

'The doctor from The Falls took the bullet out, and you never knew it, did you?' Dora asked one morning after he had begun to talk again.

He shook his head. 'But I felt a lot of pain in my right side,' he said, smiling.

After a period of silence he asked about affairs at the ranch and learned that the regular work was progressing. The men who had been captured in the upper valley the day of the forest fire had been taken to the jail in Great Falls. His uncle had gone back to the ranch, but came down to see him every other day. A relative of Martin's had arrived from the East and had assumed charge of the Double S. Ben had been buried there, as had also Martin. Dora said she understood that Pierson had made a full confession to the authorities. The homesteaders were rebuilding their shacks, Left Hand had relinquished his claim, and two others had filed on the two quarters in the north half of section twenty-two. It appeared that Left Hand had merely filed on the land to draw the fire of the combine.

His uncle told him he had suspected the combine of doing away with Swain from the first, but that no effort to fasten the crime on any one had been made at the time, so the combine could be led into the trap of their own making, which had resulted in the death of Martin and five others and the capture of the rest, except

'And Lentu?' Neil asked quickly.

'Lentu is hiding in the mountains,' replied his uncle.

'Where is Left Hand?'

'Left Hand has been on his trail for a month but hasn't been able to catch up with him yet. But Lentu can't get away; the officers all over the State are on the lookout for him, and when he shoves his nose out of the hills he'll be captured—or killed. Left Hand is waiting for him, and he's liable to hit for Angel.'

'You mean Lentu? Wouldn't he be foolish to do that?'

'Neil, my boy, Lentu is one of those men who can't forget that another has beaten him. He'll try to get even any way he can. He knows that sooner or later he must meet Smith— which is Left Hand's right name. An' Smith is not chasin' him so much as he's waitin' for him to come out—and fight.'

'I should have known all along that Left Hand wasn't a hired gunman,' Neil complained. 'I even thought once, Uncle Amos, that maybe—that maybewhat the combine said was true, and that you that you had hired him for—for protection!' Neil blushed with shame as he finished his contrite statement.

But Amos Brodick merely laughed heartily. 'I knew what Smith was here for, but he'd swore me to secrecy. It did look sort of bad for me—us—there for a while. An' I've never been much of a hand to confide in people; I should have told Swain and you and the rest more than I did.'

'Uncle, how did Swain come to shoot the light out that night of the celebration when Left Hand and Lentu met?'

'Well, I think that was agreed upon by Left Hand and Swain,' replied Amos. 'You see, Left Hand had to meet Lentu to show him he wasn't afraid of him. That play on the horse in the afternoon and the play in the saloon that night was to sort of egg him on to make the combine begin hostilities. Smith couldn't go up there an' arrest that bunch till he had a good respectable lot of evidence. An' he didn't want to kill Lentu that night, or it might lead to the establishment of his identity as an officer and scare the combine out. An' he wanted, too, I reckon, to see if Lentu knew him.'

'Why, had they met before?' asked Neil, surprised.

'I reckon they did, some time.'

'Did they have trouble, uncle? It seems as though Lentu would have recognized Left Hand without Ratty having to identify him.'

'I guess maybe Lentu had forgotten him,' said Amos with a reminiscent smile. 'But he's likely to remember him the next time they meet. Now, Neil I've got to be going; Dora will stay down here in the hotel with you until you're well enough to come back on the ranch. The hunting season has started, an' I brought you down a couple of blue grouse today. Mrs. French an' all the boys send their choicest regards, an' I'm afraid they'll try to make a hero of you when you get back for calling Lentu that a way in front of his gun an' gettin' shot up for doing it. Boy, I was right proud of you that day—'

But Neil had turned his face away. 'I'm a long ways from being any hero, uncle, but I'm willing to learn a few things from now on,' he said earnestly.

'That's the spirit, son,' said Amos as he patted him on the back with a smile of genuine pleasure. 'An' now here's your nurse to chase me away an' bring you some of that grouse, I expect.'

Neil found it hard to take his eyes off Dora when she was in the room, and often when she was reading to him she would look up to find his gaze fixed on her; then she would flush and turn disconcertedly back to her reading.

But not once as the days passed and he finally became able to sit up in a chair and then to walk a little, did he speak to her of their unusual situation and their pact. Into his mind had come a strange thought which worried him, because he felt the force of it more and more as the days went by.

Was he worthy of her?

The land now was aflame with the golden browns and vivid crimsons and saffrons of autumn, and the high slopes of Angel Butte were splashed with color. The air was crisp, cool, and invigorating. Neil felt the blood bounding in his renewed body. And then came the memorable day when he first went downstairs, leaning upon Dora's shoulders, and ate in the hotel dining room. Soon after this he went down for each meal, and his uncle announced that within a week he would be taken back to the ranch.

One warm, sunlit afternoon Dora joined him where he was sitting on the lower porch and tried to prevail upon him to go to his room. She appeared worried and excited, and at first refused to acknowledge this until he had asked her again and again about the cause for her agitation. The men about the place, too, appeared thoughtful; they were unusually keen and somewhat expectant.

Finally Dora told him.

'Lentu and Left Hand are in town,' she whispered.

CHAPTER XXIX

THE RECKONING

The news sent a thrill vibrating in every fiber of Neil's body as he contemplated its significance. The meeting, which his uncle had declared inevitable, was at hand. Lentu had come out of the hills. Whether driven out by Left Hand or by that inexorable law which decrees that men of Lentu's stamp must meet an avowed antagonist or be forever branded as a coward, mattered not. Lentu had proved he was not afraid.

From Dora, Neil ascertained that the report of the arrival of the two gunmen had been whispered about town all morning. He turned aside in a kindly manner her entreaties that he avoid any excitement—if there should be reason for excitement. He asked the hotel runner for additional details and learned that the men had ridden in from the west at dawn, Lentu arriving in advance of Left Hand.

Their horses had shown unmistakable signs of long, hard riding, the dust being caked on their flanks and seamed with the dried courses of rivulets of sweat. Lentu had eaten in the café near the Prairie Flower and had disappeared, but had not been seen to leave town. Left Hand had had breakfast in the hotel and had then gone to a room for a few hours of sleep. Neither had mentioned the other.

Neil wondered that every one appeared so calm and outwardly disinterested. Men collected on the hotel porch to comment on the weather, the time of the two daily trains, the price of sheep and cattle—anything at all save the topic which must have been on the tip of every tongue and yet remained unspoken. Neil saw the deputy sheriff, Mills, sauntering to the post office, chewing a toothpick, apparently unconcerned. Yet Lentu was wanted on several charges. He was wanted for the murder of Ratty, the dealer; for the killing of Swain; for the firing of the prairie, thus burning the property of many homesteaders and threatening the town of Angel itself; for his association with Martin, McCabe, and the others of the combine in their unlawful scheme. It was generally known he was in town, but no move was made to take him into custody.

Very plainly, by their attitude, the county authorities and the townspeople were showing that the affair was to be settled without interference at that time from them. Left Hand's demand, that Lentu be left to him, was respected.

Neil could not help but remember with a quickening of the pulse the passionate fire which shone in Left Hand's eyes when he had stood before Lentu unarmed on the summit of the butte. He recalled, too, how Left Hand had looked that night in the cabin in Wild Horse Valley when he had told the dying Ben what manner of man he considered Lentu to be. What would happen when these two met? Neil felt the conviction growing within him that there was something between these men aside from the breaking of laws; something more sinister, more terrible than the disregarding of a manmade law could possibly be.

The town seemed strangely quiet in the sunshine of early afternoon. All about it stretched the golden plains, with here and there a vivid spot of color from the turning leaves of cottonwood or willow growing in some better-watered coulee; colors that grouped and ran riot on the higher slopes of the butte in the west. The air was rich with that peculiar, dry, earthy tang which is distinctive of the prairie lands climbing to the eastern foothills of the Rockies. The occasional bark of a dog and the clang of metal from the blacksmith shop were the only sounds heard. Now and then some drifting cloud of dust upon the plain betokened the approach of a horseman or a team. Such a cloud of dust from the west brought Amos Brodick in the buckboard to take Neil and Dora back to the ranch.

When Amos had taken the team to the hotel barn to be watered and fed and rested against the trip to the ranch in the cool of the late afternoon and the twilight, he stopped to talk to Neil on the porch before going in to eat lunch.

'I expected it,' said Amos when he heard the news from Neil. 'Came down here to settle it. He showed up twice on Smith River, I heard, but they simply didn't offer to arrest him. He had to come.'

Amos looked up and down the street, shook his head thoughtfully, and without further comment, went in to eat. Dora hurried upstairs to arrange her own and Neil's belongings for transportation in the buckboard on the ride home. She, too, felt the significance of the hour, but hoped that they would be able to get started for the ranch before anything could happen.

Neil, leaning back in his chair, saw that several men were lounging around the west end of the porch, and as he looked down the street he made out other groups in doorways and before the stores and saloons. Interest seemed to be centered in the street instead of inside the various buildings, and in the very studied, listless attitudes of the groups was an intangible suggestion of tense expectancy.

Usually at this time of day there were many homesteaders and ranchers setting out for their homes, having finished the business which brought them to town. But this afternoon there was no movement to leave on the part of those who had come in in the morning. There were many horses tied to the hitching rails before the stores, while their owners, riders, or drivers lingered along the street.

Neil suddenly noticed a change in the attitude of the men about the hotel porch. Their low hum of conversation was hushed. They were looking down the street. Neil looked too, and started in surprise. Again came the hum of conversation, but it was very plainly forced and meaningless, more for effect than for any real purposes of discussion or information.

Lentu was coming slowly up the street.

He walked well within the shade of the shelters built over the fronts of some of the stores, and kept close to the buildings. He hardly glanced within the doorways he passed, as if by some subtle intuition he divined that no one whom he wished to see was within. Occasionally he replied to a guarded greeting or nodded to some one in the groups about the street.

As he came nearer Neil saw that this day Lentu wore two guns. He had removed his chaps, and the sheaths which held his weapons were strapped tight against his thighs. His big hat was pulled well down to shade his eyes; his black leather cuffs, worn smooth, gleamed with silver trappings. And ever his keen, searching, menacing gaze roved about the

238

street from group to group, meeting the looks of others without a sign of flinching; audacious, bold, at times sneering, but ever alert.

When Lentu was across the street from the hotel he halted for a look over the open square in the direction of the railroad station. Then he swung on his heel and walked quickly toward the hotel.

In the excitement which he had experienced in seeing the gunman, and in his anticipation of the meeting between him and Left Hand, Neil had actually forgotten that this was the man who had shot him, whom he had openly accused of killing Swain and thus defied. However he felt no particular anger toward the man, and it was not until Lentu actually put foot on the porch and flashed his gaze over Neil along with the others that he recollected he might possibly expect more violence.

He rose quickly to his feet with the instinct of self-preservation, but Lentu paid no further attention to him. Instead his eyes were turned toward the doorway leading into the hotel's small lobby. He stepped across the porch and seemed to slouch in a half crouch as he cautiously entered. He looked about the lobby and into the dining room and then warily stepped to the refreshment counter.

Neil, looking into the lobby through the window from the porch, saw his uncle enter from the dining room. A strange silence had

239

fallen over those on the porch and within the hotel. The jingle of Lentu's spurs had echoed loudly, and now the clink of glasses was heard clearly as the bartender set out a drink in response to what must have been a silent signal from Lentu.

Now another step was heard—a light, catlike step from the dining room. There was a faint jangle of spurs, and Left Hand glided into the lobby and paused almost in front of the door leading into the bar. Neil saw his face freeze into grim but distorted lines; it was white, furious, and held a glare of almost maniacal rage and hate in the eyes which slowly narrowed and gleamed steel-blue.

A sigh seemed to waver in the room and out upon the porch, as there was a long intaking of many breaths; and when Left Hand spoke, his words came like the crack of a whiplash.

'Don't move, Lentu. I can see you in the mirror!'

In the pause which followed Neil sensed that the two gunmen were staring into each other's eyes through the medium of the mirror behind the bar. Men who were standing directly behind Left Hand slipped silently aside. Amos Brodick was watching breathlessly from a place near the desk. Neil kept to the window, his eyes upon Left Hand's face and the left arm and hand which hung tense and as motionless as if it were modeled in bronze, above the butt of the pistol in the black sheath

240

at the man's left thigh.

Left Hand spoke again, his words coming clear with a hint of tremendous passion behind them as he kept his gaze riveted upon the image he saw in the mirror.

'Lentu, the law wants you. The government has given me the authority to arrest you. You are wanted for murder and for leading a conspiracy against settlers on government lands. If you give up and allow yourself to be taken to The Falls you will be found guilty, and you'll hang like a rat till you're dead!'

There was a short, breath-taking interval of silence.

'Lentu, you can sneer at the gallows, for you'll never hang. You'll never hang, because you won't give up. I'd hate to see you give up! If I had thought there could be no hitch of justice and that you would hang I'd have arrested you before this or I'd arrest you now. But you might have a chance that way, and you can't have a chance, Lentu—not with me.

'I told you that the night we were alone in the shack on twenty-two; and now I'll tell you why. Think back,—Lentu think back a long time. Think back to that night up on Sand Creek remember? Ah—you begin to remember, eh? The night you led the bunch that took two men out and murdered them hanged them for a crime they were accused of but never tried for hanged them after you had captured them under a white flag of truce!'

Neil glanced instinctively at his uncle, and for a brief instant Amos Brodick met his gaze with a meaning look. Neil recalled the story of the Sand Creek hanging which Dora had heard from Mrs. French and later told to him. This, then, was the thing which was between Lentu and Left Hand.

But Left Hand was speaking again in a voice that trembled with passion.

'There was a boy with those two men, Lentu, a young boy, unarmed, inexperienced, a relative of one of those men you hanged without giving a fair chance. You drove that boy out upon the prairie to die. You would have killed him, too, but you couldn't find him later in the night. You thought his bones were found bleached and scattered on the prairie the next spring.

'Lentu, that boy didn't die. He wandered, frightened and starving, until he was found and taken in by the Blackfeet Indians. He lived with them for years because you had killed his faith in white men. And to this day he has hated white men—yes, and killed them—because of that hate, and because he taught himself to shoot faster than any one of them he has ever met; learned to hate and to shoot and to kill so that some day he might pay *you*, Lentu, in hot lead.

'I was that boy, Lentu, and now I am that boy grown up. I see by your eyes that you know I am speaking the truth. I'm glad, Lentu; glad you should know all this before—the end!'

The voice seemed to mellow into a plaintive tone as Left Hand finished. After a few seconds he spoke again, softly and musically, seeming to caress the words as they left his lips.

'And this is why I have come after you, Lentu. I kept track of you, and I waited until I knew you couldn't beat me in a gun play, for I had to tell you first. When the government offered me the job of putting a stop to the range troubles hereabouts I took it because it would give me a chance to get you and get you right. It was an accident that you got Swain; it would have been an accident if you had got Brodick, and you wanted to get him and seal his lips for all time. But I'm not going to get you by any accident, for you haven't got any more chance than you gave the two men you hung and that boy—myself.'

Left Hand Smith took three steps toward the door leading into the refreshment room without lowering or shifting his gaze.

'I'm hoping this is the last time I'll have to use my gun,' he said in a low voice as if to himself. 'I'm going back up to Canada where I was born. I'm doing a real service to this country by ridding it of you, Lentu, and saving the State or government some money.'

Again the interval of silence.

'Are you coming out, Lentu?'

The speaker stooped ever so slightly,

gathering his muscles tense for a spring.

'Lentu, if you're not coming out, I'm coming in!'

A flashing instant of time and Left Hand's body shot into the doorway to the thunder of blazing guns. Neil scrambled through the window and with his uncle was among the first to enter the refreshment room, pungent with pistol smoke.

Lentu's body was still leaning backward against the counter. At his feet lay two guns. Left Hand leaned forward from just within the doorway as the body slipped to the floor. He broke his weapon and spilled the empty shells upon the huddled form, then slowly replaced it in the sheath on his left thigh.

The bartender rose from his place of safety, stared about awkwardly, and began wiping the counter before him in a foolish manner with his bare hands. A dog, awakened from his nap by the sound of the shooting, came from one of the deserted card rooms in the rear. From within the lobby came the sound of some one clearing his throat. Then a casual word was spoken, and soon arose the discord of excited voices.

Left Hand Smith immediately pushed his way through the crowd and disappeared.

CHAPTER XXX

LEFT HAND'S FAREWELL

In the cool, sweet breezes of late afternoon Amos Brodick, Dora, and Neil rode back up the long slopes of Angel Butte in the buckboard behind the best road team on the 3-X-Z, and, in the first hour of the twilight, emerged from the cañon road to the floor of Wild Horse Valley. As Amos gave the horses free rein, and as they hurried between the fields of stubble for the main gate, the ranch bell, used to call the men to meals, was heard ringing merrily.

All the men on the place, as well as Mrs. French and the boy, Louis, came out to the gate to meet them, and Neil felt a strange lump in his throat as they shook hands with him and joshed him in the best of natures about being too tough to kill, and bullet-proof, while they congratulated him and expressed their pleasure at his recovery.

It was a royal welcome, truly Western in spirit, and while Neil felt that he hardly deserved it he mentally resolved that his future life with them would never once fail to merit their good-fellowship and confidence.

They sat down to a splendid dinner with appetites sharpened by the crisp autumn air,

245

and then, while Dora assisted Mrs. French with the dishes and other household duties, Neil and Amos Brodick sat in the little office in the front of the ranch house. For the first time Neil told his uncle all the details connected with the killing of Swain.

With a blush of shame Neil confessed that he had at first suspected Swain, that he had not been altogether sure that Lentu was not telling him the truth, that he had feared Lentu and his veiled threat to kill him if he told all he knew, that he had at the time actually hoped that Left Hand was implicated. He bared his groundless jealousy of Left Hand and spared none of the details of his foolish thoughts and actions in which he had, as he now saw, been disloyal to his uncle and the ranch.

'I came out here with the wrong idea, Uncle Amos,' said Neil earnestly. 'I thought I wanted to be a gunman, and I didn't even know what a gunman was or how he was made. Left Hand's story taught me things!'

Then he explained the feeling of exultation and joy which had come over him when he saw his uncle battling with Martin before the stampeding herd and the racing fire; how a sense of loyalty and justice and right was born in him at that moment, and how he saw afterward the meanness of the combine's selfish stand against the homesteaders who had come out, veritable pioneers of an era of agriculture, to reclaim the prairie wastes.

Through it all Amos Brodick listened with sparkling eyes. When Neil had finished he laid a kindly hand on his nephew's knee.

'There was a great preacher, son, who once said in one of his sermons that "tremendous natural scenery makes the greatest natures for good or evil"—1 think that's the way it goes. An' that's sure true out here. You fell in with the evil crowd at the start, an' you can't be blamed so much. But you've learned something, an' I don't know as I would have had it any other way. Now you're on the right road with a clear track an' no more gates to open. You'll make it all right. An' now, son, we'd better go to bed. We've got work ahead of us, for we'll have to get ready to ship the beeves in a few days.'

The day following Neil was plied with questions from the men who wanted all the details of the meeting between Lentu and Left Hand. Neil described the scene and repeated Left Hand's words as best he could, never without respect for the terrible seriousness which attended the merited death of Lentu.

'Served him right, an' he got just what was coming to him,' declared Williams, voicing the sentiment of the others who nodded in strict approval. 'An', Sterret, you know I had a hunch you was bein' fed a lot of stuff by Lentu an' his gang, an' so did Swain, but he says "Let him go, an' if he's got any stuff in him at all he'll wise up to it himself." An' you did, an' the crowd's with you. Put it there.'

The handclasp strengthened the resolve which Neil had made.

There followed days of hard work on the ranch in which Neil participated more and more, willingly and happily, as his strength returned. The beeves were rounded up, and Amos Brodick went to The Falls and arranged for the cattle cars to be spotted on the Angel siding. Then the herd was driven to Angel and the cattle loaded into the cars, and Amos and two of the men went East with the stock to the Chicago market.

Neil and Walt Frost went on a hunting expedition and brought back two deer. The grouse on the slopes about the valley were plentiful, feeding now on the juniper berries. Plowing was under way, and there was fencing and woodcutting and hauling. The men on the place had plenty to do to get things shipshape for the long, cold Montana winter which would soon gather the land in its icy grip.

The first snows had fallen, melted in the valley and on the south slopes, and shone white upon the peaks in the warm sun of the late Indian summer when Amos Brodick and the men returned from marketing the cattle.

'Well, we're all squared off at the bank, Neil,' said Amos cheerfully. 'Couldn't lose out on this ranch now if we wanted to. Cattle's in fine shape for the winter, an' everything's set for a good year to come. I guess I better take you in on the secret of my books such as they are an' maybe you can help me a little with the figuring.'

Neil laughingly waved a hand in protest. 'Wait until there isn't so much outside work to do, uncle, before I have to get ink on my fingers.'

Two days later Neil and Dora were sitting on the porch in the sun. They had been together more often during the weeks following Neil's convalescence. Each seemed to sense a difference in the attitude of the other. Dora was always cheerful and smiling and perhaps a bit shy, while Neil appeared subdued and serious.

So interested were they in the casual bits of conversation in which they indulged that they failed to notice the approach of a rider until he thundered up to the gate on his big black horse.

'Left Hand Smith!' cried Neil in glad surprise.

Amos Brodick came running out upon the porch and shouted a greeting to Left Hand, who dismounted and walked rapidly toward them.

'Just dropped over to say good-by,' he said gravely. 'Had to get my pack horse an' stuff down at Angel. I'm starting for Canada tonight.'

Amos had one of the men look after the big black, and Left Hand sat down to dinner with them.

'Guess it won't hardly be necessary for any of you to go to The Falls on the McCabe and Pierson matter,' he informed them. 'Pierson an' some of the men made a complete confession of the whole scheme an' put the blame on Martin an' Lentu—as you know. Then McCabe an' the others pleaded guilty. They're all due to be sentenced tomorrow.'

After dinner on the porch Amos Brodick looked at Left Hand with regret in his eyes. 'We're right sorry to see you go, Smith,' he said. 'I was goin' to ask you if you wouldn't stay here an' take on the job of bein' my foreman for a time—'

Left Hand's laugh interrupted him. 'No use, Brodick. I'm going back to Canada an' try to forget a lot of things, an' who knows but what I'll go to farming up there! I guess maybe you've got material for a foreman right there.' He indicated Neil, who flushed under his tan at the compliment.

Left Hand advanced to Neil and, pulling a pistol from his hip pocket, offered it to him. 'Here's your gun you loaned me that day up on the butte,' he said, smiling.

Neil drew back. 'I'd—I'd rather you took it along as—as a keepsake,' he said slowly. 'I don't want it!'

Left Hand again pocketed the gun and held out his hand. Neil took it with a joyous smile as he recognized what it meant. Then Left Hand said good-by to Dora and the others, and Amos Brodick followed him to the gate as a man brought around the big, black horse.

Dora and Neil stood arm and arm watching Amos as he bade Left Hand Smith farewell. They waved as Left Hand saluted them from the saddle and galloped up the trail toward the cañon road and Angel Butte.

They were watching him out of sight when Amos came back to the porch.

'By golly,' said Amos, 'I actually believe you two are gettin' kind of chummy lately.'

Neil, taken aback, looked down at Dora, who lowered her eyes and blushed.

'There, now, what'd I tell you, young lady?' Amos went on in a hearty voice. 'Didn't I say I'd give you two till along about Christmas. By golly, I believe I hit the mark!'

Neil turned Dora around facing him as his uncle went chuckling into the house.

'What does he mean, Dora—Christmas? I guess I'll have to start all over again after what's happened. But if you still think that in another year I can—why what's the matter, girlie?'

Dora had thrown her arms about his neck and was crying softly. Her lips found his ear. 'Maybe uncle is right,' she whispered.

'What? Right—about about—'

'Christmas!' she murmured as he gathered her closely in his arms.